The Complete Book of Cat Health

The Complete Book of
CAT HEALTH

THE ANIMAL MEDICAL CENTER

William J. Kay, DVM, Chief of Staff
with Elizabeth Randolph

Illustrations by Nancy Lou Makris
Photographs by John A. Hettich

Macmillan Publishing Company
New York

Collier Macmillan Publishers
London

This book is not intended as a substitute for the medical advice of your veterinarian. The reader should consult a veterinarian regularly in matters relating to a pet's health and particularly in respect to any symptoms that may require diagnosis or medical attention.

Photograph 25 by Susan Brooks
Photographs 26 and 27 by Katherine Quesenberry, DVM
Produced by G. S. Sharpe Communications Inc.

Macmillan Publishing Company
866 Third Avenue, New York, N.Y. 10022
Collier Macmillan Canada, Inc.

Library of Congress Cataloging-in-Publication Data
Kay, William J.
The complete book of cat health.
Bibliography: p.
Includes index.
1. Cats. 2. Cats—Diseases. I. Randolph, Elizabeth. II. Title.
SF447.K39 1985   636.8′083   85-15264
ISBN 0-02-502350-0

Macmillan books are available at special discounts for bulk purchases
for sales promotions, premiums, fund-raising, or educational use. For details, contact:

Special Sales Director
Macmillan Publishing Company
866 Third Avenue
New York, N.Y. 10022

10 9 8 7 6 5 4 3 2 1

Designed by Jacques Chazaud

Printed in the United States of America

In memory of Tigger and Muffy.
And to Wilbur, the sweetest of just plain cats.

Acknowledgments

"Thank you" to all of the following:

Each of the Animal Medical Center veterinarian and staff contributors for their cooperation and care in helping prepare material for this book in their areas of expertise.

Dr. William J. Kay, Chief of Staff, and Dr. Michael S. Garvey, Chairman of the Departments of Medicine and Surgery, who made this project possible. Maija Jezina, Dr. Kay's assistant, for her very special help and care.

The others at The Animal Medical Center who helped—in particular Joan M. Weich, Director of Public Relations, Yasmine Echaves, and Rebecca Berkowitz.

Genell J. Subak-Sharpe, our producer. And our editor at Macmillan, Arlene Friedman, and her associate, Melinda Corey.

Elizabeth Randolph

Contents

Part Two: People-Pet Relationships

Part Three: Disease and Illness

ENCYCLOPEDIA OF DISEASES OF CATS, THEIR TREATMENT

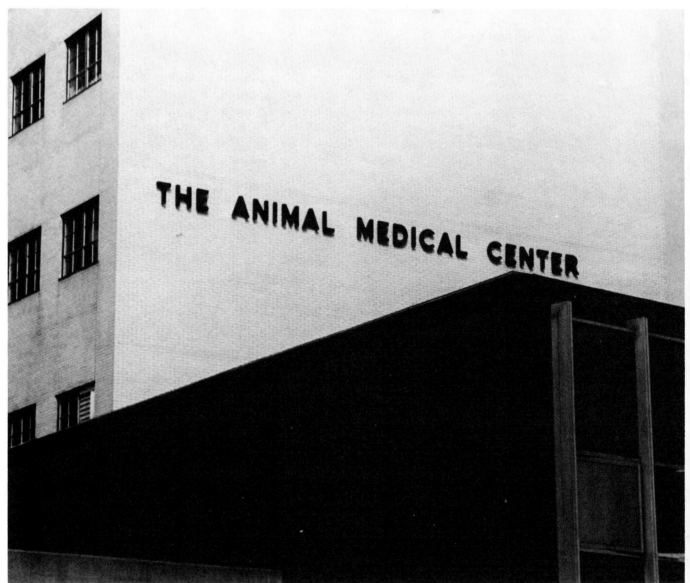

Photograph 1: The Animal Medical Center, as seen from the FDR Drive

The Animal Medical Center
Contributors to This Book

WILLIAM J. KAY, DVM
Diplomate, American College of Veterinary Internal Medicine
    Specialties of Internal Medicine and Neurology
Chief of Staff
Staff Neurologist

MICHAEL S. GARVEY, DVM
Diplomate, American College of Veterinary Internal Medicine
    Specialty of Internal Medicine
Chairman, Departments of Medicine and Surgery
Staff Internist/Gastroenterology

DAVID P. AUCOIN, DVM
Associate Staff Internist/Clinical Pharmacology

PETER L. BORCHELT, PH.D.
Director, Animal Behavior Clinic

SUSAN PHILLIPS COHEN, CSW, ACSW
Director of Counseling
Chairperson of The AMC Institute for the Human/Companion Animal Bond

PHILIP R. FOX, DVM
Diplomate, American College of Veterinary Internal Medicine
    Specialty of Cardiology
Staff Cardiologist. Director of Clinics

STEPHEN L. GROSS, VMD
Diplomate, American College of Veterinary Ophthalmologists
Staff Ophthalmologist

AUDREY A. HAYES, VMD
Diplomate, American College of Veterinary Internal Medicine
    Specialty of Internal Medicine

KAREN A. HELTON, DVM
Resident in Dermatology

DAVID T. MATTHIESEN, DVM
Associate Staff Surgeon/General Surgery

ROBERT E. MATUS, DVM
Diplomate, American College of Veterinary Internal Medicine
    Specialty of Internal Medicine
Head, Donaldson-Atwood Cancer Clinic
Staff Internist/Oncology

CHERYL J. MEHLHAFF, DVM
Associate Staff Surgeon/General Surgery

SAMANTHA MOONEY, BA, MA
Research Associate, Donaldson-Atwood Cancer Clinic

KATHLEEN E. NOONE, VMD
Diplomate, American College of Veterinary Internal Medicine
    Specialty of Internal Medicine
Staff Internist/Respiratory Medicine

MARK E. PETERSON, DVM
Diplomate, American College of Veterinary Internal Medicine
    Specialty of Internal Medicine
Staff Internist/Endocrinology

KATHERINE QUESENBERRY, DVM
Associate Staff/Director, Exotic Pets and Zoo Animal Medicine Clinic

DEBORAH SARFATY, DVM
Associate Staff Internist/Neurology

LEE SCHRADER, DVM
Diplomate, American College of Veterinary Internal Medicine
    Specialty of Internal Medicine
Staff Internist/Nephrology and Reproduction

RICHARD C. SCOTT, DVM
Diplomate, American College of Veterinary Internal Medicine
    Specialty of Internal Medicine
Staff Internist/Nephrology. Director of Education

DENNIS A. ZAWIE, DVM
Diplomate, American College of Veterinary Internal Medicine
    Specialty of Internal Medicine
Staff Internist/Gastroenterology

Introduction

The Purpose of This Book

The purpose of this book is to provide cat owners and potential cat owners with information they need to have a satisfying experience with their pets. How will we do this? By putting together an unparalleled collection of expertise to help with every aspect of cat ownership. Each contributor to this book is a recognized authority in his or her particular field. Many are recognized Diplomate (Certified) Veterinary Specialists, experts in their fields. By coupling the enormous diversity of these individuals' knowledge with The Animal Medical Center's seventy-five years of experience in veterinary medical practice, this book presents an unbeatable combination of useful information for all cat owners. The book is clearly written and is easily readable by both experienced and inexperienced cat owners (even non-cat owners!). This is not to say that the subject of cat ownership and cat health is simple, but in these pages we have clarified the most complex topics, from raising newborn kittens to the care of older cats and the death of a well-loved cat. We have included symptoms of common feline diseases and disorders and how to understand and deal with behavior problems that may arise at various stages in a cat's life. In short, we think that this is the only book anyone who owns a pet cat, or is about to own one, will ever need.

Unfortunately, cat ownership is not always a completely satisfying experience. Many cats are given up because they do not fit well into their owner's or family's life. Almost always, the fault lies in a lack of realistic expectations about what cat ownership entails, what a cat will be like, and what role a pet cat will play in the owner's or family's life. This is not surprising when we consider that many people choose a kitten or a cat without having the faintest idea of what the animal they choose will become or how owning a cat may influence and affect their lives. Many fail to take possible changes in their own lives into consideration. Children grow up, families move, and social circumstances are altered. Potential cat owners should be aware that these things may happen in the lifetime of the average cat. By the same token, people often have little or no idea what they really want in a pet. If potential cat owners would stop to think that the decision to own a cat is one that will probably be a factor in their lives for an average of fifteen or more years, they would give that choice at least as much thought as they do choosing a new pair of shoes.

1

The pages of this book are filled with information for people who already own a cat. Here, at the very beginning of the book, I would like to touch briefly on some things to bear in mind *before* choosing a kitten or cat that may help to avoid disappointment and dissatisfaction later on. Let me hasten to say that I am not discouraging cat ownership in any way. Rather, I hope to help people make more intelligent choices as to cat ownership—and I am speaking from years of personal experience!

Should You Own a Cat?

Both prospective new cat owners and experienced hands at cat ownership should be aware of several facts before embarking on a relationship with a pet cat. Some general considerations are:

• *Economic:* The expense of owning a cat may be a rude surprise to a new owner. There are certain fixed costs involved in cat ownership. Spaying or neutering operations are desirable for both female and male pet cats, and all cats require regular immunizations. Ongoing veterinary care can be expensive. Major illnesses and injuries may run into many hundreds of dollars over the course of a cat's lifetime. It costs at least $200 a year to feed one cat a good diet and provide clean litter daily. Longhaired cats may occasionally require professional grooming. An owner who travels or takes frequent vacations should also take boarding or sitter costs (or the cost of transporting a cat with him) into consideration. In addition, no matter how well trained, a cat may contribute to the wear and tear on household furnishings.

• *Time and Attention:* Cat owners should be prepared to spend time each day with their pets. Cats need daily affection and play, and many actively demand attention from their owners. Brushing and/or combing is a mutually pleasurable necessity, the frequency of which depends on the length of a cat's coat. Other necessary cat-owning routines include cleaning litter pans and going to the veterinarian for regular checkups and immunizations. These activities can take several hours a week that cat owners could spend on other pursuits.

• *Disruptions in Routine:* Cat ownership may also result in occasional disruptions and upsets in a household and in an owner's plans and routines. Cats get sick and may need medications and care. Accidents can happen. Fur will shed. People who have difficulty dealing with disruption or lack of order in their lives should probably not consider cat ownership.

What all of these considerations add up to can be summarized in one question: Are the things I will give up—time, money, tidiness (can I tolerate cat hair on my furniture and clothes?), freedom to come and go—worth it to have a cat? For most cat owners these "give-ups" are negligible compared to the satisfaction and love they gain in cat ownership.

Choosing a Cat

If your answer to the above question is "yes," the next question is: What kind of cat should I get? The reasons why a particular person or family wants a cat may be a factor in the breed and personality of the cat chosen.

One of the first questions to resolve is: Do I want a purebred cat or a mixed-breed cat?

There are advantages to both types of cat. Mixed-breed cats are usually healthy and hardy, and make wonderful pets. Nearly 90 percent of all pet cats in the United States are mixed breed. Purebred cats are healthy and hardy too and have a particular body conformation, haircoat, temperament, and personality due to careful genetic selection. Many people do not realize that there is a large difference in temperament and personality, as well as physical characteristics, between breeds of cats. It is important for potential owners of purebred cats to realize that a Persian cat is quite different from a Siamese, and an Abyssinian from a Burmese or Russian Blue, for example. A purebred kitten raised in ideal conditions by a reliable breeder will grow into an adult cat with a predictable temperament, size, haircoat, and so forth. This is very important for people who know exactly what they want in a cat, including looks and personality. Some purebred cats occasionally have physical or personality faults and diseases limited to a particular breed. Some of these problems are discussed in these pages, but careful research *before* deciding on a breed is strongly suggested.

Whether you decide on a purebred or mixed-breed animal, one of the first considerations is the environment the cat and you will share. If you are an urban apartment dweller, you may want to consider one of the quieter, calmer breeds or perhaps one that does not shed a lot (or at all). If, on the other hand, you and your cat will be living an indoor/outdoor life in the suburbs or the country, you may decide to choose a tough, energetic animal that will enjoy the freedom of the outdoors. Families with young children should probably avoid a shy breed of cat such as a Persian and opt for an extroverted Siamese or Abby. All of them can make wonderful pets.

In addition to environmental considerations, ask yourself why you and your family want a cat. Will the cat's role be primarily that of a playmate for children, or is she to be a cuddly companion for a single adult? Do you want a quiet cat or one who "talks" and meows a lot? What about looks and care? Is your image of the ideal cat one with a beautiful long, silky coat, or would you rather have a cat with short, easy-to-care-for fur or very little fur at all, like a Rex?

If you have never owned a cat before and know nothing about the various breeds and their characteristics, how do you find out about all these things? Look through books that describe and picture the various cat breeds. (See the Bibliography in the back of this book for some.) Talk to other cat owners and if possible go to a cat show. Visit and play with the breed you might be interested in and find out how it differs from other breeds. Talk to breeders. Even more important, because breeders are prejudiced in favor of "their" breed, talk to as many owners as you can; ask questions about the advantages of a particular breed, about the breed's drawbacks, if any, and if any special care is required.

Unlike the American Kennel Club for dogs, there is no single central registry of standards for purebred cats in the United States. Rather, there are several national organizations and a number of specific breed clubs and associations, most of which give shows, set standards, and issue pedigrees to their members. See the Bibliography for a listing of some of these registries and clubs/associations.

Where to Get a Cat

There are no hard-and-fast rules about the best source for a satisfactory pet cat, and a great deal depends on whether or not you want a purebred animal.

Finding a Purebred Cat

A potential buyer of a purebred kitten or cat should expect to pay a fair amount of money for the new pet and should exercise an appropriate amount of caution to ensure that the pet will turn out to have the desired characteristics.

In general, the best source for a good purebred cat or kitten is from a professional breeder who specializes in that particular breed. Breeders can usually be located through one of the registries or at a cat show. In the case of the more exotic and rare cat breeds, it may take time to find a kitten with the particular sex and coloring you wish. Sometimes cat breed associations will put a potential owner in touch with someone who will sell or give away a grown purebred cat, but this is not common. Owners of particular breeds of cat are usually so devoted to their pets that they would never think of parting with them for any reason! Breeders may offer a potential owner who is interested in a pet rather than a show cat or breeder a "pet-quality" kitten at a reduced price, one that lacks perfect markings or "points" but will still make a fine pet.

Individual owners sometimes offer purebred kittens for sale. A potential buyer should always ask to see both parents in these cases, to be sure that a kitten actually does have the desired genes, and should insist on a pedigree if the buyer has any intention of showing or breeding the pet.

There are pet stores in many areas that specialize in purebred felines. They usually differ from ordinary pet shops in that they often give very extensive guarantees, and some of them even allow a potential owner to take a cat or kitten home on a trial basis. Some even go so far as to refuse ownership to people whom they consider "unsuitable" adopters. In general, these types of establishments are very trustworthy and maintain an ongoing interest in "their" cats, often continuing to perform needed services such as grooming and boarding.

Finding a Mixed-Breed Cat

Fortunately, the time has passed when most pet cats had numerous litters and baskets of unwanted kittens could be found everywhere, from doorsteps to grocery stores. Nevertheless, it's still not difficult to locate a mixed-breed kitten in almost any desired color combination at a local Humane Society or Shelter, or advertised on supermarket bulletin boards. Grown cats can also be easily adopted or found, especially in urban areas.

For first-time cat owners and people who want a special pet, the wisest thing is to find a kitten that has been raised in a household with someone's pet cat as a mother. This way at least you can be assured that the kitten has been raised in a warm, clean environment by a mother who is well nourished and free from disease.

Small kittens are especially vulnerable to disease, and it is important to know that the pet you choose has been protected with the proper immunizations and is not incubating a serious illness which may manifest itself after you have become attached to it. If you adopt a kitten from a shelter or an individual, always

ask for a vaccination certificate and a health certificate signed by a veterinarian, then take the kitten to a veterinarian right away for an examination and further immunizations if necessary. The same holds true for an older cat, whether stray, adoptee, or purchased. If there are other cats in a household, a new kitten or cat should be isolated until given a clean bill of health. See Chapter 3 for more about this.

Choosing a Healthy Pet

Breeders and purveyors of purebred cats will usually have enough of a financial investment in their animals to assure that their cats are physically well cared for. This is not necessarily the case with mixed-breed kittens. Many owners of "plain" cats simply do not know enough about necessary health precautions; others do not opt to spend the time or money to provide them.

If possible, ask to see the mother and littermates. A great deal can be learned by observing how a kitten reacts with its siblings. A very aggressive, active kitten will probably grow up into a healthy, aggressive cat. The runt of the litter, however, may have a congenital physical defect and/or may not have been able to obtain enough of the mother's milk, and may always be sickly and weak. If the mother acts shy and afraid, it is possible that her kittens will react in the same way. In general, a friendly, responsive mother cat will have kittens that are the same. Clean, odor-free living quarters are also positive indications that mother and kittens have been well looked after.

Pick up the kitten and look it over. Check especially for the following signs of ill health: runny nose; dull, watery eyes; smelly (or any) discharge from the ears; bloated abdomen; diarrhea; rough, dull coat; listlessness; labored breathing; or coughing. Although external parasites such as fleas and ear mites can be taken care of by a new owner, they indicate a general lack of care, and a severe flea infestation can result in anemia in a young kitten.

If a kitten or full-grown cat is adopted from a shelter, it usually will not be possible to find out much about its parentage or former living conditions. A friendly, outgoing kitten or cat with bright eyes and clean, shiny coat is probably healthy and familiar with people. Again, insist on being allowed to handle any animal you are seriously considering adopting. Even little kittens will purr when picked up if they have been treated well by people. Older cats may be a bit more wary of strangers, but it is generally pretty easy to tell if a kitten or cat is outgoing and feeling well.

Cat lovers who pick up stray animals are usually well aware of the potential for health and personality problems and are willing to take their chances on being able to solve them. The neophyte cat owner with one pet as a companion should take time to choose that pet carefully to derive the most satisfaction from cat ownership.

Caring for a Cat

Once a kitten or cat is chosen and brought home, the information in this book will help an owner in making decisions about everyday care—choosing a veterinarian, feeding and grooming a cat, and so forth.

Cat owners are very often confused or unclear about specifics of health care. One of the most common health care issues is the inability of many cat owners to know at what point a pet requires medical attention. Quantifiable errors range all the way from panic over a slight limp to waiting to "see what will happen" to a cat that has been struck by a car. The emergence of the cat as an important pet means that the diseases, nutritional requirements, and care of cats have undergone a very significant revolution during the past ten years and will continue to do so. There are chapters in this book that are designed to help owners become acquainted with new developments and avoid errors about their pet's care: Chapter 12 includes the symptoms most commonly seen in cats and what their significance might be; the Encyclopedia of Diseases of Cats has more de-

tail about specific illnesses and diseases of cats. There is also a complete Emergencies section and chapters about the care of newborns and of older cats.

Many owners are under the mistaken impression that they have to live with their cat's misbehavior. Not so. Chapter 8 discusses the most commonly seen feline behaviors and helps owners to know how to deal with them.

These chapters and many more will help a cat owner know what is going on with a pet. They will also help an owner to know when to seek help and to judge the effectiveness of that help intelligently so further steps can be taken if necessary.

As I said at the start, this book is unique because of the scope, diversity, and expert sources of the information it contains. It is written to give cat owners all that is needed to have a mutually satisfying experience with a pet cat. My colleagues at The Animal Medical Center and I share the love and joy of cat ownership. This book is dedicated to cats and their owners, old and new.

William J. Kay, DVM, Chief of Staff
The Animal Medical Center

PART ONE

———

A

HEALTHY

CAT

1

Veterinary Care

William J. Kay, DVM

The Rise of Companion Animal Veterinary Medicine

People have had cats as pets for hundreds of years, but until the second or third decade of this century, companion animal veterinary medicine as a major area of professional practice was primitive and rudimentary. That is not to say that cats and other pets did not receive medical care when they were ill or injured, but this care was often performed by physicians or laymen who had little if any scientific knowledge about pets and veterinary medicine.

In the beginning of this century, most veterinarians were large-animal practitioners who treated mainly horses and food-producing animals including cattle, sheep, goats, and swine. At the time of the Great Depression in the early 1930s, several factors combined to cause more veterinarians to concentrate on small companion animals, or pets. Many farmers were unable to spend a great deal of money on veterinary care for their livestock, and by then horses had been nearly replaced by the automobile. At the same time, animal hospitals and veterinary practices devoted to small-animal care were increasing, especially in urban areas.

At this point small-animal care was generally unsophisticated. There were few standards or guidelines covering the essentials of a good small-animal hospital or clinic, and the amount of scientific information available on the care of pets was limited. In 1933, the American Animal Hospital Association (AAHA) was founded by a small group of visionary veterinarians. This group created standards for veterinary hospital facilities, equipment, and procedures. They began to serve as a continuing-education and information-sharing organ for companion animal veterinarians and the pet-owning public.

With the establishment of the AAHA, small-animal care soon became a well-defined area of veterinary medicine. The dynamic of pet practice as it is today, however, coincides with the evolution of veterinary medical colleges and the veterinary curriculum, along with the AAHA. At the end of World War II, there were only ten accredited veterinary medical colleges in the United States and Canada. Now there are twenty-seven, with others in development. As veterinary colleges developed, they began to expand their emphasis. Once they primarily trained veterinarians in the arts and skills of food-animal and equine practice; now the professional training includes the sciences, arts, and skills required for treating all

9

animal species, including pets. Today, a large segment of the curriculum in the nation's veterinary schools is devoted to the study of the diseases of pets (including small birds, reptiles, and so forth). And as public interest grows, more money is being spent to implement curriculum changes, both for reasons of public health and the growing awareness of the importance of pets in the lives and well-being of people.

A third development that has increased the basis of pet practice is the formation of specialties (areas of special skill) in small-animal medicine. Specialization in the study of specific areas of expertise in small-animal veterinary medicine began in the late 1940s and has grown rapidly. About 6 or 7 percent of the veterinarians in this country have practical and certified expertise in one of about a dozen areas. These areas of expertise include cardiology, clinical pathology, dermatology, internal medicine (which includes gastroenterology, nephrology, oncology, and so forth), neurology, ophthalmology, pathology, reproductive disorders, respiratory medicine, surgery, and zoological medicine. Veterinarians must take special training and pass rigorous examinations to become specialists, or Diplomates, in their area of expertise. These specialists often practice in large veterinary institutions including veterinary universities throughout the country. Many are in private practice. This specialization has provided the basis of continuing education for the thousands of general practitioners who continue to be the professionals that millions of cat owners and their pets see regularly.

Veterinary Medicine Today

Today, we have a large number of professionals directing a significant amount of time, energy, and talent into training young people to be veterinarians. When they graduate, these young veterinarians may go on to postgraduate studies and specialization, or they may go directly into pet practice.

We also have a higher and higher level of skill and an emerging body of knowledge, either research-based or founded on scientific clinical experience. This foundation for a larger data base allows veterinarians to build on the information known and to ascertain what can be done to cure pets and improve their health. The development of veterinary medicine in this way parallels the development of human medicine.

The diagnostic techniques and treatments available for pets today are astounding and are growing rapidly. There are continuous new scientific developments; new areas, new skills, and new methods of treatment (acupuncture and dentistry are now practiced at The Animal Medical Center, for example), and new recognized disciplines develop on a regular basis. Within each general discipline there may be six or seven different subdisciplines. As we mentioned above, there are a number of subdisciplines in internal medicine. Generally, specialists in these very specific subdisciplines limit their practice to institutions, urban areas, and large groups of veterinarians who have gathered together to form a clinic, or group practice. There are now a number of veterinarians skilled and certified in general veterinary practice, comparable to the popular family practitioner for humans. A veterinarian in this group is called Diplomate, The American Board of Veterinary Practitioners.

Cost of Veterinary Care

This brings us to an emerging problem. The cost of this new technology and specialization will in many cases outstrip the public's ability to pay. Even now, pet owners aware of what services are available have to make difficult choices about what level and amount of medical care they are able and willing to provide for their cat. This distance between what is available and the public's willingness and ability to pay for this treatment will widen as time goes by. Therefore, there will be an increasing differential in pet health care, based on owners' ability to pay, their understanding of the types of pet health care available, and their willingness to seek a particular level of care. Some owners will choose to provide as much care as is available; many others will not.

Although a large medical bill for a cat ranges only between $500 and $3,000, as opposed to much larger bills for comparable human care, it places a financial burden on many people. Pet Health Insurance (PHI) may be the answer. In the past, many PHI plans failed, leading to skepticism and mistrust. However, several companies have now developed PHI plans that are viable and relatively inexpensive. Excellent PHI is available in several states. It is a reasonable expectation that as pet health care costs rise more plans will be available within easy economic reach of the pet-owning public. Although health insurance for cats is not necessarily a life-saving issue, since a terminally ill pet may still be euthanized at the owner's discretion, PHI is an excellent investment and good value for people who want to protect themselves against large pet medical bills. Because PHI is not yet available in all areas, plans differ widely, and new plans are becoming available all the time. Owners interested in PHI should discuss it with their veterinarians.

Are There Human Medicine Implications in Veterinary Medicine?

Men and other animals share the same environment, and in the biological domain of cats and humans there are diseases common to both species and diseases similar in both species. The process of studying a specific disease in the cat and transferring what is learned to treating humans with the same disease, and vice versa, is called *comparative medicine*. Veterinarians and physicians often work together in terms of applying data from one species to another. Diseases need not be identical to be useful as study models, either by physicians if the disease is in animals or by veterinarians if the disease is in humans. More and more scientific articles are written, lectures given, and study groups discussing this cross-referencing of knowledge gained in human and animal medicine.

There are many examples in which data about a disease or condition in cats has had an impact on the further understanding or treatment of the same disease or condition in humans. For example, cats suffer with several forms of heart disease known as cardiomyopathy, a common and serious condition in cats. Humans, too, are afflicted with cardiomyopathy, and the symptoms and underlying pathological changes are very similar. Through clinical studies of cats with cardiomyopathy, we have learned a great deal about how the disease affects people. Another example is meningioma, a nonmalignant yet serious form of hair tumor that occurs frequently in both cats and people. Meningiomas can cause epileptic seizures, personality changes, and many other neurologic symptoms. We have learned much about the treatment of this disease in cats from studies of afflicted humans.

The most useful thing for cat owners to know in this context is that cats can and do suffer from many of the same diseases and disorders as humans. The study of biological systems is interrelated, and the more we know and understand about one species, the more we know and understand about another.

Choosing a Veterinarian

With all of the knowledge and specialization in the field of small-animal and companion-animal medicine, can cat owners be sure that the first veterinarian listed in the telephone book will be a satisfactory doctor for them and their pet? Not necessarily. Just as dentists, lawyers, and physicians vary in qualifications, interests, and ability, so do veterinarians. Occasionally a cat owner is disappointed in the veterinarian chosen. The discovery that a choice of doctor is unsatisfactory often doesn't occur until an emergency, serious illness, or other health crisis arises.

Cat owners should have an idea of what they expect from a veterinarian before they choose one. If what the owner wants is routine care—yearly immunizations and possibly routine surgery such as an ovariohysterectomy or neutering operation—then the choice is not crucial. All veterinarians can deliver most veterinary services. If an owner has very limited resources, low-cost clinics will perform most routine procedures. There are mobile veterinarians and veterinarians who make house calls. These veterinarians offer convenience and service for cat owners.

For the cat owner whose pet is an important part of the family, a steady and satisfying relationship is required. Most cat owners want to establish a relationship with their veterinarian, as sound as the one they have with a physician or dentist. The veterinarian, too, requires time and experience with both the animal and the owner to be knowledgeable and effective.

A good first step in selecting a veterinarian is to *ask someone who is knowledgeable about cats* and has had extensive experience with them. A local breeder is often a good source of information. Pet owners and neighbors are not necessarily the best people to ask for recommendations since their needs, experience, and standards may differ.

A prospective client should also make an *objective* evaluation of an animal hospital or clinic. The building need not be super-modern or fancy, but: Is the physical plant clean? Are the personnel dressed neatly and attractively? Does the business seem to be well run, from outward appearances, with good record-keeping and accounting? Are the equipment and facilities up to date and adequate? Can you have a tour of the hospital?

It is good to know that there are professional associations that set high standards as a prerequisite for membership. The AAHA and state and local Veterinary Medical Associations have standards regarding the equipment, procedures, and physical facilities of animal hospitals. Animal hospitals that are members of these organizations comply with strict standards and are subjected to periodic examinations. Membership in the AAHA requires a doctor to subscribe to a set of standards for pet medical care and hospital management. Interested pet owners can obtain a list of AAHA member hospitals in their area by writing to AAHA headquarters.* AAHA and state veterinary societies can also be helpful to cat owners who are moving to another community or state by providing a list of local member hospitals.

There are a variety of different types of pet medical care facilities to choose from. In large urban areas and in locations where there is a veterinary medical college, cat owners have access to large veterinary hospitals in which there are specialists in nearly every facet of small-animal medicine and surgery. In many urban areas several veterinarians with different specialties have joined together to form a "group practice." Many private practitioners have also formed group practices and have arrangements with specialists to visit on a regular basis. In smaller communities and areas, three or more veterinarians may practice together, pooling their resources to purchase sophisticated equipment and/or to subscribe to one or more of the many professional services that are now available, such as telephone-accessed electrocardiograms. About 75 percent of the veterinarians in the United States practice with one or two other veterinarians.

Before selecting a doctor, cat owners should *know what kind of veterinarian they want.* Is the veterinarian a generalist or a specialist? If he/she is a specialist, in what area? If he/she is not a specialist, what arrangements are made when one is needed? Does he/she have a working relationship or referral arrangement with a cardiologist, surgeon, ophthalmologist, and so forth, or with a larger hospital or insti-

---

* Send a self-addressed stamped envelope to: American Animal Hospital Association, P. O. Box 768, Mishawaka, IN 46544

tution with specialists on staff? (If a generalist claims not to need access to these kinds of specialties, a cat owner should probably go elsewhere.) Is the doctor's practice limited to small-animal medicine, or is it a mixed practice? These are legitimate questions to ask in order to assess a veterinarian's suitability to be a particular pet's doctor.

All veterinarians attend undergraduate college and veterinary school. The duration of university training is usually seven or eight years. With an internship and residency, a veterinarian often spends ten years or more in rigorous training. All veterinarians are licensed in the state in which they practice.

Although it is not necessary for a cat owner to like a veterinarian, it will make the relationship more workable if there is a *compatibility of objectives* between owner and veterinarian. In a relationship that may last for years, it is important for an owner to feel comfortable and at ease with the doctor. In addition to objective assessments, there are several *subjective* questions that cat owners can ask themselves before deciding to choose a veterinarian:

• Is the veterinarian easy and comfortable to talk to? Does he/she inspire confidence? Does he/she seem interested or impatient and offhand with questions?

• Does the veterinarian like the cat (and cats in general)? Does the cat seem to be reasonably at ease with the veterinarian? Or is there some underlying sense of mistrust?

• Does the veterinarian's schedule fit the owner's?

• What arrangements does the veterinarian make for emergencies? Is someone from the staff on call twenty-four hours a day, seven days a week, or must a cat be taken somewhere else if it gets sick or is injured on a Sunday?

• Are other services, such as grooming and boarding, available at the hospital, or must the cat be taken somewhere else?

• Are there facilities to keep an ill or injured cat in the hospital? If so, is there close supervision?

• Does the veterinarian keep accurate, up-to-date records of immunizations, and so forth, and send reminders when necessary? Or is it up to the owner to keep these records? (See Chapter 3 for a sample health record for an owner to keep.)

• Are there regular telephone hours and times when the veterinarian can be reached to discuss an ongoing problem or something that's worrying an owner?

Responsible cat ownership has many facets, one of which is the selection of the best available medical care. There is certainly no reason a cat owner should be unhappy or uncomfortable with a veterinarian's manner or personality. It is important to make the point, however, that charm does not equate with veterinary skill. Small-animal veterinarians should have a good relationship with an owner, in addition to treating an animal patient, in order to be truly effective. For some this has meant establishing

Photograph 2: Dr. William J. Kay listening to a cat's heart with a stethoscope

JOHN A. HETTICH

a good "bedside manner" with owners. Cat owners should use common sense in selecting a veterinarian who not only meets their needs and expectations but who meets their cat's needs as well, and should be aware that a charming manner is not always the measure of a good animal doctor.

What to Expect on the First Visit to the Veterinarian

First-time cat owners going to a new veterinarian may find it helpful to ascertain ahead of time just what the parameters are of a particular veterinary practice. Often a receptionist or secretary can answer questions over the telephone. Most veterinary hospitals have pamphlets and/or information sheets that outline their services and owners' responsibilities.

In addition to finding out about office and telephone hours, fee schedules, emergency and boarding policies, and any other services, owners will need to ask what is expected of *them*.

• What, if anything, should be brought on the first visit? Will the doctor want a stool sample, previous immunization record, if any, and so forth?

• Must a cat be in a carrying case? (See Chapter 9 for more about cat carrying cases.)

• Will the owner be expected to stay during the examination or procedure? Will the owner be expected to hold or restrain the cat, or is hospital staff available to do this?

• What are the hospital's policies about payment? Is the owner expected to pay before leaving, or will a bill be sent? Are credit cards and checks accepted?

These and other questions that may occur to an owner should be asked ahead of time so that there are no surprises.

On a first visit, the doctor will usually take an oral history of a cat from the owner, asking questions about where the cat was obtained, its parentage if known, and any observations an owner may have about the cat's appetite, digestion, sleep, and activity level. If the patient is an older cat that has been cared for by another doctor, a written health record is very helpful. Barring this, an owner's oral report of the cat's medical history will have to suffice.

(This is one reason why it is always a good idea for owners to maintain their own pet's health records. See Chapter 3.) This is the time for an owner to voice any concerns he may have and ask any questions that may have occurred to him about the cat's well-being so that the doctor can bear these questions and concerns in mind while examining the cat.

A thorough physical should entail examination of all parts of a cat's body, including the insides of the mouth and ears. The veterinarian will listen to the cat's heart with a stethoscope and palpate the animal's abdomen. The cat's temperature should also be taken. Skin and extremities will be carefully examined. If there is evidence of a problem, the doctor may suggest further testing and/or evaluation. This may be done while the owner waits, or the cat may have to be left at the hospital for a few hours or a day. Owners should never be afraid to ask questions in order to understand what any procedures entail and are intended to do. The veterinarian should apprise owners ahead of time of the cost of any test or procedure. If he does not, an owner should ask.

Young kittens visiting the veterinarian for the first time are usually examined for intestinal parasites. As we discuss in several following chapters, it can be assumed that kittens have roundworms at birth. It often requires more than one deworming to rid them of these parasites. Immunizations will also be started, according to a schedule established by the veterinarian (see Chapter 3). At this time the veterinarian may schedule future visits. It is the owner's responsibility to determine whether a reminder will be sent by the doctor's office.

If medications are to be used at home, it is very important, especially for the inexperienced cat owner, to understand how a particular medication should be given. An owner should ask for a demonstration. In the end it will save time and will assure that the cat is properly medicated. (See Chapter 13 for how to give cats various types of medication.)

In Conclusion

Outstanding veterinary medical care is readily available in the 1980s. Cat owners should know that a wide spectrum of expertise is accessible to them. An owner who wants and can afford the time and money can obtain highly sophisticated veterinary services. But in order to obtain good medical care for a cat, an owner must be willing to take time, use common sense, and pay attention to objective and subjective criteria when choosing a veterinarian.

2

Your Cat's Body and How It Works

DENNIS A. ZAWIE, DVM

This chapter contains a brief rundown of the major systems comprising a cat's body and their normal functions, so that owners can learn about the inner workings of their cats and can better understand what their veterinarians are referring to.

With a few minor exceptions, cats' bodies are made up of the same parts as other mammals' bodies, including humans'. Although their body systems also work in the same way (the heart pumps blood, for instance), cats are prone to developing diseases and illnesses that are different from those of other species. Specific problems and diseases of cats will be covered in subsequent chapters, most particularly in the Encyclopedia of Diseases of Cats.

There are, of course, some physical differences that have evolved over the ages to meet specific needs. In particular, cats have a highly developed ability to see and "sense" in the dark, to jump very high, to retract their claws, and to turn their paws inward. More about these special abilities later in the chapter.

Skeletal System

The average cat's skeleton contains 244 bones, including the skull, vertebrae, ribs, and tail. Like humans, cats have clavicles (collar bones), which dogs do not. A cat's bones perform several very important functions. They support the entire body and provide a system of levers, which are necessary for muscles to work. A glance at Illustration 19 on page 209 will show that a cat's spine is curved, providing flexibility. This allows a cat to "coil," or compress, the spine in order to spring or leap high. Bones also act as a protective mechanism for the internal organs: The skull protects the brain; the rib cage, the lungs; the spinal vertebrae, the spinal cord; and so forth. Skeletal bones also act as storage areas, housing bone marrow and minerals (primarily calcium and phosphorous), until the body needs them.

Cats have a specialized musculature in their forearms that allows them to *pronate* (turn inward) their front paws in order to bat or grasp prey (or toys). Otherwise, cats' muscles and tendons are essentially the same as those of other species, including humans.

Nervous System

Cats' nervous systems can be broken down into two parts, central and peripheral. The central nervous system includes the brain and spinal cord. Within the brain there is the cerebral cortex; it contains the intellectual capacity of a cat and enables it to see, hear, feel, and experience pain. Also, the cat's behavioral or "instinctive" patterns (sexual behavior, maternal and defensive/survival instincts, and so forth) are housed in the cerebral cortex. The brain also contains the cerebellum which is responsible for coordinated movements and equilibrium. The spinal cord is necessary for a cat to interpret sensations in its legs and feet. This interpretation of sensations is called proprioception. Damage to the spinal cord can cause an interruption in the messages to and from the limbs, and varying degrees of leg weakness or paralysis may occur. (See "Neurologic Diseases and Disorders" in the Encyclopedia.)

The peripheral nerves include the twelve cranial nerves that come out of the brain and are responsible for all of the things that occur from the neck up, including vision and hearing, and the spinal nerves that innervate the rest of the body. After the peripheral nerves branch out of the brain or the spinal cord, they transmit messages to the muscles, telling them to either expand or contract.

Eyes

A cat's vision is directly controlled by the peripheral cranial nerves. Cats' eyes have essentially the same parts as those of humans: cornea (the clear part of the eye), sclera (white part), pupil, iris (the colored part); lens, and retina (see Illustration 20, p. 216). However, there are some notable differences between cats' eyes and those of other animals, providing cats with the best night vision of all domestic species. Cats' eyes have a great many more rods than cones, while human eyes contain more cones than rods. Rods are tiny cells that respond to very dim light, which means that cats can see very well at night. In addition, the shape of cats' pupils—oblong rather than round—permits them to dilate widely in dim light to allow more light in. In bright light, cats' pupils are reduced to a mere slit to protect the eyes (see Photograph 4, page 19). Cats' acuity, or visual keenness, is also highly developed. All of these factors combine to make cats' vision extremely acute.

Another way in which cats' eyes differ from humans' is that they contain a membranous region around the retina called the tapetum which reflects light back to the retina after it has passed through once, giving the cat two chances to capture an image. This further enhances the animal's night vision. Sometimes an owner will notice a blue or yellow glare in a cat's eye when it is looking straight at the light. This is a reflection from the tapetum. This should not be confused with another phenomenon common in older cats in which the lens fibers become denser with age and refract light differently than they formerly did, imparting a bluish color. This condition, called lenticular sclerosis, or nuclear sclerosis, is often misdiagnosed as cataracts but does not affect a cat's vision. (See also "Ophthalmic Diseases and Disorders" in the Encyclopedia.)

One other thing worth mentioning about cats' eyes is that they, along with all other animals except humans, have a third eyelid, a membrane between the outer lid and the eye itself. This membrane serves to protect and clean the eyeball and sometimes appears in front of the eye, especially if the eye is slightly irritated.

JOHN A. HETTICH

Photograph 3: Dr. Philip Fox uses a small light to examine a cat's eyes.

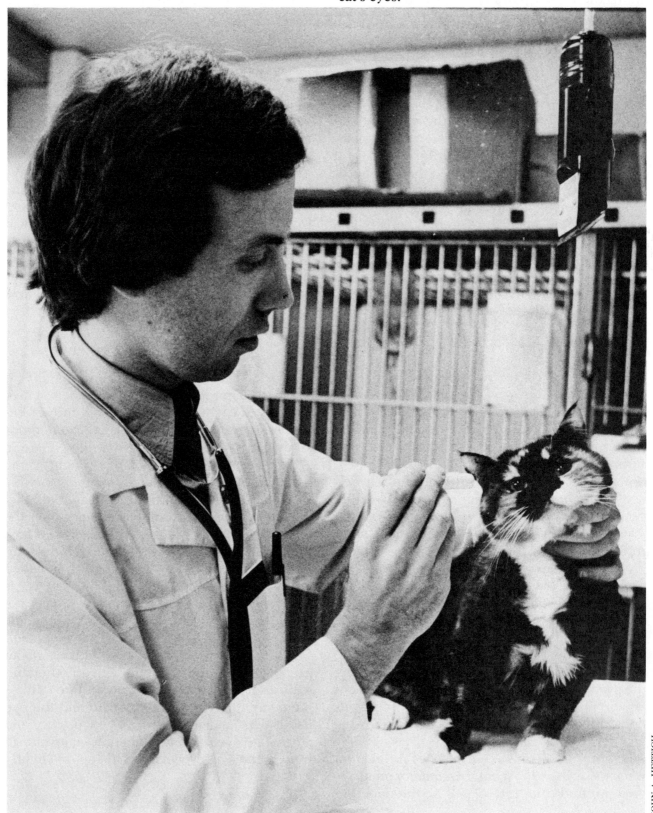

Ears

A cat's hearing is also controlled by the peripheral cranial nerves and is very acute. The ear is divided into three parts: external, middle, and inner (see Illustration 18, page 179). The outer part of a cat's ear, called the pinna, is made up of cartilage and serves to capture sound vibrations and direct them into the ear canals so that they will reach the eardrum. The middle ear contains the eardrum and three tiny bones that transmit sound vibrations from the eardrum into the inner ear, where nerves register the sounds and transmit them to the brain. The inner ear is also responsible for balance.

Photograph 4: Cats' pupils are oblong, rather than round, and can be reduced to a mere slit in bright light.

JOHN A. HETTICH

Digestive Tract

A cat's digestive tract is made up of a number of parts that transport food and water from the oral cavity where it is ingested, through the body where it is broken down, digested, and the nutrients absorbed, to the rectum from which waste material is excreted.

Before discussing the digestive process itself, we will look at a cat's oral cavity and in particular at the teeth. The teeth serve an adult cat in two ways: as weapons for both offense and defense, and as tools used to procure and cut or tear food. Cats' mouths and teeth are designed to meet their particular style of eating, grasping, and then tearing or shredding food, which is then swallowed and broken down by gastric juices. An adult cat's canine teeth incline inward slightly to trap food.

Teeth provide an excellent way to tell the age of a kitten. By four to five weeks, a kitten should have a full complement of 26 deciduous (baby) teeth, consisting of six incisors (I), two canines (C), and five premolars (PM), equally divided between each side of the upper and lower jaw, as follows:

$$I \frac{3}{3} \ C \frac{1}{1} \ PM \frac{3}{2} = 13 \times 2 = 26$$

Baby teeth should be replaced by a full complement of adult teeth by the time a kitten is six months old. Occasionally, this doesn't occur on time, and the baby teeth may have to be extracted so that the adult teeth don't become deformed. An adult cat should have thirty teeth, including molars (M), as follows (see Illustration 1, below):

$$I \frac{3}{3} \ C \frac{1}{1} \ PM \frac{3}{2} \ M \frac{1}{1} = 15 \times 2 = 30$$

A cat's tongue is very rough and is used primarily as a grooming tool.

Moving down into the cat's body from the oral cavity, we come to the esophagus, a long, tubular muscle, or organ; its only function is to propel food from the oral cavity to the stomach by means of muscular contractions called peristaltic waves which function throughout the digestive tract. At the time of swallowing, a hinged cartilage (the glottis) automatically covers up the trachea, or windpipe, to prevent food or water from entering it.

The food then enters the stomach, which acts primarily as a storage area for food but also starts breaking it down with digestive enzymes and hydrochloric acid. Very little digestion actually begins in a cat's stomach. The food then passes on to the small intestine, which is responsible for the digestion and absorption of water, electrolytes, and nutrients. Its sponge-like surface is full of folds and turns to increase its absorptive area. The small intestine consists

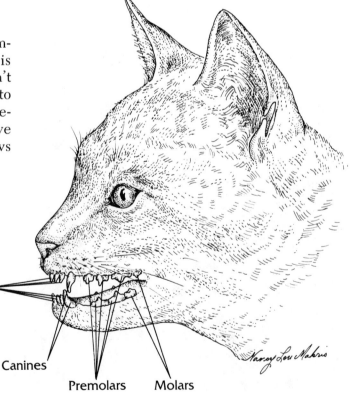

Illustration 1: An adult cat has 30 teeth.

Incisors

Canines

Premolars   Molars

of three parts: duodenum, jejunum, and ileum. In addition to the functions of digestion and absorption, hormones from the duodenum stimulate the secretion of enzymes from the pancreas. These enzymes help to digest the food as well as to stimulate contraction of the gall bladder to release bile into the small intestine. Bile serves to digest and emulsify fat.

At the junction of the small and large intestines, a cat has a small pocket similar to a human's appendix, called the cecum. This can be the site of gastrointestinal infections in the cat. The large intestine, or colon, serves mainly as a storage area for waste material, but it also reabsorbs any remaining electrolytes and water. What is left over is fecal matter, which is then expelled through the rectum.

Other parts of the digestive tract are the pancreas and the liver. The pancreas has an endo-crine function, secreting the hormones insulin and glucagon which are necessary for the regulation of glucose. It also has an exocrine function, manufacturing and releasing digestive enzymes and bicarbonate into the small intestine. A cat's liver is the largest organ in its body. It has six lobes, as opposed to the human liver which has only one large lobe. The liver is responsible for a myriad of functions, all of which are very important. It aids digestion by producing bile, which aids in the absorption of fat; metabolizing protein and carbohydrates; and acting to detoxify the by-products of digestion. In addition, the liver acts to metabolize and degrade any drugs, chemicals, or poisons that might get into a cat's body through environmental exposure, and it manufactures the major blood-clotting factors. (See also "Gastrointestinal Diseases and Disorders" in the Encyclopedia.)

Cardiovascular and Respiratory Systems

Next, let's travel to the cat's heart and lungs, which are very similar to those of all other animals, including humans.

The cardiovascular system consists of the heart, which pumps blood, and the arteries and veins, which carry it. Blood from the circulatory system enters the right atrium of the heart, passes through the tricuspid valve into the right ventricle, which pumps it through the pulmonary valve into the pulmonary artery and on to the lungs for a fresh supply of oxygen. The oxygenated blood flows back into the heart (the left atrium), passing through the mitral valve into the left ventricle, the heart's main pumping chamber, which forces blood through the aortic valve into the aorta, the body's major artery. This artery branches into smaller arteries, arterioles, and finally capillaries that carry oxygen and nutrients to every cell in the body.

The respiratory tract carries air into the lungs, where oxygen enters the bloodstream and carbon dioxide is removed from the blood. The respiratory tract begins with the nose. The primary function of the nose as far as respiration goes is to act as a filter, removing large particles the cat inhales. These particles are filtered out all along the respiratory tract, but the nose is the first and most efficient filter. The nose is also an olfactory organ, providing a sense of smell. In cats, the olfactory nerves of the brain are highly developed, and the cat has a much better sense of smell than we do.

The inhaled air travels down through an opening in the throat to the larynx, containing the vocal cords, which vibrate to produce sound when air is forced over them. Interestingly, purring does not originate in a cat's throat. It begins in the blood system. The actual sound results from vibrations of blood vessels in the cat's chest. Air then enters the trachea, or windpipe, a long tube that serves only to convey the air to the bronchi and the lungs. As we mentioned before, the windpipe is protected by a hinged membrane called the glottis, which protects against accidental choking. From the windpipe, air travels through the various bronchial tubes and then into the lungs. It is in the lung tissue that the gaseous exchange of waste and oxygen occurs. (See also "Cardiac Disease" and "Respiratory Diseases and Disorders" in the Encyclopedia.)

Genitourinary System

Some of the reproductive organs of an intact (unneutered) male cat are external. There are two testicles that manufacture sperm and are housed within a membranous pouch called the scrotum. The scrotum is located just underneath the anus and should be able to be felt by the time a cat is two months old. Occasionally, a cat may have undescended testicles, which might cause breeding difficulties; it might also cause some testicular tissue to be retained after neutering, creating a urine spraying problem. Always consult your veterinarian when this condition occurs. The penis is directly under the scrotum, pointing backwards. Intact males have tiny barbs at the end of the penis; this is one way to determine whether or not a cat has been neutered. At the base of the penis is the bulbourethral gland, which supplies the fluid in which the semen, manufactured in the testicles, is transported. The epididymis stores sperm prior to ejaculation and a duct called the vas deferens transports sperm when it is ejaculated. Male cats do not have a discrete prostate gland. They instead have disseminated prostatic tissue (or several very small glands). Therefore, they avoid the prostate gland problems that often plague other species.

The female reproductive-urinary tract consists of the external genitalia, or vulva; the vagina, a passage leading from the vulva to the cervix, the narrow outer end of the uterus, or womb, which holds the fertilized ova, or eggs, during their development as fetuses; and the two uterine horns that lead via the oviducts to the ovaries, which produce the eggs.

The urinary tract of both male and female cats contains two kidneys. They serve as filters for waste materials in the bloodstream, ridding the body of the different by-products, toxins, and poisons that can build up. The kidneys concentrate these wastes into urine by passing the blood through a system of filters. The urine is then conveyed through the ureter into the bladder, which serves as a reservoir until it is full and a certain pressure point is reached. At this point, the sphincter muscle relaxes and allows the stored urine to go out of the body through the urethra. Older cats often suffer from various urinary tract disorders. Kidney disease is a common problem, as is cystitis and feline urological syndrome (FUS). See "Renal Diseases and Disorders" in the Encyclopedia for symptoms and treatment of feline urinary diseases.

Endocrine System

The endocrine glands, located throughout a cat's body, manufacture and release hormones into the bloodstream. The pituitary gland controls and regulates many of the other endocrine glands by the hormones that it produces (there are six major hormones produced by the pituitary) and is a major control site for the entire

body. Other endocrine glands are the thyroid, the parathyroid, the adrenal cortex, the adrenal medulla, the pancreas, and the gonads. For a detailed discussion of the endocrine system of cats, see "Endocrine Diseases" in the Encyclopedia.

Hemic-Lymphatic System

Because of the feline leukemia virus (FeLV), the hemic-lymphatic system is a common area of primary disorders in the cat (see the Encyclopedia of Diseases of Cats). The hemic-lymphatic system includes the spleen, lymph nodes, and bone marrow. Bone marrow is primarily responsible for the production of the different blood cells (red and white blood cells

and platelets). Platelets are necessary for proper blood coagulation, red blood cells carry oxygen to the tissues, and white blood cells perform various tasks. They ward off infection, clear debris from the body, and produce antibodies. White blood cells live about seven days, while red blood cells average a sixty-day life span. The clearinghouse for old red blood cells is the spleen, which also serves as an organ for the secondary production of red blood cells.

There are literally hundreds of lymph nodes located in various areas throughout a cat's body. They are responsible for the production of lymphocytes, a particular type of white blood cell that controls and regulates the body's immune system. Tonsils are specialized lymph nodes (glands) or tissue in the throat necessary to ward off infections. They rarely cause cats any problems, but many cats are misdiagnosed as having tonsillitis and are given unnecessary tonsillectomies.

Integumentary System

In this category we include the cat's hair, skin, whiskers (vibrissae), anal glands or sacs, claws, and feet.

A cat's hair, or coat, is an important system of its body. It forms a physical barrier between the environment and the skin, and with the skin helps to create homeostasis (a balance between the external world and the internal cat).

Cats have three basic types of hair. Fine hairs make up a soft undercoat. Longhaired cats' coats simply grow more, because of a special inherited gene that stimulates growth. The outer coat is made up of longer, coarser guard hairs, and there are the stiff vibrissae, which project from the cat's body as whiskers (we will talk more about these later). Cats' hair is able to stand on end all over the body in response to fear or anger because of tiny erectorpile muscles that react in an action called piloerection. Exceptions to this are Rex cats, both Devon and Cornish. The Cornish Rex coat contains no guard hairs at all, and the Devon Rex has a coat of uneven length and often few whiskers. The result is a very short, often curly coat.

There is an infinite variety of cat coat colors in all sorts of combinations and shades of pure white, lavender, red, gray, brown, and black. The majority of cats have several different colors in their coats, and many breeds (the Abyssinian, for example) have two or three bands of contrasting color on each hair—known as "ticking," or agouti. Cats' coat colors can be affected by the environmental temperature: Cold areas induce dark hair growth, and hot climates produce lighter hair color. This phenomenon commonly occurs in the body color of Siamese cats, which can range from dark brownish tan to almost white, depending on the climate.

The most frequently seen coat patterns, especially in shorthaired nonpedigreed cats, are the tabby and variations of the white pattern. The combinations and variations of these two markings are too numerous to mention. Bicolor cats always have a dominant white gene, while tabby coats are made up of a background of one color overlayed by a pattern. It is interesting to note that some coat colors are sex-linked. Tortoiseshell or calico (tortoiseshell and white) cats are almost always female—the rare male is sterile—and orange cats (except for Abyssinians) are usually male. In order for a female orange cat to be produced, both the queen and the stud must be predominantly orange.

All cats shed a great deal all year long. This is a natural cycle of hair replacement and has to do with both the photoperiod and the environmental temperature. Thus, an outdoor cat may shed more in the spring as the days grow longer. Cats under stress will always shed excessively. Variations of degrees of shedding are usually due to a difference in the length and thickness of the coat and the hair itself. When left ungroomed, the shed hairs of long-coated cats will form mats and tangles instead of falling out, especially in the fall when new hair growth begins.

Under the coat is the cat's skin, a very important organ that is often overlooked. Along with the coat, the skin protects the cat's internal organs and helps to provide a balance with the external world. Because cats do not perspire except through their foot pads, their skin helps to dissipate heat. The blood vessels dilate, helping to cool the body. When it is cold, the skin's vessels constrict to retain body heat. One of the most important functions of the skin is its action as a sensory perceptor, conveying sensations of touch, pain, and so forth, to the brain. Another positive role that the skin plays is as a synthesizer of vitamin D. A cat's skin is also an important indicator of disease. Cats with jaundice, for instance, will turn yellow all over, while the skin of a cat with congestive heart failure may have a blue tinge. In addition, if there is no dermatologic problem, poor looking dry skin and coat often signal illness. A cat's skin has antimicrobial and antibacterial capabilities as well, which help to protect the body from infection. See "Dermatologic Diseases and Disorders" in the Encyclopedia.

The claws and feet are also part of a cat's integumentary system. A cat's foot pads are thick and tough, and act as a kind of shock absorber for the body. Sweat glands are located in the skin between the foot pads, causing a cat's feet to become moist when it is hot or overexcited. Usually, there are five toes on each front foot and four on each back foot; cats often have extra toes on their front feet—an inherited trait known as polydactylia. By pushing on the appropriate foot pad, each claw can be made to extend. Cats' claws serve a threefold purpose: as weapons, as a source of traction for climbing, and as tools for digging to

bury urine and feces. Cats have an ability to retract and extend their claws when needed, using specialized tendons and ligaments. To prevent them from catching on things the claws must be clipped if they do not wear down naturally. See "Grooming and Cleanliness" in Chapter 3 for how to do this. Also see "Declawing" in Chapter 4 and "Furniture Scratching" in Chapter 8.

The unique areas of the integumentary system of the cat are tactile or sinus hairs. These are stiff hairs that protrude from the body in various locations (see Illustration 2, below). They consist of the whiskers (vibrissae), eyelashes, and sinus hairs on the insides of the mid to lower forearms. The whiskers are innervated by the fifth cranial nerve of the brain. These specialized hairs act like radar, enabling a cat to "feel" air currents and judge spatial relationships when it cannot see.

The anal glands, or sacs, are two small glands located roughly at the eight and four o'clock positions on either side of the rectum of both male and female cats. At one point during the cat's evolution, the foul-smelling secretion from these glands was probably used as a territorial marker, but for the average house cat

Illustration 2: The cat's tactile hairs

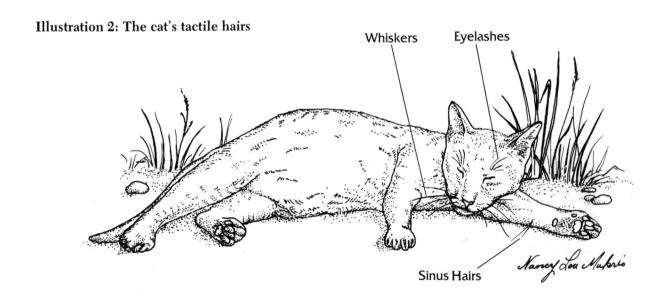

Whiskers   Eyelashes

Sinus Hairs

they now serve no useful purpose. Usually, the secreted matter in the anal glands is forced out by pressure from the feces when a cat has a bowel movement. Cats rarely have problems associated with these glands.

Physiological Differences in Breeds of Cats

Despite differences in size, ear shape, tail length, body conformation, and haircoat in various breeds of cats, all cats are essentially the same physiologically. Exceptions are Manx cats, which are born tailless, and Scottish Folds, which have ear tips that are bent forward. Manx cats often walk with a stilted gait and many suffer from spina bifida (see "Congenital Neurologic Diseases" in the Encyclopedia), and they sometimes have rectal abnormalities, such as an opening that is too small or no anal opening at all. For more information about some of these hereditary problems, see "Congenital Abnormalities" in Chapter 6.

3

Keeping Your Cat Healthy

Audrey A. Hayes, VMD

The Importance of Routine

In this chapter we will be concentrating primarily on how to provide for a cat's physical well-being through proper veterinary care, immunizations, diet, exercise, and basic grooming and cleanliness. There is more to keeping a cat healthy and well than just physical care, however.

Cats are relatively easy pets to own because of their innate cleanliness, neatness, and generally quiet behavior. For this reason, owners may make the mistake of thinking that a cat requires little thought or attention other than providing for basic physical needs. But in addition to regular mealtimes and a clean litter pan, pet cats crave and require attention and affection from their owners on a regular basis.

Although adult cats can be left alone for fairly long periods of time with food, water, and a litter pan, a pet cat should never be left for more than two days without some other care provisions being made. If unexpected delays or absences come up, arrangements should be made for someone to visit the cat at least once a day. Emergency telephone numbers—where the owner and the cat's regular veterinarian can be reached—should always

be available. Cats depend on their owners a great deal, and a pet who is ignored or left alone for too long may very well develop behavior problems. (See Chapter 8 for more about this.)

Cats really want to please and to do what is wanted, as long as they know what to expect. Even a very young kitten can be taught that her owner does not want her on furniture or kitchen counters, for instance. A spray bottle of water is a very effective training tool for cat owners. It is quiet, inexpensive, easy to use, and cats really dislike being sprayed with water. Of course, training a cat to behave in an acceptable way requires time and effort from an owner. Ideally, the owner of a new cat or kitten should plan ahead to set some time aside to acclimate the pet to the household in order to start it off right.

A cat owner who is willing to take the time and make the effort to see to it that the pet's needs for routine and affection are taken care of and who recognizes that these needs will change as the kitten grows into an adult cat will be rewarded with a responsive, well behaved pet.

Bringing Home a New Cat

Whether or not there are other cats in the household, the smartest thing that an owner can do is take a newly acquired kitten or cat directly to the veterinarian for a checkup before going home. This applies to adult cats as well as kittens and to all new acquisitions regardless of source (for example, shelter, street corner, breeder). This is because there are a number of highly infectious feline parasites and diseases that may not be outwardly apparent, even to the most experienced cat owner.

Unfortunately, even this step cannot unfailingly ensure that a cat is not incubating an infectious disease that even a veterinarian may not be able to detect. Therefore, it is very important for owners who have other cats at home to isolate a newcomer for a minimum of two weeks, until it is certain that the newcomer is not contagious. This means providing separate litter pans and food and water dishes, and preventing all direct contact between the cats. It makes no difference that the existing resident felines have up-to-date immunizations, because there are often strains of disease to which they may not be immune. This is especially true in the case of very young or elderly cats who are apt to be less resistant to disease than healthy young adult and middle-aged felines.

If the new kitten or cat is obviously not well or develops any symptoms of illness, even more care must be taken to protect other cats in the household from exposure. Because an owner can be a carrier, transporting some viruses (upper respiratory viral infections, for example) on clothing, hands, and so forth, protective clothing such as a smock or bathrobe and old socks or slippers should be worn over regular clothing when tending to the new cat; this clothing should stay in the isolation area. Hands and dishes should be disinfected with an antibacterial, antiviral, antifungal agent that you may get from the druggist or veterinarian. If all this sounds very difficult, owners should bear in mind that it is far easier to prevent infection than to have several sick cats to care for.

Checkups

When a kitten or cat is taken to the veterinarian for the first time, a stool sample should automatically be brought along so that the doctor can check for intestinal parasites (see the Encyclopedia of Diseases of Cats).

A routine physical examination of a cat is described in Chapter 1. It is important for owners to establish the habit of taking an adult cat to the veterinarian annually. When a cat is seen on a regular basis, the doctor can spot any abnormalities or differences much more easily. An office visit is also an excellent time for an owner to discuss any physical or behavioral changes that may have developed in the cat.

One of the easiest and best ways to be sure that a cat receives regular health examinations is to combine a checkup with necessary immunizations or booster shots. Since kittens require immunizations every few weeks until they are four months old, this presents an excellent opportunity for the doctor to assess a young cat's development. After that, yearly visits for booster shots allow an adult cat to be examined. Of course, special circumstances may call for additional visits, and once a cat becomes a senior citizen, more frequent exams may be needed; but, in general, an annual visit combining boosters with a checkup is a good rule to follow for all healthy adult cats.

Vaccinations: What Do They Do?

One of the most important aspects of preventive medicine for cats is periodic vaccination for serious infectious diseases. Infectious diseases are those caused by the invasion of the body by living organisms, usually bacteria or viruses. An infectious disease may or may not be contagious, depending on the organism involved and its tendency to pass from one animal to another. Most of the infectious diseases for which vaccinations are available are highly contagious through either direct contact, airborne viruses, indirect contact (such as stools of infected animals), or through an intermediate host (such as fleas).

The infectious cat diseases for which vaccines have been developed are: feline panleukopenia, rhinotracheitis, calicivirus (often combined in one vaccine), pneumonitis (included in four-component vaccines), feline leukemia virus (FeLV), and rabies (killed vaccine only for cats). We recommend the four-component vaccine because, although pneumonitis is a relatively mild disease that manifests itself with upper respiratory symptoms, it tends to linger longer than rhinotracheitis or calicivirus and can become chronic. Cats with chronic pneumonitis often become poor, picky eaters because the disease interferes with their sense of smell. More about these diseases and their symptoms and treatment can be found in the Encyclopedia of Diseases of Cats.

Vaccinations are given to "teach" a cat's immune system (defense system) about a particular disease organism. Once the body's defenses are primed or awakened to a particular bacterium or virus, the body is ready to do battle when the real disease organism is encountered. Antibodies have been manufactured.

An *antibody* is a protein that body cells manufacture in response to exposure to a disease organism or to a vaccine. Thus, when an animal has been vaccinated against a particular disease, the antibody is in its body. This antibody helps to fight off the invading infection and obviously does a better job if it is already present and circulating in the cat's body when the disease enters. This, then, is the basic rationale for vaccination. It allows a cat to have the antibody already present and ready to fight against a disease instead of having to become sick and recover in order to have that antibody form naturally.

Vaccines are *not* effective once an animal becomes infected. They are used to *prevent* diseases, not treat or cure them.

Incubation Periods of Diseases

One of the most confusing things about infectious diseases is the concept of an incubation period, or the time that lapses between exposure of an animal to an infectious disease and the first signs or symptoms of the disease. No disease organisms produce signs or symptoms immediately after they enter the body. The bacteria or viruses settle in the body and begin a process of multiplication. This period is known as the incubation period, and during it a cat may show no signs of illness. It is only after the disease organisms have reached a critical number, destroyed enough tissue, or spread to another area of the body or the bloodstream that the animal will begin to appear ill.

As we pointed out above, it is especially crucial to be aware of this when getting a new kitten. Although the kitten may show no signs of illness even to a veterinarian, it can be incubating a disease that will surface some time later. That is why it is so important to isolate a new kitten from other cats in the household. Even the most careful breeders, agencies, and owners may not be able to prevent *all* contact with disease, so it is equally important to start a kitten's vaccinations right away. So-called "temporary" shots have very limited effect against disease, as we will discuss in the next section.

When a kitten or cat is vaccinated during the incubation period of an infectious disease (in other words, after the disease has already entered its body), a race is set up within the cat's body. Will the vaccine stimulate enough immunity quickly enough to protect the cat from the disease? Or has the disease gotten such a head start that the infection will still cause the animal to become ill despite the vaccination? Usually, the disease will win out and the animal will become ill. This is often misinterpreted by owners, and they attribute the cat's illness to the vaccination itself. It is extremely rare that a vaccination causes an animal to become really ill. There is one exception to this; it has to do with the way vaccinations are given and the fact that cats are such continuous self-groomers. If just one tiny drop of modified live virus vaccine gets on a cat's fur and is then licked off by the cat, symptoms of illness will occur. That's why we are always so careful to ensure that a dry sterile needle is used to give a vaccination and that no vaccine is accidentally spilled on the outside of the cat. An observant owner should pay attention to the way a veterinarian gives immunizations, and if any vaccine is spilled, the owner must make sure that an antivirus disinfectant such as alcohol is used to remove it before the cat (or another cat) has a chance to lick it off.

Vaccinations are usually given in a series every four weeks to kittens under four months. This is necessary, for although kittens do attain *passive immunity* during the first week of life from the colostrum in their mother's milk, these antibodies are short-lived. Studies show that 95 percent of kittens have lost passive immunity by twelve weeks of age, and the remaining 5 percent by the time they are sixteen weeks old. While these maternal antibodies are alive, they will automatically inactivate a vaccination. But since we don't know exactly when passive immunity will be lost, a series of vaccinations is given to ensure that a kitten is protected at all times. After sixteen weeks it is certain that a kitten will have lost all maternal antibodies and will now be able to respond to vaccination by forming antibodies, or *active immunity*. This is why so-called "temporary" shots given to a kitten at a young age do not provide effective long-term protection.

After a kitten has been successfully vaccinated by a series of injections (see Figure 1, below), it can usually be assumed that immunity has been achieved for a period of time.

FIGURE 1

IMMUNIZATION CHART FOR KITTENS

(Note: This chart is a representative example of immunizations.
Many veterinarians recommend slightly different vaccination schedules.)

Disease	Age: 5–8 wks.	9–12 wks.	13–16 wks.	18 wks.	26 wks.	1 year
Panleukopenia	x	x	x			x
Rhinotracheitis	x	x	x			x
Calicivirus	x	x	x			x
Pneumonitis	x	x	x			x
Feline Leukemia Virus Vaccine (killed virus). For FeLV (−) cats only			x	x	x	x

Rabies vaccination: Use only killed rabies vaccine for cats. If first vaccination is given between 16–24 weeks of age, repeat vaccination needed at 28 weeks of age. If first vaccination is given between 24–28 weeks of age, only one vaccination is needed during the first year of life.

Feline Leukemia Virus test should be performed at 16 weeks of age.

However, it is important to realize that *no vaccine is 100 percent effective in all cases.* Some cats have a more sluggish immune system than others, and not all respond as well to vaccination as we would hope. It is always possible for an animal to contract a disease even when properly vaccinated, although the disease will

FIGURE 2

IMMUNIZATION CHART FOR ADULT CATS

Disease	Yearly	Every 1–3 Years	More Often When Indicated
Panleukopenia	x		
Rhinotracheitis	x		
Calicivirus	x		
Pneumonitis	x		x
FeLV vaccine (killed virus)	x		
Rabies (killed vaccine)		x	x*
Feline Leukemia Virus Test		x	x†

Adult cats who have received no previous vaccinations as kittens, or whose vaccination history is unknown, should have 2 vaccinations at 2–3 week intervals and then annual booster vaccinations for the rest of their lives.

* Depends on different state laws and import requirements when traveling to foreign countries and on the vaccine preparation used.
† If exposed to FeLV(+) cat and if required before boarding. Before breeding, both queen and tom should be tested and proved (−) for FeLV.

usually be less severe and of shorter duration than in an unvaccinated animal.

It is also important to point out that recently there have been cases of properly immunized kittens developing a strain of calicivirus, characterized by fever and swollen, very painful joints. This has been dubbed the "limping kitten syndrome." There are multiple strains of calicivirus, and manufacturers have traditionally chosen to include one strain of the virus that would protect against most of the other strains in their vaccines. However, at least two strains of calicivirus that produce the limping kitten syndrome have been isolated, and existing vaccines produce no protection against one particular strain. The result is that new vaccines must be developed. In the meantime, owners should be aware of the possibility that even properly immunized kittens, and those who have received colostrum from well-vaccinated mothers, can develop this disease and become very ill very suddenly. When properly treated with antibiotics and other medications, kittens do recover from this disease.

The most recent development in feline preventive medicine is the development of a feline leukemia killed-virus vaccine, approved by the USDA in November 1984. Because of the contagious nature of FeLV, this is a major breakthrough. Once an adequate amount of vaccine has been produced in order to supply the public at large, cats will be routinely vaccinated for FeLV, according to the schedules in Figure 1, page 29, and Figure 2, at left. Adult cats being vaccinated for FeLV for the first time should be given immunizations following the schedule given for kittens—that is, two weeks after the first vaccination, two months after the second, and then on a yearly basis. Because of its recent development, the FeLV vaccine may be expensive. We should reiterate that no vaccine is 100 percent effective, and vaccinated cats should nevertheless be tested for FeLV prior to exposure to other cats (before boarding, breeding, and showing, for example). A cat that is already suffering from FeLV or that is incubating undetected FeLV will not be hurt by the vaccine; however, the vaccine may not prevent FeLV infection in a cat that has recently been exposed.

Booster Shots

Immunity to a disease from a vaccination or from the disease itself is not a lifelong matter. Antibody levels fall, and vaccinations must be given periodically to create an anamnestic response (reminder) and make sure that immunity continues. As a rule, revaccinations or "booster" shots should be given annually, but there are some exceptions. Figure 2 shows the normal frequency of boosters for most infectious diseases, but in some instances a doctor may recommend more frequent boosters. A booster, by the way, is the same kind and strength of vaccine as the original vaccination. The name developed because it is intended to periodically strengthen or boost immunization.

Do All Cats Need Vaccinations?

"My cat never leaves the apartment, so why should I spend money on shots for her?" is a common owner question.

Regardless of living situation, every cat should be protected against infectious disease. Even a cat who "never goes anywhere" will probably make at least one visit to the doctor's office to be neutered or spayed. But a cat does not need to go anywhere to contract an upper-respiratory tract infection—its owners do. Infectious respiratory viruses can be carried on clothing, hands, and shoes even if an owner only comes within breathing distance of an infected cat. We are now recommending that even completely indoor cats be routinely immunized against rabies because of the high incidence of the disease among wildlife in many areas.

Cats that have not been properly immunized are particularly susceptible to infection from even casual exposure, and older cats can be especially hard hit. The possibilities of even the most well protected house cat encountering disease germs are so numerous that regular vaccinations are the only sensible course for caring cat owners to follow.

Keeping a Cat's Health Records

Many veterinarians keep health records for their patients and send cards or call to remind owners when it is time for a cat to have a vaccination or booster. However, cards do get lost in the mail and call messages can be forgotten, so the best and easiest thing for careful cat owners to do is keep their own records. Up-to-date records will come in very handy, too, in case of a move or change of doctor. And if there is more than one cat in the household, a ready reference of immunizations and boosters due is the only way to keep records straight!

We have included a sample health chart here (Figure 3, page 32).

Nutrition: Feeding a Cat Right

The information on pages 31–46 is adapted, in part, from Feline Nutrition, Animal Nutrition Series 2, Kal Kan Foods Inc., 1984, by Cheryl R. Dhein, DVM, MS, and Edith van Marthens, DVM.

Although there is ongoing research by the major pet food manufacturers and in university laboratories throughout the country, there is still less information about cats' dietary requirements than there is about those of humans or dogs. We do know, however, that while cats' nutritional needs are generally similar to those of other animals, they do have some unique nutritional needs,[1,2,3] including: 1) a relatively high amount of protein, 2) an inability to synthesize vitamin A and niacin, 3)

FIGURE 3

CAT'S SAMPLE HEALTH CHART

Owner's name: _____
Address: _____
Cat's Name: _____ Birth date: _____
Breed: _____ Color: _____ Sex: _____
Age when acquired: _____
Where acquired: Name: _____ Address: _____ Phone: _____

KITTEN RECORD:

Age: 8 weeks   Date: _____
Weight: _____ Length: _____ Height: _____
Remarks: _____
Immunizations given: Panleukopenia, Rhinotracheitis, Calicivirus, Pneumonitis
Stool specimen checked for internal parasites. Results: _____
Medications dispensed: _____
Next visit: _____

Age: 11 weeks   Date: _____
Weight: _____ Length: _____ Height: _____
Remarks: _____
Immunizations given: _____
Medications dispensed: _____
Next visit: _____

Age: 16 weeks to 1 year   Date: _____
Feline leukemia virus test performed. Results: _____
Date neutered or spayed: _____
Immunizations given (includes FeLV vaccine):_____

And so forth, until adulthood.

ADULT RECORD:

Age: Date: _____
Weight: _____ Length: _____ Height: _____
Remarks: _____
Feline leukemia virus test performed. Results: _____
Boosters given: _____
Next vaccinations due: _____
Medications dispensed: _____

the amino acid arginine (for adult cats), 4) the amino acid taurine for cats of all ages, 5) an animal source of essential fatty acids, and 6) a relatively large requirement for B-complex vitamins. We will discuss what a deficiency of any of these requirements can lead to later on in this section (also see Table 2, page 35). The single most important thing for cat owners to know, however, is that cats *must be fed a diet specifically formulated to meet their needs* and that they require an animal source of nutrients. Foods designed for dogs will not meet cats' nutritional requirements and should not be fed exclusively for any length of time.

A Balanced Diet

The food a cat eats supplies its body with calories (usually measured in kilocalories [Kcal], or 1,000 calories) that are transformed into energy in order to keep the body functioning and to meet special needs such as growth, gestation, lactation, and so forth. Cats' energy needs, and therefore their caloric requirements, vary at different times of their lives and in different circumstances. We will talk more about this later on. In order to understand what proportions of nutrients are needed on a daily basis, however, we need to know that fat supplies twice the Kcal per gram ingested than carbohydrates and proteins do.

Proteins

Whereas dogs and many other animals, including humans, derive their energy primarily from carbohydrates and fats, a cat's main source of energy is protein. A cat's daily protein requirements are from two to three times higher than a dog's, with a minimum requirement of 22 to 25 percent of the dry matter of diet made up of protein for kittens, and 13 to 20 percent for adult cats.[3,4,5]

Amino acids: Proteins also supply a cat with amino acids, often referred to as the body's "building blocks." There are twenty-two recognized amino acids. Ten are deemed essential for all species, but two are uniquely essential for cats because they are not manufactured in their bodies and must be supplied by diet (see Table 1, at right). In addition, proteins supply the body with nitrogen. Not all protein sources supply all of the amino acids in the same usable proportions. Vegetables, for example, are not a complete protein and do not contain an adequate balance of amino acids to meet a cat's needs.

The two amino acids arginine and taurine are essential to the cat. Arginine rids adult cats' bodies of the unusually large amount of ammonia created by their high protein intake. Because their bodies cannot make arginine, it is essential in their daily diet. An arginine deficiency will lead to immediate signs in the cat. These include depression, muscle tremors, incoordination, and even death.[6] Fortunately, deficiencies are not common, because most foods contain arginine. Exceptions are milk, cheese, and most semimoist cat foods, in which the primary protein is casein, which is deficient in arginine. If these foods are a cat's sole protein source, they must be supplemented with arginine.[1] A cat cannot convert nutrients into taurine as all other species can and therefore needs taurine in its diet throughout its lifetime.[7] A taurine deficiency will eventually lead to blindness in a cat because of degeneration of the retina. Secondary results of a taurine deficiency are heart trouble and stunted growth.[1,2,3] Meat is the best source of taurine for a cat. Milk is low in this amino acid, and vegetables contain almost none. Commercial

TABLE 1

ESSENTIAL AMINO ACIDS

Arginine*	Phenylalanine
Histidine	Taurine**
Isoleucine	Threonine
Leucine	Tryptophan
Lysine	Valine
Methionine	

* Essential for adult cats
** Essential for cats of all ages. Essential *only* for cats.

pet food manufacturers recognize the cat's need for taurine and add it to their products in adequate amounts.

Fats

Fats supply essential fatty acids in a cat's diet and provide for the proper absorption of the fat-soluble vitamins A, D, E, and K. They are also good energy sources (as we pointed out, above, fats contain twice as many calories per gram as proteins or carbohydrates do), and they also make foods palatable for cats. Although cats can tolerate high fat diets without intestinal upsets better than dogs or humans, it is still advisable to increase a cat's fat intake gradually when necessary. There is some controversy as to the ideal percentage of fat in a normal cat's diet. In special situations when more energy is required such as growth, pregnancy, or lactation, a cat's fat intake needs to be increased.

There are three essential fatty acids that the cat needs: linoleic, linolenic, and arachidonic acid. Linoleic and linolenic acid are found in vegetable oils, but arachidonic acid is contained *only* in animal fats. Unlike other animals, cats cannot convert arachidonic acid from linoleic and linolenic acids. A diet low in essential fatty acids can lead to dry skin and coat, a sparse haircoat, sterility, and low energy. An animal source of fats is essential to cats.

Carbohydrates

There are no established minimum daily carbohydrate (sugars, starch, crude fiber) requirements for cats. However, cats can utilize cooked or finely ground grains and vegetables,[7] found in many commercial cat foods. Raw vegetables and vegetable matter such as grass are often eaten by cats. Too much crude fiber in a cat's diet, however, may lead to large stools, which will rob a cat's body of essential nutrients. It is also important to remember that vegetables and grains do not contain the proper proportions of amino acids and essential fatty acids necessary to a cat.

Milk contains a sugar, lactose, that is sometimes indigestible for adult cats and may cause diarrhea. But it is a good source of nutrients and can often be tolerated by adult cats when it is introduced gradually.

Vitamins

There are two kinds of vitamins: water-soluble (C and B-complex) and fat-soluble (A, D, E, K). It can usually be assumed that those vitamins not manufactured in a cat's body are added in proper quantities and strength to quality commercial cat foods, and casual additional supplementation may lead to toxicity. (We will talk more about this later.) *The fat-soluble vitamins* are stored in the body, and an excess can therefore become toxic.

Vitamin A: Cats have a relatively high vitamin A requirement. They cannot convert carotenoids (found in green vegetables) into vitamin A in their own bodies and must have a meat source for this vitamin. Liver is a good source of A, but an excess (as in an exclusive diet of liver) can lead to severe bone disease. A deficiency of vitamin A can lead to weight loss, scaly skin, hair loss, eye (retinal) and reproductive problems.

Vitamin D: Cats can manufacture vitamin D in their own bodies through the action of the sun's ultraviolet rays, or it can be obtained through food. A deficiency of this vitamin is rare. Since D is required in the proper proportion in order for the body to properly utilize the minerals calcium and phosphorus, over-supplementation with D can lead to calcium and phosphorus deposits in the body's soft tissues (kidneys, lungs, heart, and blood vessels).

Vitamin E: Cats' vitamin E requirements are quite low and can usually be met by a well-balanced vitamin-fortified commercial diet formulated for cats. A deficiency can occur, however, when a diet contains too much unsaturated fat. It will prevent the absorption of E into a cat's body. Red tuna and other dark-meated, oily fish such as sardines and mackerel, intended for human consumption and not supplemented with vitamin E, can lead to a deficiency in a cat if eaten on a regular basis (even if not the cat's sole diet). Vitamin E deficiency results in a painful inflammatory dis-

TABLE 2   35

DEFICIENCIES AND EXCESSES OF NUTRIENTS IN A CAT'S DIET: THEIR CAUSES AND RESULTS

Nutrient	Cause of Deficiency or Excess	Result
Arginine (amino acid):		
Deficiency	Unsupplemented diet of foods high in casein (milk, cheese, semimoist cat food)	Depression, lack of coordination, muscle weakness, collapse
Taurine (amino acid):		
Deficiency	Unsupplemented diet of dog food, vegetables, milk	Blindness, heart trouble, stunted growth
Essential fatty acids (linoleic, linolenic, arachidonic):		
Deficiency	Lack of dietary animal fat source	Low energy, poor coat, hair loss, sterility, crankiness
Vitamin A:		
Deficiency	Lack of dietary source	Skin and eye problems, weight loss, impaired reproductive functions
Excess	Exclusive diet of raw liver	Severe bone disease
Vitamin D:		
Excess	Oversupplementation	Calcium and phosphorus deposits in soft tissues
Vitamin E:		
Deficiency	Diet high in unsaturated fats due to feeding unsupplemented dark, oily-meated fish	Pansteatitis, or yellow-fat disease
Vitamin K:		
Deficiency	Prolonged use of antibiotics, warfarin poisoning	Anemia, bleeding
Vitamin B_1 (Thiamine):		
Deficiency	Diet consisting of some kinds of raw or canned fish containing thiaminase; unsupplemented food that has been heated in processing	Anorexia, weight loss, convulsions, catatonia
Niacin:		
Deficiency	Lack of niacin in diet	Weakness, weight loss, mouth disorders, respiratory disorders
Biotin:		
Deficiency	Too many raw egg whites	Secretions around eyes, nose, and mouth; emaciation, dermatitis
Improper calcium-to-phosphorus ratio:	Unsupplemented all-meat diet	
Calcium:		
Deficiency		Nerve, muscle, bone, and bleeding disorders; secondary hyperparathyroidism
Excess		Soft-tissue mineralization
Iron and copper:		
Deficiency	Unsupplemented all-milk diet	Anemia
Iodine:		
Deficiency	Unsupplemented all-meat diet	Thyroid dysfunction
Magnesium:		
Excess	Too much in diet	Formation of uroliths (urinary tract stones)

ease called pansteatitis (yellow-fat disease) that is characterized by fever, anorexia, pain on being handled or touched, and fatty subcutaneous lumps.

Vitamin K: Cats manufacture vitamin K in their own bodies, so no dietary K is necessary except in special situations such as prolonged illness and antibiotic therapy. Warfarin poisoning (see the Encyclopedia of Diseases of Cats) can also interfere with vitamin K absorption.

Water-soluble vitamins (B-complex and C): Excesses of water-soluble vitamins do not occur since unused amounts are flushed out in the urine.

B-complex vitamins: Cats require two to eight times more B vitamins than dogs do.[7] Except in cases of prolonged antibiotic therapy, which may produce a deficiency of most of the B vitamins and result in anemia, deficiencies are rare, with the following exceptions. (However, we always add B vitamins to the solution given to cats on intravenous feeding.)

Vitamin B₁ (Thiamine): Thiaminase, an enzyme that destroys thiamine, is contained in certain kinds of canned or raw fish (carp, saltwater herring, smelt, catfish, and bullhead, among others) and can produce a thiamine deficiency in cats. Thiamine is also easily destroyed by heat, and home-cooked diets may be deficient in it. Commercial cat food manufacturers add thiamine to their products after processing. However, B may be lost from canned food with prolonged storage. In cats, thiamine deficiency leads to anorexia, weight loss, catatonia, and convulsions. When a cat is deficient in this vitamin, a positive response to thiamine therapy is rapid and dramatic.

Niacin (Nicotinic Acid): Unlike other animals, cats cannot convert the amino acid tryptophan into niacin and therefore require it in their diets. A deficiency of niacin results in weakness, weight loss, diarrhea, mouth disorders (including a susceptibility to herpes), and respiratory disease.[3]

Biotin: Cats require very little biotin, which is manufactured in their own bodies. A deficiency can arise, however, when a cat is daily fed raw egg whites, which prevent the absorption of biotin in a cat's intestines. To avoid this, feed the yolk along with the white or cook the

egg white.[4] A severe biotin deficiency can lead to emaciation, dermatitis, and secretions around the nose, eyes, and mouth.

Vitamin C (Ascorbic Acid): Cats are able to synthesize vitamin C, and it is therefore not normally required in their diets. There is some controversy as to the benefits of supplemental C for cats with various infectious diseases or to acidify urine in cats with previous urethral obstruction. Although no permanent damage can be done even by oversupplementation, since the excess is washed out of a cat's system, too much C in the form of ascorbic acid can upset a cat's stomach, and overlarge tablets may irritate a cat's throat or become stuck in it. Many cat food manufacturers add some vitamin C to their products.

Minerals

Minerals are required by cats in small amounts on a daily basis and are normally provided in a varied, well-balanced diet. After a food is cooked, the remaining "ash" is composed of mineral residue. There are basically two groups of minerals: the trace minerals that are required in very minute amounts (such as chromium, cobalt, copper, fluorine, iodine, iron, manganese, molybdenum, nickel, selenium, silicon, tin, zinc, and vanadium), and the major minerals that are needed in larger quantities (calcium, chloride, magnesium, phosphorus, potassium, sodium, and sulfur).

Many factors, including vitamin intake, can affect the proper absorption of minerals into a cat's body. In addition, if the proper ratio of certain minerals to others is not maintained, absorption is reduced. Improper supplementation or a poor diet can cause mineral imbalances and excesses. For example, a cat fed nothing but unsupplemented meat will probably develop an improper calcium to phosphorus ratio. This can lead to a number of diseases. Too little calcium can lead to nerve, muscle, and bleeding disorders, and secondary nutritional hyperparathyroidism (paper bone disease) can develop in which the bones become thin and brittle, and break easily. Excess calcium can create deposits in the body's soft tissues just an an excess of vitamin D can. It may also reduce the absorption of zinc, leading to skin disease, and may cause anemia due to the lack of absorption of iron and copper. Occasionally, an unsupplemented all-meat diet can lead to an iodine deficiency and impaired thyroid function.

An all-milk diet, which is rare today, can result in iron and copper deficiencies and anemia, while excess magnesium is suspect in the formation of urinary tract stones.

Sometimes owners will be advised by the veterinarian to add sodium chloride (salt) to a cat's food in order to encourage greater water intake.

Water

Many people are under the mistaken impression that cats require little if any drinking water. That is because cats can often derive all of the water they need from their food and seem to drink very sparingly. But cats require water, like all living creatures, to replace the water lost from waste, respiration, grooming, and evaporation. It is needed to flush out the body, to remove excess minerals and other waste materials, to transport nutrients throughout a cat's body, and to regulate body temperature. Some of this water is metabolically derived,[8] some is obtained in food, and the rest must be provided by drinking water. Needless to say, a cat that eats only dry food will require more drinking water than one that eats moister canned rations.[8,9,10] Excess loss of body moisture as a result of fever, vomiting, diarrhea, or very hot weather, means that a cat will need more drinking water.

Fresh drinking water in a clean glass, china, or stainless steel bowl should always be available for a cat. Cats often prefer to drink from dripping faucets and even toilet bowls, and owners of these cats should take care to rinse fixtures carefully so that residual cleansing agents can't cause problems. Despite their normal fastidiousness, some cats will drink standing water—for example, from a plant saucer. If possible, owners should discourage this. If milk agrees with a cat, it can help to fulfill daily water requirements.

Kinds of Commercial Cat Foods

Commercial cat foods come in three basic forms: dry, semimoist, and canned. The most obvious difference in these types of food is moisture content, which also affects their ability to stay fresh when exposed to air. Many owners feed their cats more than one type of food each day. It is a good idea to accustom a cat to eating several kinds and flavors of food early in life, to avoid firmly established food preferences (see "Feeding Problems," page 44). See Table 3, page 38, for a comparison of the caloric and nutritive values of these three types of food.

Dry Food

Dry cat foods are very low in moisture (6 to 10 percent) and are usually a combination of many ingredients and supplements that are cooked, dried, and then sprayed with fats and flavorings. They are convenient to use, stay fresh in a feeding bowl, are relatively inexpensive, and are very good for cats' gums and teeth. Most cats like them. Some dry foods contain insufficient fat or protein to be used as an exclusive diet (see "Reading the Labels," page 38), and supplementary water is essential for a cat that eats a lot of dry food. Small kittens should not be fed dry food at all unless it is softened with water or broth.

Semimoist Food

Semimoist cat foods contain three to four times (30 to 40 percent) more moisture than dry foods. They are also a blend of ingredients and supplements that are combined with humectants and sugars to prevent spoilage and to keep them moist. They are relatively expensive and, because they are soft, provide no gum or tooth benefits; but they are convenient to use and stay moist in the bowl for several hours, and cats usually find them very palatable.

TABLE 3

NUTRITIONAL VALUES OF CAT FOODS*

Type of Diet	% Moisture	Kcal/ Ounce Including Moisture	Protein % Dry Matter	Fat % Dry Matter
Dry	6–10	100 (97–106)	34 (30–40)	12 (9–12)
Semimoist	30–40	75 (60–90)	36 (33–39)	16.5 (12–23)
Canned	70–78	35 (23–46)	55 (31–78)	22 (3–40)

* Feline Nutrition, Animal Nutrition Series 2, Kal Kan Foods Inc. Modified from Lewis, L. D., Morris, M. L. *Small Animal Clinical Nutrition.* Chapter 1: Nutrition; Chapter 2: Pet Foods; Chapter 3: Feeding Cats. Topeka, Kansas: Mark Morris Associates, 1983.

There are several problems associated with the use of semimoist food as an exclusive diet. Owners should be aware that cats cannot metabolize the sugars used for preservatives in these foods and will flush them out in their urine, possibly causing a false positive diabetes mellitus test. As we mentioned above, casein, a low-quality protein, is the principal protein used in most semimoist foods, and an exclusive diet of these foods may create an arginine deficiency. In addition, some cats are allergic to semimoist foods. Although they will not harm an otherwise healthy cat when used as a snack and can sometimes have beneficial value in certain gastrointestinal disorders because of their bulk (see Chapter 14), we strongly recommend that owners not use semimoist foods as a cat's sole diet.

Canned Foods

Canned cat foods contain from 70 to 78 percent moisture and are usually made up of one or two main ingredients, such as meat, poultry, or fish mixed with grains or cereals and supplemented with vitamins and minerals. They are relatively expensive, but are very palatable and generally very nutritious. Because of their high moisture content, they are much lower in caloric value, per ounce, than either dry or semimoist foods and therefore more must be fed daily in order to meet a cat's energy requirements.

Reading the Labels

Pet food manufacturers are generally very responsible when it comes to the formulation of the products they sell for pets. The major companies have spent years researching cats' nutritional needs, and their products reflect that. However, it is often difficult for an owner to compare products because manufacturers include different data or data in a different form on their labels.

We should make one differentiation—between foods that are labeled "Complete and balanced nutrition for all life stages," "Meets or exceeds the minimum nutritional levels established by the National Research Council for kitten growth and adult cat maintenance," or "Complete, balanced diet," and those that do not. Foods that do not have these or similar statements on their labels, or those that are called "Treats," "Bits," "Snacks," or something similar, are *not* intended as the sole diet of a cat at any stage of life and should be used only as additions to an otherwise balanced diet.

If percentages of nutrients are included, a complete diet of dry cat food should contain approximately 30 percent crude protein; semimoist foods, 20 percent; and canned rations a minimum of 10 percent. On a dry weight basis, from 8 to 12 percent fat should be in dry and semimoist food and 5 percent in canned cat food. Foods high in "ash" (mineral residue) content are to be avoided for cats with a history of urinary disease. This may be hard to determine from the label alone, but foods recommended by the Morris Animal Foundation* for cats that have a history of FUS are: Friskies

* Morris Animal Foundation, 45 Inverness Dr. E., Englewood, CO 80112

Beef and Liver Buffet, Friskies Turkey and Giblets, and Feline c/d and s/d (see Table 4, page 40).

That is only part of the story, however. As we have pointed out, "crude protein" does not always signify *usable* protein. Because ingredients must always be listed in decreasing amounts, it is important to be sure that the primary protein source (listed first) is animal, not vegetable.

Vitamins and minerals are often lumped together, but most cat food manufacturers know the importance of adding vitamin E to fish products and list it separately on the label.

Similarly, B-complex vitamins, which may be destroyed in processing, should be listed as supplements. Meat-based diets also require mineral supplementation. If a calcium to phosphorus ratio is included, it should be approximately 1 to 1.

Although it is not necessary to buy over-priced food for a cat, it is important to note that, in general, you get what you pay for. Cheap cat food is likely to contain poor-quality ingredients that will not provide proper nutrition and may end up costing an owner more in the long run in veterinary bills.

Other Alternatives

Some owners are concerned about additives and food dyes used in commercial cat diets. In our experience, these preservatives and colorings are used in relatively small amounts and usually do not cause a problem for most cats. As we pointed out, however, some cats are allergic to the preservatives used in commercial semimoist foods, and some may not be able to tolerate other types of food. For these cats, alternative diets may be necessary.

Natural Cat Foods

In addition to the nationally known products that are distributed in supermarkets, there are several manufacturers of natural pet diets that produce cat foods in all the above forms. These products usually contain no sugar, artificial flavoring or coloring, preservatives, or other additives. But owners should check the labels for ingredients. Because there are no preservatives added, these foods have a short shelf life. Natural cat foods are generally quite expensive and are usually found only in pet stores or through mail order. See the Bibliography for a list of some manufacturers of these products.

Home-Cooked Meals

Some owners prefer to feed their cats food that has been prepared at home. There is no harm in this as long as the basic rules of feline nutrition are followed and meals are properly balanced. Sometimes a vitamin-mineral supplement is desirable when a cat is on a home-cooked diet. Be sure to obtain a preparation designed specifically for cats. The veterinarian is the best source of advice on this subject.

Problems can arise if a cat is allowed to develop a strong preference for any one food to the exclusion of all others, a syndrome that is likely to occur more easily when food is prepared at home. Owners should make sure to vary their pets' meals.

As an alternative to feeding a cat entirely home-prepared meals, an owner may opt to feed a pet a well-balanced commercial diet as its staple food and vary it with special treats. Small bits of cooked leftover chicken, meat, or fish are usually welcome additions to a cat's diet. Cats also like organ meats from poultry or meat, as well as small bits of cheese or butter. Some cats like vegetables, raw and cooked. Many will eat corn on the cob (owners should make sure the cat does not eat the cob itself, which might cause intestinal blockage).

Raw fish of all kinds should be avoided because it may contain parasites. Although raw meat is generally not recommended for cats because of the possibility of infection from toxoplasmosis, raw organ meat (heart, liver, kidney) that is very fresh is a particular favorite of cats, and many breeders do give it to their animals.

Bones of any kind, even cooked, soft bones, are to be avoided at all costs. Because cats do chew their food quite well they are often able to swallow small chicken bones, for instance, and many will end up with a bad intestinal laceration, perforation, or stoppage. Some cookbooks for cat owners are listed in the Bibliography.

Vegetarian Diets

Although cats often do like vegetables and some vegetable matter is included in almost all commercial cat diets, an exclusive diet of vegetables will not provide a cat with enough usable protein, essential fatty acids, and minerals to maintain health. As we pointed out, cats cannot utilize carbohydrates and fats for energy, as humans and some other species such as dogs can, and must have an animal source of protein for energy.

Prescription Diets

These special-formula diets, prepared by commercial manufacturers, are designed to meet the specific needs of cats with severe medical conditions such as food-related allergies, feline urologic syndrome (FUS), heart condition, kidney failure, and so forth. Their formulas are very precise, and they can be obtained only by prescription through a veterinarian. See Table 4, below, for a list of these products and their uses.

TABLE 4

PRESCRIPTION CAT FOODS AND THEIR USES

Following is a list of the most frequently used Prescription Diets for cats. These diets are all produced by Hills Pet Products, Inc., and are available only from a veterinarian. Most are available in both canned and dry forms.

Feline c/d	Low raw mineral, highly digestible diet for routine feeding; also indicated for urinary stoppage and cystitis; not for pregnant cats or young kittens	Feline r/d	Low-calorie diet for reducing
		Feline s/d	Low protein, magnesium, calcium, and phosphorus diet to prevent urethral obstruction and dissolve uroliths (urinary tract stones)
Feline k/d	Lower protein and mineral diet for impaired liver and kidney function		
		Feline Growth	Extra calories, protein, calcium and phosphorus for kittens and pregnant and nursing cats; contraindicated for FUS
Feline h/d	Low-salt diet for heart patients		
Feline p/d	Increased protein and fat for kittens, pregnant or lactating queens, recuperating cats and cats with infectious diseases	Domestic Feline	General maintenance diet

How Much of What to Feed and How Often

There is some controversy among experts about how many times a day to feed a cat. Traditionally, cats have been considered "occasional" eaters, believed to prefer snacking up to a dozen times a day rather than eating one or two large meals. Now, however, some researchers have concluded that adult cats fare better on two large daily meals (cats do not do well on only one meal a day). Many owners also object to providing a constant buffet for their pets and prefer to limit their adult cat's mealtimes somewhat. In our experience, if a cat with a big appetite is allowed to become too hungry, she will eat too fast and immediately vomit. On the other hand, some very hungry cats will fill up on dry food when given free access to it all day and then won't eat the more nutritious meal of canned rations that an owner offers. Probably the best solution is for owners and their pets to work out a mutually satisfactory feeding schedule. There are, however, special situations that preclude allowing a cat to feed at will. Cats who are ill or recuperating, lactating queens, cats who need to lose weight, and growing kittens require careful owner supervision and monitoring of their daily food intake.

If a cat is going to be allowed to snack at will during the day, dry food is the best alternative. Semimoist food can be left out only for several hours; after that it will dry up. Many owners combine a self-feeding bowl of dry food with one or two regular meals of canned rations and perhaps a snack of semimoist food. Feeding at least one regularly scheduled meal allows an owner to keep track of a cat's appetite or lack of it, especially if there is more than one cat in the household. (Canned food should always be served at room temperature, by the way. If it is chilled, it can be warmed slightly by putting the can in a little bit of water to heat on the stove. But be careful not to let it get too hot!) Remove uneaten portions of canned food right away to keep it from spoiling.

Cats' normal food intake can fluctuate for a number of reasons. Variations in the weather, seasonal changes, and stress can affect the amount of food a normal cat eats. Owners need not be concerned about the exact quantity of food that a healthy adult cat eats on a regular basis as long as the cat seems to be thriving. Read more about changes in feeding habits under "Feeding Problems," page 44.

Figure 4 on page 42 shows the average number of kilocalories per pound required by cats at various stages of life and the combinations of dry and canned food that will meet these needs. For example, a normal, active, adult cat requires approximately 40 Kcals of food per pound of body weight each day for energy. Cat food labels do not usually include caloric content, but a glance at Table 3, page 38, will help to determine this.

Special Feeding Considerations

Orphaned newborn kittens require a special diet, which is discussed in detail in Chapter 6.

Kittens: After weaning, up until four months of age, kittens should be fed four times a day; from four to six months of age, three times a day; after that, at least twice a day. In general, healthy kittens should be allowed to eat as much as they want of a high-caloric-density, high-fat diet. Supplementation is not needed unless a veterinarian recommends it.

Pregnancy and lactation: It is particularly important for pregnant queens to be fed a high-quality, well-balanced diet. A pregnant queen should be allowed to regulate her own food intake, which will usually increase up to 25 percent above normal shortly before the birth of kittens.[4] The nutritional demands made on a queen during lactation are extremely high, and she requires a densely nutritious, high-calorie diet. When it is time to wean the kittens, cutting back on the queen's food intake will help to reduce milk output.

Older cats: Reduced activity and metabolism rate usually mean that older cats require

FIGURE 4

CAT FEEDING GUIDE

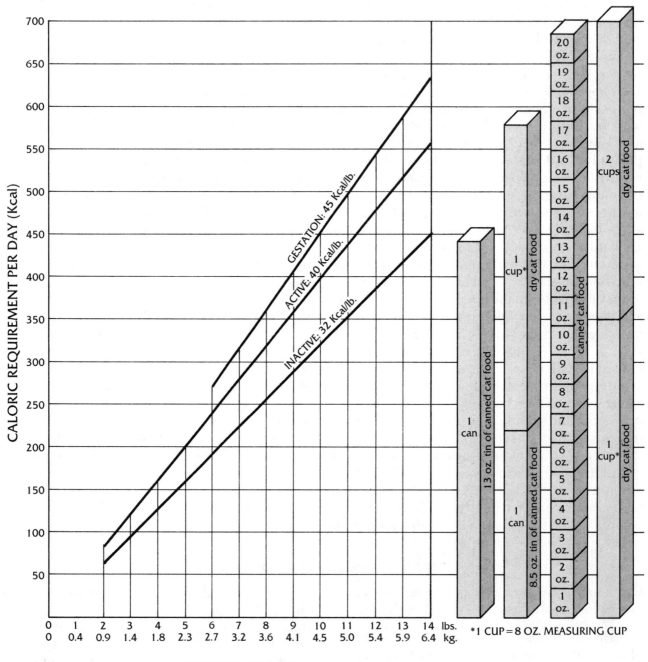

WEIGHT OF CAT

To use the Feeding Guide:

Find the body weight of the cat on the bottom scale.
Follow the vertical line until it meets the appropriate requirement line.
Follow the horizontal line to the right and read the amount of daily food
needed to meet the cat's caloric requirements.

Adapted from Feline Nutrition, Animal Nutrition Series 2, Kal Kan Foods Inc.

fewer calories per day for maintenance. However, their protein requirements continue to remain high, so their needs for a high-quality animal source of energy does not diminish. As long as an older cat continues to eat well and has no systemic disease, there is no need to alter its diet. Of course, if the veterinarian detects some problem, a cat may need to be fed a special diet. Older cats may become more fussy about their food—see "Feeding Problems" on page 44 for how to help overcome finickiness.

Food and Water Dishes

All food and water dishes should be washed daily. In general, soft plastic is not a good choice for cats' dishes and bowls as it tends to retain odors of food and washing solutions, and will melt if it needs to be sterilized. In addition, some cats are allergic to plastic, especially the soft type, and will develop contact dermatitis which appears as an acne-like rash on their chins. Double dishes, intended to hold food in one side and water in the other, are extremely impractical because the contents tend to get into each other.

If a cat's food dish is up on a counter or shelf for self-feeding (to keep it away from a dog, for instance—see Photograph 5, below) it should be weighted and preferably unbreakable. Heavy high-impact plastic is a good choice as long as a cat is not allergic to it. Weighted metal dishes are also practical.

Water bowls and bowls used for canned rations must be especially easy to wash thoroughly with soap and water. Water bowls are

Photograph 5: If there is a dog in the house, a cat's food bowl may have to be put up on a counter-top.

JOHN A. HETTICH

usually placed on the floor and therefore do not need to be unbreakable, but it helps if they are not too light and do not tip over easily. A heavy glazed ceramic bowl or one made of metal is preferable to plastic for water because it won't retain soap or detergent residue. Breakability is not a factor when feeding canned rations either because the dish will be removed and washed right away. Many owners feed canned rations on a paper plate or piece of waxed paper. China saucers or plates are also practical and easy to clean. Each cat should have its own individual serving of canned rations on a separate plate.

Supplementation

It is evident from the information above that casual, unscientific supplementation can lead to an excess of certain dietary elements and an imbalance of others. Yet supplements for cats proliferate on the market in all forms—liquids, powders, and tablets. The public concern with providing all of the best in the way of nutrition for themselves, their families, and their pets is partially responsible for this.

In our opinion, the average spayed or neutered house cat that is fed a well-balanced diet has absolutely no need for supplements of any kind. They are not only an unnecessary expense, but they often lead to vitamin and mineral imbalances; also, there is no scientific evidence that supplementation affects longevity. What's more, many cats will refuse to eat their regular food when supplements are added to it.

There are, of course, situations in which dietary supplementation can be beneficial. Orphaned kittens, small kittens that are not thriving, breeding queens, cats that are ill or recuperating from an illness, anorexic cats, and very old cats may all be able to benefit from controlled supplementation of their diets, but only under a veterinarian's supervision. Many breeders of purebred cats use supplements of some sort for their cats and recommend them to people who buy their kittens. In general, however, it is simply not a good idea to undertake supplementing a cat's diet on your own for all of the reasons we have stated. It is far better to feed a cat a good, well-balanced diet in the first place.

Feeding Problems

An owner should be concerned if a kitten or cat displays a sudden change in eating habits or food intake. Anorexia can be caused by illness, injury, or an infection. Mouth and tooth infections are very common causes of a loss of appetite. Stress and emotional upset, such as a change in the household, a move, or boarding, can also cause a cat to lose its appetite.

If a cat appears to be in good health otherwise and is not vomiting, having diarrhea, running a fever, or obviously in pain, an owner can usually perform a very simple test to find out if the cat is really ill or is simply not very hungry for some reason. Most cats have their "price" when it comes to food and will do almost anything for a favorite dish. If an owner offers the pet a small morsel of, say, roast beef, lamb, or turkey (whatever the cat's particular favorite is), and the cat eats it, then it is probably not very ill. Another favorite ploy of experienced owners is to offer a cat something very, very smelly, such as strong fish. Cats' appetites are governed almost entirely by smell, and a cat with a slightly stuffy nose, one with chronic rhinitis, or an older cat whose smell is no longer acute may not find meat or chicken appealing but will eat smelly fish. (Figaro Tuna is especially strong-smelling, and we use it regularly for this test.) Again, if a cat eats the fish, it is clear that it is not suffering too much. If all attempts to tempt a cat with favorite food fail, then an owner must seek a veterinarian's help right away. A cat should not be allowed to starve any longer than twenty-four hours at the most. (See also "Gastrointestinal Diseases and Disorders" in the Encyclopedia.)

Finicky Cats

A far more troubling problem for many cat owners is the so-called finicky cat that constantly turns up its nose at certain foods, nibbles bits of this and that, and in general has its owner running around in circles trying to please its palate.

Owners should realize that finicky cats are made, not born, and that finickiness is not an inherent trait of the feline species. In general, there are three distinct reasons why a cat becomes a finicky eater. By far the most prevalent is a conditioned diet preference for one particular food or one kind of food—usually fish. This is not harmful to a cat as long as the fish being fed is properly balanced and supplemented with other ingredients. Problems arise when a cat has been allowed to develop a preference for plain, unsupplemented fish intended for human consumption. A cat with this kind of diet preference must be retrained to accept other foods (see below).

Cats with chronic nasal stuffiness or those with a diminished olfactory sense, such as some older cats, can also become problem eaters because of their lack of smell (as we said, cat appetite is governed by the ability to smell food). Pneumonitis can often become chronic and prevent a cat from smelling its food and, therefore, from having any appetite. If an owner suspects that this may be the problem, the cat should be tested with very smelly fish, as we suggested. Chronic nasal stuffiness can usually be controlled by a veterinarian.

Emotional or behavioral causes of picky eating may be harder to solve and require that an owner become something of a detective. Obvious upsets in the household, such as the addition of a new animal or person, or the loss of a favorite companion, often cause a cat to lose her appetite. The cause can be more subtle, however: The cat may not like the location of its feeding dish or the dish itself. The cat may be easily distracted by other animals and household activity, and will eat better in a room alone; it may not eat *unless* there is a lot of bustle around; or it may want its owner to stand by and watch it eat. Another cat may be encroaching on its territory, or the running water in the sink nearby may make it nervous. Whatever the reason, an owner will have to try to discover it by trial and error.

Most cats will reject ice-cold food and will not eat from a feeding dish that smells of disinfectant or is not clean.

Sometimes there is no apparent reason why a cat suddenly seems to lose its appetite. Offering a different flavor or form of food may do the trick for a few days, at which point the cat usually goes back to eating its old diet. If a cat is not used to having another cat around when it eats, the competition of the other cat may make it eat. Again, feeding a favorite food generally induces a cat to start eating well again after being picky for a few days.

Introducing New Foods

New kinds of food should always be introduced to a cat gradually in order to avoid intestinal upsets. This is usually an unnecessary piece of advice because a cat with a well-ingrained food preference generally scorns new foods. A cat that has been allowed to form unhealthy eating habits may have to be taught to accept new foods. The cat may never get to like them as well as the old diet, but can at least be taught to eat them.

A cat's strong smell conditioning can be put to advantage by using a small bit of smelly fish to mask the odor of other foods. If this doesn't work, the switch will have to be made more gradually by mixing the cat's favorite food with a small bit of new food, and increasing the amount of new food each day. A little gravy made up of warm water and a bit of fish, poultry, or meat flavor may help a cat to accept a new food. Most cats also like the flavor of onions and garlic, and mixing a bit of their juice with food may make the food more palatable.

These problems can usually be avoided if a kitten is taught to accept a variety of foods from weaning.

Obesity

It is quite rare for active cats to become overweight, but apartment-bound pets often get fat due to inactivity. If obesity does develop, it is important for a cat to lose weight because overweight will put a strain on a cat's body and ultimately will shorten its life.

A lower caloric intake is a must for fat cats as for any animal that needs to lose weight. Cats on reducing diets must have their rations cut to about three-fourths to two-thirds of their normal intake, and they usually cannot be allowed to snack freely but must be fed controlled amounts of food. Treats must be cut out altogether, unless they consist only of vegetables.

A reducing cat should be weighed regularly to be sure that it is losing weight. If not, its rations should be further cut. When a cat has reached the desired weight, it can be fed a maintenance diet. This will consist of the proper number of calories to keep it at its present level. A veterinarian can help determine the correct amount of food to give a cat so that it does not gain again.

Fat cats tend to become very sedentary, and an owner can help to speed the losing process by encouraging play and activity to use up some calories.

Indoors or Indoors/Outdoors?

Although it *is* natural for a cat to be allowed outdoors, unsupervised outdoor activity is very likely to shorten a cat's normal lifespan of fifteen to twenty years (see Photograph 6, below). On the other hand, cats who are kept entirely indoors can be prone to problems, too.

Photograph 6: Many suburban and country cats that go outdoors never stray far from the doorstep. Note the ID tag on this cat's collar: a must for cats allowed outdoors.

JOHN A. HETTICH

For many reasons we are very much opposed to allowing cats to go outdoors unsupervised. A cat cannot be easily contained by a fence or bush and usually will not stay in its yard; it is therefore subject to accident or injury. Encounters with other cats can lead to cat-bite abscesses and exposure to infectious disease. Cars, dogs, other humans, and environmental dangers such as poisons used to kill weeds, insects, or rodents can also pose a threat to free-roaming outdoor cats.

Serious problems for indoors-only cats are boredom and inactivity. Cats that never have a change of scene may seem happy and content, but they are apt to become sedentary and overweight early in their lifetime. It is part of responsible pet ownership to help offset this problem. An owner should make the time and devote at least a few moments each day to play activity with a cat. Even when there are other cats (or dogs) in the household for playmates, a cat still requires daily human interaction.

Because cats are seasonally polyestrus (their estrous cycles are determined by the number of hours of daylight—see Chapter 5), an unspayed cat who continuously lives in artificial light and never goes out will be unaware of the seasons and may remain in year-long heat. This can pose a problem for owner and cat alike!

There are several ways to allow a cat the pleasure of the outdoors with none of the attendant dangers. One of the easiest and least expensive is to teach a cat to walk on a leash. Using a figure-8 harness that holds the cat well and won't bind or twist, a cat can be taken outdoors comfortably (see Photograph 7, at right). Kittens are easiest to accustom to wearing a harness, but even older cats will learn in time. Begin by putting the harness on the cat for brief periods indoors so that it will get used to the feel of it. When it will tolerate the harness well without simply lying down, try walking the cat on a leash indoors. After a few practice sessions, an outdoor trial in a quiet place can be attempted. Do not immediately take a cat out onto a busy street but allow it to feel safe and comfortable walking on the leash in the quiet of a park or backyard. After a while, almost all cats will feel secure on a leash and can

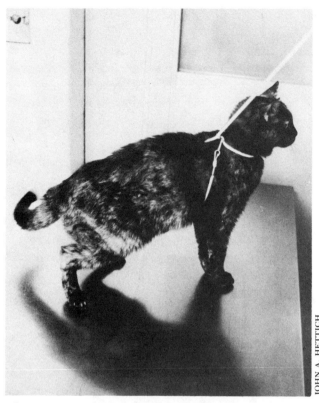

JOHN A. HETTICH

Photograph 7: A figure-8 harness holds a cat well and will not bind or twist—harness and leash are in one continuous piece.

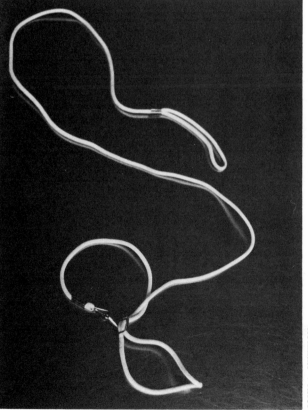

JOHN A. HETTICH

be taken for regular walks or excursions into the backyard.

For owners who live in houses or apartments with balconies or terraces, a securely *screened-in* patio enclosure is an ideal way to allow a cat to see the outside world safely. The enclosure need not be a large one, just big enough for the cat to move around in, to sit in the sun and watch the birds and leaves outdoors.

A cat that is allowed to move around outdoors while at the same time is protected from danger will be happier and more active than one that spends its entire life indoors.

Play/Exercise

Cats that do nothing but sleep and eat every day will get fat and listless. Some kind of play or exercise should be part of every cat's daily routine. If a cat does not get up and move on her own, owners may have to provide an incentive.

When cats are young, they usually need no encouragement to jump and climb and explore. As a cat ages, however, it is apt to become more sedentary, especially if it is an only pet and spends most of its time indoors. Even outdoor cats often become less active as they age and

Photograph 8: These Cornish rex cats get a lot of exercise on their indoor "tree."

JOHN A. HETTICH

spend the greater part of most days asleep in whatever patch of sun they can find.

Various types of furniture designed for cats will encourage indoor activity. There are a number of excellent kinds of cat furniture on the market. Much of it is very attractive and comes in various colors to fit in with any color scheme. A glance at a catalog or a visit to a store specializing in pet equipment will give an owner an idea of the variety of these devices, which range from simple scratching posts to elaborate tree houses (see Photograph 8, opposite page).

Much of this equipment is expensive, and many owners opt to make their own cat furniture. Whether the equipment chosen is store-bought or homemade, it must be sturdy and well balanced, with no loose parts. Nothing will discourage a cat from using a piece of equipment faster than a seemingly booby-trapped device that topples over or falls on her. Carpet or a sturdy fabric covering provides a good paw-hold and doubles as a scratching device.

It is important for cats to have an appropriate scratching device. Cats scratch primarily to remove loose bits of claw material, and some say it is also one of several territorial marking devices; at the same time they get a great deal of exercise and stretch when they claw. Some cats like to scratch horizontally, others vertically, and an owner will find out quickly if he has provided the wrong type of scratching post for a pet. Whatever it is, it must also be topple-free and long enough to provide a cat with a full-length stretch (see also Chapter 8).

Most cats prefer to sleep off the ground, so one of the many perch-type furnishings can serve the dual purpose of keeping a cat off the furniture and providing for scratching and exercise. Hassocks and tunnels (see Photograph 9, above right) are ideal for games of hide-and-seek and hide-the-toy, while a ledge that attaches to a windowsill will keep Tabby out of the ivy while serving as a perch from which to observe the outside world.

Toys can be as simple as an empty paper towel roll, a plastic straw, or a string of wine corks. Paper bags, empty cartons and boxes, and tissue paper can all provide hours of enter-

JOHN A. HETTICH

Photograph 9: A dangling rubber band entices this Abby to play. Notice the "tunnel" he is in.

tainment. For the cat who needs encouragement to play, a wiggling pencil underneath a sheet of newspaper or a Ping-Pong ball rolled across the floor may provide incentive. Even the most sedentary and sedate senior citizen can usually be coaxed into activity with a string or piece of yarn dragged across her range of vision or dangled enticingly just out of reach (see Photograph 9).

A word must be said here about safety. Sometimes cats seem so sensible that owners forget to consider safety measures for them.

Even a seemingly wise ten-year-old may swallow a loose piece of string or small metal bell in the excitement of play, and kittens are apt to swallow anything that will fit into their mouths. Boredom may lead to exploration and chewing. Small toys and playthings should be stowed carefully out of a cat's reach in a tightly closed drawer or cabinet when owners are not watching, and even enticing nonplay objects must be secured until a cat is mature enough to leave them alone. We include more about cat/kitten-proofing a house and avoiding accidents in the Emergencies section.

Whatever toys an owner provides for his cat and whatever games he invents for entertainment or exercise, he'll find that his enjoyment of his pet is greatly increased by the give-and-take of daily play activity.

Grooming and Cleanliness

Regular grooming will keep a cat clean and free from snarls and mats, and frequent brushing and combing will do a great deal to keep a cat's skin and coat healthy and free from problems. A grooming session provides an excellent opportunity to look over the animal for changes and abnormalities (parasites, lumps, rashes, wounds, or sores). The process itself is also mutually enjoyable for both cat and owner, providing a quiet time for togetherness.

The fact that cats groom themselves regularly is all the more reason why regular grooming sessions are important. Because of their constant licking, ungroomed cats swallow large amounts of hair—which will cause hairballs. In addition, if a cat's coat picks up toxins or other substances, these substances will be licked off the fur and ingested, causing intestinal upsets and possibly poisoning.

An owner should groom his cat wherever he and the pet are most comfortable. It is generally easiest to begin getting a cat accustomed to being brushed and combed while sitting down with the animal held on your lap, backside against your body. Some cats refuse to be held at all and will fare better standing or lying on a counter-top or table or on the floor. Wherever a cat is groomed, it is good practice to put an old towel or newspaper under the cat to catch loose fur and protect whatever surface is being used.

Young kittens should be accustomed to handling as soon as possible (see Chapter 6). If this has been done and you introduce grooming gradually in short sessions, there should be no problem. If, however, a cat is skittish and frightened, even of brushing, it has probably had a bad experience and will have to be shown, gradually and calmly, that there is nothing to be afraid of. Owners sometimes become irritated and upset when a cat shies from them or runs away when it is grooming time. What they need to realize is that it is not they but the routine or the tools that the cat is fearful of and that their annoyance will only frighten and confuse the cat even more. It may take some patient observation to determine the problem. With a little time and a lot of patience, almost all cats will learn to like being handled and brushed, and will soon stay still for a complete grooming.

It is a good idea to assemble whatever tools will be used for grooming and put them somewhere handy, in a box, bag, or drawer. A brush or comb, pair of blunt-nosed scissors for longhaired cats, and some cotton swabs are all that most owners will require. (If a longhaired cat is groomed regularly, scissors will probably not be needed.) Other tools, such as nail clippers, can be purchased later if needed.

Brushing and Combing

In our experience, longhaired cats are better combed while shorthaired cats should be brushed. If a longhaired cat is combed every day, mats can be avoided (see Photographs 10 and 11, opposite page). Many breeders of longhaired cats clip or shave their cats at least once a year in order to rid them of mats, but the owner of only one cat need not resort to this if the cat is groomed daily. If mats do develop in a longhaired cat's undercoat, they can be

Photograph 10: This mixed-breed longhair should be combed, not brushed, to avoid mats.

JOHN A. HETTICH

Photograph 11: A Himalayan being combed. Notice the loose hairs in the comb—these would become mats if not combed out daily.

JOHN A. HETTICH

pulled out gently—it is very easy for an inexperienced owner to cut a cat's skin while attempting to cut mats out—but the cat will end up looking somewhat moth-eaten. If the mats cannot be removed by pulling, it is best to cut down a little bit into the center of the mat, tease it apart, and cut some more to untangle it. Extreme care must be taken not to cut too far too quickly, or the cat can be pinched or its skin broken. Even if the damage is slight, it will take some time to gain back the cat's confidence.

If the weather or the inside air is dry, a damp cloth rubbed over the surface of the cat's coat after grooming will help pick up any remaining loose, flying hairs. This is especially useful for shorthaired cats.

Eyes and Ears

Cats' eyes usually do not require any particular attention, but any hardened matter along the nose side should be gently wiped away with a cotton swab or paper tissue. Longhaired cats may need to have excess fur trimmed a bit around their eyes with a blunt-tipped scissor. This requires a firm hand and a cooperative cat.

Ears should be examined in the course of grooming, and any excess wax or dirt can be removed with a moistened cotton swab. Because of the structure of cats' ears (see Illustration 18, page 179), no harm can be done to them with a gently inserted cotton swab. A foul odor, discharge, or grainy matter may indicate infection or infestation with ear mites (see "Aural Diseases and Disorders" in the Encyclopedia for details about these conditions).

Checking for Parasites

In addition to ear mites, cats are very susceptible to flea infestations, especially in warm climates. A discussion of fleas and other parasites will be found in the Encyclopedia, under "Parasitic Skin Diseases," but we want to say a few words here about finding them while grooming a cat and about flea control.

On cats, the favorite hangouts of fleas are underneath the front legs (armpits), between the hind legs, on the back of the neck, and on the back at the base of the tail. Owners often see only the flea eggs, which are white, or flea feces, which are tiny black specks. If a cat is badly infested, it may be necessary to give it a bath (see below) to rid it of the fleas or to use flea powder specifically made for cats. If powder is used, the entire cat must be covered (including between the toes), and the application needs to be repeated several times according to the veterinarian's or manufacturer's instructions. Sprays are very difficult to use on cats, and it is hard to ensure that the entire cat is covered. For everyday flea control, combing with a special flea comb will trap fleas in the comb's teeth, and then the entire comb can be dipped into alcohol or sprayed.

Flea collars, tags, and medallions may help to keep fleas off a cat, but they have no effect on those already on the animal. Some owners swear by brewer's yeast and thiamine, given orally as flea preventives, but in our experience they are not effective.

Environmental control is extremely important because fleas do not live on cats, they merely feed on them, and no matter how many fleas are killed on the animal, it will become reinfested if the environment is not rid of fleas. Even an indoor cat can become infested—dogs that go outdoors can bring fleas into the house. Sprays and bombs may be useful (be sure to read labels on bombs very carefully. It may be necessary to turn off the pilot light in a gas stove to avoid an explosion), but in the case of a really bad infestation it may be necessary to have a professional exterminator. Recently, environmental sprays with longer-lasting residual action have been developed. Sprays that formerly lasted about a week now last a month or more.

In areas where it is warm all year long, flea control can be a continuous battle. Homeowners often regularly put flea killer all around the outside perimeter of their houses. Carpets must be vacuumed daily, and flea powder should be put in the vacuum bag so that eggs do not hatch there. Two products, Proban (cythioate) and Spotton (fenthion), are often used by owners and veterinarians, especially in the South, even though neither of them has been approved for use on cats. Proban comes in tablet form and was developed for dogs. It causes the immediate death of a flea that bites the animal. Spotton, developed for use on large farm animals, is a liquid that is dropped on the back of an animal's neck. Its use on cats is highly controversial.

Mouth and Teeth

With the cat's mouth closed, pull back on her lips to expose gums and teeth. Healthy gums are pink and firm, and the teeth should be firm and free from any bad stains. Pushing gently on the corners of the jaw, open the cat's mouth and examine the tongue and the insides of the teeth. If the gums are pale or bleed when touched, or if there are any swellings or red marks inside a cat's mouth, the cat should be seen by a veterinarian.

We recommend that owners brush or clean their cats' teeth regularly to remove tartar and plaque that can cause tooth loss. An adult cat who has never had proper tooth care should have an initial scaling performed by a veterinarian to remove hard tartar, which will have built up over the years. As with all routines, the younger the cat, the easier it is to get it used to having its teeth cleaned. Begin by using a rough cloth, such as a washcloth or gauze square wrapped around a finger, and rub the teeth from gum to tip. Work up to a rougher cloth and then to a toothbrush. Using a child-sized toothbrush with soft bristles, brush each tooth from the gumline to the tip with a mixture of half salt and half baking soda, slightly moistened with 3 percent hydrogen peroxide. Don't use toothpaste designed for humans since it can cause stomach irritation and cats do not like the foaming. Sensitive, loose, or broken teeth should be seen to immediately by a veterinarian. Gingivitis (inflamed gums that become swollen and bleed easily) is a big problem for some cats, but little is known about it. (See Chapter 2, concerning the normal eruption of a cat's teeth, and Chapter 7, for problems relating to older cats' teeth.)

Litter Trays

An extremely important care routine for all cats is the proper maintenance of litter trays. Even if a cat is allowed outdoors, at least one litter tray should be kept in the house for emergencies or inclement weather.

If there is more than one cat in a household, there must be enough litter trays available so that each cat will be happy. Many cats will not use a litter tray that is soiled, or one that has been used by another animal. Older cats should have readily accessible litter trays throughout the household.

Cats usually have very definite preferences as to type of litter tray and litter. Some prefer covered litter trays, while others are afraid to go into one. Texture is very important to cats, so whatever type of litter a cat has become accustomed to will probably be the only type it will use. Kinds of litter vary from plain clay to fancy cedar products, and cats may not only reject some products, but can even develop allergic skin and foot reactions to certain types of litter. Longhaired cats usually prefer a heavy type of litter over plain clay, which sticks to their fur.

The location of a litter tray is also very important to most cats. Many will not use a litter tray that is at all "public," preferring to use the back of a closet instead.

Litter trays should be kept free of solid waste on a daily basis and should be changed completely when they become moist or smell unpleasant, or whenever the cat feels it is needed. If plastic liners are used, it is usually sufficient to rinse the tray with hot water and soap. If not, the tray should be cleaned with disinfectant and rinsed very thoroughly. But remember that any traces of disinfectant odor may offend a cat and can cause an allergic or toxic reaction.

Owners should be observant and cater to their pet's litter tray preferences. Careful attention to providing sufficient, clean litter trays in appropriate locations can usually help to avoid many house-training "behavior problems" (see also "Inappropriate Elimination" in Chapter 8).

Less Frequent Routines

Some kinds of cat care are done only on an "as needed" basis.

Bathing

Although it is generally not routine, cats *can* and often should be bathed, either for medical reasons such as a severe flea infestation or because they have gotten into something nasty or poisonous that must be removed from their coats.

We always recommend that *two people bathe one cat*. It certainly avoids many problems!

Before beginning, assemble all the equipment needed. The kind of shampoo will depend on what the problem is, but whatever type is used should be diluted in warm water. Cats are small, and only the tiniest amount of shampoo is needed. Too much will make rinsing very difficult. A cloth to sponge the cat with will be needed, and several large terry towels should be handy nearby. Because cats are often frightened by the sound of running water, it is a good idea to run two tubs of warm water ahead of time, one for washing and one for rinsing.

The cat's eyes should be protected against soap by placing a drop of mineral oil in each or by rubbing boric acid ointment around them. A piece of lamb's wool can be placed gently in each ear to protect them from water and also to cut down on the sounds that may frighten the cat.

After wetting the cat and working the shampoo into a lather all over its body, it should be carefully rinsed. Unless a nonrinse medicated preparation is used, thorough rinsing is very important to remove all soap residue. While the cat is still wet, examine it all over for fleas and/or any abnormalities that may readily show up. While the cat is still wrapped in a towel, it is a good time to check its ears and cut its claws (see below). Pat the cat dry thoroughly with several towels and keep it in a draft-free area until the undercoat is completely dry. Do not brush wet fur but comb it gently to aid in drying. Some very calm cats may allow themselves to be dried with a hand-held hair blower, but most are frightened by them.

Although "dry" cat baths are on the market, they are generally hard to use and are not nearly as effective as water baths.

Nail Clipping

Nail clipping is one of the most important routines that owners can establish with a pet cat. If a cat becomes accustomed to having its nails clipped approximately every two weeks, a number of so-called "behavior problems" will be avoided. It is not difficult for an owner to learn how to do this properly, and most cats learn to accept it with indifference, if not with grace. Nail clipping is required of any cat that is to be shown, for the protection of handlers and judges.

As we have mentioned, scratching or clawing is an instinctive behavior in cats. They cannot be trained or taught not to scratch, although most can be taught to scratch in appropriate places. If claws are allowed to grow too long, they can damage furniture, rugs, people, and other animals, and may become painfully ingrown. Overlong claws can also catch on things, break, and bleed, and can also cause a cat to twist its leg or shoulder.

An inexperienced owner should ask a veterinarian, cat groomer, breeder, or handler to demonstrate claw clipping the first time. Briefly, it consists of keeping a cat quiet and grasping a front paw in one hand, with the thumb resting on the bottom of one foot pad. By pressing gently on the bottom of the pad, a claw will be extended, and the sharp curved point can be cut off with a sharp clipper (see Illustration 3, opposite page). There are any number of appropriate cat claw clippers on the market, and some owners even use human nail clippers. At this stage, each claw can be filed gently with an emery board to remove any remaining loose scale. Usually only the front claws are clipped, but in the case of a very aggressive or rambunctious cat, the hind claws

Nancy Lou Makris

**Illustration 3: Holding a cat for claw clipping.
Below, several views of a cat's paws showing
where to push on the pad and where to clip.**

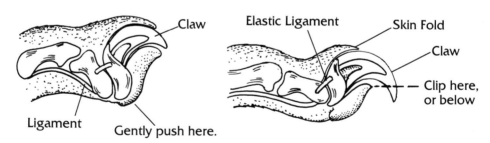

Claw

Elastic Ligament   Skin Fold

Claw

Clip here,
or below

Ligament   Gently push here.

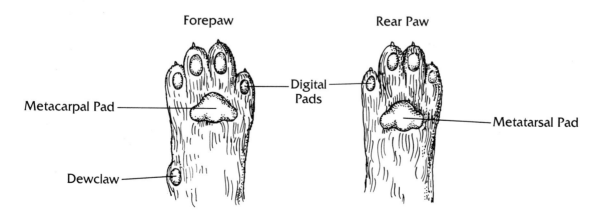

Forepaw   Rear Paw

Metacarpal Pad   Digital
Pads

Metatarsal Pad

Dewclaw

should be trimmed, too. Clipping the hind claws will also prevent a cat with a skin condition from scratching itself and breaking the skin.

Problems can arise with an uncooperative cat or if the claw is clipped too far. If too much is taken off the claw, the nerve and blood vessel, or "quick," will be cut. It will hurt the cat and may bleed a lot. No permanent damage is usually done and the bleeding can be stemmed with antiseptic, but the cat will then be wary and you will have to regain its trust.

If an adult cat is very uncooperative and refuses to stay still for a nail clipping, it may have to be restrained with a towel wrap (see Illustration 12, page 162) and its paws released for clipping one at a time the first few times until the cat learns to be trustful. A very young, wiggly kitten can be held suspended by the nape of its neck with its legs dangling, just as its mother would hold it to keep it still (see Photograph 29, page 163). This requires a helper. Well-trimmed claws can do no damage to furniture, clothing, or human skin.

References: Chapter 3

1. Morris, J. G., Rogers, Q. R. Nutritional implications of some metabolic anamolies of the cat. *Proc Am Anim Hosp Assoc*, 1983, pp. 325–331.

2. Kendall, P. Some nutritional differences between the dog and cat. *Pedigree Digest* 7 (1): 4–6, 1980.

3. Brewer, N. R. Nutrition of the cat. *JAVMA* 180 (10): 1179–1182, 1982.

4. Lewis, L. D., Morris, M. L. *Small Animal Clinical Nutrition.* Chapter 1, Nutrition; Chapter 2, Pet Foods; Chapter 3, Feeding Cats. Topeka, Kansas: Mark Morris Associates, 1983.

5. Rogers, Q. R., Morris, J. G. Protein and amino acid nutrition of the cat. *J Nutr* 108 (2): 1944–1953, 1978.

6. Morris, J. G., Rogers, Q. R. Arginine: An essential amino acid for the cat. *Proc Am Anim Hosp Assoc:* 333–336, 1983.

7. Kronfeld, D. S. Feeding cats and feline nutrition. *Compend Contin Educ Pract Vet* 5 (5): 419–423, 1983.

8. Anderson, R. S. Water balance in the dog and cat. *J Small Animal Pract* 23: 588–598, 1982.

9. Jackson, O. F., Tovey, J. D. Water balance studies in domestic cats. *Feline Pract* 7 (4): 30–33, 1977.

10. Seefeldt, S. L., Chapman, T. E. Body water content and turnover in cats fed dry and canned rations. *Am J Vet Res* 40 (2): 183–185, 1979.

(Pages 31–46 are based, in part, on information adapted from Feline Nutrition, Animal Nutrition Series 2, Kal Kan Foods Inc., 1984, by Cheryl R. Dhein, DVM, MS, and Edith van Marthens, DVM.)

4

Common Surgical Procedures

CHERYL J. MEHLHAFF, DVM

This chapter will review the surgical procedures most commonly performed on cats. In addition to simply describing some common procedures, we will also outline some of the considerations that each veterinary surgeon faces prior to recommending and performing surgery. Several classifications of surgery exist: elective procedures, semi-elective procedures, and emergency procedures.

Elective procedures are performed on healthy cats and include ovariohysterectomies (OHE, "spay"), castrations, and declaws.

Semi-elective surgeries are necessary for the sake of the animal's health and are performed in a number of widely diverse situations, for example, lacerations, fractures, bladder stones, persistent urinary tract blockage, and ovariohysterectomies for uterine infections. Both elective and semi-elective surgeries allow the veterinary surgeon time to assess the individual situation and plan the most beneficial anesthetic and surgical procedure for the cat. It is in these instances that medical data is collected (blood tests, X rays, electrocardiograms, and so forth) in order to maximize the success of the surgical procedure and minimize the risk to the patient.

Emergency surgeries are performed when a life-threatening situation occurs. As such, medical data-gathering may have to be limited in order to save the cat's life. Immediate attention is given to the procedures necessary to assure the patient's well-being. Examples of this type of situation include injury to life-supporting organs or their physiological function (for example, excessive air trapped in the chest, excessive body cavity bleeding due to internal organ rupture, and severe intestinal blockage). Despite these life-threatening situations, the veterinary surgeon does her best to *stabilize* and *assess* the patient. Intravenous fluids, antibiotics, temperature regulation, and correction of body homeostasis stabilize the patient. Laboratory tests, X rays, electrocardiograms, and other specialized tests assess the patient.

Stages of Surgery

All surgical procedures can be divided into four distinct stages: The preoperative period is the evaluation or planning stage; the induction stage is when the anesthetic is given; the intra-

57

operative stage is when the surgery is actually performed; and the postoperative stage is when the pet is recovering. Each of these stages will now be discussed in detail.

Preoperative Period

The preoperative stage or period begins when a decision to perform surgery is made. It is a planning and information-gathering time for the veterinarian. The veterinarian reviews the indications for surgery, alternatives to surgery, and the risks involved in surgery for the particular patient.

Young, healthy cats require a minimum of preparation. A thorough physical examination is given, and weight and immunization status are taken into consideration. If no compromising physical or health problems are determined, a recommendation for surgery can be made.

Older cats may require a more extensive preoperative screening. The veterinarian may recommend blood and urine tests, X rays, and other selected diagnostic procedures to minimize the risk of anesthesia. Because anesthesia is a *risk* in any surgery, the veterinarian will assess the overall body function of the cat. This will aid her in choosing a method of anesthesia and specific surgical procedure.

Because a cat that is going to have elective surgery is usually allowed to remain at home until the morning of surgery, it is important for an owner to remember that the *animal's stomach must be empty.* This is advised to prevent vomiting during the recovery period, which might result in inhalation of the vomitus into the lungs. *Food should be withheld for eight to ten hours prior to anesthetic induction. Water should be withheld two to three hours prior to surgery.*

Induction Period/General Anesthesia

The purpose of anesthesia is to block the perception of pain and to keep the patient still while surgery is in progress. General anesthesia rather than local anesthesia is almost always necessary for cats. A cat cannot understand the need to stay still, so many procedures that might be performed on people with a local anesthetic (for example, stitching a cut finger or dental work) require a general anesthetic for cats. General anesthesia renders the patient completely unconscious, relaxes the muscles, eliminates pain, and prevents recall of the procedure once the patient is awake. If appropriate steps have been taken to evaluate the patient during the preoperative period, general anesthesia carries a minimum of risk for most animals, even those that are seriously ill.

A cat may be given an intramuscular tranquilizer or sedative to relax it a few minutes before being brought into the prep room to be anesthetized and prepared for the OR—the operating room (see Photograph 12, opposite page). Other preanesthetic drugs may also be given at this time as needed to help maintain heart rate, control salivation, and so forth.

In the prep room, the now calm cat is placed on a table and a catheter is inserted into a leg vein. Hair is often clipped from the area where the catheter will be placed. A general anesthetic is then carefully injected through the catheter, and the animal is relaxed and unconscious in seconds.

Once the cat is under anesthesia, it must receive a maintenance anesthetic for the duration of the operation. For short procedures it may simply be small additional doses of the injectable drug. For longer surgeries, a gas or inhalant anesthetic is used. The gas is a mixture of oxygen and one or more modern drugs —*not ether*—and is administered via a rubber or plastic endotracheal tube that is gently passed down the cat's trachea toward its lungs and fastened in place. Occasionally when an endotracheal tube is used, a cat may have a transient sore throat and a cough after surgery. This will usually resolve without treatment and should not concern an owner unduly. But if it is severe or persists for more than twenty-four hours, consult the veterinarian.

Under anesthesia a cat may breathe on its own spontaneously or in certain cases its breathing may be assisted or controlled by the anesthetist. This can be done manually by squeezing a bag containing the anesthetic gas or by use of a mechanical ventilator called a respirator.

Once the cat is under anesthesia, an intravenous drip of fluids is attached to the catheter. Blood transfusions are rarely necessary and are almost never used in routine operations.

Before being moved to the operating room where the actual surgery will take place, the cat's hair must be shaved from the area intended for surgery. The area shaved must be large enough to prevent any hair from encroaching on the surgical field during the operation and must allow for lengthening the incision if necessary. The shaved hair is vacuumed away and the patient then transferred to the operating table.

Intraoperative Period/Surgery

At The Animal Medical Center we have a standard surgical procedure that is followed by each doctor with every surgical patient. This procedure may vary in individual practices but, in general, certain operational procedures should be followed. The animal is carefully monitored during surgery. This includes monitoring with a cardiac oscilloscope, administration of intravenous fluids, and continuous monitoring of anesthetic levels. The patient's breathing, pulse, and color are frequently checked, and the cat is kept warm with a special warm-water circulation pad.

Photograph 12: A cat that has been given an intramuscular tranquilizer to relax it prior to preparation for surgical excision of a tumor.

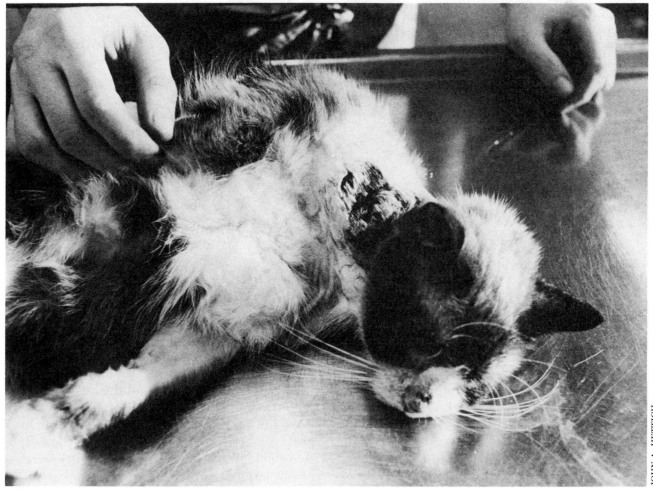

JOHN A. HETTICH

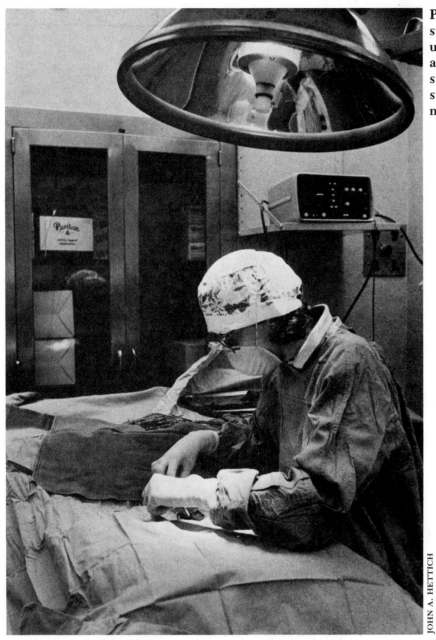

Photograph 13: During surgery, sterile drapes are used to cover all of the table and the cat, except for the surgical field itself. The surgeon wears a sterile cap, mask, gown, and gloves.

JOHN A. HETTICH

Before the operation actually begins, the shaved area is repeatedly scrubbed with a soap solution and then alcohol to sterilize the skin. Special sterile towels and drapes are used to cover the table, instrument stands, and the entire animal except for the surgical field itself (see Photograph 13, above). The surgeons, dressed in sterile caps, masks, gowns, and gloves, then move in to perform the operation. Care is taken to prevent contamination or contact with anything that is not sterile.

Postoperative Period/Recovery

When the operation is completed, the anesthetic is turned off and the patient is allowed to wake up. Depending on the type of anesthetic used, the nature of the surgery, the length of the operation, and the age of the cat, the return to consciousness can take anywhere from minutes to several hours. This is why a postoperative hospital stay of anywhere from several hours to several days is necessary to ensure an uncomplicated recovery.

Bandages are not usually necessary. Cats do not tolerate them well, and they are rarely used except for support in certain types of orthopedic cases. (See Chapter 13 for bandage care.)

After a cat is released from the hospital, postoperative care is continued at home by the owner. Even routine surgery such as an ovariohysterectomy is a major operation and requires a certain convalescent period. Animals should be allowed to rest and not encouraged to play, jump, or run when they first return home. This must be strictly enforced, especially when small children and/or other pets are at home eagerly awaiting a pet's return.

The entire experience of having surgery is very apt to upset a cat's stomach. This is perfectly normal, and owners should not expect a pet to be hungry when it first comes home. Rewarding a brave postoperative cat with extra treats is only inviting trouble. The best thing to do is feed small amounts of the pet's regular diet at frequent intervals until it can gradually be returned to a normal schedule after a few days. Of course, if the veterinarian prescribes a particular diet and feeding schedule, these instructions should be strictly followed.

Check the incisions once or twice a day. Pay attention to the sutures, if present, and look for evidence that the cat is licking or chewing them. Excessive swelling, redness, or any discharge are all warning signs and should be called to the veterinarian's attention as soon as possible. The doctor may put an Elizabethan collar on the cat. This is a plastic cone that fits around the pet's neck and prevents it from reaching around and licking the incision (see Illustration 17, page 168). An alternate device used by some veterinarians is a side brace that mechanically prevents a pet from reaching an incision.

Most cats show few signs of postoperative discomfort or pain. Analgesics or painkillers are rarely indicated and should never be given to a cat except under a veterinarian's supervision. These drugs will cause grogginess and may mask signs of complications; in addition, many of them are highly toxic for cats (see the Appendix for more about this).

Ovariohysterectomy (OHE, "Spay")

The main reason this operation is performed is that it provides permanent sterilization of female cats. Although there are other medical means of contraception, they are not without potential side effects (see Chapter 5). Besides the very important benefit of preventing unwanted periods of "heat" and pregnancies, there are several extremely important medical benefits to be gained by an OHE. These include avoiding uterine infections, tumors of the reproductive tract, certain dermatologic problems, and the unpleasant behavioral changes that can accompany the estrous cycle. There is also evidence that an early OHE (before the first heat) may be instrumental in preventing mammary gland tumors, a common malignancy in cats.

As an elective procedure, an OHE is usually performed on cats at about six to eight months of age. The only requirement is that the cat be relatively mature in growth. This can vary depending on the breed of cat but usually occurs at around six or seven months of age. If a cat is spayed at this time, the procedure will usually precede the first heat. (See Chapter 5 for a detailed explanation of why cats come into heat for the first time at different ages.)

The Operation

The cat is prepared for the operation as described above. Even though the incision is usually only one or two inches long, hair is clipped in a wide area to prevent contamination and to allow for a longer incision should it become necessary.

The surgeon uses a sterile scalpel to cut the skin just below the belly button. Several layers of fat and muscle are divided until the abdom-

FIGURE 5

GRAPH OF THE HEALING PROCESS, DEMONSTRATING WHY SUTURES ARE REMOVED 10 TO 14 DAYS FOLLOWING SURGERY

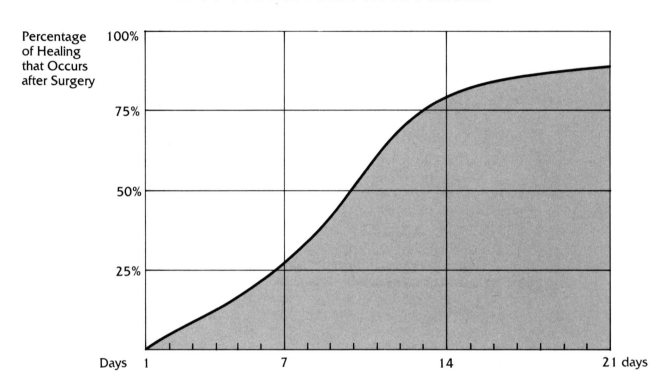

inal cavity is reached. The uterus is located and brought out, along with the attached ovaries. Sutures are placed around the blood vessels connected to these organs, and the ovaries and uterus are then removed. The surgeon makes sure to remove all the ovarian tissue because the ovaries are the source of the female hormones that cause heat-like behavior. Only a stump of the uterus is left behind. The surgeon sutures all the layers previously opened with materials that do not have to be removed later.

The skin is closed in one of two ways. The usual method is to place stitches that are removed approximately ten to fourteen days later. See Figure 5, above, for a graph of the healing process. An alternative method is to place stitches below the skin level. These subcuticular sutures dissolve in the body over time and need not be removed. The choice is based on the surgeon's preference as well as the personalities of the cat and the owner.

Owners should remember that there are multiple layers of stitches. If the skin stitches come out or the edges of the incision gap, there is no need to panic. Cover the wound with a clean dressing or leave it alone, and prevent the cat from chewing, licking, or scratching it. Call the veterinarian as soon as possible.

An OHE *is* a major abdominal surgical procedure and requires all of the postoperative rest and care previously outlined.

With proper care at all stages of surgery, complications following a feline OHE are uncommon. Very rarely a cat may come into heat after an OHE. This may indicate the presence of ovarian tissue somewhere in the abdomen and may require a second exploratory operation. Even more rare is an infection of the tiny stump of the uterus left behind during the operation. Should this occur, a second operation is required in order to remove the infected stump.

Personality Changes/Weight Gain Following an OHE

Since an OHE is usually performed just as a cat is going into puberty, normal changes in temperament, playfulness, and sleeping habits that occur at this age are sometimes attributed to the surgery. Some owners notice that their pet is calmer, less anxious, and more responsive to them after an OHE, but there is no real evidence to link these changes to the operation.

Similarly, many people believe that cats routinely gain weight after an OHE. As with personality changes, the age at which most cats are spayed is the primary factor in this observation. All cats approaching maturity undergo normal changes in metabolic rate, activity level, and food utilization. A one-year-old cat requires less food per pound than a kitten does. The problem of weight gain is easily controlled by adjusting the amount and frequency of feedings and by regular exercise (see Chapter 3).

Castration (Neutering, Altering)

Castration involves the removal of a male cat's testicles which, like the female's ovaries, are the main source of sex hormones. Removal of the testicles also eliminates the source of sperm cells and is the most effective means of birth control for the male. In addition, castration reduces aggressive behavior toward other cats and virtually eliminates roaming in outdoor cats. Castration is also recommended to prevent a male cat from spraying urine to mark his territory. Once a cat forms this habit, it may be difficult to stop. Therefore, early castration (around the age of eight months) is highly recommended.

The Operation

Preparation and anesthesia for the operation are described above. Once anesthetized, the cat is placed on his back and the area around the scrotum and groin are shaved and sterilized. A small scrotal incision is made over each testicle through which the testicles are removed. The vessels and vas deferens (a duct that carries sperm into the urethra) are clamped and tied off, and the testicles are removed. The incision site is not sutured.

Because the scrotum is left intact and may swell, it may appear to the owner that the cat was never castrated. Over time, the scrotum usually shrinks, and hair will eventually grow over it (see Photograph 14, page 64).

Complications are rare following routine castration. On occasion a cat's scrotum may be irritated by the shaving or develop a rash in reaction to the surgical iodine solution. More often, persistent licking leads to swelling and inflammation of the scrotum. This problem can be controlled with an Elizabethan collar (see Illustration 17, page 168) and the use of warm compresses for several days. If swelling of the scrotum is severe, take the cat to the veterinarian.

The cat should be kept indoors for several days, and clay litter replaced with shredded paper to prevent contamination of the scrotum.

Personality Changes/Weight Gain After Castration

As with OHEs and female cats, castrations are usually performed just as a male cat is maturing. Some owners falsely attribute normal changes in activity level, food utilization, and so forth, to the surgery. We have noticed that some cats have an increased appetite following castration. To avoid weight gain, owners must be careful not to indulge their pet's increased desire for food and should feed their adult male cat balanced, nutritious meals in the amounts described in Chapter 3.

Photograph 14: A while after castration, the scrotum usually shrinks, and hair will grow over it.

JOHN A. HETTICH

Declawing

Unlike ovariohysterectomy and castration, declawing is not recommended as a routine operation for most cats. This is an operation that requires careful thought by an owner. A veterinarian (and possibly an animal behaviorist) should be consulted ahead of time to help make a decision about whether or not this operation is necessary.

To prevent the cat from scratching furniture, carpeting, plants, people, and so forth, removal of the front claws is often done at the same time as spaying or castration, but it may be performed at a later date. (See nail clipping under "Less Frequent Routines" in Chapter 3 and "Furniture Scratching" in Chapter 8 for some alternatives to this operation.)

Rear claws are rarely used for any of these actions, and so most veterinarians discourage removal of the rear claws except in extraordinary situations, such as in the case of large exotic cats (see Chapter 11). Although a cat *can* defend itself with its rear claws in a real fight and can even climb trees with only rear claws in an emergency, the front claws are the major defensive weapons of the cat, and an owner who has a cat declawed must commit himself to keeping the cat safely indoors afterward.

The procedure entails removal of a structure analogous to a person's fingernail. After the operation the feet are bandaged for at least twenty-four hours. Cats are generally hospitalized for two or more days for observation and care after the operation. Even after a cat goes home, slight tenderness of the feet may be noticed. This is to be expected but should resolve itself within one to two weeks.

When properly performed, complications after a declawing procedure are very rare. Infection of the toes is the most common complication and shows itself by swelling or discharge from the toes, lameness, and a loss of appetite. If any of these signs are noticed, consult the veterinarian.

Home care in most cases consists of changing the litter in a cat's box to shredded newspaper to help avoid contamination and infection. Some veterinarians routinely prescribe antibiotics after the operation.

Perineal Urethrostomy (PU)

Questions often arise concerning the perineal urethrostomy operation. This surgery is occasionally recommended for male cats that have had severe or repeated episodes of blockage of the urethra (see "Feline Urologic Syndrome [FUS]" in the Encyclopedia).

The urethra is a tubelike structure through which urine passes from the bladder during normal urination. The urethra of some male cats becomes plugged with a substance that resembles sand. In order to prevent this from occurring as easily, the urethra is reconstructed to form a wider opening. Since the narrow portion of the urethra is within the cat's penis, the penis is removed and a new opening is constructed just below the cat's anus. Because of the anatomical position of these structures, a cat that has not been castrated must have that operation performed at the same time.

While this operation is commonly performed, it requires delicate reconstructive surgery. Each owner should discuss the benefits and risks of this procedure with the veterinarian before it is performed.

5

Breeding and Reproduction

Lee Schrader, DVM

This chapter provides a cat owner with the information he needs to make an intelligent decision about breeding a pet cat. It also contains a description of the normal breeding process and outlines health care for the queen (female cat) during pregnancy and the birth of kittens. Chapter 6 will cover the care of newborns, or neonatals.

Because cats usually give birth very easily and avoid most of the genetic predispositions toward diseases or deformities that dogs can be prone to, most cat owners have traditionally paid little if any attention to their pets' breeding and reproductive processes. They have simply allowed "nature to take its course." There are problems inherent in this casual attitude, however—most particularly, the enormous number of unwanted kittens.

Despite this, there are a number of reasons why a cat owner may think that a cat should have one or two litters of kittens before she is spayed. Some owners think that it is good for a female cat to experience motherhood, others want to have the fun of having a litter of kittens around, and still others think that their children will benefit from the experience of seeing birth. It is important for these owners to seriously consider the question of what will happen to the kittens. A visit to any pound or shelter will give ample evidence of the fact that cat overpopulation continues to be a major problem. Owners of a pet cat who are thinking of breeding her or owners of an unspayed female who stands a chance of becoming accidentally pregnant should think very carefully about the need to provide good homes for all of their cat's kittens.

Cat owners should also realize that having an unspayed queen or unaltered tomcat around is not pleasant. Cats that have not been neutered do not make very good pets. In addition to being very restless and sometimes testy, tomcats often spray foul-smelling urine all over in order to mark off their territory, especially if there are other male cats around. If a tomcat is allowed outside, he may fight with any other male cat that ventures into his territory and, as time goes on, he may try to enlarge his territorial boundaries, finding more and more rivals to battle. Unspayed females come into heat many times throughout the year and will be very vocal and restless during each cycle. A female cat that is allowed outdoors will continuously attract battling tomcats and will have litter after litter of kittens. It is possible for a female cat to have two litters of kittens a year

66

for up to ten years, a process that would not only put a terrible strain on the cat's entire body but could produce more than one hundred kittens!

In addition, although queens in general care for their young very well, an owner who allows a cat to have kittens must be willing to devote some time, energy, and money to provide proper veterinary care for both the queen and her kittens.

Birth Control

Unless a tomcat is going to be used strictly as a breeding stud, an owner of a male kitten will most certainly want him to be neutered or castrated not only as a means of birth control but in order to have a pet they can live with. The operation itself, which is described in detail in Chapter 4, is usually performed when a cat is between seven and nine months old. It is a regularly performed surgical procedure of minimal risk.

Owners of female kittens that are not going to be bred will usually have an ovariohysterectomy (OHE) or "spay" operation, performed when the cat is between six and eight months of age (see Chapter 4 for details). If the operation is performed before a cat has her first estrous cycle, it can help to minimize her risk of developing mammary gland tumors later in life, in addition to providing permanent birth control. A spayed cat will also avoid uterine and ovarian diseases.

Temporary birth control methods are some-times used by owners of females who want to breed a cat at a later date. These forms of birth control can also be used if a cat is a poor surgical risk and cannot safely have a spay operation. There are two types of nonsurgical birth control that can be used for cats. Ovaban, or megesterol acetate, is a synthetic hormone that prevents the pituitary gland from producing the hormones which control the estrous cycle. It should be used only under a veterinarian's supervision, but it is relatively safe for cats. Side effects such as diabetes mellitus or changes in the mammary glands are possible if an inappropriately high dose is used or if the drug is given over a long period of time. Mibolerone, which is an androgen (male hormone), can also be given to cats to postpone the estrous cycle. It should never be given to a pregnant cat because it will masculinize the female fetuses, and it should not be used on a long-term basis. Again, a veterinarian's supervision is necessary.

Accidental Breeding

Owners of an unspayed or unprotected female cat must face the possibility of accidental breeding, especially if the cat is allowed outdoors.

The safest thing to do if an accidental mating occurs and the cat is not a breeding queen is to have an ovariohysterectomy performed. The operation should be done two to three weeks after the cat has come out of estrus, before her uterus becomes greatly enlarged.

The queen can also be allowed to go through with the pregnancy and birth, and homes found for the kittens.

There are mismating injections, which consist of a strong dose of estrogen. They will alter the transit of the egg through the reproductive tract and change the receptivity of the uterus, causing it to become an unsuitable environment for the eggs so that they do not become fertilized. We do not recommend using these shots because of the risk of side effects. Estrogen shots have a high potential for upsetting the body's hormone levels and may cause a serious uterine inflammation, or pyometra (see the Encyclopedia of Diseases of Cats). They can also predispose a cat to future mammary gland problems. In addition, if estrogens are used at too high a level, they can cause bone marrow destruction, leading to aplastic anemia (see the Encyclopedia).

The Cat's Estrous (Heat) Cycle

NOTE: "Estrus" refers to the actual heat period of about seven days. "Estrous" refers to the entire cycle (consisting of proestrus, estrus, and so forth), described below.

The cat is seasonally polyestrus; that is, the photoperiod (number of hours of daylight) determines a cat's estrous cycle. Most cats will begin to cycle in February or March and continue cycling every two or three weeks until the days begin to get shorter in the fall. Approximately twelve to fourteen hours of light a day is usually the measure used. The time when a female cat enters puberty and comes into her first estrus depends on the time of year she is born. A kitten born in September may be only five or six months old when she begins to cycle in February, while a kitten born in June will be eight or nine months old at her first heat. This explains the wide range of ages (from four to nine months) at which female cats can become sexually mature. The one exception is Persian cats; they tend to enter puberty later, when they are anywhere from a year to a year and a half old.

This reaction to the photoperiod can cause problems for strictly indoor cats who live with artificial lighting. Often these cats will cycle continuously all year, and owners will either have to have them spayed, breed them, or have ovulation induced by a veterinarian, which will provide a temporary respite from cycling for owner and cat alike. Cats are what is termed "induced ovulators," meaning that they will ovulate and progress through their entire estrous cycle (which usually takes about sixty days) only if they are stimulated to do so, either via coitus or by manual stimulation of the cervix. If a cat is continuously going through the heat or estrus, a veterinarian may be able to get her to ovulate via manual stimulation of the cervix repeated several times over a twenty-four-hour period. After ovulating, the female cat will complete her estrous cycle and not go through another heat period for approximately forty to sixty days. Often, cats who have been artifically induced to ovulate will go into a false pregnancy (see below).

A cat's estrous cycle basically has three stages. There is a proestrus of about one to two days, which owners may not notice. A can may start to cry a bit, knead, tread the floor with her rear legs, and elevate her rear end, but she will not accept a male cat. She then enters estrus, which lasts about seven days. During this time a cat will pace and yowl loudly, or "call," all day. She will tread with her rear legs, elevate her rear, and rub insistently against her owners and furniture.

As we have said, cats are induced ovulators and usually will not ovulate unless they are bred and have stimulation of the cervix. Occasionally, a cat will ovulate when she is petted, but this is uncommon. A cat who has not ovulated will come back into estrus in from ten to fourteen days and will continue to cycle throughout the entire photoperiod or, in the case of some indoor cats, throughout the entire year.

If a cat ovulates, she will then go into the luteal phase when she is under progesterone rather than estrogen influence. This phase occurs whether or not she becomes pregnant and terminates either in birth or pseudopregnancy.

Pseudo-, or false, pregnancy: A cat that has ovulated and not become pregnant may enter a stage when her body feels as if it is pregnant but actually is not. This is referred to as pseudo-, or false, pregnancy. It usually occurs forty to forty-five days after ovulation. The cat may have milk in her mammary glands, may have some abdominal enlargement, will indulge in nesting behavior, and may carry a toy or old sock around in her mouth. If she is uncomfortable due to breast enlargement, alternate warm and cold compresses will soothe the discomfort, but otherwise there is nothing that needs to be done. Usually, a cat will come out of false pregnancy by herself. Unlike dogs, which always ovulate during estrus, cats do not necessarily have more false pregnancy incidents unless they are again ovulated and no pregnancy occurs. If a cat in false pregnancy is extremely uncomfortable, a veterinarian may be able to help. There has been some research done using androgens, such as mibolerone (see previous section on birth control), to bring a cat out of false pregnancy.

Breeding

In general, cats do not have any difficulties mating, and there are fewer inherited problems to consider in choosing a proper mate than there are with dogs. Even so, inbreeding and direct line breeding should be avoided. It is always better to be sure that one of the two partners is experienced. Two cats that have never been bred before or that have never socialized with other cats may have some initial difficulty knowing what to do, although this is usually not a serious problem with cats. Sometimes longhaired cats are shy and may need time to get used to each other. It is better to bring the female cat to the male, rather than vice versa, so that the male does not have territorial problems in a new environment.

Owners of queens that they want to breed can usually find a suitable stud from their veterinarian, a breeder, or through advertisements in cat magazines. Always ask for references, and be sure that the stud is in good health.

Health Measures

The male and female cats should have complete physical examinations before breeding. They ought to be dewormed, and their immunizations brought up to date. It is important that both cats (and the entire cattery, if they come from one), are checked for feline leukemia virus (FeLV) and feline infectious peritonitis virus (FIP). (See the Encyclopedia of Diseases of Cats for more about these diseases.)

Both cats should be examined for any obvious genetic disorders such as a cleft palate or umbilical hernia. The reproductive tracts of queens should be palpated by the veterinarian, and they should also be checked for vaginitis, vaginal strictures, and any other physical abnormalities, such as a badly healed pelvic fracture that might cause pain during mating and problems during birth. Although tomcats have very few penile and reproductive disorders, they should also have a genitourinary examination to be sure that the penis is normal and both testicles are descended. A longhaired male can sometimes develop little rings of hair around his penis that must be removed before mating, or they will cause pain.

There are no serious venereal diseases in cats.

Age to Breed

Females should be mature before their first breeding. It is a good idea not to breed a queen during her first heat but to wait until she is at least a year old. Very young animals tend to ovulate only a few eggs and have small litters, which can lead to very big fetuses and a difficult birth.

The Mating Act

There is usually no problem determining when a female is ready to breed. Her physical demeanor is very distinctive when she is in estrus. The cats should be placed in a room together and be left in privacy. Very shy cats may refuse to copulate. It is possible to hold a reluctant queen, but the handler risks being bitten or scratched.

The male will approach the female, grab her by the back of her neck and bite her, and then mount her. Intromission usually occurs within five minutes. Cats do not have a prolonged coitus, and intromission itself is usually very quick, generally lasting only for about four seconds. A forceful male may prolong intromission for up to twenty seconds, but no longer. The female's reaction to mating, called an after-reaction, is very severe. She will scream, turn, and try to scratch the male, and then roll over and thrash around, trying to lick her vulva. This is a normal reaction that is related to cervical stimulation, which affects the cat's central nervous system. Experienced studs will back away from the female immediately after coitus to avoid being scratched. See Illustrations 4, 5, and 6, page 70.

Because a queen needs multiple matings (often two or three) in order to ovulate, the cats should ideally remain together several hours a day for three days. Intervals between matings are brief (about five to thirty minutes), and a queen may permit up to thirty copulations in twenty-four hours and up to thirty-six copulations in as many hours.

Illustration 4: First step in the mating act. A female cat's physical demeanor makes it obvious when she is ready to breed.

Illustration 5: Second step in the mating act. The male grabs the female by the back of the neck, bites her, and then mounts her.

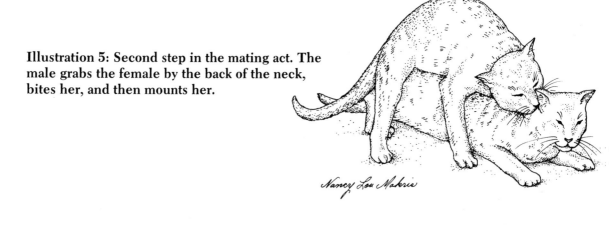

Illustration 6: Third step in the mating act. The female's normal after-reaction to the mating act is very severe and occurs because cervical stimulation affects her central nervous system. An experienced stud will back away to avoid being scratched.

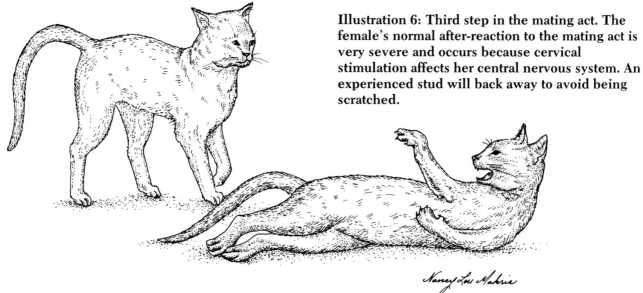

Infertility

If a successful mating has apparently taken place and no pregnancy occurs, the first thing to do is to make sure that the male cat is fertile. If he has successfully impregnated other females within the same time period, then the female must be evaluated by a veterinarian. It is possible that the female is not cycling because the photoperiod is not long enough. Some very inbred cats, such as Persians or Himalayans, may not cycle regularly.

Hypothyroidism, which is very rare in cats, can also cause a cat to either not cycle or have difficulty conceiving, as can congenital anomalies such as hermaphroditism, in which a cat has both male and female sex organs present in its body (but this is also rare in cats).

More often, a chronic uterine infection, such as metritis or endometritis, can cause failure to conceive. Cats with FeLV or FIP may fail to conceive. These two diseases can also cause early fetal death, fetal resorption, stillbirth, and abortion any time throughout gestation. Kittens born alive to queens with FeLV or FIP will probably die very young.

If a cat is cycling but not conceiving, an internal examination can be performed, although it is a difficult procedure with cats because they are so small. Dye studies are sometimes utilized but, again, not on a usual basis.

Artificial insemination is rarely performed for queens who either will not stand to be bred or who have some structural abnormality that prevents normal mating. It is done only at a few select universities and veterinary medical schools. The main problem with this procedure is that it is difficult to cause a male to ejaculate in order to collect sperm.

Pregnancy

The gestation period for kittens is sixty-three to sixty-five days on average, with a possible range of sixty to seventy. Differences occur because the queen may not actually become pregnant on the day that she is bred (sperm can live in the female reproductive tract for as long as four days after mating). A veterinarian can usually determine pregnancy by palpation of the female's abdomen approximately twenty-eight to thirty days after mating. Sometimes this can be difficult because the fetuses are very small. The fetuses start to calcify at around thirty-six to thirty-eight days and can then be seen on X rays. However, X rays should not be taken of a pregnant queen unless absolutely necessary because of possible fetal damage.

Care During Pregnancy

During the last half of pregnancy, the queen's food intake should be increased by 20 to 30 percent over normal. She should be fed more frequently—up to three times a day. If a cat is eating a complete, balanced diet, supplementation with vitamins and minerals is not necessary. Oversupplementation can lead to nutritional imbalances, and supplementation should be undertaken only under a veterinarian's supervision. Medications should also be given only under a veterinarian's direction because some drugs can interfere with fetal development.

Moderate exercise is very good for a pregnant queen and will help to make delivery easier. Most cats will regulate themselves as their size increases; the fetuses are very well cushioned and will not be hurt by normal activity. Owners should protect pregnant queens from violent, aggressive play, however. If necessary, the expectant queen should be isolated from other cats, dogs, and small children who may be too rough with her or involve her in wild activity. If a cat becomes too sedentary, the owner can encourage gentle play.

The queen's mammary glands will start to enlarge during the last third of pregnancy and will start to fill with milk one or two days before birth.

If a queen has had a thorough medical examination before breeding and seems to be in good health during pregnancy, there is no need for checkups unless there are signs of a problem.

Problems During Pregnancy

Abortions are not uncommon in cats. An early abortion may seem to be simply a failure to conceive. The fetuses may be aborted, or they may die *in utero* and be resorbed. In this case the only sign that an abortion has occurred will be the cat's failure to come into heat again right away.

When there is a later abortion, at four to six weeks of gestation, there may be a bloody vaginal discharge containing little bits of fetal tissue. This may not be evident, however, because the queen cleans herself so thoroughly. After a later abortion the queen may not cycle again for up to six weeks. Later abortions are often due to systemic disease such as toxoplasmosis, FeLV, or FIP.

A queen that has aborted may not feel well for several days and may lose her appetite and her energy. She may become pregnant again if she is bred on her next cycle. But if the cause of abortion was a systemic illness, she may abort again. It is important for a veterinarian to examine a queen that aborts more than once.

Preparing for Birth

About a week and a half before birth is expected, an owner should prepare a queening box for the cat so that she can get used to it. Select a box that is large enough for the queen to lie down in comfortably, and line it with towels that can be removed and washed after the birth. The sides of the box should be high enough to protect the kittens from drafts. Because it is so important for the kittens to be kept warm, place a small thermometer in the box. It may be necessary to put a heat lamp over the box if the house is kept cool. The box should be placed in a private spot away from family activity and the queen encouraged to get into it and become familiar with it. If the box does not suit the queen because of its size or location, she is likely to make a nest and give birth in a highly impractical spot such as on top of the bed or in the back of a closet.

Shortly before birth occurs, the queen will begin to prepare a nest somewhere, and she may become restless. She may cry out, and often she will not eat. She may even vomit.

It can be difficult to determine just what stage a cat is in before birth begins because, unlike dogs, cats do not necessarily have a temperature drop immediately before birth.

Delivery

Most queens have no difficulty with delivery. Amazingly, a queen can spread out the time between deliveries of kittens if something happens and she has to move, for instance. Queens have been known to stretch out the delivery of a litter for as long as a day or two.

Usually, however, once a queen goes into active contractions (labor), the first kitten appears within four hours. Most queens lie on their sides at this time, but a few may prefer a squatting position. A small amount of greenish discharge (lochia) may appear, and then the kitten, which is usually contained in an amniotic sac, will be seen. Most kittens are born with their head in front, feet first, but it is not unusual for a kitten to be born tail first, upside down, or sideways. This should present no problem because cats generally queen very easily.

After the kitten is born, the placenta appears. Usually the queen eats the placenta. She bites off the umbilical cord close to the kitten's umbilicus and licks the kitten rather roughly to dry it and remove all of the amniotic sac. The kitten should then begin to nurse. The nursing action causes a reflex that increases the contractions of the queen's uterus and makes the remaining births easier.

It can be difficult to determine when all of the kittens have been born. Usually, if the queen stops straining and seems calm and relaxed, an owner can safely assume that the birth has been completed. If possible, it is a good idea to keep track of the placentas as they appear, to be sure that one has not been retained.

One of the most interesting things about cats is that there can be several different fathers for one litter of kittens. This is called superfecundation and is not uncommon. It occurs when a cat is bred by two or more toms during the same twenty-four-hour period and eggs from the same ovulation surge are fertilized. This explains why kittens from the same litter can look so different. Very rarely, a phenomenon called superfetation can occur when fetuses of different ages are in the uterus at the same time. This can only happen if a queen comes into estrus and is bred when she is already pregnant.

Helping

There is usually nothing that needs to be done to help in the birth process. Some cats want to be left completely alone while giving birth, and others want some company. An owner will have to decide on the best course to take based on the queen's own personality and relationship with her family. No matter how calm a queen is, however, it is not a good idea to allow a lot of people to visit during the birth process. A queen who becomes nervous and gets up and runs around, or moves the kittens to another spot, should be left undisturbed until the birth is completed.

Problems During Delivery

When it is a queen's first litter, it is possible that she will not know how to care for the first kitten. If this happens, an owner should tie off the umbilical cord with soft string, about an inch to an inch and a half from the kitten's

belly button, and then cut the cord on the side of the knot away from the kitten. This must be done very gently—pulling could cause an umbilical hernia. The kitten should be rubbed and dried thoroughly with a rough cloth, its mouth cleared out, and its head hung down until normal breathing starts. The placenta can be thrown away. The kitten should then be given back to the queen, who will probably begin to lick it and allow it to nurse. Usually even first-time queens will then know instinctively how to care for subsequent kittens.

If the queen is actively straining and a kitten appears to be stuck in the birth canal, an owner may have to help. The kitten can be grasped with a clean, dry cloth and pulled very gently in a downward direction, toward the queen's rear legs, while she is straining. Extreme care must be taken not to injure the kitten or the queen. If the kitten does not move, a veterinarian's help is needed.

Caesarean sections are rarely necessary for cats. Exceptions are the brachycephalic breeds (Persians, Himalayans) with broad, domed foreheads, cats that have had pelvic fractures, and those with a vaginal stricture. These cats can have dystocia, or difficult birth. Often a veterinarian can help a cat with dystocia to deliver normally without surgery by using drugs to increase uterine contractions.

If more than four hours pass before the first kitten appears or more than four to six hours lapse between kittens, and the queen is actively straining or appears ill or weak, she needs immediate veterinary attention. Any vaginal discharge should be thin and greenish in color. There may be a slight tinge of blood, but if it becomes very bloody, dark, brown, yellow, or purulent and smells foul, it is a sign of trouble.

Postpartum Care of the Queen

A lactating queen's caloric requirement reaches its peak at about two or three weeks postpartum. During lactation her daily food intake should be increased to reach two to three times her basal food requirement, and she should be fed three or four times a day. She should also have access to as much water as

she will drink. If she can tolerate milk without diarrhea, she can have it, but it is not necessary. She will get all of the calcium that she requires from a well-balanced commercial cat diet. Supplementation is usually not necessary unless a home-cooked diet is fed, and then it should be given with care and under a veterinarian's direction. As the kittens begin to be weaned at about six weeks of age, the queen's food intake should be tapered off. This will reduce her milk output so that it has almost stopped by the time the kittens are completely weaned.

All of the queen's mammary glands (eight) should be checked daily for redness, swelling, warmth, and pain when touched. If possible, express a little bit of milk from each gland. It should look like normal milk. If it is bloody, very thin and watery, has clumps or flecks in it, or looks yellowish and purulent, it is abnormal.

It is all right for a queen to have some vaginal discharge for two to four weeks postpartum, and this should also be checked daily for abnormalities (see above). It may be hard to check this because cats usually lick themselves clean. If necessary, the lips of the vulva can be spread slightly in order to see the discharge.

If a postpartum queen fails to keep herself clean, acts ill, loses her appetite, or has an abnormal vaginal discharge, she may have an infection. We recommend that owners take a postpartum queen's temperature twice daily. If her temperature goes above 103 to 103.5 degrees F., it may be an early sign of an infection. Most cats do not tolerate temperature-taking with much grace, but if it can be managed, it would be helpful in detecting an infection early. (See Chapter 13 for how to take a cat's temperature.) If the queen is ill, she should be seen immediately by a veterinarian. The kittens can either be taken along with the queen or left to be cared for at home. They should never be left alone for long periods of time.

Postpartum Problems

Most queens will not neglect their kittens unless they become very ill or are continuously disturbed. A high-strung queen can become frantic if she is bothered a lot, and some very nervous queens will continuously fuss over their kittens but will not allow them to nurse. In both of these instances, the veterinarian may recommend a mild tranquilizer to help calm the queen.

Agalactia: Agalactia is absence of milk. Little is known about this condition. Signs are obvious: The kittens continually try to nurse but cry all the time and become weak. Sometimes continued suckling will stimulate milk production. If it does not, the only thing to do is to make sure that the queen is getting enough food and water and is not sick. If no milk can be stimulated, the kittens will have to be hand-raised (see Chapter 6).

Hemorrhaging: Severe postpartum hemorrhaging is not a common problem with cats. If it does occur, it may indicate a tear in the uterus or vagina and requires immediate veterinary attention.

Hypocalcemia, or Eclampsia: This condition, which is rare in cats, occurs when a queen's high calcium requirement during pregnancy and lactation is not met. It usually develops in cats during lactation. The queen will develop muscle tremors, followed by stiffening of the muscles, panting, restlessness, vomiting, diarrhea, and eventual collapse. The kittens must be removed and intravenous calcium must be given to the queen by a veterinarian. After that, the queen can be supplemented with extra calcium orally, and the kittens can usually be put back to nurse.

Mastitis: Mastitis is an infection of the mammary glands while a queen is lactating. It is usually an ascending infection, originating in the nipple and getting into the gland, but it can originate somewhere else in the body and travel through the bloodstream to the mammary gland. It is characterized by fever, enlarged, firm, warm, painful mammary glands, and abnormal milk that appears to be curdled or discolored. The queen will usually push the kittens away when they try to suckle because it hurts her to have them nurse. The kittens may also develop diarrhea and become sick from the milk. A veterinarian will diagnose the condition based on visual signs and will usually perform a culture of the abnormal milk to determine bacteria present and study the cells present in the discharge. In the absence of a large abscess that can be lanced, he will usually give the queen antibiotics and warm compresses for the affected gland. If the kittens are not made sick from the milk and abscesses are not present, they can be allowed to continue to nurse.

Metritis: This is a postpartum bacterial infection of the uterus that can occur after a difficult birth or after abortion. Signs include a fever, appetite loss, depression, neglect of kittens, and a foul-smelling vaginal discharge. Usually, the kittens will have to be weaned and the queen treated with antibiotics. Sometimes it is necessary to hospitalize the queen for intravenous feeding, and occasionally she will require an ovariohysterectomy.

Retained placenta: A retained placenta will usually disintegrate in the uterus and be passed out in the lochia (postpartum vaginal discharge). If an owner knows that a placenta has been retained, the veterinarian can give an injection that should help it to pass normally. An owner should suspect a problem if the vaginal discharge is not normal or if the queen starts to run a fever.

Uterine prolapse: This is not a common problem with cats. It occurs when an animal strains so hard during birth that the uterine horn comes out through the vagina. If an owner sees what looks like tissue protruding from the vagina, the tissue should be covered with a wet cloth and the cat kept from licking it, using an Elizabethan collar if necessary. The cat should immediately be taken to the veterinarian for treatment, which may involve surgery.

Postpartum Care of Kittens

We discuss the care of newborns, or neonatals, in detail in Chapter 6, but it bears repeating that it is extremely important for kittens to nurse for at least the first forty-eight hours after birth in order to get colostrum, which gives them antibodies to fight infection. Even if the queen is sick, every effort should be made to allow the kittens to nurse for at least two days. If the kittens must be taken away from the queen or if the queen dies, the kittens should be isolated from contact with all other cats and their immunizations begun at an early age—according to a veterinarian's schedule.

Excessive handling of neonatals may sometimes cause a queen to reject them or to move them out of harm's way into an unsuitable place. Other animals in the household should be kept away from the kittens for the same reason. Once the kittens' eyes are opened and they begin to move around on their own a bit, the queen will become less protective.

During the first week of life, newborn kittens do not regulate their own body temperatures but rely on their mother and littermates for warmth. If the temperature in their environment drops below 85 degrees, they can become chilled and their mother will reject them. That is why it is extremely important to protect newborns from drafts and to use a heat lamp, if necessary, to keep the kittens warm.

6

Care of Newborns

SAMANTHA MOONEY, RESEARCH ASSOCIATE

As we pointed out in the previous chapter, preparation for a litter of kittens begins with special care for the expectant mother. A well-vaccinated, nutritionally fed queen who is free of parasites (both internal and external) and disease will be better equipped to deliver and care for a healthy litter of kittens. The nutritional requirements of a pregnant cat are more than twice the caloric needs of an average adult cat (see Chapter 3 for more about this). During pregnancy the queen will benefit from supplemental feedings and veterinary-approved vitamin supplementation. In order to maintain both her normal body weight and milk production, the queen may consume two to three times her normal amount of food.

Gestation

The normal gestation period is sixty to seventy days. Most kittens are born sixty-three or sixty-five days after pregnancy occurs. Kittens born before fifty-six days are unlikely to survive. The queen's mammary glands increase in size primarily during the last week of gestation, and the cat usually begins to secrete milk two or three days before parturition.

During gestation the queen's basic needs will remain the same. They will change only to meet specific needs for food, water, warmth, love and attention, and privacy. In order to provide privacy, some owners prepare a box for the birth—see "Preparing for Birth" in the previous chapter. With even greater respect for their pet's privacy, many owners watch as the queen frequently ignores the box and selects her own birthing spot.

Typical signs that birth is imminent may start approximately twenty-four hours prior to delivery and include pacing, circling, accelerated nesting behavior, crying, decreased appetite, possible vomiting, and vaginal licking. Abdominal contractions may begin a couple of hours before the first kitten is born. In a normal delivery the owner's role is limited to observation and emotional support.

The normal delivery process, problems during delivery, postpartum care of the queen, and possible postpartum problems that can occur both to the queen and to the newborns are discussed in detail in the previous chapter.

Care of Newborn Kittens

A concerned owner will want to ensure that the queen is able to meet the needs of her kittens, especially if this is her first litter. If a queen is extremely high-strung, it is a good idea to keep a close watch on the kittens for at least twenty-four hours after birth to ensure that they are being properly cared for.

Kittens need a clean, warm environment. The queen will clean her kittens after stimulating them to urinate and defecate, but the owner should keep the living area (incubator, box, or basket) clean by changing the towels and papers frequently to prevent dampness and bacterial growth. The sense of smell appears to be the dominant sense in neonates, and nest odors, including the scent of the mother cat and her productive nipples, are essential to the kittens' adaptation to the environment. So, although the living area should be kept clean, it is possible to confuse the kittens by eliminating familiar odors through overzealous cleaning. If the nest is scrubbed with a full-strength disinfectant, the kittens may become disoriented. If the queen's nipples become blocked, for instance, bathing the queen may also disorient the kittens. Usually it is sufficient to bathe a blocked nipple with warm water and massage it gently.

The mother and littermates will generate warmth, but the environment itself should be kept free of drafts and maintained at a constant temperature. If one kitten in the litter is rejected, that kitten should be rubbed and warmed and returned to the queen while the litter is nursing. (The queen will reject a cold kitten.) It may take repeated efforts before the queen accepts the kitten back; if necessary, the owner should feed the newborn with milk replacer until this happens.

In addition to meeting her kittens' nutritional needs, the queen supplies the kittens with colostrum when they nurse. Colostrum from a well-vaccinated queen contains antibodies that protect the kittens against disease. Although these antibodies protect the neonate, they may also interfere with the effectiveness of vaccinations. For this reason, we recommend a series of vaccinations, usually beginning when the kittens are fully weaned and continuing every two weeks until sixteen weeks of age. (See Chapter 3 for more about immunizations.)

Supplemental Feeding

If the litter is large, it may be necessary to further supplement the queen's food intake and to monitor the kittens' weight. If nursing kittens do not gain weight daily, it will be necessary to supplement their diet with a commercial queen's milk replacer.

In most circumstances, continued nursing is desirable. Since the neonates will be returned to the queen if possible, the preferred means of feeding is the nursing baby bottle and nipple. This method simulates the natural nursing process because it requires the kitten to use a sucking reflex. Bottles made for animals are available, or dolls' bottles can be used. The hole in the nipple should be adjusted to let the kitten ingest a sufficient amount of nourishment with minimal sucking effort. To avoid indigestion, the kitten should be burped by gently massaging its stomach to expel swallowed air.

If a nursing bottle is not available, a syringe or eye dropper can be used. The liquid must be administered slowly, and caution must be taken so that the neonate does not injure its mouth by trying to nurse on the inflexible equipment.

The preferred formula for supplemental or replacement feedings is commercial formula kitten milk replacer (KMR-Borden). Formulas made for dogs or whole milk alone should not be used for kittens because they do not meet cats' necessary protein, fat, and caloric requirements (cats' milk has approximately 40 percent protein on a dry weight basis). In addition, some kittens may not tolerate cow's milk, and it may cause diarrhea. If cow's milk is used, as in the homemade formula below, it should be discontinued if diarrhea results.

Some homemade formulas can be used as substitutes for commercial products if they are high in protein. An acceptable formula is:

1 large can evaporated whole milk (12 ounces)
1 large can evaporated skim milk
6–7 egg yolks
Liquid vitamins, according to package directions

This makes one quart of formula. Freeze unused portion in ice cube tray and store cubes in an airtight freezer bag. Defrost and warm to room temperature as needed.

Another formula, this one using cow's milk:

½ cup cow's whole milk
1 hardboiled egg
1 teaspoon calcium carbonate
Liquid vitamins according to package directions

Mix in blender until smooth.

Kittens should gain about 10 grams daily, averaging an increase of 70 to 100 grams per week. A small gram scale, available from the pharmacy, will be helpful in keeping track of the kittens' weight gain. (Note: Well-fed kittens will not constantly cry or whine.)

Handling, Weaning

The queen who is nursing will let the owners know when the kittens may be handled. She will not be disturbed by the human scent on her kittens if she is present when they are handled.

Kittens' eyes generally open between seven and ten days after birth. By two weeks of age they are rolling, walking, grooming, and playing. As early as three weeks, they can begin to eat soft food. Baby food, milk, or a cat food gruel can be offered on a fingertip or placed in a kitten's mouth to generate interest. Most kittens will discover soft food if the queen is fed

solid food in a shallow dish in the incubator or box. They will walk across the plate, slip in the food, and lick their paws, thereby making the transition themselves.

The time to wean kittens depends on several factors including the number of kittens in the litter, the queen's health, and the queen's willingness to be suckled. In the weaning process, soft food and milk are initially offered as supplements only, but the kittens' meals must be completely balanced by the time they replace nursing entirely. Most kittens are fully weaned when they are six to eight weeks old.

Care of Orphaned Kittens

Because orphaned kittens are deprived of the immediate care and prolonged maternal attention essential to their survival, an owner must do his/her best to substitute for these necessities. A healthy queen not only feeds her kittens and thereby offers temporary protection against contagious disease, she also stimulates them, exercises them, cleans and warms them.

Neonates are unable to regulate their own body temperatures and are *hypothermic* at birth. Neonates that are denied a radiant heat source such as the queen's mammae (breasts) at birth risk slipping into deep *hypothermia* (reduction of body temperature below the normal range). Early signs of hypothermia include

increased activity, agitation, crying, coldness to touch, and an increased respiration rate. If the condition is not corrected, neonates will make weak attempts to suckle, experience a lack of coordination, and eventually collapse, gasping onto their sides. Kittens can be revived after as long as twelve hours of hypothermia by gentle rewarming. All efforts should be made to restore body temperature in a hypothermic kitten.

A high-sided, draft-free box can be used as an incubator for orphaned neonates. A thermometer should be placed in the corner of the box to monitor the environmental temperature. For the first post-birth week, the temperature should be maintained at between 85 and 90 degrees Fahrenheit. A heating lamp placed at a safe distance above the box will ensure a constant temperature. One area of the box should be covered to offer shelter from the constant light. After the first week, a constant temperature of 75 degrees should be maintained.

An owner should change the kittens' bedding frequently to ensure a clean, dry environment for the neonates. It is necessary to stimulate a motherless neonate to urinate and defecate—a job that is normally performed by the queen. To do this, massage the genital area with a warm, moist cloth or Q-tip after every feeding (see Illustration 7, below). Wipe the kitten's mouth after each feeding. To clean the kitten, use a cloth moistened with warm water and gently rub the kitten dry; also wipe its unopened eyes daily with a cotton ball dampened with a saline solution or mineral oil, to prevent stickiness.

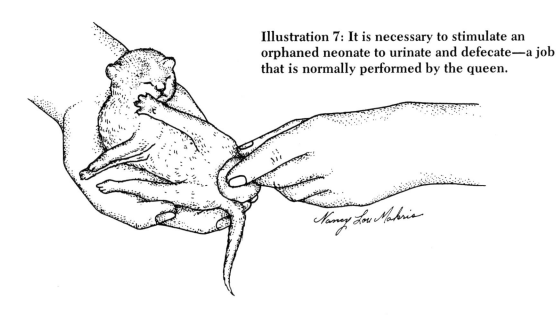

Illustration 7: It is necessary to stimulate an orphaned neonate to urinate and defecate—a job that is normally performed by the queen.

Feeding Orphaned Kittens

Tube-feeding is an alternative to the nursing bottle, and the only alternative for a sickly neonate that will not nurse or suckle. A kitten born with a cleft palate or any congenital deformity that prevents normal nursing must be tube-fed. In a cleft palate, the bones in the roof of the mouth fail to join together, leaving an opening or a partial opening. A tube bypasses this aperture, enabling nourishment to reach the stomach directly. In some cases the defect can be corrected surgically, but the kitten must be supported by tube-feeding until it is old and large enough to be considered a good surgical risk. A gastric or stomach tube is most beneficial for those neonates that are unable to suckle and need immediate nourishment.

A sixteen-inch polyethylene feeding tube should be used, its length sufficient to reach from the kitten's nose to its stomach. The tube should first be marked at the appropriate length, located at the last rib, and cut off about six inches beyond the mark at the flared end of the tube. See Illustration 8, page 80, for how to measure and mark the tube.

The tube can be moistened with warm water to pass into the kitten's throat more easily. With the kitten in an upright position or on its stomach with its head tilted slightly upward, the tube is inserted along the roof of the mouth into the esophagus. The tube should not be forced if resistance is felt or if the kitten gags or chokes but should be removed and re-

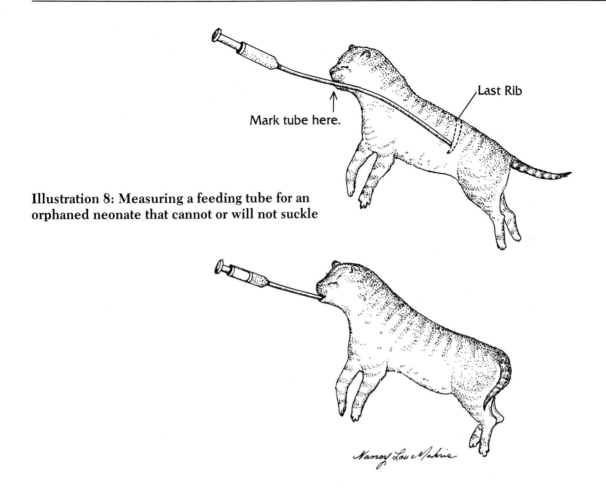

Mark tube here.

Last Rib

Illustration 8: Measuring a feeding tube for an orphaned neonate that cannot or will not suckle

started. The tube is in the correct place in the stomach when the premeasured mark is level with the kitten's mouth.

Orphaned neonates need to be fed immediately after birth because they have no fat reserves. They should then be fed at regular four-hour intervals for the first week. The formula (see page 78 for various recommended formulas) should be given at room temperature and administered slowly.

Neonates weigh approximately 90 to 135 grams (3 to 4½ ounces) at birth. A 120-gram (4-ounce) kitten requires approximately one ounce (30 ml or cc's) of liquid formula every twenty-four hours. If feedings are scheduled every four hours, the kitten receives 5 cc's (approximately 80 drops) per feeding. If KMR (kitten milk replacer) is used, 3 to 5 ml should be given to each kitten per meal and slowly increased over the first week to 7 to 10 ml per meal per kitten. Small, frequent feedings are

necessary in order to avoid regurgitation. When a kitten regurgitates liquid into the mouth, it runs the risk of aspirating that fluid into the lungs, which could lead to pneumonia.

During the second and third weeks the intervals between feedings can be extended if the kittens continue to gain weight and are not constantly hungry. The amount and frequency of feeding can be adjusted to ensure continued weight gain. Generally, by the end of the first week, neonates should double their initial weight. A four-ounce kitten, for example, fed 5 ml of kitten milk replacer every four hours for the first week should weigh at least eight ounces after seven days. It is important to weigh the kittens daily in order to recalculate the amount of formula necessary. An eight-ounce kitten should receive 10 ml of milk replacer per feeding every four hours by the end of the first week. After the first week most neonates can be fed every six hours.

Liquid formula should be fed at room temperature (68 to 70 degrees). As the liquid sits in the stomach it assumes the kitten's warmer body temperature (99 to 100 degrees). The interval between feedings should be long enough to allow time for the previous meal to pass from the stomach into the intestines. If sufficient time does not elapse between feedings (at least four hours), the cooler room temperature of the following feeding will curdle any warmed liquid remaining in the stomach. Crying and abdominal bloating are signs of the painful colic that can result from this.

Weaning Orphaned Kittens

Hand-reared neonates can be introduced to soft food as early as two and a half to three weeks of age, regardless of whether they were bottle-, dropper-, or tube-fed. An owner can whet the appetite of a reluctant motherless kitten by placing a fingertip coated with a small amount of food in the kitten's mouth.

Kittens should be fed soft food four to five times a day. Lacking a mother to teach them the ways of the world, orphaned kittens must be guided by their owners. When they are eating on their own, they are old enough to discover and use a shallow litter pan kept close to their feeding and sleeping area. After each meal, kittens should be immediately placed in the litter box so that they know where it is. (See Chapter 8 for more about this.)

Kittens that a healthy queen has nursed will have received temporary antibodies from the colostrum in her milk. Hand-reared kittens will not have ingested any of these protective antibodies. They should be isolated from other cats and from visitors until they have received their complete immunization series (see Chapter 3).

Diseases and Illnesses

Young kittens can sicken very quickly and, because of their tiny size, often require immediate veterinary intervention in order to save their lives. The following are the most common medical problems that can occur in young kittens:

Dehydration: Immediate attention must be given to a kitten that refuses to nurse or to eat on his own after weaning. Dehydration can occur rapidly if the fluid intake derived from food and water consumption is decreased. Diarrhea is another source of dehydration and, coupled with anorexia, can quickly debilitate a young kitten. This is an *emergency* and requires immediate veterinary attention to rehydrate the kitten and maintain normal body temperature while the veterinarian locates the cause of the problem.

Hernia: A young kitten can develop a hernia, which is the enclosure of an organ or part of an organ in a pouch of skin outside the body cavity and appears as a small bulge in the skin. A veterinarian should examine the hernia in order to determine the best treatment.

Hypoglycemia (low blood sugar): This is a medical *emergency.* A neonate that is trembling, depressed, weak, and unwilling to nurse can be given emergency treatment at home by administering as much honey or Karo syrup as possible orally by the teaspoonful (up to a tablespoonful at least) until a veterinarian can be consulted. (See also the Encyclopedia of Diseases of Cats and the Emergencies section.)

Infections: Although uncommon, neonates can develop an umbilical cord infection. Bluish discoloration around the navel is evident, and death can result if medical attention is not sought. A clean environment will generally prevent this and other bacterial infections.

Repercussions resulting from poor hygiene can affect an entire litter of kittens. Neonates nursing a queen that suffers from untreated vaginitis or mastitis (see Chapter 5) may exhibit the following warning signs: crying, tenesmus (feeling an urgent need to defecate or urinate, accompanied by straining), and abdominal tympany (a distended, taut abdomen). In addition to the queen's illness, all nursing kittens are affected, and these conditions, if untreated, can lead to convulsions and death of the kittens.

Acid, or toxic, milk syndrome in the queen (see Chapter 5) shows itself in neonates by crying, tympany, nausea, salivation, inflamed anal region, green feces, and decreased interest in suckling. Take the queen to the veterinarian and have her examined for infection. While she is being treated, the kittens will have to be hand-raised.

Viral diseases: Kittens are susceptible to a variety of viral diseases, including panleukopenia and several upper respiratory tract viruses. The most common *upper respiratory infections (URI)* are caused by the following viruses: rhinotracheitis, calicivirus, and pneumonitis. These viruses are contagious among cats and can be fatal if a sick kitten is not given immediate and continued nursing care. (See Chapter 3 and section on Infections/Contagious Diseases of Cats in the Encyclopedia for more about these diseases.)

Feline panleukopenia virus can cause abortion or fetal resorption in the queen. In late-term pregnancy and in young neonates the panleukopenia virus causes cerebellar hypoplasia (brain underdevelopment) and has been associated with severe pulmonary edema (fluid buildup) in neonatal kittens. Panleukopenia can be prevented by vaccination. A well-vaccinated queen can supply her kittens with passive immunity through the colostrum they ingest in the first few days of nursing that will last until they are old enough to be vaccinated.

URIs are characterized by sneezing, ocular and nasal discharge, and fever. Newborns may experience severe conjunctivitis, manifested by purulent ocular discharge and glued eyelids. Corneal deformity may result if this condition is untreated (see the Encyclopedia of Diseases of Cats). Ulcerative glossitis, a condition in which the superficial epithelium (tissue) of the edges of the tongue sloughs, is often seen with URIs and may be manifested as excessive salivation. The tongue lesions may contribute to the kitten's anorexia, and combined with the neonate's inability to smell, may necessitate supplemental or forced feeding.

Queens that are *feline leukemia virus test positive* (FeLV+) may experience abortion or resorption of their kittens. If the queen delivers, however, she can pass the virus to her kittens through the placenta and through her milk when they nurse. FeLV+ queens frequently produce weak kittens with thymic hypoplasia or aplasia. These kittens do not develop normal cell-mediated immune responses and experience decreased resistance to secondary infectious diseases caused by viruses, bacteria, and fungi. They often die of infections such as pneumonia and enteritis within a few weeks of birth.

Congenital Abnormalities

Many of the same factors responsible for causing genetic damage in unborn human offspring have the potential to cause similar damage in unborn kittens. Several factors present in or acting upon the queen prior to delivery can cause birth defects in kittens.

Chemical agents: Congenital defects can result from the administration of certain drugs such as corticosteroids and griseofulvin (an antifungal drug given orally to treat infections such as ringworm) during early pregnancy. If you suspect that your cat is pregnant, check with a veterinarian before giving her any drugs. Cleft palates, shortened tails and hind limbs, and fused or absent phalanges (bones of the toes) have been reported in kittens born of queens treated with griseofulvin.

Hereditary defects: Some deformities and disabilities are associated with particular breeds, and inheritance of these traits may prove fatal. Taillessness, for example, is caused by a mutant gene that can also affect the vertebrae, producing varying degrees of spina bifida (see "Congenital Neurologic Diseases" in the Encyclopedia) in Manx kittens as well as an abnormal anal opening. A kitten that receives identical mutant genes from both parents is said to be homozygous (not heterozygous). Kittens that are homozygous for the dominant Manx gene for taillessness die in embryo.

The dominant gene responsible for the downward-turned ears of the Scottish Fold is also associated with skeletal deformities in cats that are homozygous for this trait. A gross congenital head defect believed to be associated with a recessive gene carried in a particular line of Burmese results in varying degrees of deformity in kittens. Even severely deformed Burmese kittens are alive at birth. This inherited condition is fatal.

Infectious agents: Viruses that affect the queen, especially in early-term pregnancy, are the most significant agents responsible for malformation and congenital defects among neonates (see FeLV and panleukopenia, for example).

Metabolic factors: A cat that is undergoing treatment for diabetes mellitus or any other metabolic or endocrine-related disease should not be bred. The primary consideration should be the cat's continued response to therapy and, even though abnormal kittens may not result, the cat's health should not be jeopardized by breeding her.

Nutritional deficiencies: Nutritionally deficient queens may produce weak and/or deformed kittens. A vitamin-poor diet in the queen may cause bony defects such as flattened chests, skull or vertebral deformities, or may lead to hydrocephalus, deafness, and ataxia (see the Encyclopedia of Diseases of Cats) in kittens. Queens deficient in iodine reportedly produce kittens with open eyes and cleft palates. Iodine-deficient kittens may cease to grow, are hypothyroid, and develop a sparse, short coat and thickened skin. They are reported to be slow moving, lethargic, and gentle, affectionate kittens.

Physical agents: Extreme variations in temperature may have adverse effects upon a queen and her embryonic kittens. Hyperthermia caused by environmental conditions (heat and humidity without ventilation) or by illness may cause embryotoxicity (poisoning of the embryo). It is also generally recommended that elective X rays on the queen be postponed until the time of delivery to decrease the possibility of embryonic malformation.

Socializing Kittens

Kittens should be allowed to feel secure in their small living quarters—to know where their food and water dishes, their bed, and the litter pan are—before their horizons are expanded. Make fresh water available at all times. Introduce a variety of foods, at first moistened with baby food, milk, and/or water and gradually made more solid. Dry food for kittens can be left out for snacks and for play.

In addition to climbing out of the box, beginning to eat, and discovering the litter pan, kittens will be discovering one another and developing their coordination through play. As their curiosity grows, both queen-raised and hand-raised kittens will want to explore and should be encouraged, within reason, to discover the rest of the household. If a sick kitten is nursed back to health by a conscientious owner, the tendency may be for the owner to become overprotective. Sheltering a kitten from loud noises and unexpected happenings will only make its eventual adjustment to the real world more traumatic. A healthy, well-loved kitten that feels as secure as possible in its world will be a good match for the challenges that await it.

When an owner takes a kitten to the veterinarian for its first immunizations, a stool sample should be submitted for microscopic examination for internal parasites. Depending on its history, the kitten should also be checked for ticks, fleas, and ear mites. If it has been exposed to ringworm or has lived in a crowded cattery, the veterinarian should look for ringworm lesions.

If a kitten is handled frequently at home, the medical examination may be easier. Owners can easily examine ears, mouth, foot pads, and nails. The familiarity of these routines will dispel some of the kitten's fear sometimes associated with a visit to the veterinarian.

Other routines such as grooming, nail clipping, and tooth cleaning (see Chapter 3) will be much easier to perform later on if a kitten is accustomed to them when young.

7

Care of Older Cats

KATHLEEN E. NOONE, VMD

ntil about two decades ago, a domestic cat's normal life expectancy was only ten or twelve years, and a cat of eight or nine was considered old. Today, a well-cared-for cat's lifespan ranges anywhere from fifteen to twenty years, and it is not considered a senior citizen until fifteen or sixteen years of age. This greater longevity is the result of our increased awareness of cats' needs—better veterinary care and a more complete knowledge of cats' nutritional requirements.

General Signs of Aging

Like all animals, individual cats age at differing rates. The age at which a cat becomes old can be influenced by a number of factors: care and nutrition, genetics, environment, stress, and disease. Although inherited traits can affect a cat's lifespan, there is no evidence that purebreds and mixed breeds differ in this respect. Signs that a cat is getting old can be both *physical* and *behavioral*. Probably the most obvious behavioral sign is that a cat may sleep more and become less active as it ages. The cat may also be more set in its ways and therefore less accepting of change.

There are a number of physical indications of advancing age: As a cat gets older, tartar begins to form on its teeth, making them appear yellowish. The cat may also lose one or more of the small incisors in the front of its mouth. As long as there is no obvious pain or soreness, this should not be a cause for alarm, but regular dental checkups during veterinary visits will assure proper oral health. Mouth and tooth care are discussed later on in this chapter and in Chapter 3.

A cat may develop age changes in its eyes. The pupils may become cloudy, and the irises can lose some of their brilliant color. An owner may even notice dark areas and/or wrinkles in a cat's irises. (See also "Ophthalmic Diseases and Disorders" in the Encyclopedia.)

The coat quality of an older cat may become diminished. The loss of luster need not be of concern unless a cat is acting ill or the coat change occurs suddenly.

As a cat ages and loses muscle mass, its hips and spine may appear more prominent. Again, if the change is gradual, an owner does not need to be worried, but if there is rapid weight loss in any cat, especially an older animal, it should be cause for concern.

Routine Health Care

One of the most important things that owners of older cats can do is observe their pets. Change of any sort can be an early sign that something is not right, and an owner should make it a practice to look a pet over thoroughly on a regular basis. An all-over hand check while grooming can often detect small lumps or bumps at their inception, and a complete visual scan may reveal outward changes in a cat's eyes, ears, nose, or even posture. Different eating, drinking, or bathroom habits can be significant in an older cat, and behavior or personality changes may also be a sign of trouble. Early detection and treatment of disease is particularly important for older cats, as their resistance is not as strong as it used to be and the risk of serious illness can be greatly diminished by quick action.

Veterinary Care

It is important that older cats continue to be immunized on a regular basis. Usually boosters are given once a year (see Chapter 3). At this time the cat should also be given a thorough checkup that should include taking its temperature, weighing the cat, examining its mouth, and listening to its heart. Some veterinarians will also perform a routine blood test to determine if any early, subtle organ failure has developed that can be dealt with before it becomes a real problem. Owners should ask any questions and voice any concerns that may have occurred to them about their older cat's condition.

A once-a-year visit to the veterinarian for a checkup and immunizations is probably sufficient for a normal older cat. Of course, if changes occur or the cat becomes ill, it may have to visit the doctor more frequently.

Feeding an Older Cat

Cats are usually good self-regulators when it comes to eating, and dietary changes are not necessary just because a cat is becoming older. A cat that is obese has been allowed to overeat all its life. A well-balanced diet, as outlined in Chapter 3, should prevent this. Unless there are specific medical problems that require a special diet, a cat should be allowed to continue eating whatever it has been used to.

Exercise and Activity

As a cat ages and becomes less agile, it will automatically limit physical activity to suit its ability. It will probably not jump as high or as often as before, especially if it is arthritic, and owners may need to adjust the household to suit the cat's capabilities. Food and water bowls may have to be moved from the counter to the floor, and a favorite blanket may need to be moved from the bed to a low chair. Other than that, owners need do nothing to restrict an older cat from whatever activities it feels able to do.

If a cat seems to become too sedentary, owners can try to encourage some activity with a favorite toy or game, but as any cat owner knows, a cat cannot be forced to play.

Grooming

Unless very ill, a cat will automatically keep itself clean. Daily brushing or combing is a good idea, however, especially if a cat has a tendency to shed a lot. Hairballs, which may not present much of a problem when a cat is young, can cause problems in an older cat, especially if it has any other underlying physical disorders.

At the same time, a cat's mouth and teeth should be examined. We recommend that an owner clean a cat's teeth on a regular basis (see Chapter 3 for how to do this). If an older cat's teeth have never been properly cleaned, they will have to be initially scraped by the veterinarian to remove accumulated plaque before regular maintenance is started.

Litter and Water

Thoughtful owners will provide enough clean litter trays and water bowls so that an old cat does not have to search for them. A sedentary older cat or one not feeling too well may not have the energy to find water when it should be drinking regularly or to look for a litter tray when it needs one.

Avoiding Stress: Emotional and Psychological Needs of Older Cats

As we said, some older cats tend to become very set in their ways and are less adaptable to change. A sudden switch in routines or an uprooting from familiar surroundings may take an elderly cat longer to adjust to than a younger one. An owner should pay special attention to the cat during this period to make sure that it continues to eat and drink normally.

If an owner needs to be away for long periods of time, an older cat can ideally be cared for in the home by a family member or friend. The cat "sitter" should be instructed about the details of the cat's normal daily routine so that the owner's absence will be made as easy as possible for the cat.

Sometimes it may be necessary for an older cat to spend time in a strange house because an owner is unable to arrange for its care at home, due to a move or vacation, for instance. Owners can ease the trauma of this kind of situation for an old cat by arranging for familiar objects to be brought along, such as bedding, food and water dishes, litter trays, and so forth. The cat's normal routine should be upset as little as possible, with mealtimes carefully observed. If the cat is to stay in a strange household where there are other animals or unfamiliar children, it is probably a good idea to confine the cat in one room for a few days until it adjusts, before it is given free run of the home. For some cats this is not necessary, and owners will be the best judge of this. Common sense and a cat's-eye viewpoint can help to

prevent an older cat from becoming too upset in this type of situation.

Common sense should also apply when it comes to boarding a cat in a kennel. Some cats that have been boarded regularly since kittenhood will have no problem staying away from home in a kennel situation. Others that have never been boarded before may have some difficulty adjusting. An owner can help to minimize the strain on an older cat by apprising kennel owners of the cat's particular habits. Most kennel owners are very conscious of the problems of boarding senior citizens and will be cooperative in providing any special care that is necessary. There are a number of boarding facilities nowadays that cater specifically to cats.

If possible, an owner should visit a new boarding facility ahead of time to look it over, talk to the owner or manager, and check on the details of care, such as:

• Are up-to-date immunizations and FeLV tests required of all boarders? This is particularly important for older cats, to lessen the risk of infection.

• Will the kennel give medications if necessary?

• Does each cat have its own litter tray, and feeding and water dishes?

• What about climate control (for example, air conditioning or heat)?

• What are the cats fed? Will special diets be given if necessary?

• How often are the animals visited each day? Is there anyone there at night?

• What arrangements are made for emergency medical care?

• Are owners allowed to bring blankets or beds? If so, are they actually used?

These are not unreasonable questions for an owner to ask of a boarding facility. If they cannot be answered to your satisfaction, another facility should be found. The American Boarding Kennels Association (ABKA) is an association of boarding kennel operators devoted to providing good care for their charges. They will provide a list of member kennels to cat owners.*

A New Cat for Company and Entertainment?

There are dangers of introducing illness along with a new kitten or cat. It is highly possible that a seemingly healthy newcomer is incubating a germ and will then bring it into the household. This can present a problem to an aged cat that will not be able to throw off the infection as well as it could have when young.

Another problem with introducing a new cat into the home is that many cats are not especially social with new felines. Therefore, the introduction of a new, young cat into an older cat's "territory" is apt to cause some resentment and stress. Some cats never get along well, while others will ignore each other. Other cats will do just fine together.

The commonly held theory that a younger animal will energize and entertain an older one really does not hold true for all cats. Owners who are considering the idea of bringing home a new playmate for their senior citizen cat should weigh the disadvantages thoroughly. If they do decide to bring home a new cat, the choice should be made very carefully to ensure as much as possible that the new cat is well. (That is, select a healthy looking kitten or cat and have it examined immediately by a veterinarian.) Proper isolation routines should be strictly followed (see Chapter 3). The older cat should be protected against assault on itself, its favorite spots, and its belongings in order to avoid too much stress. Usually, the two cats will come to some kind of understanding, but the first few days can be hard on the older cat.

Common Physical Disorders of Older Cats

Most of the problems listed here are not confined to older cats but can be more serious in an old animal and should be attended to as soon as they are noticed so that a diagnosis can be made and treatment begun. Trouble should be suspected with a cat of any age when there is a change from the norm, such as excessive water drinking, excessive urination, diarrhea, constipation, rapid weight loss, or loss of appetite.

Arthritis (see the Encyclopedia): Old cats can suffer from arthritis in their hips and spines. Cats with this disorder will show some discomfort and may not want to jump as much or as high as they formerly did.

Constipation: This may be the result of hairballs or other problems. If it becomes chronic or severe, it can lead to obstipation (stoppage). Owners can often ease the problem with some kind of lubricant (Vaseline, butter, mineral oil) placed on the cat's paws so that the cat will lick it off, or at the top of its mouth (see "Medicating a Cat" in Chapter 13). If this does not work, the veterinarian should be consulted.

Dental disease: As a cat ages, dental disease may develop and be a source of infection for the entire body. Root abscesses can also cause

---

* Write to: American Boarding Kennels Association, 311 N. Union Blvd., Colorado Springs, CO 80909

a chronically runny nose. As we said before, a cat's mouth and teeth should be checked on a regular basis for signs of trouble. Any growths or sores in the mouth or tongue, bleeding or excessively pale gums, and loose or broken teeth should be treated immediately. Dental work can be performed on a cat, regardless of age, as long as the proper precautions are taken and severe internal problems are not present.

Diabetes mellitus (see the Encyclopedia): Diabetes mellitus is a disease of the older cat characterized by frequent water drinking and urination. It is diagnosed by means of urine and blood analysis.

Heart murmurs: Older cats can also develop heart murmurs, which can often be initially detected with a stethoscopic examination and then evaluated with an electrocardiogram (EKG) and chest X ray. (See "Cardiac Arrhythmia" in the Encyclopedia).

Hyperthyroidism (see the Encyclopedia): Sudden weight loss and an increased appetite may indicate hyperthyroidism, which usually develops in middle- to older-aged cats. This disease is diagnosed with a blood test.

Kidney (renal) disease (see the Encyclopedia): Often seen in older cats, kidney disease can be diagnosed by means of a urine sample and appropriate blood tests. Signs of kidney problems include more frequent or excessive water drinking and frequent urination.

Tumors: Tumors in all parts of the body are common in older cats. Any external lump or bump should be examined immediately and a biopsy performed if indicated. Internal tumors may manifest themselves in gastrointestinal tract symptoms (see "Gastrointestinal [GI] Diseases and Disorders" in the Encyclopedia), such as weight loss, loss of appetite, diarrhea, and vomiting. Should any of these signs develop in an older cat and not go away spontaneously, the cat should be evaluated with a blood test and X ray. If a tumor is diagnosed, a biopsy may be performed for confirmation. Various tumors may be treated surgically or with chemotherapy.

Caring for an Invalid Older Cat

Once a diagnosis has been made, an older cat may require hospitalization for treatment and/ or surgery. Owners are often very concerned about the dangers of surgery for an older cat, no matter how minor, and are especially fearful about the use of anesthetic.

Although anesthesia still holds more risks for older animals than for younger ones, presurgical testing procedures and new methods of giving anesthetics lessen the risk. Older cats can safely be given anesthesia if their evaluation by the veterinarian finds no major abnormalities (see Chapter 4). Most veterinarians perform a complete medical workup on an older cat before even minor surgery. Owners should be aware that testing does involve additional cost.

Owners are also often concerned about the stress on an older animal that a stay in the hospital may produce. In some cases, of course, there is no choice. If a cat requires aggressive

medical treatment or management, she is better off in the hospital with proper care, and in our experience most cats fare very well in the hospital once they adjust. In some instances, however, a veterinarian and owner may decide that a sick cat is better off being treated and cared for at home. In this case, the owner may have to provide maintenance care.

Essentially, the home care of an ill older cat will differ very little from the care of a sick cat of any age. Owners may have to administer medications and force-feed an animal according to the veterinarian's instructions and following the various methods described in Chapter 13.

It is especially important to keep an ailing older cat's litter box and water bowl clean, and they should be placed nearby so that the cat does not have to walk around to find them. Also, ample heat and a cozy bed should be provided.

The Decision to Euthanize

The reasons for euthanasia, how it is performed, an owner's presence during the procedure, ways of memorializing a beloved cat, and the ways in which a pet's death can affect an owner are all discussed in detail in Chapter 10. It seems appropriate, however, to briefly touch on how to make that choice for an old cat here.

As we emphasize in Chapter 10, the decision to euthanize must be an individual one. There is no right or wrong involved. Some pet owners are unable to cope with disease and/or illness of any kind and find it distasteful or even impossible to medicate or treat an ailing animal. For them, the decision to euthanize a sick cat is based on the remembrance of the joy of their relationship with their cat when it was well and the fact that the sick pet's daily care now that it is ill would only serve to rob them of their happy memories.

For others, concern that a cat is suffering leads them to consider euthanasia. In our opinion, a cat that continues to show pleasure in being alive and still enjoys daily life can be allowed to continue to live as long as it can do so with dignity.

When this is no longer true, the final decision to euthanize an old cat should be made by an owner together with the veterinarian.

Emergencies

Michael S. Garvey, DVM

The word *emergency* can be very frightening in its implications of a sudden, life-threatening occurrence. For a cat owner, the sense of panic and helplessness can often be heightened by the fact that animal accidents and sudden illnesses usually seem to happen at off-hours, when the regular veterinarian's office is closed. One thing that cat owners can do to alleviate part of the problem is to find out ahead of time what to do in this situation. What does the veterinarian recommend doing? Where is the nearest emergency veterinary clinic or hospital? What is the telephone number? This information can be placed in a convenient spot along with other emergency information so that time is not wasted wondering what to do should the need arise. Cat owners who travel with their pets or take them to vacation homes should take a few moments to obtain the same information wherever they are.

The fact remains that the best thing to do for any cat in almost every kind of emergency is to *get it to a veterinarian right away.* Owners have neither the knowledge nor the equipment to accomplish much in the way of real help when a cat is seriously ill or injured. In our estimation, the many so-called emergency techniques and measures for animals that have been touted in the past and are still put forth in many pet-care books and articles at best serve no constructive purpose and at worst only tend to make things worse by wasting precious time.

There are, however, some steps that can sometimes be taken by owners in certain situations to make a cat comfortable and possibly prevent further damage until a doctor can be reached. We will outline these steps and will also talk about what the signs of a real emergency are so that cat owners can make intelligent judgments regarding their pets' well-being. (See also Figures 6 and 7, pages 105–106.)

Feline emergencies can be the result of a traumatic accident. Falls from windows (the "high-rise syndrome") are often seen in urban areas. Other traumatic accidents, both external and internal, include being hit by a moving vehicle, which may involve fractures and other injuries, and wounds from animal bites, and so forth. Cats also sometimes ingest poisons or other harmful substances, and they can sustain burns and electrocution. In a category of its own, heat prostration can also be a serious emergency for cats.

Any illness can become an emergency in cats. It can be acute or of sudden onset. Usually, however, an illness may have been present in a cat's body for some time before it suddenly appears with acute symptoms. The difference between cats and dogs in their reaction to disease is quite dramatic. Cats usually seem to develop disease in a very acute, life-threatening fashion. Very few diseases in cats appear to be chronic, developing over a long period of time. This is due in part to the fact that cats tolerate and compensate for disease states much better than many other animals do. A cat can have serious medical problems that it will compensate for itself by restricting its exercise and resting until the disease process becomes too widespread to be offset. Then the cat will seem to have an acute problem. In other words, cats send out very few warning signals that all is not well and will therefore often appear to become very ill very suddenly.

This can be especially true in the case of systemic, metabolic diseases such as renal failure, liver disease, and diabetes mellitus (see entries in the Encyclopedia of Diseases of Cats). Although these diseases are not usually acute in nature, cats often compensate so well in the early stage of illness that symptoms can easily go unnoticed by an owner. These diseases will then seem to suddenly manifest themselves in much the same way: The cat will be severely depressed, dehydrated, lethargic (reluctant to get up and move around), may vomit, have diarrhea, and other associated symptoms. In other words, the cat will show signs of being severely metabolically ill, and these diseases may appear suddenly as medical emergencies. We will see more examples in the following pages.

Avoiding Accidents

Cat owners can often avert an emergency situation if they are aware of the kinds of accidents that frequently occur to kittens and cats, and use common sense to try to prevent them. First-time cat owners especially should realize that kittens and cats have no way of knowing about the possibilities of injury. They should remember to anticipate danger for a pet, just as they would for a small child. We often see the following accidental causes of injury to cats:

1. *Trauma from falls from windows.* The "high-rise syndrome" is a very common cat accident. It is not necessarily limited to animals who live in large cities but can occur in suburban apartments as well. Neither kittens nor full-grown cats should ever be left unattended in a room above the second floor with unscreened open windows. Even when people are present, screens or closely spaced bars are necessary.

2. *Trauma from being hit by a car or motorcycle.* Cats that are allowed outdoors can easily be hit, especially at night; they tend to "freeze" in headlights and then run in an unpredictable direction. Owners should be aware of this and keep cats in after dark. If this is impossible, a reflector collar or tag may help the cat to be seen. When traveling by car it is essential to keep windows and doors tightly closed, or the cat should be securely leashed or in a carrying case at all times, especially when the car stops.

3. There is a related danger to outdoor cats from cars. Cats often sleep underneath cars. Even worse, they may climb underneath a car hood and sleep on the warm engine block at night and can be severely hurt by the fan when the car starts up. Cat owners should make it a habit to know where their outdoor pet is in order to avoid this kind of accident.

4. *Scratch and bite wounds from other animals* can be prevented only by keeping a cat indoors. Neutering of males can help to cut down on territorial fighting with other cats.

5. Because of their innate curiosity, young kittens (and even older cats) often climb into appliances such as refrigerators or clothes dryers. This can be fatal if they are not noticed in time, and owners should make it a habit to check before closing the doors or turning on appliances.

6. *Swallowed objects* such as strings and other small things can become lodged in a cat's esophagus and have to be removed by a veterinarian. Strings can also become twisted around the back of a cat's tongue and cause severe damage to the entire gastrointestinal tract. Owners should always be sure that

strings are not left lying around and that toys with strings on them are securely attached at one end.

7. *The ingestion of substances,* such as human medications and so forth, *can cause drug intoxication, and cats can be poisoned when they eat or drink various other substances.* Cats are highly sensitive to medications, and no medications should ever be given to a cat except on the advice of a veterinarian, especially anything containing acetaminophen or phenactin, which can be fatal to cats (see also the Appendix). It is particularly important for cat owners to know that antifreeze (ethylene glycol) is extremely attractive to cats and potentially fatal. Antifreeze should be kept in tightly sealed containers and disposed of immediately, not left lying around the garage or property. Cats can worm their way into very small spaces and can jump very high. Therefore, cleaning substances, antifreeze, and other potentially harmful chemicals must not only be stored very carefully but should be tightly sealed as well.

8. Kittens' curiosity can also get them into trouble with electric cords. Chewing on a plugged-in cord can result in *electrocution.* Until an owner is sure that a kitten will not be tempted to chew electric cords, it is best to unplug them when no one is around.

9. Despite a great deal of publicity about this problem, owners still take their cats with them in the car on hot days. *Leaving a cat closed in a carrying case in a car in the sun for even brief periods of time can quickly result in heat prostration.* In warm weather, cats are best left at home.

These are some of the accidental emergencies that occur most frequently with cats and kittens and that can often be avoided by thoughtful owners.

WHEN IS IT AN EMERGENCY?

It is an emergency requiring immediate veterinary attention when:

- **A cat has received any kind of traumatic injury—a fall, being hit by a car**

- **A fracture is suspected**

- **There is significant bleeding from any part of the body, including in the stool and urine**

- **Any kind of eye injury has occurred, no matter how seemingly slight**

- **A cat's gums/mouth are pale and/or purplish blue**

- **A cat is having difficulty breathing**

- **A cat is severely trembling, shaking, or in obvious discomfort**

- **A cat collapses, seems suddenly weak, loses consciousness, and/or has more than one seizure**

- **There is sudden onset of depression, fever**

- **Vomiting and/or diarrhea lasts for more than twenty-four hours**

- **A cat is unable to urinate**

- **A cat is choking or is known to have swallowed a foreign object**

- **A cat is known to have ingested drugs, medications, or poison**

Any of these signs or occurrences or any combination of these signs constitutes an emergency.

Some Common Symptoms of Many Emergencies

The signs or symptoms listed at the beginning of this section can often be caused by one or more conditions. Two particular symptoms that frequently appear as a result of a number of emergencies should be defined in detail, and these are:

Dyspnea (Difficult Breathing)

This symptom is commonly seen as the result of a number of different causes, both medical and accidental. There are many reasons why cats develop dyspnea, which is usually an acute emergency situation even though in many cases it arises from a chronic, unnoticed illness that a cat has had for some time. As we discussed in the beginning of this section, a cat's ability to compensate for an illness for a long time is particularly applicable to dyspnea.

Pneumothorax: This is commonly referred to as a collapsed lung, a condition in which air escapes from the lung and enters the chest cavity around the lungs, resulting in breathing difficulty. It is caused by a number of different conditions and traumas.

Hydrothorax: This is an accumulation of fluid around the lungs that causes breathing difficulty. It can occur as a result of bleeding, heart failure, an infectious disease, or low blood proteins.

Lung Disease: Other conditions that create breathing problems are an accumulation of fluid inside the lungs or an infiltration of abnormal or diseased cells into the lungs. This can be a result of cancer, bronchial asthma, a fungal infection, pneumonia, and pulmonary edema.

Shock

Cats can be in shock from trauma, including fractures and severe bleeding or hemorrhaging. Shock is a collapse of the cardiovascular system and is characterized by rapid heartbeat, confusion, collapse, shivering, weak pulse, and pallor. Pallor can be detected by lifting up a corner of the cat's lip and examining the gums and mucous membranes in the mouth. Normally, the insides of a cat's mouth are bright pink. If they are pale pink, there is a problem. If they are white, the problem is serious. Shock brought about by severe blood loss is called *hemorrhagic shock.* Cats suspected of being in shock should be kept quiet and warm and be given prompt veterinary attention. Treatment for shock includes rapid intravenous fluid therapy. Without prompt treatment for shock, the damage to the cardiovascular system will be irreversible.

Emergency Conditions/Situations

NOTE: DISEASES AND DISORDERS IN CAPITAL LETTERS WILL BE FOUND
IN THE ENCYCLOPEDIA OF DISEASES OF CATS.

Bleeding or Hemorrhaging

A cat's blood volume makes up only about 6 percent of its total body weight, so we must be particularly concerned about blood loss in cats. Bleeding or hemorrhaging from any part of a cat's body can be an emergency if the bleeding is profuse or if it is at a slow pace and lasts for a long period of time. Owners can often assess the seriousness of bleeding by checking for pallor and other signs of shock.

Nasal or oral bleeding: If profuse, nasal or oral bleeding can be life-threatening. Packs or cold compresses over the nose or mouth area may help to slow bleeding, but it is usually impossible to get a compress to the problem area. Therefore, there is very little that an owner can do to stop this kind of bleeding ex-

cept get a cat emergency veterinary attention as quickly as possible.

Skin or surface bleeding: Lacerations, wounds, and punctures (see below) in any part of the body can cause bleeding. Usually wounds in the skin surface cause minimal bleeding. The exception is a deep wound, which involves a vein or blood vessel underneath the surface. This is most likely to occur in the neck area where the jugular vein is or with cuts of the leg or foot. If there is significant bleeding from the skin, manual pressure should be applied in places that are not easily bandaged, using a clean cloth or bandage and applying pressure over the wound until the bleeding stops (see Photograph 15, opposite page). A compression bandage should be used in areas that can be readily bandaged (see Il-

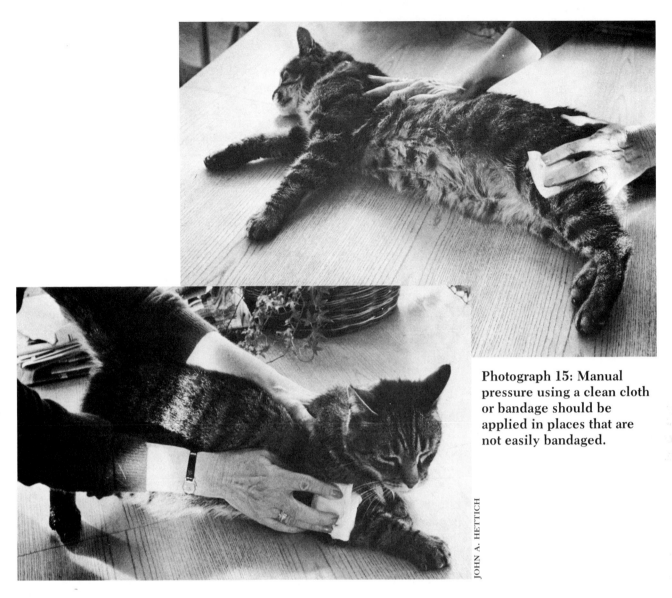

Photograph 15: Manual pressure using a clean cloth or bandage should be applied in places that are not easily bandaged.

JOHN A. HETTICH

Nancy Lou Mohrus

Illustration 9: A compression bandage to control bleeding

lustration 9, page 95). *We do not advocate the use of tourniquets.* They are very dangerous, may cause the loss of a limb due to prolonged interruption of the blood supply, and are not as effective as properly applied pressure.

Bleeding on feet and legs: Because they walk lightly, cats do not tend to cut their feet often, but if they do, lacerations of the foot pads tend to bleed a lot. This is very spongy tissue, and while the bleeding will often stop, it may begin again as soon as the cat steps on the foot and spreads the foot pad. If this process continues for too long, a cat can lose a significant amount of blood. Foot pad lacerations should be treated with a compression or pressure bandage, if possible.

Vomiting blood: This can be a cause of great concern for cat owners. However, if fluid is being vomited or vomiting is infrequent or the extent of the bleeding is flecks or streaks of blood in the vomitus, this is not a life-threatening emergency. If there is a profuse amount of blood thrown up or if there are blood clots present, it can indicate significant bleeding in the stomach. In this case, seek veterinary attention quickly. There is no emergency treatment for this condition, and oral medication is not advised.

Bloody diarrhea or stool: If the blood is confined to streaks or flecks, with normal stool or diarrhea, it is not a severe emergency. If, however, a cat passes a lot of blood rectally, veterinary attention should be sought immediately.

Blood in the urine: This is usually a sign of a urinary tract infection such as BACTERIAL CYSTITIS, and it is not usually a significant emergency. When there is profuse bleeding, the urine becomes very dark red, or blood clots are passed. This is a sign of significant bleeding that requires prompt veterinary attention. Again, there is no first aid or medication that can be given at home.

Spontaneous bruising: This type of bleeding can be the most difficult for an owner to recognize, but it can be significant. Large purple splotches on the skin, particularly on dependent areas such as the abdomen, can indicate a bleeding disorder. Small purple or red spots on the insides of the cat's ears or on the gums may indicate a low platelet count, rat poisoning (WARFARIN POISONING), or some other type of bleeding disorder. The animal can bleed into areas that can cause acute problems, such as the brain, and so all of these types of bleeding disorders should be taken very seriously and considered medical emergencies.

Burns

Cats are rarely burned with fire, but a cat can fall into a tub of scalding water or, more likely, boiling water or grease may fall onto a cat, scalding the animal all over its body and causing diffuse burns that can be extremely serious. No first aid but prompt medical attention is advised.

Cardiomyopathy

CARDIOMYOPATHY is the most common category of feline heart disease. It can be present for years before symptoms show up in a cat. In HYPERTROPHIC CARDIOMYOPATHY (HCM), for instance, the heart will fail suddenly and cause pulmonary edema and dyspnea (difficult breathing). Another form of cardiomyopathy, DILATED (CONGESTIVE) CARDIOMYOPATHY, will cause a buildup of fluid in the chest cavity outside the lungs, very similar to FIP although in this case the fluid arises from heart failure; it will cause acute dyspnea even though the fluid may have been building up for some time. Immediate veterinary help is required.

Collapse

As we have said before, cats can suddenly become acutely ill and collapse because of an ongoing systemic or metabolic disease, or because of poisoning. They can also collapse as the result of shock following a traumatic injury or severe blood loss, or of dyspnea (difficult breathing) due to fluid buildup in the lungs following a trauma or because of an illness. Collapse can also be caused by ANEMIA, SEIZURE DISORDERS, or a thromboembolism.

Diarrhea

Cats occasionally get diarrhea. Usually, it should be of no serious concern. For treatment of common diarrhea, see GASTROINTESTINAL DISEASES AND DISORDERS in the Encyclopedia. Diarrhea becomes an emergency when it is bloody or contains blood clots (see Bleeding disorders above), or is accompanied by any or a combination of vomiting, listlessness, DEPRESSION, loss of appetite, fever, and seeming or acting ill. In any of these cases, immediate veterinary help is necessary.

Drug Intoxication

Cats should never be given any medication without the owner first checking with a veterinarian. Even drugs that are generally considered to be safe in other species (e.g., aspirin, acetaminophen, tranquilizers, antihistamines) can cause serious problems in cats. Cats are not apt to swallow unfamiliar substances, but if a cat does ingest a lot of any human medicine, including heart medications, blood pressure pills, antidepressants, tranquilizers, and so forth, it is an emergency. In addition, drugs such as marijuana, hashish, hallucinogenics, and so forth, can cause severe problems for a cat. Reactions of cats are highly unpredictable. The ingestion of any of these things requires a rapid trip to the veterinarian. When an owner is sure that a cat has eaten medicine or other drugs, an appropriate first-aid measure is to get it back up out of the cat before significant absorption takes place. If an owner is sure that the material is not caustic (see Poisoning below), he can induce vomiting by giving hydrogen peroxide orally, by the teaspoonful, until vomiting occurs. Hydrogen peroxide will not harm a cat and is usually effective. See also the Appendix.

Dystocia (Difficult Birth)

This is not very common in the cat. Signs of dystocia are continued labor with no kittens born and continued labor with no birth after only one kitten has been born. Any birthing difficulties need immediate veterinary attention.

Electrocution

This is a problem that is usually confined to kittens who may chew on a plugged-in electric cord. They will sustain a nasty shock to the mouth area and electrocution. Electrocution can be mild and present very few signs, but as a rule it will cause shock and significant pulmonary edema (fluid in the lungs) resulting in labored, difficult breathing (dyspnea). Owners should be sure that electric cords are not accessible, especially to young kittens. Cyanosis (blue mucous membranes) is often noted, or white mucous membranes, indicating shock. If treatment with diuretics and oxygen is fast enough, the kitten can usually be saved. If an owner comes home and finds a kitten lying prostrate unable to move and having difficulty breathing, he should suspect that the kitten has bitten an electric cord and get immediate help.

Eye Trauma

Because eyes are very intolerant of trauma, any eye injury must be handled quickly and appropriately, or the eye may not be savable. In addition, any injury to the cornea can be very painful. See also Wounds below.

Falls from Windows (the "High-Rise Syndrome")

As we said above, cats are especially prone to falls from windows. There are a number of theories as to why this occurs as often as it does. One is that a cat will go after a bird or insect; another holds that cats do not have highly developed depth perception and therefore do not realize that the ground is far away. A third theory is that a cat can become dizzy or lose its balance and fall when sitting on a windowsill. Whatever the reason, the end result is usually the same.

Interestingly, the distance of the fall is not always in direct proportion to the seriousness of the injuries sustained by a cat. A study done at The AMC in 1984 showed that cats that fell five to nine stories tended to have worse injuries than those that fell fewer than five stories

Photograph 16: Although city cats like to sit on fire escapes, it is a dangerous place for them!

or *more* than nine stories. Those that fell more than nine stories often had either milder injuries or a greater incidence of survival than those that fell only six stories. One reason for this seeming contradiction has to do with how cats fall. The higher survival rate for short falls (under five stories) can be logically explained by the fact that the higher up a cat is when it falls, the more likely it is that it can achieve a terminal velocity as it reaches the ground. However, when cats fall a long enough distance (for example, over nine stories), they orient themselves, and then they can straighten themselves out and spread their limbs to increase wind resistance to fall. Thus, they slow themselves down and manage to absorb most of the concussion in their chest and abdomen, which seems to minimize the amount of really serious damage done.

Because of the way cats land, the most common injury associated with falls of this sort is pneumothorax (see Dyspnea above), the presence of air in the chest cavity outside the lungs. When this happens, the negative pressure that usually keeps the lungs inflated disappears, allowing the lungs to collapse inside the chest and producing breathing difficulty. Since most of the concussion when a cat falls is absorbed by the chest hitting the ground, this is a likely explanation for the incidence of pneumothorax.

The second most common injury is a fracture of the hard palate or roof of the mouth. This arises because as a cat hits the ground its head snaps forward in response to the sudden stop and it smacks its nose on the pavement, causing the fracture. A bloody nose is also often present.

The third common injury occurring from a fall of this type is skeletal FRACTURES—fractured pelvis and long bones.

In 1984, a new record was set of a cat surviving a fall with minimal injuries—thirty-two stories. The cat was released from the hospital two days later!

Feline Bronchial Asthma

Asthma in the cat is very similar to asthma in humans. FELINE BRONCHIAL ASTHMA can be a serious or life-threatening emergency and probably arises from an allergic reaction to some airborne pollen or antigen, or perhaps is aggravated by dust from the environment, cat litter, and so forth. Bronchial constriction or an acute onset of dyspnea (difficult breathing) may develop. After diagnosis, it can be controlled but never cured.

Fractures

Virtually every bone in a cat's body can be affected by FRACTURES. Usually, cats with fractured limbs are not in a great deal of pain provided they are not walking around or the fracture is not being moved around. Attempts to immobilize a fracture with splints or any other kind of hard apparatus usually causes more discomfort and pain to the animal than leaving it alone. What's more, many of the fractures that are high on the leg cannot be splinted appropriately. The splint is usually placed where it is convenient for the owner, and the end of the splint comes right at the fracture, which then causes the fracture to distract more than it would have normally. The best thing to do for a cat with a suspected fracture is to pick it up by the chest and/or abdomen, place it in a carton, carrying case, or even a litter tray, and transport it to the veterinarian (see Photograph 17, below). Sometimes shock is involved when there is a fracture, so a cat should be kept as quiet as possible, wrapped in a blanket for warmth, and brought to the veterinarian with as little jostling and movement as possible.

Photograph 17: A cat with a suspected fracture can be transported to the veterinarian in a cardboard carton.

JOHN A. HETTICH

Gastrointestinal Upsets

Intestinal upsets can be caused by a variety of problems, many of which are not emergencies (see GASTROINTESTINAL DISEASES AND DISORDERS in the Encyclopedia). Most serious emergency situations, however, will cause a cat to suffer from some form of gastrointestinal upset, and sudden loss of appetite is almost always a sign of illness or pain. Owners must use their judgment as to cause, and severity, of these kinds of upsets. See also Diarrhea, Poisoning, Pyometra, and Vomiting.

Heat Prostration

This is an emergency that naturally occurs in warm weather. Heat prostration develops in cats very quickly because they are small and do not sweat. The only way they have to remove excess heat from their bodies is by panting, which allows moisture to evaporate from the tongue, mouth, and mucous membranes, providing some cooling. This is obviously a very inefficient system to try to get rid of heat from a cat's entire body, and there's a limit to how fast an animal can breathe and pant and continue to oxygenate itself. Heat prostration in cats commonly occurs when an owner closes a cat in a carrying case and places it inside a car that is in the sun. The poor ventilation in the carrying case combined with the heat in the car results in heat prostration. A cat with heat prostration will breathe rapidly with its mouth open and tongue hanging out. In severe cases, the cat's mouth will become cyanotic as well, and the animal's body temperature will be very high. It is best to rush the cat to the veterinarian as quickly as possible so that the animal can be cooled, receive medication to protect the brain from the heat and the hypoxia (deficiency of oxygen), put on fluids if in shock, and given oxygen if necessary. It is all right to try to cool a cat by misting it all over with a plastic spray bottle, but if it is not done well, this may lose valuable time. The leading cause of death from heat prostration is cardiovascular collapse, shock, and also DIC, a bleeding disorder that can be turned on by prolonged excess body heat. It usually starts with trickles of blood from the nostrils and progresses to profuse hemorrhaging. Once DIC starts, there is usually nothing that can be done to save the animal.

Hypoglycemia

The most common cause of HYPOGLYCEMIA, or low blood sugar, in cats is the complication of insulin treatment for DIABETES MELLITUS. Signs of hypoglycemia vary. It usually begins with weakness and mental confusion. The animal may pace, wander aimlessly for a period of time, and be unresponsive. There is a variant form in which there is an acute onset of seizures or convulsions. A cat will roll over on its side, make rapid jaw movements, salivate profusely, let go of bowel and bladder, and violently shake its limbs. If hypoglycemia is too severe and goes on for too long, seizures and eventual COMA are inevitable. Sometimes there will be brain damage, even after proper treatment. This is a condition in which first-aid treatment may help. Some honey, Karo syrup, sugar water, or anything containing sugar given orally may reverse the problem quickly. There is no necessary dose. It would be nice to get at least a tablespoonful of honey or syrup into a cat, a little bit at a time. Do not attempt to give oral substances if a cat is unconscious!

Pneumonia

PNEUMONIA, or infection of the lungs themselves, usually appears in other animals as a severe cough or another sign of respiratory disease before it becomes life-threatening. In many cases, this is not true with cats. Pneumonia itself can occur without any coughing at all in the cat and with such severe infiltration that severe labored breathing may develop. *This is an emergency requiring immediate veterinary treatment.*

Poisoning

Although cats are not as apt to eat poisonous substances as dogs are, they can ingest poison directly or by killing and eating poisoned rats and mice. As with dogs, owners are often not aware that a cat has eaten something poisonous until the animal begins to show symptoms. If an owner knows that a cat has ingested something caustic, such as Drāno or another acid, no attempt should be made to make the animal throw up. Milk can be given to provide protein for the acid or caustic alkali to work on so that it will leave the stomach and esophageal lining alone. When in doubt and if a veterinarian cannot be reached immediately, owners can *call the nearest poison control center* to find out what to do for known ingestants. Ethylene glycol, the active ingredient in antifreeze, is one of the most toxic substances for cats. Any animal that gets anywhere near antifreeze should be brought to the veterinarian immediately. Symptoms are usually mental confusion, vomiting, and eventual collapse. If symptoms begin before treatment is started, the animal usually goes into KIDNEY FAILURE and dies. Cat owners should be warned that antifreeze should be disposed of or locked up in tight drums or closed-cap containers. Once a cat tastes antifreeze, it starts a craving, and a cat may drink an entire container of it. This is a seasonal problem, occurring in both the fall and spring, when people normally add antifreeze to or flush it out of car radiators.

Toxic plants can be a problem with cats because many will chew plants (see Chapter 8 for ways to prevent this). Fortunately, most plants, even the poisonous ones, only have irritating saps that cause cats to vomit or perhaps get diarrhea. One exception is dumb cane (*Dieffenbachia*), which contains an ingredient that can cause profuse swelling of the tissues in the mouth and throat, and could cause a cat to suffocate if it gets enough. This is a rare problem (see GASTROINTESTINAL DISEASES AND DISORDERS in the Encyclopedia). With all poisonings, rapid treatment by a veterinarian is helpful, particularly in case of caustic substances, so that the cat can be given cathartics, flushes, or whatever is needed to neutralize or remove the poison before it is absorbed.

Pyometra

PYOMETRA is a surgical emergency that occurs in older, unspayed female cats. It is an infection of the uterus and is characterized by appetite loss, VOMITING, DIARRHEA, DEPRESSION, possibly fever, and increased thirst and urination (see Chapter 5 and the Encyclopedia of Diseases of Cats). It must be treated immediately by surgical removal of the uterus.

Pyothorax

PYOTHORAX is an infection in the chest cavity that can be produced from penetrating wounds or from a systemic spread of bacteria. This may arise from a simple bite wound that has abscessed; the bacteria becomes bloodborne and deposits in the chest cavity, producing a raging infection. Cats with pyothorax are usually quite ill and have a fever. The fluid in the chest cavity is life-threatening and may cause acute dyspnea (difficult breathing).

Respiratory Difficulty

Whenever a cat is having difficulty breathing, it should be considered a very severe emergency. Breathing difficulty can be caused by CARDIOMYOPATHY, FELINE INFECTIOUS PERITONITIS (FIP), severe PNEUMONIA, or a traumatic chest injury that produces dyspnea or pneumothorax. Air outside the chest, after a trauma, fall, car accident, penetrating chest wound, will manifest itself as an acute onset of dyspnea. A cat will make deep excursions of the chest to try to get oxygen, and will often be cyanotic as well. *Immediate veterinary help is essential to draw the air and/or excess fluid out of the chest cavity.* See also Dyspnea above.

Other causes of respiratory difficulty are:

Feline leukemia virus (FeLV): Cats with FELINE LEUKEMIA VIRUS positive may develop tremendous tumors in the anterior mediastinum (space in the chest cavity between the lungs). This will cause either an accumulation of fluid in the chest or severe compression of the organs in the chest; it can appear again as an acute dyspnea.

Lung cancer: LUNG CANCER can also produce an acute onset of labored breathing.

Smoke inhalation: Cats that have been in burning buildings can develop serious respiratory problems from smoke inhalation even though they have not actually been burned. Sometimes the problem is not obvious right away, but within a few days a cat may have severe difficulty breathing. Again, veterinary help should be sought.

Seizure Disorders/Convulsions

See EPILEPSY in the Encyclopedia. Although not as common in cats as in dogs, seizures or convulsions can occur. Any seizuring animal should be attended to very quickly because seizures can be repetitive, are often violent, and can be fatal. If a cat is in status epilepticus (repeated seizures with no return to consciousness between them), or if it is having multiple seizures (sequence clustering), hospitalization and intravenous administration of anticonvulsants are necessary before oral anticonvulsant medication is begun. Diazepam is safe and effective in control of acute seizures. If the seizures continue, a second injection can be given. Should the seizures *still* persist, phenobarbital is given intravenously. In extreme cases when an animal is resistant to diazepam and phenobarbital, general anesthesia is necessary. Because of the serious nature of repeated seizures and the sedative effect of the anticonvulsants, a neurologic examination must be postponed by the veterinarian for twenty-four to seventy-two hours. In these instances, the veterinarian will require a detailed history from an owner in order to determine whether or not the cat has a potentially treatable disease.

Swallowed Objects

Strings, yarn, tinsel, needle and thread, and other linear objects are very attractive to cats. Very often, in the process of playing, these things will be swallowed. If a needle is swallowed, it will usually lodge somewhere in the mouth or throat. String, if long enough, will often wrap around a cat's tongue and go down into the intestinal tract. When the string is anchored somewhere in the body, the normal intestinal motions of the cat's gastrointestinal tract tend to cause the intestines to bunch up on the string, which will then cut through the intestinal tract or cause strangulation of the intestinal tract. This can turn into an extremely serious emergency situation. Symptoms include gagging, retching, vomiting, anorexia, DEPRESSION, abdominal pain, and dehydration (see GASTROINTESTINAL DISEASES AND DISORDERS in the Encyclopedia).

Thromboembolism of the Iliac Arteries

This occurs in the arteries in the back of the cat that give rise to blood supply in the rear legs. Usually, it occurs in association with CARDIOMYOPATHY. Cats may suffer from an acute collapse of the rear legs, which looks like paralysis, and there may be a lot of pain from swollen muscles. *This is a severe medical emergency.* The heart disease must be treated and circulation improved if possible. The prognosis is very poor for this when the heart disease is severe, although if the heart disease can be controlled, a cat may become able to use its legs again.

Urethral Obstruction
(FELINE UROLOGIC SYNDROME [FUS])

This common feline emergency is discussed in detail in the Encyclopedia of Diseases of Cats. Immediate veterinary attention is required if symptoms of straining to urinate or inability to urinate are noticed. Sometimes the first signs of a problem are when a cat becomes very ill. Left untreated, potassium elevation can cause cardiac arrest. Emergency treatment involves treating the potassium elevation, relieving the obstruction with a catheter, and administering intravenous fluids. This disease often recurs and requires ongoing treatment and possibly surgical correction.

Vomiting

Vomiting becomes an emergency when there is a profuse amount of blood or blood clots in the vomitus (see Bleeding or Hemorrhaging above) or if it persists for more than twenty-four hours and is accompanied by one or more of the following symptoms: diarrhea, fever, abdominal distention, listlessness or weakness, loss of appetite, obvious discomfort or illness. In these cases, vomiting can be a symptom of many conditions and/or illnesses (see GASTROINTESTINAL DISEASES AND DISORDERS in the Encyclopedia).

Wounds, Lacerations, Trauma

Wounds associated with fighting are quite common in cats that are allowed outdoors. Most commonly we see bite wounds; these can be simple skin breaks or severe wounds that penetrate into the lungs or abdominal cavity and cause a tremendous amount of underlying damage. The latter are obviously the most serious and usually occur when a cat fights with larger animals, although other cats can cause a lot of damage as well.

Secondary to the bite wounds we also see anything from minor bleeding to FRACTURES. There can be a tremendous amount of soft-tissue damage and subsequent infection and abscess if the wound is not properly cleaned, and there can even be a threatening emergency if body cavities are penetrated and sensitive organs are damaged (see Pyothorax above). Because of the way cats fight, damage around the head and face is most common. Eye damage, torn ears, and so forth, must be treated promptly for cosmetic reasons and in order to restore normal use.

Small lacerations and bite wounds usually do not bleed a great deal unless a large blood vessel in the neck or leg, for instance, is lacerated. See above for treatment of bleeding of any kind. ABSCESSES secondary to bite wounds may become an emergency. Signs of trouble include lethargy, fever, and loss of appetite. Without prompt veterinary attention, a cat can become toxic and die.

A FIRST-AID KIT FOR CATS

The following items should be kept handy in a box or
bag at home, in the car, or when traveling with a cat:

Gauze pads

Gauze rolls

Old sock or two to protect foot bandaging and hold it in place

Adhesive tape—athletic tape is very good

Sterile cotton or cotton swabs

Tweezer

Blunt-tipped scissor to cut away hair, especially for longhaired cats

Hydrogen peroxide—to induce vomiting and to use as a wound cleaner

Veterinary ointment for superficial wounds or burns

Ophthalmic drops or ointment

Tablespoon or syringe for administering liquids

Old towel, blanket, or carton to transport a hurt cat and/or to serve as a wrap while medicating

Rectal thermometer

Any medications cat usually or sometimes takes

Handling an Injured or Very Ill Cat

Common sense is the basis for handling an injured or very ill cat. Owners must realize that a cat in shock and severe pain is also probably very frightened. Even the best-tempered pet may strike out in this kind of situation. Before approaching a cat that has been injured, protect your hands and arms if possible, and avoid putting your face close to the animal. If a cat tries to bite or scratch and does not have an obvious fracture, it can be wrapped tightly in a pillow case or blanket in order to pick it up.

A cat that is very frightened may try to run off despite its injuries. If possible, the owner should stay with the animal while someone else goes for help. Talking to the animal in a soothing manner may help to calm it, but a cat that is really frightened and hurt may not even hear.

It is safe to assume that a cat that is injured or seriously ill will be suffering from shock and should be kept warm, dry, and as quiet as possible.

Under no circumstances should an injured or ill cat be given anything by mouth or forced to take liquids or medication. At best, they will do no good, and at worst, the animal may choke. (Exceptions to this are in the case of hypoglycemia and the ingestion of caustic substances.)

If an owner is in a strange place and doesn't know where the nearest veterinarian or emergency veterinary clinic is, a local branch of the ASPCA or Humane Society, or the local police or fire department, may be able to help.

FIGURE 6

Chart of Accidental Feline Emergencies

Injury	What to Look For	First-Aid Measures	Degree of Emergency*

Animal bites:
  Known animal
  Unknown/wild animal
	Excessive bleeding
	
	Locate biter—check for rabies
		Clean with antiseptic
		Pressure bandage
			e to E
			E

Secondary abscesses	Lethargy, fever, excessive swelling, appetite loss	Hot compresses to encourage draining	E to LTE
Arterial bleeding	Spurting blood	Manual pressure Compression bandage	LTE
Burns	Shock	Keep warm and quiet	E to LTE
Drug/medication ingestion	Reaction	Induce vomiting	SE
Electrocution	Unconsciousness, shock, cyanosis, breathing difficulty	Keep quiet and warm	LTE
Eye injury Scratch or cut	———	Keep eyeball moist with ophthalmic drops/ointment. Wet compress.	E to SE
Foot/leg bleeding	Arterial bleeding	Manual pressure Compression bandage	E to LTE
Fractures	Shock	Keep quiet and warm	E to SE
Heat prostration	Respiratory difficulty, excessive panting, cyanosis, high body temperature, collapse, bleeding from nose	Spray with cool water	LTE
Mouth, nasal bleeding	Shock	Ice packs/cool compresses	SE to LTE
Poisoning/caustic substances	Vomiting, collapse	Milk	LTE
Skin or surface bleeding Neck area	Significant bleeding	Manual pressure Compression bandage	E to SE
Swallowed objects	Choking/difficulty breathing, vomiting	———	E to SE

Trauma:
  Fall from height
  Hit by vehicle
	Shock, fractures, difficulty breathing, inability to urinate, weakness, collapse	Keep quiet and warm	E to LTE

* e = *emergency*—requires *prompt* veterinary attention (within 24 hours)
  E = *Emergency*—requires veterinary attention *as soon as possible*
  SE = *Serious Emergency*—requires *quick* veterinary attention
  LTE = *Life-Threatening Emergency*—requires *immediate* veterinary attention

FIGURE 7

Chart of Feline Medical Emergencies

Illness/Condition	Symptoms	First-Aid Measures	Degree of Emergency*
Asthma, feline bronchial	Difficulty breathing	Keep quiet	LTE
Bleeding disorders	Easy bruising, bloody stools/urine, anemia, pale mucous membranes, nosebleeds, difficulty breathing	Protect from trauma and jostling	SE to LTE
Bloody diarrhea/stool	Foul-smelling, dark	——	e to E
Blood in urine	Clots, dark-colored	——	E to SE
Bruising	Purple splotches on skin/abdomen; purple/red spots on insides of ears or gums	Protect from trauma and jostling	SE
Cardiomyopathy	Difficulty breathing (dyspnea)	Keep stress-free	LTE
Convulsions/seizures	Shaking, rolling over on side, paddling with limbs, loss of bladder/bowel control	Protect from harm	E to SE
Repeated seizures			LTE
Dystocia	Birthing problems	——	SE to LTE
Hypoglycemia	Weakness, mental confusion, aimless wandering, collapse, possible seizures (cats with diabetes mellitus)	Oral sugar	SE to LTE
Pneumonia, severe	Difficulty breathing, cyanosis, collapse	——	LTE
Pyometra	Loss of appetite, vomiting, diarrhea, depression, fever, increased thirst and urination (unspayed females)	——	SE
Pyothorax	Fever, difficulty breathing	——	SE
Thromboembolism	Rear-end collapse; pain (associated with cardiomyopathy)	——	LTE
Urethral obstruction	Inability to urinate, vomiting, very quiet, sick	——	LTE

* e = *emergency*—requires *prompt* veterinary attention (within 24 hours)
  E = *Emergency*—requires veterinary attention *as soon as possible*
  SE = *Serious Emergency*—requires *quick* veterinary attention
  LTE = *Life-Threatening Emergency*—requires *immediate* veterinary attention

PART TWO

PEOPLE-PET

RELATIONSHIPS

8

Feline Behavior

PETER L. BORCHELT, PH.D.

Cat owners are interested in and curious about their pets' behavior. There are several questions that cat owners ask frequently. Some questions have to do with personality: Does a cat have a "personality"? Do cats differ in "personality"? What do these differences mean? A related question is about the cat's independence or reported lack of social attachment. Another question concerns the cat's ability or lack of ability to be trained. This question also involves the uses and misuses of punishment. And, of course, there are questions about scratching furniture, plant eating, aggression toward people and other cats, and eliminating out of the litter box as well as other behavior problems.

These questions provide a framework for discussion of some of the basics of behavior; they allow us to point out information in the scientific field of behavior that is relevant to cats and to highlight some recent findings regarding the prevention and treatment of feline behavior problems. Using the scientific data about feline behavior as a springboard, we will also show cat owners how to deal with some everyday behavior problems in a practical way.

Cat "Personality"

The word *personality*, as used in everyday language, has several meanings. If we say of a human, "She has a wonderful personality," we are probably using the word to connote social skill (adroitness or the capability of that person to elicit positive reactions from a variety of people under different circumstances). Another aspect of the common definition of personality focuses on the most obvious or salient impression that a person gives to others. For example, a person may be described as aggressive, boring, fearful, or shy. There is often an element of evaluation involved in these assessments, and a given personality may be deemed "good" or "bad." These definitions of personality aim at what the nature or essence of a person is. That question has intrigued and puzzled philosophers and others since before the time of the ancient Greeks.

You might ask what this has to do with cats. We will start with a short review of the scientific study of human personality and show how it is relevant to the pet cat. From the beginning of the science of psychology over one hundred years ago, a major area of interest has been the description and measurement of human personality. Originally, this study was closely related to the science of human medicine. Clinicians such as Freud were interested in individuals who had obvious personality "problems"; there was a concern for how those people were or were not functioning in or adjusting to the environment. The focus was on what motivates a person to act the way he does and to observe the whole person in his natural habitat.

Later on, as psychology became more experimental, data from laboratory studies of humans and other animals such as rats, pigeons, and monkeys would be used to try to help answer these theoretical and practical questions. At the present time the question of what personality actually is literally involves everything we know about psychology from behavioral genetics, biochemistry of the nervous system, early experience, and learning and conditioning to social and environmental influences.

The science of animal behavior has also been around for over one hundred years, and thousands of animal behaviorists have labored to describe the behavior of many hundreds of species of animals in their natural habitats. People who are concerned with what animals do in the "real world" as opposed to laboratory situations are called comparative psychologists, animal behaviorists, or ethologists.

The question of a cat's "personality" (what makes up an individual animal's nature and behavior) is really very complicated and cannot be fully answered yet. But one simple idea makes understanding a cat's behavior somewhat easier: Cats are less complex than humans. With cats we can safely ignore the complicated areas of language and symbolic thinking and can concentrate on behavior and emotions.

An important beginning concept in animal behavior is the ethogram, a descriptive list of the various behaviors of a particular species. An ethogram can be general, very specific, or a combination of both. For instance, an important behavior of animals is an ability to eat. This can be classified generally as feeding, or we could list all of the various behavior patterns involved in feeding such as biting, chewing, and swallowing. Preparatory feeding behavior such as searching for, stalking, and chasing prey could also be included. Even more specifically, particular muscle movements involved in feeding could be described. Most ethograms comprise several different levels of description simultaneously, arranged into behavior systems and subsystems. A behavior system is a functional class of behavior; that is, it includes important behaviors the animal is motivated to do that have an evolutionary base and occur in most or all members of the species.

Table 5, opposite page, is a general ethogram of the major classes of behavior or behavior systems of the cat. When we speak of a cat's personality we will be considering (at least potentially) all of these behavior systems. At a general level, several major classes of behavior that apply to most animals are listed. These systems are then subdivided into additional behavior subsystems and then further subdivided into specific behaviors that apply only to cats or related species such as lions and tigers. This list of behaviors and behavior systems can be very useful because it allows us to define and agree on what we are talking about. It forces us to give specific descriptions of what an animal is doing, and it often leads to discovering either general principles of behavior or relationships between and among behaviors. More on all of this later on.

Two classes of behavior, locomotion and social, are not included in Table 5. This is because neither of these types of action is a functional system of behavior. Locomotion can occur at some point in just about any behavior system. For instance, a cat may walk or run to food, water, novel areas, toys, other cats, and so on. By the same token, several major behavior systems are always social (for example, reproduction), and others (such as grooming) are sometimes social activities and sometimes not. Moreover, as we shall see later, there are large individual differences between cats with respect to how social they are or are not.

TABLE 5

ETHOGRAM OF MAJOR FELINE BEHAVIOR SYSTEMS

System	Subsystem	Behavior	Problem(s)
Ingestion	*Feeding*	Stalking, pouncing, neck biting, chewing, swallowing	Predation on birds, mice, etc.
	Drinking	Licking	
Elimination	*Defecation*	Digging, squatting, covering	Elimination out of the litter box
	Urination	Squatting, sometimes digging/covering	
	Urine marking	Tail up and quivering, back legs stepping alternately	Spraying
Care of the Body Surface	*Self-grooming*	Licking, washing	Anxiety-induced, self-injurious grooming (rare)
	Social grooming	Licking, washing	
Contacting	*Investigating ("curiosity")*	Sniffing, pawing	Jumping on furniture, table
	Play	Stalking, inhibited biting, pawing, pouncing, chasing	Play "aggression"
	Social attachment	Maintaining body contact or proximity, rubbing head or flank, vocalizing	Jumping on table, desk, couch—separation anxiety problems are rare
Reproduction	*Mating*	Courting (howling, rolling over)	
	Care of young	Nursing, retrieving	
Agonistic	*Attack*	Slowly approaching, staring, head turning, ears turning out, biting	Inter-male threat/fight
	Self-defense	Ears flattened, rolling on back, kicking/scratching with back feet, piloerection, swatting with paws or running away	Defensive ("fear") aggression
	Territorial defense	Chasing, swatting with paw	Territorial aggression

This table of behavior systems serves as the start of a list of what cats *can* do. What they *actually* do at any given time is more complicated and harder to understand. We know that cats do not engage in these various behavior systems in a random manner and that observable environmental stimuli are important predictors of what an animal is likely to do. For instance, cats do not eat just anything at just any time. Rather, they generally eat when food is available and they are hungry. Two general sets of stimuli interact here: an external stimulus perceived in the environment (food) and an internal stimulus that we label hunger. High hunger will lead to a less restrictive definition of food—a starving animal will eat just about anything it can. However, when a cat is full, it may not even eat a tasty morsel right in front of it.

An important part of the job of an animal behaviorist is to understand what internal and external stimuli are involved in each behavior system. Some behavior systems, such as feeding, drinking, and mating, have been extensively researched, whereas other systems, such as grooming and play, have not. In spite of the fact that the science of animal behavior has learned a lot, there is much that remains a mystery. However, some general principles can be stated. One principle is that each behavior system is influenced by a large number of factors. There is evidence that each behavior system is influenced by genes, by learning, by early experience, by social variables such as the presence or behavior of other animals, as well as by complicated internal physiological and biological factors. Behavior is very complicated because it involves the functioning of a living organism in a complex and intricate world.

This means that every cat will be unique. Each animal starts off different because of its genes (identical twins, however, may start out with the same genes). Further variation is introduced cumulatively because each animal's pre- and post-natal environment is different and this environment changes constantly. Cat owners should expect different cats to be similar in some respects (after all, a cat is a cat—they all have four legs, hair, and a full list of normal behavior systems). But each individual cat is different from every other physically, behaviorally, and in many other respects.

A second principle makes it a bit easier to understand each cat's unique personality: Animals usually do only one thing at a time. So even though a cat may shift from one behavior system to another rather quickly, the stimuli to which it is responding at any given time are somewhat restricted. If we understand what stimuli a cat is paying attention to, we can more accurately predict the animal's behavior. Another way of saying this is that an animal's behavior is generally stimulus-specific and that the stimuli often can be observed by us. But in observing those stimuli we must not forget that despite many sensory and perceptual similarities between cats and humans, there are profound differences. For instance, a cat's sense of smell and its visual acuity in the dark are much more sensitive than ours.

How do these principles relate to personality in the pet cat? We now know that there are many dimensions or behavior systems that we can use to measure personality. We know that behavior is influenced by a multitude of external and internal factors. We also know that an animal is perceiving and responding to a rather limited set of stimuli at any given time. So, your cat's personality is a complex interaction of its genes, early and later experiences, and environment. And all of these factors may lead to a different personality depending on which behavior system you consider. A nice way to tie this information together is to look at how behavior develops in cats.

Development of Personality in the Cat

The process of development from kittenhood to maturity is central to the issue(s) of personality because so many factors in a cat's life can operate to influence its behavior. We will begin with an overview of the development of the cat. Table 6, opposite page, is a general schematic chart indicating the development of various sensory and behavioral systems (remember that there are large individual differences).

Most kittens are adopted into the home at about two months of age. From birth to two months the kitten will have developed considerably. It entered the world as a relatively helpless, blind creature that could suck, crawl forward looking for the mother's nipple, cry when hungry, and purr when content. It could show rudimentary reflexes but was not able to eliminate by itself.

The kitten develops rapidly. By two months of age it eats solid food, has developed independent elimination (it digs, eliminates, and

TABLE 6

A SCHEMATIC CHART SHOWING THE DEVELOPMENT OF SENSORY AND BEHAVIOR SYSTEMS IN THE CAT

	Birth	1 wk.	2–3 wks.	3 wks.	1 mo.	2 mos.	6 mos.	12 mos.	2–3 yrs.
SENSORY	blind	eyes open	use of vision		eye-paw coordination focus on movement of small, inanimate objects (toys, food)		permanent canine teeth family (in wild) breaks up		
MOTOR	suck-paddle (knead) nuzzle crawl	stand, walk		lick fur	batting, pawing in play running, jumping, rough play with mother eats solid food aggressive competition over food with littermates (seize, run with, defend) elimination reflexes develop	rolling play highly developed frequent play		sexual maturity urine marking	behavioral maturity

covers in the litter), and engages in vigorous play behavior. In contrast to the new puppy, which chews when teething, has to be housebroken, and must learn to tolerate being alone, the kitten doesn't chew much, is already housebroken, and gets along fine in most cases with moderate amounts of play behavior and contact with the owner.

It is important to note that the development of the kitten up to the time it usually comes into the home (two months) has been organized essentially with respect to the feeding system. Initially and for the first several weeks, behavior such as crawling forward, crying, suckling, and paddling/kneading with the front paws function to get milk from the mother. As the kitten's visual and motor skills develop, so does play behavior, at first with itself and littermates and then with the mother. Play behavior initially focuses on moving small objects, running and jumping up to an object, and eventually engaging in vigorous attack-like play with the mother at about six weeks or so. Play serves as the basis for the development of predatory behavior which is, of course, the preliminary component of feeding in the adult cat in the wild.

This is an important junction in the behavioral development of the kitten. Certain circumstances and experiences can bias its development in the direction of a relatively asocial, independent, self-sufficient predator. Other circumstances and experiences can lead the cat to become a relatively social, playful pet that relishes proximity to and contact with the owner.

In the wild, the kitten will aggressively compete with its littermates for the single item of prey that the mother cat brings back to the nest. The kitten that manages to get the food item from the mother will run away with it and growl at the other kittens if they attempt to take it away. As the kitten matures, it is weaned from the mother, and as the litter disperses, each kitten's food-seeking behavior develops into hunting, capturing, and killing of live prey. The kitten thus develops into a cat that "makes its living" as a solitary predator with a history of competing with other cats for food. As it reaches sexual and behavioral maturity, it will begin to exhibit territorial behavior and/or intense aggressive competition with other males (depending on its sex). In either case, the only real social behaviors it subsequently displays are courtship and mating, maternal behavior to kittens, and perhaps occasional social interaction with "friends." Cats have developed and lived like this for a long time now, and the early sequence of play leading to skilled predation ensures that cats can survive in the wild.

The development of the cat in the wild is usually in marked contrast to the development of a cat in the human household. With humans, the "mother" (owner) supplies an abundance of food to the kitten or kittens, and thus there is no need to compete aggressively for food. The kitten is often encouraged to follow and maintain bodily contact with the owner. It is held and petted throughout its life. The cat may engage in social grooming with other cats and in frequent play with other cats or the owner. Its social and greeting responses are continuously elicited and maintained by an attentive owner who "talks to" or responds to the cat. Moreover, the pet cat is neutered so that intense inter-male aggression and territorial marking behaviors are less likely to develop.

Thus, the cat's social behavior and its personality are quite flexible. Its personality is highly dependent upon its early and later experiences and the environmental circumstances that prevail. However, there are also individual differences in temperament and behavior that are apparent from birth. Some cats are more likely to vocalize and explore new and unfamiliar stimuli than are other cats. There is also evidence that some cats tend to become shy and neophobic (afraid of new stimuli). When we get to the section on behavior problems later on in this chapter, we will discuss some common factors that also can dramatically change a cat's personality or behavior toward people and other cats.

Social Behavior of Cats

Are cats basically social, or are they generally independent? We already have seen from the section on personality and the development of personality that there is great flexibility as to how a cat may and does develop. In the wild a cat is likely to become a solitary, asocial predator. In the human household a cat is much more likely to be social and responsive to people, other cats, dogs, and even pet rats and mice! Cats that are handled frequently by humans at a very early age (about two to three weeks) tend to be much more attentive to and socially interactive with people. It is not known what factors lead to cats becoming socially responsive to other cats, but certainly it is true that kittens or younger cats raised together are very likely to engage in frequent social behavior—for instance, eating together, sharing food, and sleeping, grooming, and playing together. Animal behaviorists occasionally encounter cases of cats that have become depressed (reduced eating, playing, grooming, and so forth) when a "friend" cat has died or been taken away.

Probably the most frequent basis for comparison of the cat's social behavior is dogs, and the most common judgment is that cats are relatively aloof and nonsocial compared to pet dogs. This is partially true. Dogs are obligatorily social animals; they will naturally seek out the company of others, whether people or other dogs. Cats, on the other hand, are able to live quite well by themselves if the need arises.

Most cat owners, however, seem to think that cats are, indeed, pretty social. A survey of over eight hundred cat owners in two large East Coast metropolitan areas indicated that most owners considered cats as part of the family and described their cats as friendly and affectionate. Most stated that their cats enjoyed being with people and sought human attention every day. Many said that they talk to their pet cat and feel that they are aware of the cat's moods and that the cat in turn is aware of their moods. Most cat owners report that their cats sleep in bed with them, rest or sleep on or near them when they sit on the couch, and greet them when they come home by meowing, running toward them with tail up, and rubbing against their legs. The average cat is probably in body contact with its owner more hours per day than the average dog.

Cats and Training

The topic of training cats is related to the previous topics of personality and social behavior. And again, the basis of comparison is usually the training of dogs. The basic difference between these two species centers around the type and complexity of social behavior typically exhibited in the wild. Dogs, as social hunters, have had to be good at communicating between and among each other regarding in-group behaviors such as dominance/subordinance, protection and care of young, and defense of the group, as well as communicating during the hunt about where to search, what to chase, how to capture, and so forth. They have had to be able to perceive and understand all sorts of intricate visual, auditory, and olfactory signals. Moreover, dogs have been selectively bred by humans for over fifteen thousand years to hunt with us, protect our homes, and be companions to our families.

Cats, as solitary hunters in the wild, have had relatively less need for perceiving and understanding complicated social signals. They have not been domesticated as long as dogs, but perhaps most important they have not been selectively bred for specialized tasks, particularly social tasks. So it is relatively easy to teach a dog to come (rejoin the group), sit or lie down on command, and do tricks for praise or petting. It is more difficult to teach a cat to respond in these ways.

On the other hand, cats do learn and can be readily taught if we select the right stimuli and responses. In fact, as we will see later in the chapter, there are some things that cats learn immediately, even faster than dogs. For instance, cats very quickly learn to associate an unpleasant or frightening experience with the place or location where it occurred or with something animate that is perceived at the same time. This can lead to very rapid learning of fear or aggressive behavior. More about this later on.

Cats *can* be taught to do tricks, and there are many opportunities for using behavior modification techniques for changing behavior problems in cats. To teach tricks, all you have to do is get the cat's attention (food often works well), prompt or elicit the behavior you want, and then reward the cat appropriately—again, food often works well, but play, curiosity, or petting often works well, too. Cats do not seem to be motivated by the subtle social signals that dogs respond to, and it is therefore easy to assume that they are untrainable. However, cats readily learn to run to the kitchen when they hear anticipatory food signals such as the sound of can openers, refrigerator doors, or rustling of cardboard boxes. Very playful cats can learn to retrieve if bringing the toy back to the owner means it will be tossed again so they can chase it. Playful cats easily learn that paper

JOHN A. HETTICH

Photograph 18: To teach this Abby to sit up, his owner rewards him with a treat.

"crinkling" means a fun chase game is forthcoming.

In a sense dogs are prepared by their evolutionary history to respond, or they easily learn to respond, to human social signals. They seem to know what we want them to do (at least in many cases), and they are described as "wanting to please their owners." Cats, on the other hand, are not prepared by evolution, or as well prepared by it, to respond to human behavior. But with proper socialization and opportunity for learning, they can learn much more than is commonly supposed, particularly if the owner is clever about learning what motivates the cat, is knowledgeable about the principles of learning, and has a modicum of patience.

This chapter will not discuss some of the "tricks" (sitting up, rolling over, etc.) that cats can be taught but will concentrate on how some of the principles of learning and behavior can be used to prevent and solve some common behavior problems. Some of those specific behavior problems are furniture scratching, plant eating, aggression (both toward humans and toward other cats in the household), and inappropriate elimination.

Furniture Scratching

Cats in the wild claw at tree bark and other textured surfaces. This can be a means of removing the sheaths of the claws as they are periodically shed. It is thought that some wild cats claw objects as a means of marking territory. It is not clear if domestic cats claw furniture for either of these reasons, or perhaps some other reason.

There are generally two effective solutions to the problem of the cat scratching at furniture, stereo speakers, rugs, and so forth: scratching posts and declawing. Keep in mind that people—not cats—design, fabricate, and buy scratching posts. The type of scratching post that is easy to manufacture, looks good,

and is commercially available may not be made of the material the cat likes to scratch. Think about it—most scratching posts are covered with rug. They look attractive, but if the cat scratches your speakers, table legs, or the arm of the couch and not the living room rug, then a rug-covered scratching post may be a waste of money, even if it is inexpensive.

It helps to know what type of material(s) cats typically prefer to scratch. Most of the time cats seem to prefer scratching and clawing at tightly woven, fibrous surfaces such as bark or the back side of a carpet. If your cat does not use the rug-covered scratching post you bought, you might try taking the rug off and

Photograph 19: A rug-covered scratching post obviously suits this Abyssinian very well.

JOHN A. HETTICH

turning its underside out. It might not look as attractive, but the chances are the cat will like it better and will stop scratching where you do not want it to. Also, you can buy scratching posts covered with fibrous materials such as sisal, and these appear to be preferred by many cats. If this doesn't work, you can try covering the scratching post with material that is the same or similar to the material on the surface the cat is presently scratching. You should also place the post at or near the location that the cat is presently clawing; cats develop location preferences for certain activities such as clawing. Sometimes, changing the position of the post will help—some cats prefer to scratch in a horizontal, rather than vertical, position.

Many people try punishment—yelling at the cat or spraying it with a plant mister when it scratches. In order for such a technique to work, you have to catch the cat in the act, and at the very least you have to punish this behavior most of the time it occurs. This is difficult or impossible to do, and even if it can be done, the cat may simply look for something else to scratch on, or it may scratch only when you are not around.

Many owners find that if they can learn to clip their cat's front claws properly so that there are no sharp points, the damage to furnishings is diminished almost entirely. Even owners with cats that regularly use scratching posts instead of furniture should clip their pets' claws to prevent overgrowth and possible damage to themselves when playing with their pets. See Chapter 3 for how to do this.

If all the above steps fail and the cat is destroying your home, you can consider declawing the cat (front feet only; the rear claws are not used for scratching furniture). Declawing involves surgery, and it must be done by a good veterinary surgeon who is experienced in the procedure. The operation itself is as unlikely as neutering to cause the cat any permanent negative side effects. (See Chapter 4 for a description of the operation.) Although a prudent owner will keep a declawed cat indoors, declawed cats *can* defend themselves (in a real fight, the back claws are used), and owners typically do not report any changes in behavior as a result of declawing. The declawed cat usually continues to "scratch" on the furniture as before but does not do any damage.

Plant Eating

Some, but not all, cats seem to take special delight in chewing on and eating the favorite plants in the house. Of course it is not true that the cat is really trying to get you angry or to tell you something by doing this. The cat is eating *its* favorite plant, not yours, although sometimes the two coincide. It is not really understood why cats eat plants. We know that some plants they eat are dangerous for them (see "Gastrointestinal Diseases and Disorders" in the Encyclopedia). It might be true in some cases that plant eating is due to a nutritional deficit, but this probably is not the major reason for it since most cats will be very healthy and fit even when they cannot find plants to eat. There seem to be no health problems among non-plant-eating cats or among former plant eaters when the plants are removed. Plants might be used as an emetic; that is, a way of inducing vomiting, perhaps to get

rid of hairballs. But that probably is not the major reason either, since many cats that eat plants and vomit do not vomit hairballs.

What to do about this problem? The easiest and most obvious step is to make the plants unavailable to the cat. You might hang them high or place them on a shelf that the cat cannot reach. However, another solution is to give the cat a plant of its very own. Sometimes a cat will eat growing greens or grass that can be purchased in specially designed pots which allow a cat to happily chomp at the continually sprouting top growth without destroying the roots of the plants. Another possibility for solving this problem, but one less likely to be satisfactory, is to punish plant-chewing behavior by yelling at the cat or spraying it with a plant mister. This means you must catch the cat in the act of chewing. If you do not catch it in the act but instead take it to the chewed plant and then yell or spray it, the cat will merely learn to stay away from plants when you are either in the house and/or are near the plant. This means the cat has learned to associate the presence of the owner and the owner's nearness to the plants with the likelihood of being yelled at, swatted, or sprayed with a plant mister.

In truth, even if you do catch the cat in the act several times in a row, the cat is still likely to avoid plant eating only when you are around. Cats are highly attuned to associating any frightening or unpleasant stimulus (yell, swat, water in the face, and so forth) with something or someone animate, if there is something animate or moving in the vicinity. Another punishment technique that might work is to have a bad taste or an aversive smell associated with the plant that the cat chews. Of course, the cat might just switch to another plant, and you have to be careful that the substance used is safe for the plant(s).

Aggression
(Toward People and Other Cats)

Most cases of cats becoming aggressive toward people involve the (usually young) cat's stalking and biting the owner's legs and hands in the context of play. These cats often have no other cats to play with, and they go after the only moving thing in the house—the owner. Owners often provide toys for the cat, but the toys are usually "dead"; that is, they do not move by themselves. A second cat is an obvious possible solution, but some people do not want another cat and there may be problems in introducing a new cat to a resident cat (see below and also Chapter 3). Most of the time the owner can solve the problem by providing lots of active, moving, interesting toys for the cat. This involves time and energy, however. Most cats tend to have location preferences, remember, and may wait for the owner and/or may stalk in certain rooms or areas of the home. A smart owner will realize this, and when he or she walks by the area carry a string that is then wiggled. A quickly moving string provides a better "chase stimulus" than feet or legs, particularly if the owner does not move until the cat starts chasing the string. Then the owner can begin to move slowly while keeping the cat occupied with the string toy. This accomplishes two things: It saves wear and tear on feet, legs, and clothing, and it tends to teach the cat to go after inanimate, moving toys rather than the owner.

Some young cats, in particular, will have to be played with a lot simply to reduce their aggressive play motivation. As a general rule, play behavior will decrease only by being expressed or exhausted. Punishment techniques may work temporarily but are about as effective as trying to get children to play quietly in the house. Punishing rough play behavior might stop the play at the time, but it also deprives the cat of play, which means that it will certainly occur later. Punishment may also make the cat afraid of the owner.

Cat aggression toward other cats is another matter entirely. Cat fights are very different from cat play-fights. The most common type of aggressive behavior between cats involves fear or defensive behavior. Paradoxically, fear-related aggression problems often occur between two or more cats that previously had been living together as friends in the home. Something frightens one of the cats, the other cat mistakes the first cat's fear response as aggression (there is overlap in the postures of fear and aggression), and a fight starts, all within a second or so. For example, in one case a cat was sitting on the windowsill when a neighbor boy accidentally threw a ball through the window. This frightened the cat, which ran out of the room with its eyes widened and its fur all "puffed up" (this is called piloerection —see Chapter 2). Just as it jumped off the window ledge, the second cat entered the room. The second cat saw the first in what looked like an aggressive attack, and it too became frightened—its eyes widened, its fur puffed up, and there was an immediate fight. In a split second, each cat learned that the other was "aggressive," and for months afterward they would growl and/or attack each other on sight.

The chances of solving this problem are pretty good, but it will take some time. The most important thing to do is separate the cats so they cannot see each other. Do not "let them fight it out." All this does is make the problem worse. It is a mistake to assume that any fighting between two cats is due to establishment of territory or dominance. Territorial- or dominance-related aggression in previously friendly cats, if it develops, will develop very slowly.

Visual separation for a few days or weeks will often result in each cat becoming curious and looking for the other. You can then gradually reintroduce them, perhaps getting them to play together first. Gradual introduction means that the cats are gradually exposed to the *sight* of each other. Cats are very visual creatures, particularly when engaging in or anticipating aggressive behavior with another cat. They pay close attention to the other cat's visual features or signals. So, for this kind of problem, gradual introduction means that, rather than one cat seeing the other cat only for a few seconds or minutes, one cat sees only *part* of the other cat. This can be accomplished by allowing the two cats to play with each other's paws, for instance, under a closed door or a partition. As the cats learn to anticipate play with each other's paws, then the gap under the door or par-

tition can be gradually increased in size so that the cats can see more of each other. Doors with windows or partitions with wire mesh screens make ideal barriers because the amount of visual contact can be increased as slowly or as quickly as necessary to resolve the problem.

Done slowly (so that even mild aggressive behavior is kept low and infrequent), this technique will work most of the time.

Introducing a New Cat into the Home

The same procedure can be used in introducing a new cat into the home. The initial hissing, spitting, and piloerection most often are also the result of fear, which will usually dissipate if the cats are exposed to each other in a gradual manner.

Territorial aggression, however, does *not* usually involve piloerection and vocalization. If this occurs, most of the time the new cat will be promptly chased and kept in or out of specific areas in the home by the original resident. This can be an extremely difficult problem to solve. You can try separating the cats and then gradually introducing them. This might work in some cases, but it usually fails. Then the best solution is to find a good home for one of the cats.

Inappropriate Elimination

One of the most surprising and distressing behavior problems in cats is eliminating outside the litter box. To understand this problem we first have to distinguish *elimination* (urination and defecation) from *urine marking* or spraying behavior. These two different behaviors are caused by different factors and are treated differently.

First, the posture the cat takes when it urinates is not the same as the spraying posture. When urinating, the cat squats with the tail held out, parallel to the floor and curving up a bit. The urine is deposited on a *horizontal* surface—bottom of the litter box, floor, tub, and so forth (see Illustration 10, opposite page). When urine marking or spraying, the cat does

not squat, the tail is straight up in the air and wiggling, and the cat may step alternately with the back legs. The urine is sprayed onto a *vertical* surface such as a wall, speaker, or edge of furniture, several inches or more off the ground (Illustration 11, opposite page).

Second, the causation or motivation for urinating is different from marking. When the cat urinates, it simply "has to go." When the cat sprays, it does so in the context of territorial, aggressive, or competitive behavior.

Let us first discuss the motivation for spraying. It is well known that males of many species mark much more frequently than females and do so at the time or times of the year when the hormone levels are highest. So if you have

Illustration 10: A cat squats, tail parallel to the floor, when urinating. The urine is deposited on a *horizontal* surface.

Illustration 11: When urine marking, or spraying, a cat stands, tail straight up in the air, and deposits the urine on a *vertical* surface.

an unneutered male cat, it is highly likely to spray. But neutered males and even neutered females will spray also. This usually happens only when there is aggressive or competitive behavior between two or more cats. For instance, the new cat in the house may be aggressive toward or be harrassed by the resident cat. One or both of the cats may then begin spraying as a territorial or aggressive signal. Sometimes this happens between an inside cat and an outside cat. The inside cat may hear or see the outside cat or smell its spray near the house and then begin spraying in the house in response. Occasionally, an inside cat may spray as an aggressive or competitive signal in response to a person. When this happens, the cat is also either aggressive toward that person or afraid of the person.

There are several ways to treat marking behavior in cats. Obviously, if the cat is an intact male, the first step would be to have him neutered. If the cat is an intact female, it would probably be a good idea to have her spayed also, particularly if the spraying occurs when she is in heat. If the cat is spraying in only one area in the home, it might work to place the cat's food, water, and/or toys on the spot, in the hope that feeding, drinking, and playing in that location will inhibit spraying. An alternative is to place some aversive odor (cat repellant) or aversive material such as aluminum foil, plastic, or newspaper on the spot. However, these techniques often fail if the motivation to spray is high, because the cat will simply spray in a new location. Catching the cat in the act and yelling, hitting, or squirting it with water will usually result, at best, in the cat not marking when the owner is around. At worst, the cat will become afraid of the owner or aggressive, and perhaps spray more frequently.

Some cats spray because of outside cats. This is indicated by the cat's alert attention (for example, running up to the window) and/or aggression (hissing, growling) at the sight of outdoor cats. The cat usually sprays near windows or doors leading to the outside but may spray elsewhere in the home. If outdoor cats are clearly a stimulus for an indoor cat's spraying, it will be necessary to somehow get rid of the outdoor cats (easier said than done) or pre-

vent the inside cat from seeing, hearing, or smelling them. In some communities the sheer number of outside cats is far too high to hope to get rid of them by any methods. If the inside cat is responding to outside cats in only one area in the home, such as a front porch, then it might help to deny the inside cat access to that room by closing the door, or perhaps opaque shades or curtains can be placed over the windows so that the outside cats cannot be seen.

An inside cat can also be stimulated to spray because of another inside cat. Often there is an obvious aggressive interaction between two or more inside cats, but sometimes the mere presence of another cat is sufficient to stimulate spraying. Sometimes the only option is to find a new home for one of the cats—some cats just do not like other cats in general or maybe do not like one cat in particular. In many cases the spraying can be reduced by getting the two cats to become friends. Some behavioral techniques to accomplish this are outlined in the section on aggression.

In other cases of spraying the best results are obtained by using drug therapy combined with the appropriate behavioral technique. This, of course, should be discussed with your veterinarian. It is important to bear in mind that any drug therapy for spraying or any other behavior problem is *short-term* only. Behavioral techniques of some kind must be relied upon to allow the cat to be slowly tapered off the drug without the problem returning.

The motivation for urinating (and defecating) is bladder or bowel pressure. The cat has to "go to the bathroom." But why does it pick the rug or tub rather than the litter box? This problem has nothing to do with the mother not having taught the kitten to eliminate properly. Contrary to common belief, the cat does not have to be taught by the mother to use the litter box; kittens instinctively begin scratching in diggable material and eliminate, scratch, and cover up in this material on their own. Likewise, it is not necessary for the owner to take the cat or kitten to the litter box and scratch its paws in the litter to get it to use the litter box, and this will not help the cat to start using the litter box if it has begun to eliminate outside it.

Just like claw-sharpening behavior described above, cats have preferences for the feel of the material they like to dig in and cover their urine or feces with. Sometimes these preferences do not match the material we provide for the pet. People also manufacture and buy cat litter. Fortunately, most cats use commercial cat litter, but some prefer not to and others hate the stuff. If a cat does not dig and cover in the litter (some do so for urinating, most for defecating, and some for both), the cat is telling you something—that the litter you are providing does not feel right. Indications that the cat may not like the feel of the litter (other than not eliminating in it and not scratching or covering in the litter) are shaking the paws after coming out of the litter box, standing on the edge of the litter box so the paws do not touch the litter, and running quickly out of the litter box. Like other animals, cats are highly individualistic, and you might have to adjust the cat's environment to suit it rather than wasting time trying the reverse. Most people try to find another type of cat litter by switching brands of commercial, clay-based litter or trying deodorized or non-deodorized clay products. This often fails because, from the cat's standpoint, they all generally feel the same. Some cats, however, can tell the difference and prefer one brand to another. If clay-based litters do not work, you might try something entirely different, such as clay and top soil mixed, top soil alone, sand, wood-chip products, and so forth. If and when you find a material that the cat likes to dig and scratch in, you can be pretty sure that the cat will eliminate in it.

Many other factors might be involved in this problem, and it is often necessary to seek professional help from an animal behaviorist (see the list in the Bibliography). But let's look at a few of these other factors and see how interesting and complicated litter box problems can be.

Some cats do scratch and cover in the litter but proceed to scratch on the side of the litter box, the wall, the floor or carpet near the litter box. From observations in hundreds of successful treatments of these problems, it appears that the cat can learn to associate the feel of the materials it scratches on with the act of eliminating. For example, if the cat scratches and covers in the litter and then reaches out and scratches the bathmat, it might learn to associate the feel of the bathmat with the act of eliminating and then proceed to eliminate (urinate, defecate, both, or alternate) on the bathmat. In this case we would probably treat the problem by trying to reassociate the feel of litter (assuming the litter is not disliked) with the present preference for bathmat. This can be done by putting the bathmat or similar surface near or even in the litter box and then gradually changing the amount of carpet and litter available. The carpet material is gradually reduced and the litter material gradually increased. For these types of problems this technique is usually effective, but unfortunately there are almost an infinite number of variations and each case is a little bit different.

Another common factor in elimination problems involves location preferences. Animals generally tend to do certain things such as hunt, eat, drink, sleep, and eliminate in certain locations, which may change over time. Some cats that eliminate outside the litter box do so in only one spot or area. If a location preference is presently the major underlying factor involved in the cat eliminating outside the litter box, placing a litter box with litter in it on top of the area usually results in the cat using the litter box. Then the box may be gradually moved back to the location the owner prefers. However, most problems are not as simple as that, and a combination of factors is involved. In these cases, the help of an animal behaviorist may be required.

We have not mentioned keeping the litter box clean because I have rarely met a cat owner whose cat had an elimination problem who did not keep the litter box clean, so that is not a common causal factor. Cleaning up the spot or area will cut down on objectionable odors, but it is not likely to solve the problem. Moreover, there is an inherent paradox in the idea that dirty litter boxes can lead to this problem and that at the same time the cat is attracted to the odor of urine on the carpet. Why would urine in the litter box be aversive and the odor on the carpet attractive? It is not likely. Instead, the cat's attraction to the spot where it urinates or defecates is a location preference and not due to the odor.

We have also not mentioned anything about the cat being "emotionally upset" by all sorts of innocuous things such as guests, furniture rearrangement, a move to a new house, and so forth. Cats that are "emotionally upset" generally spray (see above) or become afraid or aggressive, all of which are obvious behaviors. However, there are cases in which the cat eliminates due to an emotional state; these involve separation anxiety. Cats, in fact, can become very attached to their owners. Unlike some dogs, they readily tolerate being alone all day when the owner is at work. But if the owners leave the cat or cats alone for a day or two, then the cat may tend to urinate or defecate outside the litter box. Of course, if the owners pack suitcases every time they leave for a long vacation, it will not take too long for the cat to learn that suitcases lying out on the floor mean an upcoming period of anxiety. Some cats even tend to eliminate in the suitcases any time they are left out. Generally, the elimination occurs only after being alone for eighteen to twenty-four hours or more, so behavioral techniques such as gradually getting the cat used to longer and longer absences is much too time-consuming for most owners. About the only way to solve this type of problem is to take the cat with you or have a friend or neighbor cat-sit for a while. This might involve only a few hours a day but should include interacting with the cat so that normal levels of play and petting are achieved.

But, since these cases are rare, it doesn't pay to waste your time trying to blame the cat's failure to use the litter box on some mysterious emotional response to normal human behavior or typical changes in the household.

The general rule when working with cats is to try to understand the animal's natural behavior characteristics and the motivations for its actions. If this can be achieved by an owner, sometimes with the help of a professional animal behaviorist, even the most stubborn feline behavior problems can usually be solved.

9

Cats as Companions

WILLIAM J. KAY, DVM

Not all societies, people, and countries recognize and accept the naturalness of loving pets. The reasons for this are usually socio-psychic or economic. Cats in particular have been regarded by different societies in widely dissimilar ways. While granted an exalted status in some cultures, they have been relegated to a position of ridicule and have suffered cruelly in many parts of the world.

Traditionally, pets have not played as great a role in Eastern countries as they have in Western nations. But interesting changes are taking place, especially in Japan, as that country becomes increasingly westernized. Pets are now extremely popular in Japan. The Japanese Veterinary Society is among the fastest growing Veterinary Societies in the world, with Japanese veterinarians rapidly increasing their skills and commitments as pet doctors.

Economic considerations are among the biggest reasons why pet ownership is neither condoned nor fostered in many countries. When human living conditions are at a subsistence level, there is neither enough money nor enough food to share with a cat.

Pet ownership and all of its attendant services, from veterinary care to pet food and pet accessories, has flourished primarily in countries where people are not only predisposed but comfortable enough to provide for the care of pets. In affluent societies in Western Europe and the United States, cat ownership often takes on elaborate forms, culminating in cat shows, cat clubs and competitions, grooming salons, toys, special play and exercise equipment, and so forth.

When society encourages and condones pet ownership and when people have sufficient leisure time, money, and interest to provide proper care for pets, the relationship between people and pets flourishes.

Why People Own Cats

People own cats for a variety of reasons, including ego satisfaction and friendship. But the single most fundamental reason for cat ownership is the love cats provide and the opportunity to love they present to the people they live with. Cats have many special charac-

Photograph 20: Cats like this Abby are quiet, clean, and easy to care for.

teristics possessed by few of us and can often meet needs that society does not.

The cat has become an enormously popular pet. The number of pet cats is increasing dramatically. One reason is the ease of cat ownership. Cats are small, quiet, clean, and easy to care for. They do not disturb neighbors or soil the environment. With the increasing urbanization of the United States and other countries throughout the world, the cat is an ideal pet, and millions of people now recognize and enjoy the friendship and love of pet cats. Contrary to the preconceptions of many, cats can be true, faithful friends who demand and give affection. They are very easy to be with and are loyal, nonjudgmental, companionable pets. Cat owners, especially those who have never

known a cat before, are often surprised to discover just how much they have missed and are gratified and enriched by their relationship with their pets. Those of us who have enjoyed cats for many years know just how special they are. Cats add to the human dynamic and are good for people. It is not hard to understand why people own them. Cats are the pets of the future.

This is not to say that there cannot be negative aspects associated with cat ownership. Opponents of cat ownership (and pet ownership in general) are quick to point out that some owners substitute a relationship with a cat for meaningful human relationships because it is so much easier and less demanding. Cat owners may become so involved with their pets that they suffer a great deal of pain and grief when the animal dies or becomes ill. In our opinion, the relatively few cases of negative dependence are far outweighed by the majority of cases in which cats play a positive role in their owners' lives.

Acknowledging the Role Cats Play in People's Lives

The Human/Companion Animal Bond (HCAB) is a term that has emerged in recent years as the result of society's new or reawakened interest in and awareness of the important positive role that pets play in people's lives. The investigation of this role in its many aspects has become a new social science. It is being studied by a variety of professional disciplines, many of which have a special interest in it for reasons ranging from economic to socio-medical. Among these professional disciplines are animal behaviorists, animal trainers, human health-care specialists, psychologists, social workers, physicians, and veterinarians.

Although the importance of pets to people is not new, the tremendous publicity received by The Bond in the past few years has had many positive results. Recognition that a person's relationship with a pet is significant has allowed grief over a pet's death to "come out of the closet." Not only are bereaved pet owners permitted to display their grief, but they may also bury a beloved cat in a pet cemetery or memorialize a cat in some way without society's rejection (see Chapter 10).

This new awareness of cats' value to people has helped them to receive better understanding. Cats are *not* worthless throwaways, although we still have a long way to go in this respect.

Another important aspect of this new concept of the importance of cats to people is a movement that is gaining momentum to allow people to have pets in public housing. In November 1983, President Ronald Reagan signed a bill prohibiting owners or managers of federally funded housing from denying occupancy solely on the basis of pet ownership. Some time must pass before the bill is implemented, and guidelines must be set, but it is a step in the right direction. By recognizing the value of pets to people, they are no longer automatically considered a "nuisance," forbidden completely as they once were. There are, of course, several problems associated with allowing pets to live with people in close proximity. Now, at least some thought is being given to working out a solution to this problem. The day will soon come when a lonely eighty-year-old woman will no longer have to give up her only friend, a twelve-year-old tabby cat, in order to move to or remain in a decent apartment.

Solutions must be worked out for older pet owners facing hospitalization, a move to a nursing home, or death. Often, concern about what will happen to a beloved pet overrides these people's concerns about what will happen to them. At The AMC, The Surviving Pet Maintenance and Placement Program was initiated in 1983; a pet owner in one of the above situations can be guaranteed that his or her pet will be well cared for for the rest of its life.* Society in general should be aware that pet owners facing personal situations of great significance and stress often become additionally upset if their pet's well-being has not been attended to.

Special Roles of Cats

Although there are isolated instances in which cats have been taught to act as the "ears" of hearing-impaired owners, their helping role is primarily that of loving companions. Because of their size, softness, inherent cleanliness, and ease of care and handling (they do not require walking, for example, and are not apt to be rambunctious or physically demanding), cats are especially suitable as companion pets of the elderly and of bedridden and housebound people of all ages.

---

* Write to: The Animal Medical Center, 510 E. 62nd Street, New York, NY 10021, to the attention of The Development Department

JOHN A. HETTICH

Photograph 21: The cat is an ideal city pet. This city cat spends many quiet hours looking out the window.

Many different "pet therapy" programs with various names exist and are developing across this country. In these programs cats are used as therapeutic tools in hospitals, nursing homes, homes for the elderly, hospices, and other health-care and caretaker institutions, either as visitors or as live-in "mascots." Programs under the aegis of ASPCAs, humane societies, veterinary medical schools, Junior Leagues, schools, and colleges abound. They are far too numerous to list here. Interested people can find out about these programs through one of the organizations listed above or in their local telephone directory. Two organizations that serve as national information centers on the human-animal bond are The Delta Society, an educational, research, and service resource on the interaction of people, animals, and the environment, and The Latham Foundation, which is concerned with humane education of all kinds but particularly in the field of the HCAB.*

More and more, doctors, social workers, and other health professionals recognize the posi-

---

* Write to: The Delta Society, 212 Wells Ave. S., Suite C, Renton, WA 98055, and The Latham Foundation, Clement & Schiller, Alameda, CA 94501

tive role cats play in the lives of lonely or isolated individuals, in their physical as well as emotional and psychological well-being. It is not only the elderly, ill, or physically handicapped who can benefit from a cat's companionship, devotion, and tactile comfort. Healthy adults can find themselves in situations in which they are alone and cut off from contact with familiar people and surroundings. Divorce, job loss, transfer to a strange city, death or illness of a mate or relative are only a few of the circumstances that can lead to a sense of isolation and loneliness. Children, too, can feel bereft when their mother suddenly goes back to work, leaving them to come home to an empty house after school, or a beloved older sibling goes away, a parent's job transfer entails a move to a new town and school, or a divorce or separation of parents occurs. In all of these situations the companionship of a cat can help. A pet can become a confidant, an ally, simply a warm presence in the absence of the people one loves. A cat can also be a catalyst that gets a person up and out, to shop for food for instance, and can form a basis for conversation and contact with other people. It is well documented that people with pets weather emotional storms and unrest in their lives better than those who are completely alone.

If mental and physical health is more than the absence of illness but includes by definition a feeling of well-being and comfort, then many people of all ages are healthier because of the companionship of a pet cat.

Photograph 22: Another city cat, oblivious to the world outside

JOHN A. HETTICH

Traveling with a Cat

In this jet-age society, more and more pet owners are traveling and taking their companion cats with them. Unfortunately, it is not quite as easy to take a cat as a favorite suitcase, and many owners are bitterly disappointed upon arriving at a motel or airport to find that Tabby is not welcome or doesn't have the proper traveling documents. An owner who plans to take a cat on a trip, either overnight to a neighboring state by car or to the other side of the world for a month, needs to plan ahead for the pet's safety and acceptability.

One of the most important pieces of equipment for cat owners to obtain is an appropriate carrying case. Cats should always travel in a box or case, never held in an owner's arms or merely leashed. Even the rare cat who has learned to wear a harness and walk on a leash may be able to squirm away in panic when faced with strange noises and people. The best type of carrying case is made of rigid, waterproof material (both of these are usually airline requirements), with wire on one side (see Photograph 23 below). The wire allows air to circulate when it is hot, and carrier covers can be purchased for cold-weather use or in the case of a particularly nervous cat. Plastic tops are not recommended because they allow the inside of the carrier to become too hot in warm weather. Latches are better than zippers, which can snag fur and pinch skin. Soft-sided carrying cases provide little protection for the animal and are apt to collapse with repeated use. The temporary cardboard carriers often

Photograph 23: The best type of carrying case is made of rigid, waterproof material with wire on one side.

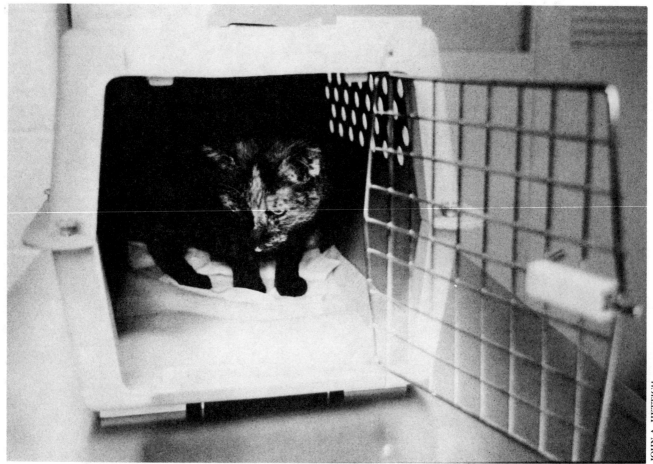

JOHN A. HETTICH

provided by pet stores and shelters are virtually useless. A two-pound kitten can punch its way out of one of these in ten minutes!

If a cat is accustomed to wearing a collar or harness with identification, it can be left on for short trips. However, for longer journeys, especially if a cat will not be accompanied by an owner, collars and harnesses should be taken off. It is too easy for a cat to become entangled in them, especially if frightened. A cat that is not thoroughly broken in to wearing a collar should *never* be left alone with one on. Some form of identification should be on the carrier, in case the owner and cat are somehow separated.

Short practice trips in the carrying case and the car will help accustom a cat to travel. Some high-strung cats may benefit from calming medication such as a tranquilizer prior to a long trip. Concerned owners should ask their veterinarians about this. Food should be withheld for several hours before a trip.

A cat can become overexcited in a strange place and panic and run away. Owners should be very careful to have a good grip on a cat before opening a carrier wide. It is generally best not to open the carrier until the final destination is reached, the cat is in a closed room, and a thorough check has been made to see that all doors and windows are closed and that the room is escape-proof. Cats are also very apt to scoot out of an open door in a strange place. It is *very important* to put a Do Not Disturb sign on a motel or hotel door so that maids or other personnel do not inadvertently let a cat escape.

Cats can get lost or stolen when they travel. There are pet-finding services throughout the country, but they generally rely on a cat wearing a collar with an identifying tag. Although at this time there is no good central registry for tattoo identification of pets, tattooing does serve a purpose in that petnappers are often wary of stealing a cat with a tattoo because they are not certain whether or not the animal is registered. Also, a cat with a tattoo is hard to pass off on an unsuspecting buyer. Recently a system was introduced using tiny microchips with identifying codes that can be injected under the skin of a cat and read by a special electronic device. The system, developed by a private company and endorsed by some humane societies, is already being used for livestock and may become available to the pet-owning public in the future. In the meantime, the best insurance against a lost or stolen pet is an owner's awareness and care.

Any animal that will be traveling long distances or going overseas must have a complete medical examination and up-to-date immunizations, especially against rabies. For entry into many countries, a current immunization record and health certificate (dated in the last ten to thirty days), signed by a veterinarian, is a must. Some states have immunization regulations for any animal entering via public transportation.

A first-aid kit or bag containing needed medications, including antidiarrhea medicine, bandaging, thermometer, and so forth, is a good idea (see the Emergencies section). A veterinarian can advise pet owners on the contents of a first-aid kit based on knowledge of the cat and the proposed trip. Changes in water and diet can have the same effect on cats as they do on human travelers. Consult with the doctor about drinking water—many owners take water from home—and take along a full-trip supply of whatever food your pet prefers.

Pet entry and departure regulations vary widely from country to country, and cat owners who plan to take their pets abroad should plan well ahead of time and know exactly what to bring with them. Some countries, especially islands that are rabies-free, require lengthy (up to six months) quarantine periods for any entering animal. The ASPCA has prepared a booklet outlining regulations for 177 nations and dependencies, and all fifty states. See the Bibliography for how to obtain a copy. Specific up-to-date requirements can also be obtained by telephone from the consulate of the country of destination.

Going by Car

In addition to the above general rules for traveling with a cat, there are a few additional particulars about car travel.

With the exception of a few seasoned travelers, cats usually dislike car travel a lot. The noise and motion can throw even the calmest cat into a panic. For this reason, cats should always be left in a carrying case for an entire trip. A loose cat in a car is a danger to itself and to the human occupants. It will try to get out any open window and will often mindlessly scratch whoever gets in its way. We know of at least a half-dozen accidents and near-accidents caused by formerly docile cats suddenly sinking their claws into a driver's legs or shoulders. If the carrier *is* opened while en route, owners should be sure that it is secured before the car stops and windows and/or doors are opened, or the cat may bolt.

An ample supply of drinking water should always be brought along, and owners should be especially careful not to let a cat become overheated. Air circulation is impeded in a carrier (especially those with plastic tops and solid sides), and because cats are relatively small, it does not take long for them to develop heat prostration (see the Emergencies section). Travel in a car without air conditioning should be avoided in hot weather, and a cat should never be left in a parked car, even for a few minutes, when it is warm. It is a good idea to take along a spray bottle of water that can be used to moisten the cat's coat if the cat begins to pant in hot weather.

Many motels and hotels *do not* welcome pets. Smart cat owners will make reservations ahead of time in a place where they know their pet can stay in the room with them; see the Bibliography for a guide. (In general, Holiday Inns are good about accepting cats.) Of course, in addition to bedding, food and water dishes, and food, cat owners will also have to bring along disposable litter tray liners and an ample supply of litter. When traveling in the South, especially, it is a good idea to take a can of flea spray with you.

Going by Train

Every railroad line has different rules and policies about allowing pets to travel. Many do not allow pets at all, while others permit an animal to travel first-class. Some will allow

them only in carriers or crates in the baggage car. Check ahead of time. If travel is in very hot or very cold weather and a cat is required to ride in the baggage car, determine if the car is cooled and/or heated.

Going by Bus

Again, bus lines differ on pet travel rules, but most do not allow pets. Locally-based carriers are apt to be more lenient than the large national chains. Those that do allow cats require them to be confined in carrying cases.

Going by Plane

Airlines also differ greatly in their pet policies. On short domestic flights, some carriers permit a small pet in a carrying case if it has a reservation and accompanies an owner in the passenger compartment, often at full fare. The usual rule is one cat per cabin (that is, first class and tourist). Sometimes two cats are allowed per cabin in wide-bodied planes or when there is no first class. Reservations to book a cat in the cabin must be made ahead of time, and travel agents should know (or can find out) which airlines will allow this. Other airlines put all animals in the baggage compartment. Usually, the cat will go at excess baggage rates ($21 to $25). Every time you change carriers, you must again pay for the cat.

Many airlines have very rigid regulations as to dimensions and material of shipping cases, and almost none will allow an owner's own case to be used. Most will sell a shipping case to an owner by prearrangement, but owners who arrive at an airport without having made arrangements ahead of time may find that there are no cases available and therefore they are unable to ship a cat. Some airlines (TWA, for example) have pamphlets that outline carrying case requirements, availability, and costs of traveling with or shipping a pet. They are usually obtainable free from travel agents or airline representatives and offices. Cat travel arrangements should always be made well ahead of time so that they can travel in off-peak hours if possible, when they will receive more attention from airline personnel. Also arrange for a direct flight to the final destination, if possible, so that a cat is not left behind when a change is made.

There are agencies specializing in animal travel in almost every large city and adjacent to all international airports. They help owners ship a pet by air to almost anywhere in the world. Some will arrange pickup and delivery to and from the airport and will make arrangements for in-transit and stopover care of a cat. In the New York City area, the ASPCA has a very well-regarded Animalport at JFK International Airport (see the Bibliography for more information).

Identification tags should be on both the inside and the outside of a shipping crate. If the owner will be in transit on a different carrier and/or on a different schedule, a third-party telephone number as well as the owner's final destination should also be included. Any special feeding/watering/medicating instructions should be attached firmly to the *outside* of the crate or case in at least two clearly visible places.

A Final Word

Cat owners should bear in mind that everyone does not necessarily love their pet, and there are many who may object to being in close quarters with a cat. When traveling in public carriers with a cat, stick to the rules and leave the cat in its case until the final destination is reached. Otherwise, in the future, even fewer carriers will permit cats to travel with their owners.

10

When a Cat Dies

Susan Phillips Cohen, CSW, ACSW

Some people are able to calmly accept the death of their cat because they realize that this is part of the natural life cycle. Others, however, may be very surprised to find themselves gripped by powerful emotions. They may be stunned at how swiftly time has passed. When did that tiny, fluffy kitten who could endlessly amuse her human friends chasing her tail and stalking imaginary mice begin to spend most of the day sleeping?

A cat owner whose pet lives a normal life span and dies in old age can take comfort and pride in the fact that his devotion and good care, together with luck and his pet's good genes, combined to help the cat have a long and happy life.

An owner who endures the premature death of a cat because of accident or illness, however, often feels cheated or even punished by his pet's early death. Other owners may have difficulty believing that their pet will ever die. Instead of accepting a cat's limited life span, these people seem almost to believe that if they give their pet perfect love and care, she will live as long as they do, or at least set a record for feline life expectancy! These people in particular often blame themselves for a pet's death. It is important for them to remind themselves that, despite the best of care, no creature can live forever, not even a beloved pet.

Why the Death of a Cat Can Be Especially Painful

There are several factors that can make the death of a pet cat especially painful. Unfortunately, cat owners in particular often have to deal with a society that does not understand the depth of their pain. To many people who do not know or appreciate cats, they are easily replaceable pets. They are not usually thought of as "heroes" who save people or helpers who guide; yet there are many stories about cats that have warned their owners about a fire in the house, and some cats *do* respond to sounds for deaf owners.

Some people actually consider cats evil or sneaky—for years, cartoons have portrayed them as villains. At the least, ordinary cats are deemed inherently worthless, and only expensive purebreds have any true value in many people's eyes. "If you miss Taffy so much, why

134

don't you get another cat?" is an all-too-frequent piece of advice given to people who are hurting over the death of a pet. Even sympathetic friends may have difficulty knowing what to say and resort to the too-cheerful cliché, often applied to human death, that it is "for the best."

Another reason why a cat's death may be especially hard for an owner is the exceptionally strong bond that people are apt to form with their cats. Many cat owners are converts who once disliked cats but are now fiercely devoted to their pets. They find cats easy to care for yet constantly graceful, charming, companionable, and entertaining. Because of their size, cleanliness, ease of care, and lack of boisterous activity, cats are often the ideal companions for the elderly and for those who are bedridden or infirm. In addition, cats have a longer natural life span than many other pets and therefore share a lot with their owners. As one owner who had just lost her nineteen-year-old cat said, "Kitty and I lived a long time together. When I first got her, there were no Japanese cars in this country, no home computers, and no supersonic air travel. I was a young woman with a husband and teenaged children at home. Today, I'm a sixty-year-old grandmother living alone now that Kitty's gone. She and I grew old together, and it's really hard to imagine life without her."

Unfortunately, even a young cat may sicken and die quite quickly, having been seriously ill for some time before displaying any obvious outward signs that all was not well (see Chapter 13). If this should happen, a conscientious owner may be burdened with guilt as well as grief, even though there was no fault or negligence involved.

After a well-loved cat has died, owners can be bewildered at the intensity of their grief. They should realize that it is not surprising they are so upset, considering what most cats contribute to their owners' lives. Who is always glad to see us and greets us with a purr or rub? Who keeps us company when we are lonely or blue? Who listens to our everyday joys and sorrows, and never interrupts? Who cuddles up to keep us warm and cozy? Who never complains about the money we have lost or the wrinkles we have gained? Who does not criticize our taste in clothes or furniture? Who does not take offense when we are crabby and likes us even when we do not even like ourselves? Our cat. Of course it hurts to lose a friend like that.

Feelings at the death of a cat can be confusing and painful to many people. Sometimes, these people consider themselves "odd" or "different" because of these strong emotions. In the following pages we will tell grieving owners what to expect of themselves during this sad time and will try to help them to help themselves and others through the period of bereavement.

Stages of Bereavement

Even though each individual's situation is unique, bereavement itself almost always follows a fairly regular pattern. For most people the stages of bereavement differ only in intensity and length.

Many people experience anticipatory grief from time to time: "What will I do when Tabby dies?" Unfortunately, this does not save anyone from experiencing real grief when it arises.

Once it becomes clear that a cat is too sick or hurt to live much longer, an owner often goes through a bargaining period, similar to a child's "I'll be good if. . . ." The bargain can be unspoken, or it can take the form of a plea to the doctor: "I'll give your hospital a big donation if you can keep Tigger alive until my child comes home from school."

The first stage of grief is numbness, shock, and denial. How long this stage lasts depends, in part, on the nature of the death. If, for example, an old cat has gradually gone downhill, there will still be surprise and shock at her death, but these feelings may not be as intense or last as long as the complete disbelief felt when a healthy young animal is suddenly killed by a car or an unexpected illness.

The middle period of grief is generally a mixed-up, upset feeling characterized by depression and anger. Depression often hits people when they first get up in the morning momentarily forgetting their loss, which then comes rushing back full force in a few seconds. Cat owners often find returning home to an empty house without their pet's welcome greeting the worst part of the day. People are often angry with themselves, the driver of the car that killed their pet, or the veterinarian for not having been able to save the cat. Guilt or anger at themselves can be insidious emotions, causing people to feel terrible for a long time. Those who are inclined to take responsibility seriously often feel guilt intensely, blaming their own shortcomings for their pet's death. Because cats can sicken and die quite suddenly, often seemingly without warning, even a careful owner can have shock and surprise added to grief at the pet's death.

The third and last stage of bereavement is acceptance. Acceptance does not imply that a person is happy that the death occurred or feels that life is just as it was. It means believing that the death happened and beginning to build a new life without the pet.

Otherwise sane people can do and experience seemingly "crazy" or unusual things during the bereavement process. They may hear, see, and feel the presence of a cat that has recently died. They often talk to their dead pets. It is important to remember that these are normal parts of bereavement.

It is possible that someone may become stalled in any of these stages of bereavement for a long time—constantly bursting into tears, unable to shake the feeling that the cat is still alive somewhere, or having problems getting up in the morning. This does not signify weakness or a complete emotional breakdown, but if any of these stages is troubling and persistent, it may be a good idea to seek counseling or other outside help.

Getting Help

The services of counselors who specialize in helping bereaved pet owners are available in only a few locations in the country at present. Here at The AMC we have a full-time social

Photograph 24: Susan Phillips Cohen counsels a concerned cat owner in her office at The Animal Medical Center.

JOHN A. HETTICH

worker on staff as well as graduate social work interns; there are social workers and students connected with the University of Pennsylvania and the University of Minnesota Schools of Veterinary Medicine. The San Francisco SPCA has held free monthly seminars for grieving pet owners, given by a health professional. It is hoped that soon more programs of this sort will be established in other parts of the country. There are a few therapists with a special interest in the subject who treat bereaved pet owners in their private practices. More and more veterinarians are becoming aware of the importance of taking owners' grief seriously, and they are learning how to help.

Barring access to professional help, the best solution for a grieving pet owner is self-help. If families, friends, and business associates offer little real solace when a cat dies, talking to someone else who has been through the same experience can often be comforting. If asked, veterinarians can sometimes put grieving pet owners in touch with one another. Although it can be very hard to do, letting other people know about the hurt and its cause can be a step in the right direction. What is most important is to do whatever is necessary in order to feel better.

One way that everyone can help is to try to educate society in general to take this kind of grief seriously and not dismiss people's pain when a pet dies with: "It was only a cat."

Helping a Child Deal with A Cat's Death

Parents can anticipate problems and help their youngsters better when a pet dies or must be euthanized if they recognize the various stages of children's development as it affects their ability to understand death. In general, the older the child, the more he should be made aware of details and the more he should be allowed to participate in and control ultimate plans concerning a cat.

Children under five usually don't have a very clear idea of what death is, nor do they recognize cause and effect. Often, they cannot tell the difference between what has really happened and their dreams, fantasies, wishes, or something they saw on television. Phrases like "put to sleep" are more than confusing, they can be terrifying to a child this age who may then think that every bedtime may be his last. Children this age have a hard time understanding that death is final and that their pet is never coming back. Because of their tenuous grasp of cause and effect, they can often suffer guilty pangs and believe that something they did, such as dressing the cat up in doll clothes, or some angry thought they had, killed the animal.

Children between five and ten or twelve usually understand a bit of what death is all about but can have trouble really comprehending it. They often shock adults by wanting a lot of gory details about a pet's death. Parents should realize that this is not heartless curiosity; these children really want and need to know the details in order to grasp what happened. Straightforward, honest answers will usually help a child this age come to terms with the reality of a cat's death.

Young teenagers may be the most difficult to help when a pet dies. For years they have been told that a cat is "their" pet, to care for and love; however, they are usually still not considered old enough to make serious life-and-death decisions about that pet, especially if these decisions involve financial considerations. Parents should be completely honest with a youngster this age and try to give the child as much control over the situation as possible. It can help a lot to take the child along to the veterinarian to hear about the cat's condition firsthand from an objective source. Allowing a child to participate in decisions about a pet and to plan some sort of memorial service, for example, can help a great deal in his acceptance of the inevitable. Children who are not consulted in making decisions about "their" cat may never forgive their parents.

Parents often think that it is better to make up a story about what happened to a pet than to be honest with their children. Often, they wait until a child goes away to summer camp or school before giving away a cat or having it euthanized. When the child returns, she is told that the pet "ran away." Children are much too intelligent and sensitive to accept these kinds of stories. A friend's ten-year-old son was given a grown cat by a neighbor. The boy was devoted to his pet, but the cat developed a severe behavior problem and sprayed urine all over the house. His parents decided that they had to get rid of the cat. They waited until their son was visiting his grandmother in another city before having the cat euthanized; when he returned, they told him that Oliver had disappeared. He said nothing but immediately went out to search the neighborhood. For days he wandered all over calling his pet. Several years later, when his mother suggested that they might get another cat, he replied, "No, I don't ever want another animal. You'll only throw it away again when I'm not here." It would have been far better if those parents had faced the situation squarely with their son, explained why they felt they could no longer live with the cat, and let him help to make the decision. Even though it might have been difficult, he would not have felt that they tried to put something over on him.

Children should never be kept in the dark about final arrangements for a pet that has died. It can be helpful to allow a child to see the cat's body after euthanasia or an accidental death. In our experience, children are more upset by their fantasies about what happened to a pet than they are by reality. If Pickles is buried in a nearby field, tell the youngster where—do not let him wander around looking for the grave. If the cat was cremated, be honest about it. Let a child have a memorial service, or sit down as a family and talk about Tommy, just as a recently departed cat is memorialized in *The Tenth Good Thing About Barney* (see the Bibliography).

In other words, let children do as much or as little as they wish about the death of a cat—but give them the option to choose and plan what they really want to do.

Euthanasia

Cats are euthanized for several reasons: because of failing/failed health, because owners can no longer keep them, and because of behavior problems.

Many healthy, young cats are euthanized yearly because of behavior problems. Faced with scratched, torn furniture or an odorous spraying problem, an owner may feel that the only answer is to have the cat "put to sleep." There are solutions other than euthanasia to almost all cat behavior problems. If an owner really cares about a cat who is misbehaving and would like to keep her, Chapter 8 may help.

Another reason owners euthanize healthy cats is their inability to keep the pet because of some outside circumstance, such as a move to an apartment with a no-pet rule (see Chapter 9 for a discussion of legislation to prohibit this type of discrimination in housing). If possible, owners and their families should try to face facts and anticipate this kind of situation ahead of time, rather than waiting until the last minute to come to terms with it. It may be hard to admit that Whiskers could be happy with someone else, but it is really unfair to the cat not to at least try to find her a new home, especially if she is young. Perhaps a relative or friend would take Whiskers if her food and medical bills were subsidized by her former owner. Maybe the veterinarian knows someone who would like to have an adult cat as a pet; this is often a wonderful solution for an elderly person who has recently lost a pet cat and who would be more comfortable with a grown cat than a kitten. In some communities pet placement services will match older animals with new owners for a fee. Even if none of these solutions turns out to be viable, at least an owner can feel that he tried everything possible.

Thoughtful owners should also plan ahead for the care of a cat in case they develop a serious, unanticipated illness or injury that forces them to give up their pet. Barring the happy solution of the cat's adoption by family or friends, some people in this situation would not give a beloved cat to a shelter or pound because they would have no control over who might adopt her. Nor would caring owners ever consider turning a pet loose to fend for herself. When all of the alternatives have been exhausted in these instances, euthanasia may well be the the kindest solution, especially for an older cat.

When a well-loved older cat no longer enjoys life because of illness or constant pain, an owner must consider letting her go. The cat's regular veterinarian should always be consulted about the option of euthanasia, and if an animal is not suffering or if her pain can be alleviated by medication, a doctor may often suggest waiting a while to take this step. Taking time to get used to the idea can help and allow all family members to say goodbye and to finish the relationship, especially if a cat has been a family pet for a number of years.

Even so, it is never easy, especially when a cat is connected with particular people or times of life in an owner's mind and heart. A successful, well-respected engineer we know recently spoke of how hard it had been for him to make this decision, even though his cat was very ill. He was shocked at the depth of his grief when the cat who had been his late wife's special favorite had to be euthanized. "Fluffy was, in a way, a part of my wife. Each time I looked at her I remembered the happy times when Fluff was still a little kitten and my wife was still here. Saying goodbye to Fluffy was like saying goodbye to my wife all over again." Not only was he grieving about the death of the cat, but he was grieving doubly because she had been his late wife's pet.

Many families ask whether or not it is a good idea for an owner to be present when a pet is euthanized. Veterinarians have different feelings about this. For some, it would be person-

ally disturbing to have owners present. They feel that most people would be upset by the experience, and that it is neither necessary nor desirable to allow anyone to witness a pet's death. An owner who feels strongly about wanting or needing to be there can certainly find a veterinarian who will allow it. Before rushing off to a new doctor, however, owners should discuss their feelings honestly with their regular veterinarian. If they let the doctor know how strongly they feel and why, they may be able to help the doctor change his position. Owners should realize also that the doctor may want to say goodbye to a cat that he has taken care of for years.

Each individual should follow his or her own feelings and instincts about this. For some it would be terrible to watch a pet leave, and these people should never feel guilty or ashamed if they do not choose to be present. They will do better remembering their cat as she was. Very responsible owners sometimes feel strongly that they owe it to their cat to be there. Others may suffer if they are not present because they will imagine terrible scenes of what happened to a pet. The important thing to know is that there are options.

If an owner does opt to be with a pet in her final moments, the doctor should be asked to explain ahead of time what may happen. Even though the shot is painless, a cat may cry out or urinate, and sometimes the medication does not act immediately. Some veterinarians have a policy of requesting an owner to sit in a chair during the process—it helps to relieve their anxieties about the possibility of having a fainting person on their hands.

Any family member who wishes should be allowed to be present, but many families select one person to act as a representative during the actual euthanasia. As we mentioned before, it often helps owners a great deal to see the cat's body afterwards—the reality is never as bad as their fantasies might be.

Memorializing a Cat

There are many options concerning what to do with a cat's body. When a cat dies at the doc-

tor's office, the veterinarian will have some sort of cold storage in which an animal can be

Photograph 25: One way to memorialize a beloved cat that has died. A section of Bide-A-Wee Home Association's Pet Memorial Park in Westhampton, Long Island, New York.

kept at least overnight, and owners should never allow themselves to be rushed into making a decision. If a cat dies at home, the veterinarian may be willing to hold the body in storage briefly if the owner transports it to the premises.

People tend to feel the same way about burial for a pet as they do for any human family member. For some, once a pet is dead the body is just an empty hull that no longer represents their friend, and what happens to it is not terribly important. For others, what happens to a cat's body *is* very important. There are no right or wrong answers about what is best to do with a cat's body. Again, individuals and families should do whatever seems right to them. The simplest thing to do when a cat has died is to leave the disposition of the body to the veterinarian who will take care of it in whatever way is usual.

If an owner lives where it is legal to do so, it may be possible to bury a cat in her favorite spot in the yard. A casket can usually be pur-

chased from a pet cemetery, or the cat can be wrapped in her favorite blanket or sweater. Many families like to place a homemade marker over the grave, fashioned from natural stone, or perhaps plant a flowering shrub over the grave.

If this is not possible, arrangements can be made for cremation or burial with an outside agency. Cremations can be handled in two ways: There are group or individual cremations. In the latter case, the ashes are returned to the owner. In many places, owners can choose a memorial park, country, or farm burial, in which either a cat's ashes or body is buried in a certain area in the country. Usually there are no markers allowed with this type of arrangement, but people can visit the cemetery where a pet is buried. Some owners prefer a formal burial for a pet. Once more, there are choices as to how this is done: A cat can be buried with or without a casket and/or a marker in a pet cemetery. Pet cemeteries also offer a wide variety of options to suit different tastes.

In some, owners can erect any type or size of memorial marker they wish, while other cemeteries limit markers to one or two models.*

There are many other ways of memorializing a well-loved pet, ranging from donations to animal hospitals or to organizations that help needy pet owners to a simple family memorial service.

Other Pets

At times, having another household pet can help to alleviate the loss felt when a cat dies, but for some people the remaining pet only serves as a constant reminder of the one who has gone. There is no question that pets do grieve for each other. There are too many stories about animals refusing to eat, losing weight, and looking depressed to deny it. Remaining animals will often look all over for a departed cat for a while, checking places that she used to frequent.

After a while the remaining pet may start to take over the role of the cat who has gone, becoming more affectionate and vocal or starting to sleep where the other pet did.

Some people get a new cat very shortly after a pet has died because they are used to the companionship of a cat. Their life-style is organized, in part, around cat ownership—feeding and caring for a cat. For others, changes in family makeup and life-style mean that pet ownership is no longer practical. Many people need time after the death of a cat before getting a new pet. They may feel disloyal to their old pet by getting a new one, or they may simply need time to adjust before making a decision.

The worst mistake that grieving cat owners can make is trying to actually replace a departed cat by getting another that is the same breed, sex, and color, naming it the same, and pretending that it is a clone of the first pet. This will lead to nothing but heartache for the owner and unhappiness for the new cat who, after all, has a right to live her own life in her own way and not as a carbon copy of another animal.

Family and friends can also make a bad mistake by presenting a grieving owner with a new cat. People should choose their own pets, and the recipient may not be ready or able to care for a new cat right away. What starts out as a kind, loving gesture may lead to unhappiness all around. A far better solution is to give a gift certificate that can be cashed in for a new cat whenever the person is ready.

Conclusion

Most people will outlive their pets, and if a cat is well loved, losing her will hurt. A period of bereavement over the death of a cat is normal, but even if the grief is severe, it can be survived. People can help themselves and seek assistance from friends and family, the veterinary profession, organizations devoted to helping pets, professional counselors, and especially from other cat owners.

Certainly parents and other adults need to be sympathetic and helpful to children who are feeling pain, and possibly guilt in this situation.

People also need to know that it is all right to do whatever is necessary in order to come to terms with their grief and should not allow themselves to let others put them off or make them feel foolish.

There are several books listed in the Bibliography that may help both adults and children deal better with the pain caused by the death of a beloved pet cat.

---

* For information about reputable pet cemeteries, contact: International Association of Pet Cemeteries, P.O. Box 1346, South Bend, IN 46624. For information about cremation, write: Professional Animal Disposal Advisory Council (PADAC), P.O. Box 22, South Bend, IN 46624

11

Exotic Cats

KATHERINE QUESENBERRY, DVM

Exotic, or wild, nondomesticated cats have been appreciated and admired throughout history for their beauty, grace, and power. Because of this, people have often desired to "own" and "tame" these cats. In some societies they have been successfully kept and *trained,* but not *tamed.* Cheetahs, for example, have been trained as hunters' assistants in parts of Asia and Africa. There is a wide difference between training and taming an animal. Training consists of teaching an animal to respond to a certain stimulus, usually a reward but sometimes punishment—to act in a particular fashion in anticipation of or reaction to that stimulus. Taming, on the other hand, implies domestication or gentling of an animal and the development of a desire to conform or please regardless of stimuli. Thus, the term "lion tamer" is incorrect; "lion trainer" should be used instead.

In the United States, the vogue of a decade or two ago of keeping wild cats as novelty "thrill" pets has fortunately subsided, victim to the law and common sense. Public awareness of animal welfare and of the inappropriateness of wild cats as pets has made it difficult for even the most dedicated individualist to indulge in casual exotic-cat ownership. Unfortunately, however, there is still some illegal trade in wild animals, and some states are more lenient than others in legislation governing the ownership of exotics.

This chapter is intended for general information and as a guide for people who already own an exotic cat, to help them to better care for their charges. It is in no way intended to encourage exotic-cat ownership, which is dangerous, expensive, usually illegal, and generally unsatisfactory, as readers of the chapter will find out.

Classifications of Felidae

All felines are in the same family as the domestic cat. The many species fall into six genera or classifications, which are:

1) *Felis:* Cats in this genus are small to medium in size, have retractable claws, and are generally nocturnal. They are indigenous throughout the world. Included in this classification are domestic cats, Geoffroy's cats, margays, mountain lions (cougars or pumas), and ocelots.

2) *Neofelis:* Native to Nepal and China, the rare clouded leopard is the only member of this classification.

3) *Lynx:* Members of this genus can be found throughout the world. They include the bobcat (North America), the caracal (Africa and the Middle East), and the Canadian lynx. They are characterized by long hair tufts on the ear tips and/or cheeks and vertical eye pupils.

4) *Acinonyx:* This genus includes only the cheetah, indigenous to India and Africa. Cheetahs are exceptionally fast short-distance runners.

5) *Uncia:* The snow leopard, or ounce, is the only member of this classification. This rare, endangered cat is native to the Asian highlands.

6) *Panthera:* The big cats are all in this genus. They include jaguars, leopards, lions, and tigers. These cats roar rather than purr due to a specialized adaptation of their vocal apparatus.

Problems of Owning Exotic Cats

The problems of owning exotic cats are legion. Before talking about specifics of care, feeding, and housing, let's talk about some general problems.

First, in order for a private individual to keep any exotic cat *special permits must be obtained.* Laws vary from state to state and between municipalities. In addition, many species, especially those that are endangered, also come under Federal regulation. Even where ownership is permitted, the purpose (that is, breeding or selling for profit) must be stated. Today, most zoos prefer to obtain their stock from other zoos throughout the world, and the business of privately breeding rare cats for sale to zoological parks, which used to flourish, has diminished greatly.

Anyone contemplating getting an exotic cat must realize that *these are not domestic cats.* While they may be cute and seem manageable as kittens or cubs, they will become unmanageable, aggressive, and destructive in a very short time! Even the smaller species are very strong and can be dangerous to their owners and others, especially if they escape from restraint. Often an owner thinks that he can control his exotic cat. This may be true under ideal circumstances and in familiar territory. But these wild cats are unpredictable and easily frightened in strange surroundings and/or with unfamiliar people and will attack people or other animals out of fear/defensive behavior. Many owners who have become too trustful of their wild "pets" have been badly mauled. These cats can also inflict serious damage to their surroundings if not properly housed.

Finally, exotic cats are extremely expensive to feed and maintain properly.

Housing

A major problem for owners of exotic cats is adequate housing. Even the smallest of the exotic cats is very wild and unpredictable, and they are all very agile and destructive. Though some owners have made it a practice to allow their exotic cats freedom of the house when they are around, they do not leave them alone unattended. A determined adult exotic cat can destroy the average living room in a matter of minutes.

Therefore, strong caging is a necessity. Ideally, the cage should be easy to clean, with concrete or tile floors that can be hosed out. (Although some of the smaller species, such as margays and Geoffroy's cats, have been litter-trained, most cannot be successfully taught to use a litter box.) Most cats need perches or ledges to get up on and a "hide box" so that they can get away from it all and be by themselves. If the cage is outdoors, adequate shelter must be provided. Cats that still have claws need a sturdy scratching post or large log for exercise and to prevent ingrown claws.

It is important for potential exotic-cat owners to realize that a small kitten or cub will grow alarmingly fast and that a cage or pen must be large enough so that an adult cat can move around and jump comfortably. Even a medium-sized cat, such as a cougar, will require a lot more space than the average household can provide.

Nutrition/Feeding

Adequate nutrition for all but the smallest exotic cat is also a serious concern. The lack of proper nutrition is the most common cause of disease problems among exotic cats.

Exotic cats generally have the same nutritional requirements as domestic cats (see Chapter 3). While some of the smaller species (under twenty-five pounds) can be adequately nourished with a balanced commercial cat food diet intended for domestic pets, this food will be rejected by larger cats.

All cats are *carnivores*. Feeding mistakes usually occur because of a misunderstanding of what this means. A carnivore in the wild does not eat an all-meat diet but a *whole-animal* diet that includes organ meats and bones, not red meat alone. A diet consisting solely of chopped red meat, which is frequently fed to large cats, is deficient in several vitamins and minerals, has an inadequate calcium/phosphorous ratio, and will lead to growth problems and skeletal abnormalities. In young exotic cats that have been fed an inadequate, unsupplemented red meat diet, we all too frequently see a condition known as paper-bone disease or nutritional secondary hyperparathyroidism (see the Encyclopedia of Diseases of Cats).

Chicken necks, also a popular diet for exotic cats because of availability and low cost, do provide sufficient calcium but do not supply adequate protein or vitamins, and therefore also lead to health problems.

Whole, healthy, fresh-killed small-animal carcasses contain the proper nutrients for exotic cats, but it is essential that no disease is present and that the carcasses are very fresh. It is both difficult and extremely expensive to obtain fresh small animals on a regular basis. "Road-killed" carcasses are usually contaminated and unacceptable.

Several companies in recent years have developed fresh-frozen or canned commercial diets specifically designed to meet the nutritional needs of exotic cats. These foods contain all the necessary vitamins and minerals and are used very successfully by the majority of zoos. Sources of these diets are listed in the Bibliography.

It is important to wean young cats directly onto a commercial diet in order to avoid acceptance problems later on. Owners of cats that have become accustomed to other foods will probably have to introduce a commercial diet gradually, mixing it with the animal's usual feed a little at a time. (See Chapter 3 for more about introducing new foods to cats.)

In addition to adequate nutrition, the larger cats also need large bones for chewing. (See discussion on dentistry under "Veterinary Care" below.)

Veterinary Care

While most veterinarians are willing and able to treat smaller species of exotic cats, finding a doctor to care for a larger exotic cat may be a problem. Owners faced with this problem should call their local zoo or the nearest state veterinary medical school for references.

Smaller species of hand-raised exotic cats and young animals can usually be manually restrained for a veterinary examination. Even so, owners should realize that they may be bitten or scratched by their pets. Even the mildest-mannered domestic cat may balk at a physical examination or vaccination! Owners should always come prepared with protection for them-

Photograph 26: Handlers must protect themselves with gloves, even when working with a young exotic cat. This Margay kitten is being restrained for vaccination.

KATHERINE QUESENBERRY, DVM

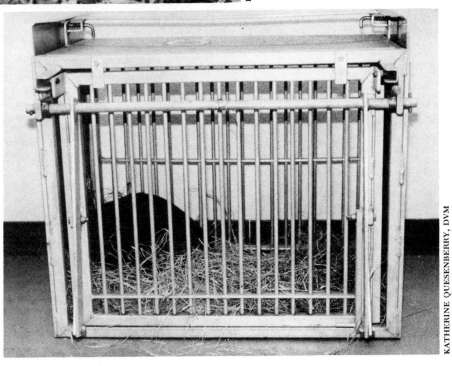

Photograph 27: A "squeeze cage" is often used in treating exotic cats. The barred side portions of the cage can be moved inward to immobilize the cat. Here, a Jaguarundi awaits treatment.

KATHERINE QUESENBERRY, DVM

selves, such as heavy gloves and thick, long-sleeved garments. Some veterinarians also use nets in order to restrain recalcitrant cats.

Large species and especially wild or timid smaller cats will probably require chemical restraint in order to be thoroughly examined and/or treated. Special cages are often needed in order to properly work on these animals. (See above.)

Routine Health Care

Exotic cats are subject to many of the same diseases as domestic cats, both infectious and noninfectious. In general, the most frequent causes of illness and disease in exotic cats are poor nutrition and inadequate housing. General signs of illness include loss of appetite, vomiting and diarrhea, depression, fever, dull or unthrifty haircoat, mouth ulcerations, nasal or ocular discharge, problems in walking or jumping, and so forth. All of these signs call for immediate veterinary attention.

Juvenile cataracts are a disease problem in some species. Exotic cats are also subject to gastrointestinal disorders as a result of hair balls, foreign body ingestion, or dietary indiscretion.

It is important for exotic cats to be immunized against disease, beginning with a series of vaccinations as kittens, or cubs, and continuing with boosters as adults. (See Chapter 3.) In most cases, killed rather than modified-live vaccines are preferred for exotic cats. One major difference from domestic cats is that the National Association of State Public Health Veterinarians does *not* recommend vaccination for rabies in exotic animals, as the safety and efficacy of the vaccine in nondomestic species is unknown.

Young exotic cats are also susceptible to intestinal parasites, especially if there are other cats around or they are living in unsanitary conditions. Treatment for intestinal parasites such as worms and coccidia is usually similar to that used for domestic cats. However, exotic cats may have toxic side effects from some drugs, so treatment should always be under veterinary supervision.

Surgical Procedures

The most common elective surgical procedures performed on large cats—extraction or cutting down of the canine teeth and declawing—are usually performed to reduce the danger of damage to owners and handlers. In addition, big cats are often subject to tooth damage that must be repaired properly. Although exotic cats are usually not neutered routinely, the operation may be requested in an effort to curb aggression.

Dentistry: Dental procedures on exotic cats should only be attempted by an experienced veterinarian. Large cats often have dental problems due to too-soft diets, malnutrition, and aggression or rough play that breaks the teeth, especially the canines.

A diet consisting of soft foods alone allows dental calculus (tartar) to build up on the teeth, leading to gum disease and tooth decay. Large bones or other chewing objects will help offset this problem.

Broken teeth can also be caused by a calcium-poor diet. Many well-nourished large cats, however, often suffer from broken teeth. When a tooth is broken, it must be properly treated and sealed to prevent infection and abscesses.

Owners of exotic cats often request extraction of the canine teeth or cutting off of the canines at the tip to decrease the potential of severe bites. These procedures must also be performed properly to avoid infection.

Declawing: The declawing procedure for exotics is similar to that for domestic cats. As with domestic cats, it is preferably performed when the animal is young. Usually, all four feet are declawed because the rear claws of big cats can do just as much damage as the front ones. Again, this procedure must be done by a veterinarian who is experienced with big cats in order to assure that all of the claw is removed and that adequate pressure bandaging is utilized.

Neutering: Usually requested in male cats to reduce aggression, castration will only affect sexual aggression and will *not* have any effect on fear-induced aggression or predatory behavior. It has limited effect in odor control. The procedure is similar to that used in domestic cats (see Chapter 4).

Ovariohysterectomy (OHE) is usually not performed on nondomestic female felines for birth control because owners rarely let their cats loose, and these females are generally kept for breeding purposes. Hormonal implants are commonly used on exotic female cats to prevent conception on a temporary basis. Of course, an OHE is necessary when a female develops a pyometra (see the Encyclopedia of Diseases of Cats).

Routine: Behavior Problems

Exotic cats are very demanding and are creatures of habit, as all cats are. Owners must provide a lot of regular activity and entertainment for them. If an exotic cat is ignored or if its routine is abruptly changed, it will become upset and probably develop behavior problems. These problems may be as overt as heightened aggression and increased, frantic pacing or as subjective in nature as self-mutilation and anorexia. For example, a frustrated or stressed cat may lick its paw raw or chew its tail until it bleeds.

An owner who is aware of a cat's demands will vary activities on a regular basis so that the animal does not become accustomed to a too-rigid schedule. When a change in routine becomes necessary, the owner should introduce it as gradually as possible.

One of the biggest problems surrounding exotic cats' need for attention and routine is: What if the owner has to be away, even for a short time? An owner will have to anticipate any absence well in advance in order to introduce a "sitter" very gradually. Even then, an exotic cat may not accept any substitute gracefully.

What to Do with an Unwanted Exotic Cat

This, of course, is the biggest problem surrounding exotics as "pets." People often find that they can no longer afford the money, time, and energy inherent in owning an exotic cat. Circumstances change, moves occur, and they can no longer house or care for an exotic cat. Or they simply did not know what owning an exotic cat entailed and are not prepared to cope with the enormous responsibility.

Most people with an unwanted exotic cat think first of their local zoo. In general, most zoos have already reached their limit, especially of the more common varieties of large cats, and cannot afford to feed, house, or care for any more. In addition, exotic cats who have been living with humans often have problems adjusting to life in a zoo with other felids, especially if they have been hand-raised. Many zoos are simply not willing or able to take on a behavioral problem such as this.

A limited number of wildlife rehabilitation centers in some states are licensed to take over cats that can no longer be kept by their owners. They usually operate on donations and will provide food and shelter for unwanted exotics. Zoos, veterinarians, or wildlife associations may be able to provide owners with the name of one of these organizations. Owners will normally be asked to provide transportation of the cat to one of these centers and to contribute to the animal's upkeep on a regular basis.

It is not easy to rid oneself of an unwanted exotic cat, and it can be even harder to find a really satisfactory solution to the problem. As we said in the beginning of this chapter, publicity about the difficulties of exotic-cat ownership has fortunately succeeded in deterring most people from considering it.

PART THREE

DISEASE AND ILLNESS

12

Symptoms of Illness

MICHAEL S. GARVEY, DVM

I t can be very difficult for a cat owner to judge whether or not a pet requires veterinary care. As we have discussed throughout this book, cats handle illness differently than other species do (see Chapter 13 and the beginning of the Emergency section). In addition, cats tend to be very private about elimination, and it may not be possible for an owner to keep track of defecation and urination. This is especially true in the case of an indoor/outdoor cat or if more than one cat shares a litter tray. Even if this is not the case, litter trays are often kept out of sight, and a day or more can pass before an owner is aware that a cat is not urinating, for example. Thus, cats' natural tendency to keep to themselves and show no obvious, overt symptoms, coupled with their inherent privacy about elimination, can make it very hard for an owner to spot early signs of illness. As we mention in Chapter 13, if an owner does become aware of a change in a cat's behavior or habits, no matter how slight, it is a good idea to seek veterinary attention.

In the Emergencies section of this book we have included feline disorders and illnesses that must be treated by a doctor right away. In other chapters many diseases, disorders, and illnesses that can affect a cat are mentioned. The Encyclopedia of Diseases of Cats contains an alphabetical listing of most of the major feline diseases and disorders that can occur in every part of a cat's body. In each instance, symptoms, or clinical signs, of each specific illness or disorder are described. This chapter will serve as a cross-reference so that an owner whose cat is evincing certain symptoms can have an idea of what the trouble might be and look it up in the appropriate section. We must hasten to add, however, that cat owners should *not* attempt to diagnose a pet themselves. There are far too many variables for anyone but a trained professional to judge and, especially with cats, observable outward clinical signs are often only the "tip of the iceberg." In order to make a firm diagnosis it is usually necessary to perform one or more diagnostic tests as described in various chapters, including Chapter 13 and Glossary 2. What follows is aimed only at helping a cat owner make an intelligent decision about when to seek veterinary help.

Signs of Pain

Cat owners are often uncertain about how to know if their pet is in pain, and they can misinterpret pain for other problems. In general, cats very seldom show pain—they rarely cry out or complain; usually, a hurting cat will simply go off alone.

A cat that is experiencing mild discomfort after minor surgery or because of a passing stomach upset, for instance, may simply not want to be touched or handled. It probably will not be hungry and will prefer to sleep undisturbed until it feels better. Owners need not be upset if this "leave me alone" attitude does not last longer than twenty-four hours.

A cat that hurts because of an arthritic joint condition or immediately following surgery for a fracture repair, for example, will exhibit all of the above signs more strongly. It may limp, have difficulty getting up, or refuse to go outdoors. If a cat continues to hurt for more than a day, a veterinarian should be consulted.

If a cat is experiencing severe pain, the signs will be more dramatic and obvious. The cat may collapse or even cry out. Cats in severe pain will often hide underneath things or in a corner or closet. Others may growl or even scratch when approached. Cats may pant when they are in discomfort. A cat displaying severe pain symptoms should have immediate medical attention (see also the Emergencies section).

Signs of Illness

Except for obvious, overt symptoms, the single most common sign that all is not well with a cat is a change in habits, personality, or activity level. As we have said, a cat may show no sign of illness until it suddenly collapses and is very ill.

Symptoms of illness, like signs of pain, can occur in varying degrees, and cats can have widely different ways of handling them. Signs or symptoms of illness frequently occur in combination with one another, and it is often not until a second symptom manifests itself that an owner is aware of a problem. For example, by itself chronic diarrhea may not seem significant, but coupled with weight loss and an increased appetite it could indicate hyperthyroidism.

A list of the major signs/symptoms of illness in cats follows, cross-referenced to a listing in the Encyclopedia, and/or the Emergencies section. We must emphasize that this is intended only as a general guide and that all the illnesses mentioned may not manifest themselves in the expected ways, nor do the symptoms listed necessarily mean that a particular animal is suffering from a given illness.

Symptoms of Illness

NOTE: CAPITALIZED DISEASES/DISORDERS WILL BE FOUND IN THE ENCYCLOPEDIA.
THOSE WITH AN * ARE INCLUDED IN THE EMERGENCIES SECTION.

Abdominal:

Discomfort: FELINE INFECTIOUS PERITONITIS (FIP), linear foreign body,* PANCREATIC DISEASE, RENAL (KIDNEY) DISEASE, urethral obstruction.*

Distention: Enlargement, swelling, or puffing up of the abdomen usually indicates enlargement of an abdominal organ, an abdominal mass, or a buildup of fluid in the abdominal cavity. It can be due to CONGESTIVE HEART FAILURE, FELINE INFECTIOUS PERITONITIS (FIP), LIVER DISEASE, LYMPHOSARCOMA, pregnancy, PYOMETRA, RENAL (KIDNEY) DISEASE, ruptured organs, toxic milk syndrome (neonatals —see Chapter 6), tumors.

Balance, Loss of; Lack of Coordination: Usually of neurologic origin. See ATAXIA, BALANCE DISORDERS, DYSMETRIA, NEUROLOGIC DISEASES AND DISORDERS. See also Gait Changes below.

Behavior Changes:

General: Brain damage (in NEUROLOGIC DISEASES AND DISORDERS), EPILEPSY,* NEOPLASTIC NEUROLOGIC DISEASES, RABIES.

Aggression: Behavioral problems (see Chapter 8), VASCULAR NEUROLOGIC DISEASE, RABIES.

Depression: Many systemic diseases can cause depression in a cat. If it is severe, it may be a sign of DIABETES MELLITUS, FELINE PANLEUKOPENIA, other systemic diseases (liver disease, heart disease, etc.).

Lethargy/listlessness: This is a nonspecific sign that can be associated with any illness.

Viciousness: Behavioral aggression, RABIES.

Bleeding:* Abnormal bleeding occurs with cuts and wounds (see the Emergencies section), bleeding tumors and cancers, and infections. It can also occur with WARFARIN POISONING* and blood disorders such as APLASTIC ANEMIA, HEMOPHILIA, and FELINE LEUKEMIA.

Bowel Movement Changes/Irregularities:

Blood in stool: Indicates a problem in the upper or lower gastrointestinal tract. If there are streaks or flecks, it is far less serious than pools of blood. See the Emergencies section, COLITIS, and GASTROINTESTINAL DISEASES AND DISORDERS. Upper gastrointestinal bleeding may appear as *melena* (black, tarry stools), indicating digested blood. Streaks or flecks may indicate COLITIS or INTESTINAL PARASITES.

Diarrhea: Cats can get diarrhea from dietary indiscretion. It need not be of concern unless it persists for more than twenty-four hours or is accompanied by other signs or symptoms of illness. See GASTROINTESTINAL DISEASES AND DISORDERS for how to treat common diarrhea. If it persists, it can be a sign of COLITIS, EOSINOPHILIC ENTERITIS, FELINE LEUKEMIA, FELINE PANLEUKOPENIA, HYPERTHYROIDISM, INTESTINAL PARASITES, LIVER DISEASE, LYMPHOSARCOMA, pancreatic insufficiency (see PANCREATIC DISEASE), and other systemic illness.

Fecal incontinence: SPINAL CORD DISEASE.

Increased bowel movement frequency: COLITIS and INTESTINAL PARASITES.

Straining to defecate: COLITIS and INTESTINAL PARASITES. Diseases of the rectum may be confused with straining to urinate (see Urinary Problems below).

Breathing Difficulty (dyspnea* and pneumothorax*): Breathing difficulty should always be taken seriously. It can be a sign of CARDIAC DISEASE, electrocution,* FELINE BRONCHIAL ASTHMA,* FELINE LEUKEMIA VIRUS (FeLV),* FELINE INFECTIOUS PERITONITIS (FIP), heat prostration,* LARYNGEAL DISEASE, LUNG CANCER,* LYMPHOSARCOMA, NASAL CANCER, NASAL DISCHARGE, PERIPHERAL NEUROPATHY, PNEUMONIA,* PYOTHORAX,* RESPIRATORY DISEASES AND DISORDERS, shock,* smoke inhalation,* swallowed objects,* TRACHEAL DISEASE, traumatic chest injury,* and WARFARIN POISONING.*

Shortness of breath: Severe ANEMIA, CARDIAC DISEASE, LUNG CANCER, or LUNG DISEASE.

Wheezing: FELINE BRONCHIAL ASTHMA,* FELINE BRONCHITIS, or LARYNGEAL DISEASE.

Bruising: Abnormal bruising may indicate a bleeding disorder. See in the Emergencies section, Bleeding or Hemorrhaging, for a description. See also HEMOPHILIA, thrombocytopenia (under FELINE LEUKEMIA VIRUS [FeLV]), and WARFARIN POISONING.*

Collapse:* See shock;* see also ANEMIA, CARDIOMYOPATHY,* DIABETES MELLITUS, drug intoxication,* electrocution,* HYPOGLYCEMIA,* KIDNEY FAILURE, LIVER DISEASE, NEOPLASTIC NEUROLOGIC DISEASE, severe infections in any part of the body, poisoning,* SPINAL CORD DISEASE, thromboembolism,* and trauma.*

Coughing: This is not a common symptom in cats. Often, it is a sign of hairballs (in GASTROINTESTINAL DISEASES AND DISORDERS). It can occur in conjunction with BRONCHIAL DISEASE, FELINE BRONCHIAL ASTHMA,* FELINE BRONCHITIS, LUNG CANCER, lung worms, PNEUMONIA,* TRACHEAL DISEASE, and UPPER RESPIRATORY INFECTION (URI).

Dehydration: This is associated with inadequate water intake or increased water loss and can be part of any serious feline disease, but is often seen with congestive CARDIOMYOPATHY,* DIABETES MELLITUS, FELINE PANLEUKOPENIA, LIVER DISEASE, RENAL (KIDNEY) FAILURE, POLYURIA, or VOMITING.*

Drooling/Excessive Salivation: Can be a sign of nausea, car sickness, or a foreign body in the mouth. May also indicate dental disease, ESOPHAGEAL DISEASE, FACIAL PARALYSIS, oral tumors (in SQUAMOUS CELL CARCINOMAS) or poisoning.*

Ear Problems:

Blisters: PEMPHIGUS GROUP.

Discharge/odor: Sign of EAR MITES, foreign material in the ear, or an ear inflammation or infection.

Flap: Tenderness or soreness can be a sign of an AURAL HEMATOMA when accompanied by swelling or of an ear inflammation or infection.

Inflamed: EAR MITES, infection, or PARASITIC SKIN DISEASE.

Masses in: CERUMINOUS GLAND ADENOCARCINOMA, polyps.

Eating Disorders:

Anorexia (appetite loss): Loss of appetite may occur in cats for a variety of reasons. Owners should be concerned only if it lasts as long as twenty-four hours or is accompanied by other signs of illness. The exception is with young kittens who cannot go without food for more than a few hours (see Chapter 6). It can occur during pregnancy/gestation (see Chapter 5 and Chapter 3), or on hot, humid days. It can be a sign of many illnesses, from a mild intestinal upset (see GASTROINTESTINAL DISEASES AND DISORDERS) to a number of diseases/illnesses occurring in all parts of a cat's body.

Choking/gagging: This can be caused by a swallowed object* but can also be a sign of ESOPHAGEAL DISEASE, LARYNGEAL DISEASE, or PHARYNGEAL DISEASE.

Hunger, excessive: DIABETES MELLITUS, HYPERTHYROIDISM, intestinal disease (in GASTROINTESTINAL DISEASES).

Inability to eat: Dental disease, MUSCULOSKELETAL TUMORS, RABIES, oral tumors or ulceration, UPPER RESPIRATORY INFECTIONS.

Swallowing difficulty: ESOPHAGEAL DISEASE, PHARYNGEAL DISEASE, poisoning,* or RABIES.

Eye Problems:

Absence of blink: If *one* eye is involved, it could be an ophthalmic problem such as OCULAR TUMORS or CORNEAL ULCERATION, or a neurologic problem such as FACIAL PARALYSIS. If *both eyes* are involved, it is usually a neurologic problem such as FACIAL PARALYSIS on both sides or PERIPHERAL NEUROPATHY.

Blindness: Signs of acute blindness include walking into walls or other objects or a reluctance to move from one spot. Acute blindness can be caused by ANTERIOR CHAMBER INFLAMMATION, brain damage (in NEUROLOGIC DISEASES AND DISORDERS), CATARACTS, CONGENITAL NEUROLOGIC DISEASE, CORNEAL TRAUMA, CORNEAL ULCERATION, EPILEPSY, GLAUCOMA, or VASCULAR NEUROLOGIC DISEASE. *Chronic* blindness usually has less dramatic signs as cats can adjust to it gradually. See NEOPLASTIC NEUROLOGIC DISEASES, also taurine deficiency (in OPHTHALMIC DISEASES AND DISORDERS and RETINAL DISEASE).

Clouding/discoloration/changes: This can be caused by ANTERIOR CHAMBER INFLAMMATION, CATARACTS, CORNEAL SEQUESTRUM, DIFFUSE IRIS MELANOMA, FELINE LEUKEMIA VIRUS (FeLV),* FELINE INFECTIOUS PERITONITIS (FIP), GLAUCOMA, HORNER'S SYNDROME, LYMPHOSARCOMA, OCULAR TUMORS, TOXOPLASMOSIS.

Corneal ulcers: RHINOTRACHEITIS, trauma.*

Discharge from: CONJUNCTIVITIS, CORNEAL TRAUMA, *ophthalmis neonatorum* (newborns) (see Chapter 6), UPPER RESPIRATORY INFECTION (URI)—watery CALICIVIRUS, REOVIRUS; more purulent PNEUMONITIS, RHINOTRACHEITIS.

Lesions around: PEMPHIGUS GROUP.

Redness: ANTERIOR CHAMBER INFLAMMATION, CONJUNCTIVITIS, CORNEAL TRAUMA, GLAUCOMA (requires immediate attention; can be painful), OCULAR TUMORS, THIRD EYELID PROLAPSE.

Facial Abnormalities:

Distortion: Various types of facial distortion can be caused by FACIAL PARALYSIS, facial tumors, HORNER'S SYNDROME, LYMPHOSARCOMA, NASAL CANCER, and rodent ulcers (in EOSINOPHILIC GRANULOMA COMPLEX).

Paralysis: Damage to the brain stem (in NEUROLOGIC DISEASES AND DISORDERS) and VESTIBULAR DISEASE.

Swelling: ABSCESSES, ALLERGIC SKIN DISEASE, BACTERIAL SKIN DISEASES, tumors.

Twitching: EPILEPSY.

Fever: Fever is often accompanied by anorexia and/or vomiting and diarrhea, and should always be medically evaluated. It can be caused by agitation and a hot environmental temperature. It can be a sign of: AUTOIMMUNE DISEASES, cancer (in ONCOLOGY), heat prostration,* and SYSTEMIC LUPUS ERYTHEMATOSUS. It can be caused by any kind of systemic viral or bacterial infection, including ABSCESSES, ENDOMETRITIS, FELINE INFECTIOUS PERITONITIS (FIP), FELINE PANLEUKOPENIA, INFECTIOUS ARTHRITIS, PNEUMONIA,* PYOMETRA,* PYOTHORAX.* All of the UPPER RESPIRATORY INFECTIONS can cause a cat to run a very high fever, especially CALICIVIRUS and RHINOTRACHEITIS.

Foot Problems:
    Nail bed infection: Paronychia, dewclaw infections.
    Pad swelling: CALICIVIRUS and PEMPHIGUS GROUP.

Fragile Bones: NUTRITIONAL HYPERPARATHYROIDISM, renal hypoparathyroidism.

Gait Changes: Can have neurologic origins such as brain damage or be a BALANCE DISORDER (ATAXIA or DYSMETRIA), SPINAL CORD DISEASE, or VASCULAR NEUROLOGIC DISEASE. It can also be due to a MUSCULOSKELETAL DISEASE OR DISORDER such as FRACTURES,* dislocations, or OSTEOMYELITIS.
    Lameness/limping: Cats do not limp very often. When they do, it can be because of a leg or paw injury. It can also be due to any of the many types of ARTHRITIS, CALICIVIRUS (kittens), COXOFEMORAL LUXATION, CRANIAL CRUCIATE LIGAMENT RUPTURE (rare), GROWTH PLATE DISORDERS, limb FRACTURES,* MUSCULOSKELETAL TUMORS, OSTEOMYELITIS, and PATELLAR LUXATIONS.

Hair Loss (alopecia): ALLERGIC SKIN DISEASES, alopecia universalis (in CONGENITOHEREDITARY SKIN DISORDERS), EOSINOPHILIC GRANULOMA COMPLEX, feline endocrine alopecia (see HORMONAL SKIN DISEASES), FROSTBITE, FUNGAL SKIN DISEASES, hypotrichosis (in CONGENITOHEREDITARY SKIN DISORDERS), NUTRITIONAL SKIN DISEASE, PARASITIC SKIN DISEASES, and STUD TAIL.

Head Abnormalities:
    Shaking/rubbing: Usually an ear problem—see AURAL DISEASES AND DISORDERS and EAR MITES.
    Tilt: Sign of a NEUROLOGIC DISEASE OR DISORDER (vestibular disorder), especially a BALANCE DISORDER or IDIOPATHIC NEUROLOGIC DISEASE.

Itching (pruritis): ALLERGIC SKIN DISEASES and PARASITIC SKIN DISEASES.

Jaundice (icterus): Yellow color to eyes, inside of ears, mucous membranes, skin, and so forth. Also may have dark yellow urine. Indicates AUTOIMMUNE HEMOLYTIC ANEMIA, CHOLANGIOHEPATITIS, LIVER DISEASE, or PANCREATIC DISEASE.

Joint/Limb Swelling: All kinds of ARTHRITIS; limb FRACTURES* or MUSCULOSKELETAL DISEASES AND DISORDERS.

Licking/Scratching/Biting: Evidence of skin disease. See DERMATOLOGIC DISEASES AND DISORDERS, ALLERGIC SKIN DISEASES, EAR MITES, and PARASITIC SKIN DISEASES. Can also indicate pain or discomfort in the area.

Lumps/Bumps/Masses: Tumors, cysts, cancers in any area. Often the only way to differentiate between them is by surgical biopsy (see Glossary 2). See also DERMATOLOGIC DISEASES AND DISORDERS, LIPOMAS, MAMMARY GLAND TUMORS, MAST CELL TUMORS, MILIARY DERMATITIS, pansteatitis (in NUTRITIONAL SKIN DISEASE), SKIN TUMORS, and ticks (in PARASITIC SKIN DISEASES). See also Mouth Problems below.

Mouth Problems:
    Discomfort: If a cat shows pain when touched on the face or when eating, it can be a sign of dental disease, ORAL TUMORS (for example, oral SQUAMOUS CELL CARCINOMA), or a foreign body in the mouth.
    Odor: Can be a sign of dental disease, ORAL TUMORS, or RENAL (KIDNEY) DISEASE.
    Pale mucous membranes: ANEMIA, CARDIAC DISEASE, or shock.*
    Sores/ulcers (oral): CALICIVIRUS, KIDNEY DISEASE, or RHINOTRACHEITIS.

Nasal Problems:

Discharge: Can be caused by a foreign body in the nose or NASAL CANCER, infectious diseases such as UPPER RESPIRATORY INFECTIONS (URI), fungal infection, LYMPHOSARCOMA, or tooth abscess.

Nosebleeds: Bleeding disorders,* FRACTURES*—hard palate ("high-rise syndrome"),* NASAL CANCER, thrombocytopenia, or WARFARIN POISONING.*

Sneezing: Not a problem unless continuous or very frequent. Can often affect cats that have a foreign body in the nose or UPPER RESPIRATORY INFECTIONS (URI). Also may be a sign of NASAL CANCER.

Panting: Breathing difficulty,* discomfort, excitement, exercise, or fear. Excessive heat prostration.*

Paralysis (of neurologic origin): See CONGENITAL NEUROLOGIC DISEASES, FACIAL PARALYSIS, LYMPHOSARCOMA, PARESIS, PERIPHERAL NEUROPATHY, PLEGIA, SPINAL CORD DISEASE, and TOXOPLASMOSIS.

Seizures/Convulsions:* Brain damage (in NEUROLOGIC DISEASES AND DISORDERS), CONGENITAL NEUROLOGIC DISEASES, EPILEPSY,* HYPOGLYCEMIA,* Hypoparathyroidism (in ENDOCRINE DISEASES), IDIOPATHIC NEUROLOGIC DISEASES, INFLAMMATORY NEUROLOGIC DISEASES, LIVER DISEASE, RENAL (KIDNEY) FAILURE, thiamine deficiency (in NUTRITIONAL NEUROLOGIC DISEASE), and TOXOPLASMOSIS.

Skin Problems: See also Itching and Lumps/Bumps/Masses above.

Abscesses: BACTERIAL SKIN DISEASES and wounds.*

Eruptions/redness: See DERMATOLOGIC DISEASES AND DISORDERS, AUTOIMMUNE SKIN DISEASES, FROSTBITE, PARASITIC SKIN DISEASES, ringworm (in FUNGAL SKIN DISEASES), and SQUAMOUS CELL CARCINOMAS.

Lacerations: Cutaneous asthenia (in CONGENITOHEREDITARY SKIN DISORDERS) and wounds.*

Urinary Problems: Any urinary problem in a cat should be taken very seriously.

Blood in urine (HEMATURIA): Indicates a problem in the kidney, ureter, bladder, or urethra (in RENAL DISEASES AND DISORDERS). It can be a sign of a bladder infection (BACTERIAL CYSTITIS), FELINE UROLOGIC SYNDROME (FUS),* HYDRONEPHROSIS, PYELONEPHRITIS, RENAL SUBCAPSULAR CYSTS, UROLITHS, URINARY TRACT TRAUMA,* and UROGENITAL TUMORS.

Inability to urinate: FELINE UROLOGIC SYNDROME (FUS), urethral obstruction,* UROLITHS, and URINARY TRACT TRAUMA.*

Increased frequency of urination (POLLAKIURIA): BACTERIAL CYSTITIS, FELINE UROLOGIC SYNDROME (FUS),* PYELONEPHRITIS, PYURIA, and urinary tract infections (in RENAL DISEASES AND DISORDERS).

Straining to urinate (STRANGURIA): BACTERIAL CYSTITIS, FELINE UROLOGIC SYNDROME (FUS),* HEMATURIA, PYURIA, UROLITHS, and URINARY TRACT TRAUMA.* See also RENAL DISEASES AND DISORDERS.

Urinary incontinence: See ECTOPIC URETER, SPINAL CORD DISEASES, and URINARY INCONTINENCE.

Urine volume increased (POLYURIA): DIABETES MELLITUS, UREMIA, CHRONIC INTERSTITIAL NEPHRITIS, PYOMETRA,* and HYPERTHYROIDISM (usually accompanied by increased water drinking).

Vaginal Discharge: ENDOMETRITIS, normal estrous (heat) cycle (see Chapter 5), postpartum infection/problem (also Chapter 5), or PYOMETRA.*

Voice Change: LARYNGEAL DISEASE, PERIPHERAL NEUROPATHY, and RESPIRATORY DISEASES AND DISORDERS.

Vomiting:* Cats vomit occasionally without being ill, usually as a result of hairballs (in GASTROINTESTINAL DISEASES AND DISORDERS). It should not be of concern unless it persists or is accompanied by other symptoms of illness or by lethargy. See GASTROINTESTINAL DISEASES AND DISORDERS for treatment of ordinary vomiting. It can be a sign of a BALANCE DISORDER but most commonly is due to a bacterial, viral, or other type of systemic disease. *Acute* vomiting can be caused by hairballs, swallowed objects,* esophagitis, FELINE UROLOGIC SYNDROME (FUS),* GASTRITIS, linear foreign bodies,* PANCREATIC DISEASE, and RENAL (KIDNEY) DISEASE.

Water Drinking, Increased (POLYDIPSIA): DIABETES MELLITUS, HYPERTHYROIDISM, LYMPHOSARCOMA, RENAL (KIDNEY) DISEASE, or UREMIA.

Weakness: ABSCESSES, APLASTIC ANEMIA, blood loss,* CARDIOMYOPATHY,* DIABETES MELLITUS, HYPOGLYCEMIA,* infection, INFLAMMATORY NEUROLOGIC DISEASE, LIVER DISEASE, NEOPLASTIC NEUROLOGIC DISEASE, PARESIS, PERIPHERAL NEUROPATHY, shock,* RENAL (KIDNEY) DISEASE, traumatic injury,* VASCULAR NEUROLOGIC DISEASE. In the *hind limbs:* spina bifida (in SPINAL CORD DISEASE) or thromboembolism.*

Weight Change:
Gain: HYPOTHYROIDISM or obesity.
Loss: Cancer, CARDIOMYOPATHY,* DIABETES MELLITUS, EOSINOPHILIC ENTERITIS, FELINE LEUKEMIA, LIVER DISEASE, old age, GASTROINTESTINAL DISEASE, pancreatic insufficiency (in PANCREATIC DISEASE), RENAL (KIDNEY) DISEASE, METABOLIC HEART DISEASE (old cats).

13

Care of a Sick Cat

Robert E. Matus, DVM

Cats and Illness

It may be a while before even the most observant owner notices any overt symptoms of illness in a cat such as those listed in the previous chapter. This is no one's fault; it is mainly because of the nature of cats, as they tend to compensate very well when they are not seriously ill and may simply go off alone when they are feeling bad. Often, by the time a cat shows any outward signs of illness that can be identified and related to specific body areas or systems, the disease or illness has progressed quite far.

This is why we recommend that owners try to be alert to subtle changes in a cat's behavior and habits. The first signs that all is not well with a cat may seem minor. A cat's behavior may change in subtle ways. A cat that is not feeling well may prefer to be left alone and will not be around with owners and family as much as usual; or it may be more demanding of attention and affection. Changes in habits may occur, too. A cat may become a more picky eater or eat a great deal more. If an owner is aware of these changes, it is always a good idea to have a cat checked by the veterinarian. Even if a disease process or illness has not progressed to the point where it is detectable in the course of a physical examination, an initial visit at this time can form the basis for evaluation later on when symptoms become more evident, and this history may help a veterinarian make a diagnosis in the future when and if an illness does develop.

To Hospitalize or Not?

Once an owner realizes that there may be a health problem with a cat, regardless of symptoms, and the cat is taken to the veterinarian, the first step is a complete physical examination for the cat, and then the doctor will decide whether or not further diagnostic tests are necessary.

When there is no emergency, several considerations will determine whether or not a cat requires hospitalization. In general, if a cat is self-supportive and eating and drinking enough to maintain its own hydration (balance of water retained in the body), is not suffering from severe diarrhea or vomiting, and is not in obvious discomfort or pain, it can usually be maintained at home while diagnostic tests are performed and the results obtained. If physical support is needed, such as intravenous fluids, blood transfusion, or oxygen therapy, then hospitalization is indicated.

This is a decision that must be made by the owner and veterinarian together, however, because sometimes home maintenance requires an owner to perform certain tasks, such as medicating or force-feeding a cat (see "Home Care of a Sick Cat," page 161). If an owner feels uncomfortable about performing these tasks or is unable to carry them out because of an uncooperative or fractious cat, hospitalization may be the best course.

Hospitalization is also necessary if a cat must be anesthetized so that specialized diagnostic tests can be performed. A cat that has been heavily sedated should be observed for at least twenty-four hours afterwards in order to make sure that it has not been adversely affected and has come out of the sedation completely before being allowed to go home. Thus, the decision about whether or not to hospitalize a cat is based on several factors: the type of diagnostic tests required, the condition of the cat at the time of examination, and the ability of an owner to maintain a cat's homeostasis (physiological equilibrium) at home.

Diagnostic Tests

There are a number of different diagnostic tests that a veterinarian may give to a cat in order to determine its condition. A definition of these tests and procedures is found in Glossary 2. It is important to note that unless a cat is taken to a veterinary medical institution that has in-house laboratory facilities and available technical support, it can take anywhere from twenty-four to seventy-two hours for test and X-ray results to be obtained from an outside laboratory. During this time a cat may be able to be maintained at home, as we discussed above.

We often find it best to advise an entire workup, or panel of tests, as indicated, on a cat right away in order to get a more complete picture of what is going on and also to prevent the animal from having one or two tests one day, only to find that more tests are needed later on. An initial diagnostic workup for a sick cat will usually entail X rays, a urinalysis, a Complete Bood Count (CBC), and Biochemical Profile (SMA-20). Based on the results of these, further or more specialized tests may be indicated.

X rays, angiograms, electrocardiograms, echocardiograms, and other diagnostic tests used to obtain a "picture" of internal organs and their functions require that a cat be kept still, and in some cases a mild tranquilizer may have to be given to the animal to ensure correct positioning and minimal discomfort.

A urinalysis is performed to examine the urine for glucose, protein, bile, and other constituents, including red and white blood cells. It is collected by catching a voided sample or by fine needle aspiration (cystocentesis) of the bladder.

Blood samples are obtained by venipuncture. A needle is inserted into the vein and blood is drawn. Most cats resist the restraint needed more than they mind the actual bloodtaking. Because many blood tests can be performed from one sample, only one venipuncture is usually needed for these tests. With cats we must be concerned about blood loss, however, because a cat's blood volume makes up only a little less than 6 percent of its total body weight. For example, a ten-pound cat has less than a pint of blood. Therefore, if serial blood tests are necessary, we often will try not to take blood on a daily basis as we would with most dogs but may alter the routine and take only a sample every other day. In many instances we will use a central venous catheter, described below, to do this.

Hospitalization

The majority of cats do very well in the hospital, although exceptions exist, of course, in which certain protective behavior patterns (for example, biting, scratching) may make life difficult for both veterinarian and patient. In general, however, cats are affectionate and

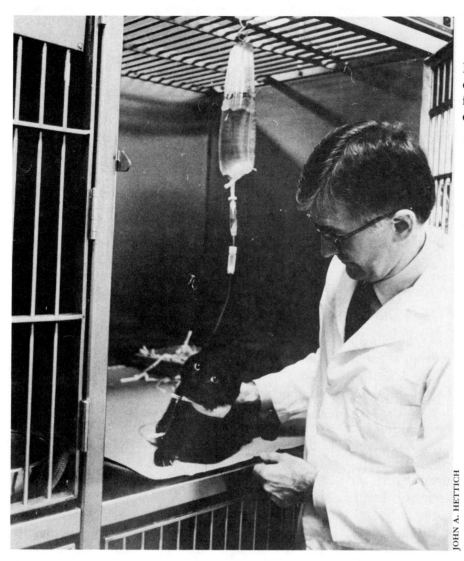

Photograph 28: Dr. Kay checks a cat that is receiving fluids through a jugular vein catheter.

JOHN A. HETTICH

respond positively to the trained people taking care of them.

Here at The AMC, cats are usually housed in small banks of cages that contain litter trays and individual water and food bowls. Because they prefer to be up high, cats are usually placed on the top tier of cages or at eye level, rather than in the bottom row on the floor. We find that cats often feel more secure in small spaces. We try not to put cats near noisy dogs.

If a cat requires medication, fluids, or blood tests on a regular basis, we usually insert a central intravenous catheter in the cat's jugular vein, through which fluids can be dispensed easily using flexible tubing. Once the catheter is in place, a cat feels no pain and little discomfort and is able to move around freely in its cage. For most cats this method of dispensing fluids and medications and taking tests is far less disturbing than constant handling and re-

straint would be. We also sometimes have to use a central vein catheter for extremely fractious cats that are not very ill in order to medicate them (see Photograph 28, above).

When chemical restraints are necessary in order to examine or treat a cat, we most commonly use ketamine, a disassociative cataleptic agent that disengages the central nervous system so that it is no longer able to coordinate the rest of the body. When this drug is used, care must be taken afterwards to protect a cat from environmental stimuli such as light and noise, to which it will be abnormally sensitive for a while.

If a cat reacts badly to a hospital situation, is unmanageable, or won't eat, we make every effort to send it home as soon as possible as long as the owner is willing and able to care for it properly.

Should Owners Visit Hospitalized Cats?

Whether an owner's visit to a hospitalized cat is desirable or not depends on the circumstances.

If a cat is in the hospital for a routine procedure or for a short stay, we usually discourage owners from visiting. An owner's visit can disrupt normal hospital routine and may upset a cat. A cat that is feeling fine may expect to be taken home if its owner visits and will be further upset when the owner leaves without it. We also ask owners not to visit on the day of surgery or during diagnostic testing when a cat is still under the influence of anesthetic or tranquilizers.

If a cat will be hospitalized for a long time, is suffering from a chronic illness, or is not doing well, visits by owners are always allowed. Here at The AMC, a cat is brought out to an examining room for a fifteen- to twenty-minute visit with its owner. Sometimes owners bring special food from home, a practice that we encourage as long as oral feeding is not contraindicated. When a cat is not eating as well as it should be, owner contact often hastens recovery.

When visits are allowed, owners must use common sense and cooperate with the hospital. Most hospitals request that only one or two people visit at one time, and only one visit a day is usually allowed. Visits must be scheduled at a time when there is adequate staff on duty to supervise.

Home Care of a Sick Cat

As we said at the beginning of this chapter, cats are often kept at home by owners during the course of diagnostic testing. They may also return home for maintenance care after diagnostic tests have been made in the hospital or surgery has been performed.

In all of these instances, owners may be required to medicate a cat, force food or liquids, take a cat's temperature, or perform various other sickroom tasks. In the case of a chronic illness (for example, diabetes mellitus), minor treatments such as insulin injections may continue for the rest of the animal's life. In other cases, medication and treatment may be required only until the disease or illness has been brought under control.

Especially in the case of a chronic or serious illness, owners may be concerned about whether or not they will be able to continue to medicate a cat. The veterinarian should always be consulted in these situations.

Veterinarians are always willing to give careful instructions about how to medicate or treat a cat. Owners who are inexperienced should also ask for a demonstration in the doctor's office. However, some cats can be extremely difficult to treat, and sometimes owners simply cannot medicate them. They should never hesitate to ask the veterinarian for help if this is the case. The solution may be as easy as changing the form of the medication—many medicines are made in several different forms, one of which may be easier to use. Sometimes a cat may have to be taken to the doctor's office for regular medications or even hospitalized for a course of treatment. There are some extremely fractious cats that may even require tranquilization in order to be medicated. Owners should not feel guilty if they cannot manage to treat a cat.

Restraints and Tricks to Use When Medicating a Cat

In the first place, cats are escape-and-hide experts. They always seem to be able to sense when a treatment or medication is due and make themselves very scarce. An owner who realizes this can make it a point to confine the cat in one room well ahead of time.

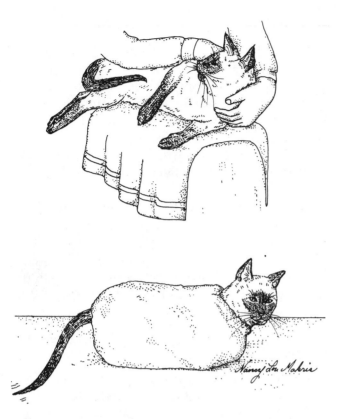

Illustration 12: A towel wrap works very well when a cat's head or tail area requires treatment. One leg or paw at a time can also be worked on.

Illustration 13: A cat can be restrained for an examination or treatment by stretching it out on the examining table.

It is always best to have an assistant to help, even with the best-natured cat. The assistant can hold the cat while the owner dispenses the medication. If an assistant is not available, an owner can put the cat up on a counter or table, and hold the animal against his body with one arm while medicating with the other. Putting a cat up on a table or counter-top before beginning medication or treatment will put the cat at a slight disadvantage and prevent it from escaping easily.

In our experience, most good-natured cats do best with minimal restraint. Too much restraint can make an otherwise calm animal panicky. Sudden, rough movements can also turn a gentle cat into a frightened, uncooperative patient. A cat that is up on a counter or table should be held gently, talked to calmly, and allowed to grab the edge of the counter with its front feet if it wants to.

If a cat is uncooperative, very frightened, or the procedure is moderately unpleasant or painful, more restraint may be required. It is always a good idea for anyone who is handling a cat in this situation or treating a strange or very high-strung cat to protect himself with heavy gloves and long sleeves.

A towel wrap (see Illustration 12, at left) works very well when a cat's head or tail area requires treatment. It can also be used to work on one foot or leg at a time. There are also cat bags with zippers, but we have always found these difficult to use.

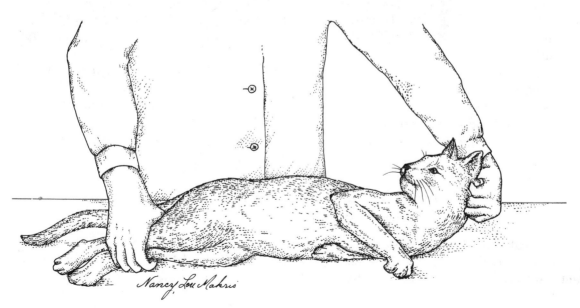

Photograph 29: Small kittens are easy to treat when they are picked up by the scruff of the neck.

JOHN A. HETTICH

Small kittens are easy to treat when they are picked up by the scruff of the neck (see Photograph 29, above). Even full-grown cats usually remain quiet when held by the loose skin at the back of the neck. Shaking a cat slightly while holding it this way will often distract it enough so that an injection can be given or blood sample taken.

Another method of restraining a cat for an examination or treatment is by stretching it out on the examining table by holding it by the scruff of the neck with one hand while holding its rear legs with the other, extending the cat's body to its full length. This does not hurt a cat at all and can often keep it still enough for treatment or examination (see Illustration 13, opposite page).

Because a cat's nose is so short, muzzling is neither practical nor effective, so if none of the above methods works, chemical restraint or tranquilization (described before in "Hospitalization") must be used instead. This, of course, would be administered only in a hospital setting.

General Care

Common sense should prevail when a sick or recuperating cat is being cared for at home.

Unless a cat has an infectious disease and lives in a multi-cat household, isolation is not necessary. Cats usually have one or two favorite sleeping places and, if possible, should be allowed to continue to use them as long as they are secure and warm. It may be necessary to provide a heat source for the cat, such as a heat lamp, above its sleeping place, especially if the house is kept cool.

A cat that does not feel well will usually send out a "leave me alone" signal to other pets, but overeager dogs and children should be kept away and the cat protected from rough play. Some cats crave a lot of attention from their owners when they are not feeling well. Others want to be left alone. An owner will have to take his cue from his own pet about this.

Illustration 14: Water, liquid nourishment, or medication can be administered with a large plastic dropper or syringe.

It is especially important for a cat that is not feeling well to have easy access to ample water and a clean litter tray. After some kinds of surgery (neutering, declawing), it is necessary to substitute shredded paper for other types of litter. More about this in Chapter 4. Indoor/ outdoor cats should, of course, be confined indoors until they recover completely.

Sometimes it may be necessary to encourage an anorexic cat to eat. As we mention in Chapter 3, cats' appetites are directly related to their ability to smell food. If a cat's sense of smell has been affected by illness, very strong smelling fishy food (Figaro tuna, for example) will often appeal to it. If a cat has not been eating well, an owner should offer a little bit of very fishy food at a time until the cat's appetite returns.

Forcing Food and Water

If the above method does not work, it may be necessary to force-feed a cat in order to provide it with enough calories to maintain energy and hydration. There is a nutrient preparation in paste form called Nutri-cal which is high in calories and available through veterinarians, or a strong gruel can be made in liquid or paste form from cat food, water, and perhaps some Nutri-cal.

These nutrients can be given in several ways. If they are mixed so that they are liquid, they can be administered with a large plastic dropper or a syringe with the needle removed, available from the veterinarian. With one hand on the top of the cat's head, tilt it upward and pull the animal's cheek out by grasping it gently with thumb and forefinger. Administer the liquid slowly into the cat's mouth through the funnel made by the cheek pouch (see Illustration 14, at left). This method can also be used if it is necessary to force water.

Nutrients in paste form are easy to administer to a cat by the following method: A strip of paste can be put on the tip of a finger and simply wiped onto the roof of the cat's mouth, which will force him to swallow it (see Illustration 15, opposite page). This works much bet-

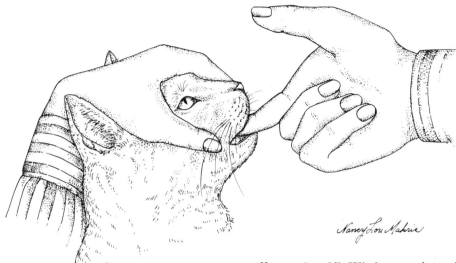

Illustration 15: Wiping nutrients in paste form on the roof of a cat's mouth

ter for most cats than the often-recommended method of placing the paste on the cat's paw to be licked off. In our experience, many cats will not lick the substance off their paws but will wipe it off on the nearest rug or chair.

Taking a Cat's Temperature

An owner may be required to take a cat's temperature to report any fluctuations to the veterinarian. Again, two people are recom-mended, especially the first time. Cats' anal-rectal muscles are very strong, and there may be a good deal of resistance when attempts are made to slip the thermometer in. A well-lubricated rectal thermometer should be placed against the rectum and gentle pressure ap-plied. Once the thermometer has penetrated a little bit, the resistance will usually ease up and it can be inserted without difficulty. A cat's normal temperature is between 100 and ap-proximately 102.5 degrees F.

Medicating a Cat

Cats do not take kindly to being medicated, and even the best-tempered pet may surprise its owners by the degree of its resistance. As we mentioned above, cats are excellent escape artists, and if an attempt to medicate a cat fails, it will be extremely difficult to get the animal to stay still for another try or even to find the cat. It bears repeating here that it is a very good idea to confine the cat to a small area or room before it becomes aware of what is about to happen. Cat owners usually have to learn to think like a cat and anticipate its moves in order to be successful at giving med-icine. It is also important to stay calm and be very patient when treating a cat.

What follows is a general description of how to give various kinds of medication. An owner should always ask the doctor to give a demon-stration of the proper way to administer any type of medicine before attempting to do it himself.

Pilling a Cat

Usually, a veterinarian will give the first dose of medicine by injection and then send an owner home with pills to dispense. Pilling a cat can be an extremely exasperating experi-ence even for old hands. Pills cannot be hid-den in food for cats as they can for dogs because a cat will usually find the pill and re-move it or push it aside. In order to make a cat swallow a pill, it must be placed in the back of the cat's mouth, the mouth held closed, and the chin stroked until the animal's tongue comes forward and the pill is swallowed. To get the pill in the back of the mouth, the cat's head has to be tilted upward by holding it from above; at the same time the cat's mouth must be opened by applying gentle pressure on the front of the lower jaw with a finger. Simultaneously, the pill has to be placed on top of the cat's tongue in the extreme back of the mouth. If it sounds as if at least three hands are needed, they usually are, at least for inexperienced owners. Experienced cat owners often have tricks for accomplishing this alone, but most people require a helper. Many medications come in both pill and liquid form, but not all of them are suitable for cats because of their extreme sensitivity to alcohol-based medicines (see the Appendix for details). If there is an appropriate liquid version of a medicine, it will undoubtedly be easier for an owner to use.

Illustration 16: Applying eye medication

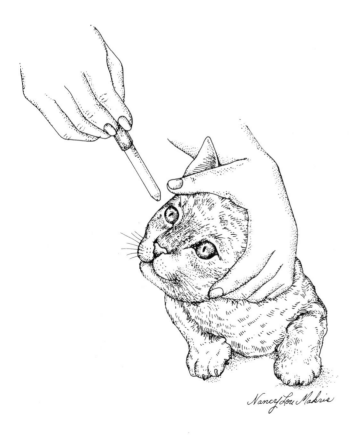

Giving Liquid Medicine

Liquid medicine can be given to a cat the same way that liquid nourishment is, by placing it into the animal's mouth with a syringe or plastic dropper. Because of cats' very strong sense of smell, it is not a good idea to put liquid medicine in a cat's food since the whole thing will probably be rejected.

Applying Eye Medicine

Eye medicine usually comes in either liquid drops or ointment. It is given with one hand placed on the top of the animal's head to tilt it upward. With the other hand, drops are put into the corner of each eye or ointment is squeezed in a fine line on the inside of the lower lid (see Illustration 16, below left).

Applying Ear Medicine

Most owners find it fairly easy to apply ear medicine to a cat. Ear medicine also comes in liquid or ointment form and is usually packaged in a squeeze tube or bottle with an applicator tip. Holding the cat's head still with one hand, place the applicator tip firmly into the opening of the ear canal and squeeze out a small amount of medicine. Then massage the ear canal, which runs down the side of the cat's head (see Illustration 18, page 179), to spread the medication up and down.

Giving a Subcutaneous Injection

When owners feel competent to do it, fluids may be administered subcutaneously at home in order to maintain a cat's proper hydration. Subcutaneous injections are most often given to cats suffering from diabetes mellitus and certain kinds of kidney disease, and to geriatric cats during an acute stage of an illness. A subcutaneous injection is given beneath the skin by picking up a fold of skin in a loose area (the back of the neck is usually best), making a dimple or dent with one finger, and inserting the needle into the dent. Care must be taken that the needle goes beneath the skin and does not come out on the other side of the fold. With practice, most cat owners do not find this extremely difficult to do.

Other Procedures

It can be hard to keep a cat from licking off any topical skin medications right away. If the medicine is rubbed in well and a cat can be distracted from licking for ten to fifteen minutes, the medicine will usually have time to do its work. A favorite game, delicious meal, or perhaps brushing the cat to distract it may prevent it from licking for a sufficient amount of time.

Occasionally a cat will have to have a medicated bath. In Chapter 3 we describe how to give a cat a bath.

Care of Bandages and Casts

Owners are not generally asked to change bandages or casts on a cat, but they do have to keep them as dry and clean as possible and check for any foul odor or redness or swelling around them. If there is a bad smell or any swelling or redness, or if the area around a cast or bandage is extremely warm or cold to the touch, a veterinarian should be seen right away. Of course, indoor/outdoor cats should be confined until the bandage or cast is removed.

Photograph 30: A cat will adapt very well to wearing a cast, hardly seeming to notice it after a few days.

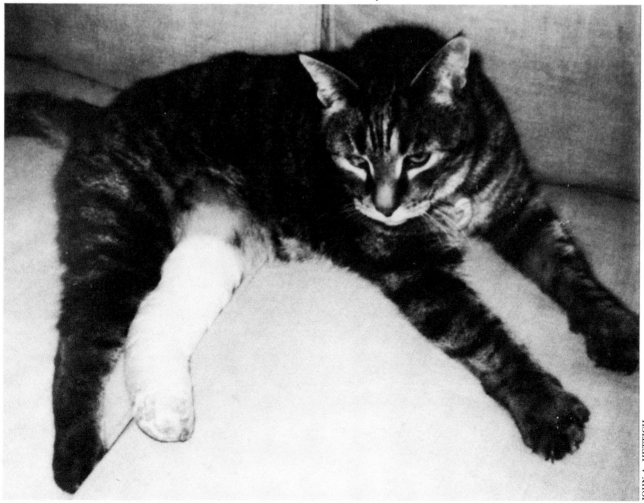

JOHN A. HETTICH

It may be necessary to use an Elizabethan collar to prevent a cat from biting at a bandage or cast. Veterinarians usually have commercially made collars, or an owner can make a temporary one from cardboard. See Illustration 17, at left, for how this is done and how it should look when in place. Remember that the collar must be flexible enough to allow a cat to eat and drink.

Illustration 17: An Elizabethan collar will prevent a cat from biting a bandage, cast, or incision.

Tender Loving Care

A sick pet can present a very difficult situation for a concerned owner. Sometimes a sick cat seems to be so upset at the affront to its independence and the indignity of having to be cared for that it may seem to want to simply go off by itself and give up. That is when an understanding owner can make a big difference in a cat's recovery—by giving the cat enough loving care and attention and at the same time knowing when to leave it alone. A caring owner can be just as important as many medicines in giving a cat the will to recover from an illness.

Encyclopedia
of Diseases of Cats,
Their Treatment and Prevention

I) Infectious/Contagious Diseases of Cats, MICHAEL S. GARVEY, DVM
   Feline Zoonotic Diseases

II) Diseases and Disorders of Cats: Symptoms, Diagnosis, Treatment, Prognosis

Aural Diseases and Disorders, KAREN A. HELTON, DVM

Autoimmune and Blood Diseases, AUDREY A. HAYES, VMD, and ROBERT E. MATUS, DVM

Cardiac Disease, PHILIP R. FOX, DVM

Dermatologic Diseases and Disorders, KAREN A. HELTON, DVM

Endocrine Diseases, MARK E. PETERSON, DVM

Gastrointestinal Diseases and Disorders, DENNIS A. ZAWIE, DVM

Musculoskeletal Diseases and Disorders, DAVID T. MATTHIESEN, DVM

Neurologic Diseases and Disorders, DEBORAH SARFATY, DVM

Oncology, AUDREY A. HAYES, VMD, and ROBERT E. MATUS, DVM

Ophthalmic Diseases and Disorders, STEPHEN L. GROSS, VMD

Renal Diseases and Disorders, RICHARD C. SCOTT, DVM

Reproductive Disorders, LEE SCHRADER, DVM

Respiratory Diseases and Disorders, KATHLEEN E. NOONE, VMD

For many years, even after the rise of companion animal veterinary medicine after World War II (see Chapter 1), the study and treatment of feline disease took a back seat to research into diseases of dogs and the development of preventive medicine for canine illnesses. In recent years, however, as cat ownership has increased, our knowledge of feline medicine has grown by leaps and bounds, and new diagnostic and treatment methods are being discovered regularly. For example, a vaccine has just been developed to protect cats against the feline leukemia virus (FeLV), the number one cause of cancer and many other diseases in cats.

Cat owners are now aware of the need for regular veterinary care for their pets, including immunizations and yearly boosters to protect them from many contagious and infectious diseases. More about the need for proper vaccinations will be found in Chapter 3. Because cats have not traditionally been bred as closely as dogs, purebred cats suffer from fewer genetic defects than purebred dogs do. However, a few genetic predispositions toward disease among some kinds of purebred cats will be found in the pages that follow.

It bears repeating that because of their nature cats usually react to illness and disease differently than dogs do. In many cases a disease or condition may have progressed quite far before even the most observant owner is aware of it. The preceding chapter and Chapter 12 will help cat owners be more aware of some subtle signs that a cat is not well. In the case of many of the infectious diseases that follow, however, symptoms are usually quite evident fairly early in the course of the illness.

Infectious/Contagious Diseases of Cats

An infectious disease is caused by the invasion of a cat's body by a disease-producing organism—a bacterium, fungus, virus, protozoon, or parasite. A contagious disease is an infectious disease that can be transmitted from one cat to another. All contagious diseases are infectious diseases, but not all infectious diseases are contagious. As a general rule, viral diseases are

171

highly contagious (except for FeLV and FIP) and bacterial diseases have a much smaller chance of being contagious.

Today, most feline infectious viral diseases can be prevented almost entirely with appropriate immunizations. Many other infectious diseases can be treated if prompt medical attention is provided. Parasitic diseases can usually be cured with appropriate medication.

We will begin with those diseases against which cats are now routinely immunized.

One of the most serious infectious diseases of cats is *feline panleukopenia* (feline distemper, feline infectious enteritis). This disease should not be confused with canine distemper, which is a totally different disease organism/syndrome. However, feline panleukopenia *is* similar to canine parvovirus in that the viral agent that causes both diseases is classified as a parvovirus. The feline panleukopenia virus has been known to exist since the turn of the century, and canine parvovirus was not identified until 1978. Thus, it is possible that the canine parvovirus may have mutated from the feline panleukopenia virus. Since the awareness of canine parvovirus has grown, we have learned more about this particular viral class. It is highly contagious and very easily transmitted from one cat to another. Live virus is passed in the diarrhetic stool, and contact with an infected cat usually leads to infection of an entire group or litter. Feline panleukopenia virus can live outside the body for extended periods of time and is very resistant to attempts to kill it in the environment. Regular disinfectants are ineffective against it, and environmental disinfection with a dilute chlorine bleach is recommended. Feline panleukopenia has an incubation period of about a week.

The classical symptoms are vomiting, severe diarrhea, dehydration, and severe depression. Just as in canine parvovirus, two sites of the cat's body are affected. The primary affected site is the gastrointestinal tract, which can be seriously damaged, causing the severe vomiting and diarrhea characteristic of the disease. The second site affected by the infection is the bone marrow, which is profoundly suppressed. Most blood cells are produced in the bone mar-

row, and since white blood cells have a life span of only about forty-eight hours (as opposed to the much longer life spans for platelets and red blood cells), the first sign of bone marrow suppression seen in cats is a severe depression in the white blood cell count. "Panleukopenia" means depression of all the different kinds of white blood cells. The coexistence of these two particular phenomena will cause severe problems for a cat. When the intestinal tract is severely damaged by the viral infection, it allows bacterial invasion of the body via the bloodstream. This would normally be handled by white blood cells which would phagocytize (eat) the bacteria as they enter the bloodstream and destroy them. With a deficiency of white blood cells in the bloodstream, the bacterial infection can become systemic, leading to septicemia (bacterial infection of the bloodstream). This is probably the cause of death in most cats, although most untreated cats would eventually die from dehydration caused by the vomiting and diarrhea.

At the time of diagnosis, infected cats usually have high fevers and are very, very ill. This disease is much more common in kittens prior to vaccination and in those with poor immune systems, although it can occur in adult cats if their immunity fails and they are exposed to a virulent strain of the virus. Treatment consists of intravenous fluids to rehydrate the cat and control water balance in the face of an inability to eat and drink properly, some supplemental nutrition if the disease lasts long, and systemic antibiotics to control the bacterial invasion that is secondary to the viral damage to the intestinal tract. The prognosis for adult animals with prompt, aggressive, proper treatment is quite good. In very young kittens this disease still has a high mortality rate and is therefore classified as a very serious infectious disease. This is one of the diseases that cats should be routinely vaccinated for (see Chapter 3).

Upper Respiratory Infections (URI)

This is a group of four different organisms that can produce signs of an upper respiratory infection which primarily affects the nose, eyes, throat, and perhaps the lower respiratory tract (lungs) as well. The four different diseases involved are: *rhinotracheitis*, a herpes virus, not to be confused with human herpes, genital herpes, or any other kind of herpes; *calicivirus*, which also produces a very severe respiratory infection; *reovirus*, which produces a mild form of URI; and *pneumonitis*, which differs from the three organisms above in that it is not a viral infection but is produced by an organism called a *chlamydia*, which is similar to a bacterium and a virus but is neither.

The classical signs of all four URI infections in cats are sneezing and runny eyes and nose. URIs can then be divided into two groups: the two very serious infections, rhinotracheitis and calicivirus, and the two much milder forms of URI, pneumonitis and reovirus. Most veterinarians do not usually take a diagnosis any further than that—viral isolations to fully identify the offending organism are not performed very often because, practically speaking, it is enough to observe how ill the animal is and to treat it accordingly. Interestingly, the two most serious of the URIs (rhinotracheitis and calicivirus) probably each account for about 45 percent of the incidence of URI in cats, while the two milder forms cause only about 5 percent of cats' respiratory infections. This flies in the face of historical thinking because at one time pneumonitis was considered a very common disease, but once rhinotracheitis and calicivirus were identified, it became clear that pneumonitis did not occur as often as was previously thought. It can occur more often in cattery situations, however, where milder URI can go through an entire population in a short time.

Typically, reovirus infection is the mildest URI. Cats will normally just sneeze and have watery eyes and nasal discharge. There are usually no complicating secondary infections —an infected cat very often will not even lose its appetite, will not have a fever, and the symptoms pass in a very short time. This particular viral URI really requires no treatment at all, as long as it is certain that is what a cat has. However, it is standard practice to treat a cat with these symptoms with antibiotics just to make sure; also, salve or drops are usually prescribed for the eyes. Remember, though, that antibiotics are not primarily useful against a viral infection, they are merely used in order to prevent a secondary bacterial infection.

Pneumonitis also usually has rather mild symptoms, although an infected cat can be more seriously affected than one with reovirus. For example, ocular discharge may be somewhat purulent, and therefore the eyes may require more treatment. Because the organism involved is a chlamydia, certain antibiotics may well be effective against it (tetracycline, chloramphenicol, for example). Cats with pneumonitis are usually not very ill; they may continue to eat and have only mild fever, if any. With some supportive treatment, cats with pneumonitis tend to do very well.

Rhinotracheitis and calicivirus have the most severe symptoms. These characteristically are very high fever (sometimes in excess of 104 or 105 degrees—see Chapter 13 for how to take a cat's temperature), very purulent ocular or nasal discharges, and coughing. A common complication is severe ulcerations or open sores in the mouth, which cause cats to become profoundly anorexic. Dehydration can follow quickly, and the disease will then become more complicated as the cat's resistance goes down. In addition, rhinotracheitis virus will sometimes cause corneal ulcers—little ulcerations on the clear outer part of the eye—which can be painful and cause the eyelids to stick together because of the amount of exudation. This is another serious complication that can lead to corneal scars which may or may not resolve over time. See Chapter 3 for a description of a calicivirus strain that has been dubbed the "limping kitten syndrome." It is safe to say that the death rate with both calicivirus and rhinotracheitis is high, particularly in very young kittens. The older the animal, the more the likelihood of survival, but surviving animals may require therapy for some time—at least a week or two of antibiotics and support and perhaps force-feeding while the ulcers in the respiratory tract and oral cavity heal.

All four of these organisms are highly contagious. It is not uncommon for them to run through an entire household or cattery. There is also some significant evidence that cats that have recovered from these infections, particularly rhinotracheitis and calicivirus, may become carriers, able to infect other cats.

The most common vaccination given to a kitten and cat on an annual basis is the three-in-one feline vaccine that contains panleukopenia, rhinotracheitis, and calicivirus, the three organisms we worry most about. Sometimes pneumonitis is also included in a four-in-one vaccine, especially in catteries where the infection has been known to exist. There is no vaccination for reovirus—it is such a simple infection that one probably never will exist. Vaccination schedules for kittens and boosters for adult cats are discussed in detail in Chapter 3.

Rabies

Historically, rabies has been of concern in dogs. Almost all localities and municipalities throughout the United States have laws requiring that dogs be vaccinated against rabies in order to be licensed; most have no such laws affecting cats. Therefore, the cat has been a forgotten species when it comes to rabies control programs, and because of this we now have noticed a startling increase in the number of reported cases of rabies in cats. Over the past few years, cats have overtaken dogs as the domesticated species in the United States with the highest number of reported rabies cases in a year.

Any warm-blooded mammal can become infected with the rabies virus, but for some reason it has not been a problem in rodents such as rats, mice, squirrels, and so forth. The carriers of rabies that pets in the United States are most likely to come in contact with are bats, skunks, raccoons, and foxes. Because of cats' natural habits of hunting and stalking and their natural high level of curiosity, the potential for exposure to any of these carriers includes all cats that are allowed outdoors, even in cities. However, even cats that live in suburban or country houses and do not regularly go outside should be immunized—cases of rabid bats getting into homes via the chimney or an open window have been reported in several localities. Rabid bats and other wild animals are likely to indulge in uncharacteristic behavior and are more apt to come in contact with a cat than are healthy wildlife. We therefore recommend rabies vaccinations for all cats.

The incubation period of rabies virus in animals is extremely variable—it can be several months or longer. (Classically, it is described as three months, but that is an average which does not apply to all animals.) This is one of the major problems with the disease. If a cat is scratched or bitten by a suspect rabid animal, there is no way to tell when that cat will begin to show symptoms of the disease. It is very difficult, if not impossible, to quarantine a cat at that stage for a specific period of time and then release it with any guarantee that the disease will not develop in the future. In most situations, then, if a nonvaccinated animal is exposed to a rabid animal or even suspected of having been exposed to one, there is really no choice but to suggest that the animal be destroyed. From a public health standpoint it would be highly negligent to release that animal.

Signs of rabies in cats are also variable, as they are in other species. Classically, there are two forms of rabies: the vicious form in which animals will become quite perturbed and overreact to environmental stimuli in a vicious manner, biting and scratching without provocation; and the dumb form in which the animal will usually become very depressed, have changes in mentation and behavior, and will usually be unable to eat or drink because of paralysis of the muscles in the back of the throat. Foaming at the mouth is *not* a classical presentation of rabies in any species—this may arise in animals with dumb rabies who cannot swallow saliva and in the process blow bubbles. Any neurologic signs and aberrations in behavior can also be symptoms of rabies. Because the signs of rabies are so variable, they can be very difficult for the average person to recognize.

Vaccination and booster protocols for rabies are discussed in Chapter 3. Local rabies control groups, rather than the Federal government, are responsible for laws about rabies immunizations.

Feline Leukemia Virus (FeLV)

This is one of the few known viral causes for cancer in any species, including humans. It is contagious from cat to cat but usually only as a result of prolonged, intimate contact because the virus lives for only a short time outside an infected animal. Therefore, as opposed to URIs, it cannot be transmitted from one cat to another by humans on clothing or hands, and so forth, and is not contagious to humans or other animal species. As discussed earlier, an FeLV vaccine was introduced in late 1984. A detailed discussion of FeLV and FeLV-related diseases and cancers, their symptoms and treatment, will be found in the following section on Diseases and Disorders of Cats.

Feline Infectious Peritonitis (FIP)

This disease can affect all cats but is not a problem for any other species of animal. It is caused by a cat's immune system's response to one strain of corona virus (see Diseases and Disorders of Cats) and is not highly contagious. When a cat's body begins to make antibodies against the virus, the antibodies combine with the virus. These combined virus/antibody complexes line the walls of the blood vessels and cause the disease process. Even though FIP is a viral disease, it acts like an immune-mediated disease (see Diseases and Disorders of Cats). There is apparently some relationship between the feline leukemia virus (FeLV) and FIP, as about 40 percent of cats with FIP are FeLV(+), but researchers believe that FIP may develop because FeLV(+) cats are more susceptible to all other viruses.

Although FIP can affect all parts of the body, there are two distinct primary forms of the disease. In one (the "wet" form), clinical signs include fever, lethargy, anorexia, mild anemia, and fluid in the abdomen, which causes distention, or in the chest cavity, resulting in difficult breathing. There is also a "dry" form of the disease in which there is no fluid buildup, but the abdominal lymph nodes, liver, and kidneys may be enlarged and a clouding of the eyes may occur. In these cases the cat eventually becomes mildly anemic, runs a fever, is an-

orexic, loses weight, and is usually dehydrated and depressed.

Although a feline corona virus-titer test has been used in the past as a diagnostic tool, it is not specific for antibodies to FIP. It is far more accurate to diagnose FIP based on clinical signs and on a cytology of fluids, if they are present, or a biopsy of the affected organs when the disease takes a dry form.

The prognosis for a cat with FIP is extremely poor, and the disease has a high mortality rate. Exceptions can occur when the disease is detected very early, before the blood vessels have been damaged by vasculitis. FIP is treated symptomatically with aspirin, immunosuppressants, and anti-inflammatory drugs. Because of the high fatality rate associated with FIP, there are several so-called miracle cures on the market, but in most instances when cats have been cured by these miracle drugs, the original diagnosis of FIP was never confirmed. There are no preventive vaccines for FIP.

Intestinal Parasites

These are not as common in cats as they are in dogs, probably as a result of the different life-styles in cats and dogs. Roundworms, particularly in newborn young kittens, are seen rather frequently, and these respond very well to the proper deworming medications. Occasionally, hookworms and whipworms are found in cats, depending a great deal on the environment and life-style of the cat. For instance, in a northeastern urban environment, hookworms are rare in pet cats, and whipworms almost never seen. In the South, however, cats allowed outdoors will have a much higher incidence of these two diseases. Tapeworms, especially those transmitted by fleas, are also seen more often in warm climates where fleas are a year-long problem. See more about intestinal parasites in Diseases and Disorders of Cats.

Toxoplasmosis

This is caused by the protozoan organism *T. gondii* and is contagious to cats via fecal matter, raw meat, the killing and eating of rodents, and infected soil (it can be picked up on the paws, for instance, and ingested while grooming). In clinically affected cats, lesions are seen most commonly in the lungs, liver, gastrointestinal tract, and brain. Seizures, behavior changes, and paralysis are common neurologic signs of infection. Neurologic signs may be irreversible even after treatment successfully eliminates the disease. See below for the zoonotic implications of this organism.

Feline Zoonotic Diseases

Zoonotic diseases, or those diseases that can be transmitted from other species to humans, are quite rare in the cat. Many of the diseases affecting cats that share common names with diseases of humans are not transferrable between species but are what we call species-specific. There are, however, a few infectious feline diseases that can affect people and, given the close proximity in which owners and their cats usually live, it is surprising that this crossover does not occur more often. In fact, the incidence of zoonoses is relatively small. Veterinarians, breeders, groomers, and handlers who work and live in close daily contact with cats have no higher incidence of illnesses or diseases that also occur in cats than the general population.

Rabies (see above) is the most dreaded zoonotic disease because it is deadly to humans. That is why, with the increased incidence of rabies among cats, feline rabies vaccinations are so important not only for the health of pet cats but for peace of mind of owners and the population in general.

External parasites (fleas, ticks, and so forth) and some fungal skin diseases such as ringworm can be transmitted from cats to humans. Cats can have ringworm with no overt symptoms. In general, good habits of hygiene (hand washing for humans, proper care and control for cats) will prevent these parasites and diseases from spreading. Proper medications, environmental control, and so forth, will rid both animals and humans of these diseases should they occur.

Although it occurs very rarely, the danger of human contamination with toxoplasmosis via cats (see above) has been receiving a great deal of publicity. People can become infected with *Toxoplasma gondii* by ingesting the tissue cysts or the sporulated oocysts. This can occur by handling or eating raw meat, or via contact with feline feces, contaminated soil, or litter containing the organisms. It is important to note that humans cannot acquire this infection through contact with the feces of any other animals (dogs, for example) except cats. The primary concern is that if a pregnant woman acquires a toxoplasmosis infection, the fetus may sustain lesions of the eyes and central nervous system. If the disease is found to be present in a pet cat, a pregnant woman should have an examination. Several simple recommendations can all but eliminate any risk of contamination: Pregnant women should not eat uncooked meat, should always wash their hands thoroughly after gardening, and should avoid all contact with cat feces and soiled litter. It bears repeating that the incidence of toxoplasmosis in humans is *extremely* low.

Diseases and Disorders of Cats: Symptoms, Diagnosis, Treatment, Prognosis

NOTE: CAPITALIZED WORDS WITH ENTRIES ARE CROSS-REFERENCED AND HAVE AN ENTRY OF THEIR OWN.

See Glossary 2 for definitions of various diagnostic tests/procedures referred to in this section.

A

ABSCESSES (CELLULITIS): Abscesses are the most common skin disorder seen in cats. Typically, they are swollen, red, painful masses and may be accompanied by loss of appetite and depression. They are often due to cat scratches and bites, and are therefore especially frequent among intact male cats. Abscesses first appear as large firm masses and later become swollen and contain copious amounts of purulent material (pus). They should be allowed to open and drain. Occasionally they must be lanced by a veterinarian if they are very painful or the swelling is especially large. Treatment with hot packs and appropriate antibiotics will usually clear up an abscess. An untreated abscess can become an emergency (see the Emergencies section). *See also* BACTERIAL SKIN DISEASES.

ACQUIRED HEART DISEASE: Acquired heart disease develops during the course of an animal's life. This is different from congenital diseases that are present at birth. The vast majority of cats affected with heart disease develop or acquire heart abnormalities as they get older even though they are not born with a heart problem. Acquired heart diseases may be due to abnormalities in the heart muscle (cardio–heart, myopathy–muscle), that is, CARDIOMYOPATHY or heart valves (valvular heart disease). Certain systemic or metabolic disease (thyroid gland tumors, infections, kidney failure, toxins, and so forth) can also secondarily affect the heart. *See also* CARDIAC DISEASE and METABOLIC HEART DISEASE.

ACUTE RENAL FAILURE (ARF): ARF can be the result of any disease or agent that abruptly results in kidney damage. UREMIA ultimately follows. Causes of ARF include toxins such as mercury, lead, arsenic, and ethylene glycol (antifreeze); solvents such as carbon tetrachloride; dehydration due to severe loss of body water from diarrhea, vomiting, or lack of adequate fluid intake; and infectious agents such as acute bacterial PYELONEPHRITIS. Clinical signs of ARF are similar to those of UREMIA but are very acute and abrupt in onset. Treatment consists of parenteral fluids, antibiotics, and supportive care. Prognosis for ARF is guarded; however, with prompt therapy a cat can recover. RENAL FAILURE can also become chronic.

AGALACTIA: Absence of milk after queening. *See* Chapter 5.

ALBUMINURIA: *See* PROTEINURIA.

ALLERGIC SKIN DISEASES: Allergic skin diseases in cats usually produce severe pruritis (itching). Among the allergic skin diseases to which cats are prone are:
Inhalant allergy (Atopy): This can be either seasonal or nonseasonal and is caused by inhaled allergens. It will produce excoriation (destruction and removal of the skin's surface) of the face, ears, neck, and limbs, MILIARY DERMATITIS, and small discrete focal scabs throughout the skin or ulcerated areas. It is diagnosed by skin testing and treated with systemic steroids and/or hyposensitization. The latter is a process in which the allergen(s) is/are incorporated into a vaccine.
Food allergy: Food allergies are recognized in the cat. They can occur at any time and are not necessarily associated with the introduction of a new food. They commonly produce pruritic lesions around the neck and facial area, and may or may not involve gastrointestinal signs. Diet testing is usually performed to determine the particular food to which the cat is allergic.
Drug allergy: Drug allergies are occasionally seen in cats and can mirror any kind of dermatosis. Treatment consists of determining and removing the cause.
Contact allergy/irritant: This is relatively uncommon in cats. When it does occur, a few of the possible causes are topical medications, cleansers, and prolonged contact with an irritant surface such as a carpet or rug. Treatment consists of local medication and removal of the cause.
Parasitic allergies: *See* MILIARY DERMATITIS.

ALOPECIA UNIVERSALIS: *See* CONGENITO-HEREDITARY SKIN DISORDERS.

AMYLOID GLOMERULONEPHRITIS (Amyloidosis): This is a RENAL (KIDNEY) DISEASE caused by the abnormal formation of amyloid, which deposits in the glomerulus after the normal filtration action of the kidneys and causes damage. All the glomeruli are involved in some cases, but amyloid also deposits around the tubules in other cases. (*See* RENAL DISEASES AND DISORDERS entry for definitions.) The cause of amyloid formation is unknown. The signs of this disease can be similar to those of GLOMERULONEPHRITIS (GN), but some cats develop only signs of UREMIA. There is no current treatment that is efficacious, and the prognosis is poor.

ANAL SAC (GLAND) IMPACTION: There are two sacs on either side of a cat's anus in which secretions accumulate. These secretions are usually released due to pressure when a cat defecates. Cats rarely have a problem with these glands, but occasionally they do not empty properly, become impacted with glandular material, and may become infected or form an abscess. Signs of a problem mimic those of tapeworm infestation (in INTESTINAL PARASITES), and a cat will lick its rectum excessively and drag its rear end on the floor. The gland should be expressed during routine examination. Treatment of an abscess consists of lancing the gland to remove the infected material, hot packs, and antibiotics.

ANEMIA: Anemia is a condition in which there are too few red blood cells present in a cat's bloodstream to carry enough oxygen throughout its body. It is characterized by shortness of breath, weakness, and lethargy. It may be caused by a number of factors, including severe infestation of INTESTINAL PARASITES or of external parasites, such as fleas, especially in young kittens. It can also be the result of a systemic disease. It is diagnosed by means of a blood test and is treated symptomatically.

ANTERIOR CHAMBER INFLAMMATION: The space between the cornea and lens of a cat's eye is called the anterior chamber. Many diseases that affect the cat's entire body (systemic diseases) can cause inflammation of the anterior chamber, which is normally filled with a very clear liquid. When there is inflammation, the anterior chamber becomes cloudy and hazy, sometimes contains flecks of white debris, and occasionally hemorrhages. Inflammation can be caused by a blow to the eye by something blunt as well as by infectious diseases such as FELINE LEUKEMIA VIRUS (FeLV), FELINE INFECTIOUS PERITONITIS (FIP), and TOXOPLASMOSIS.

Any clouding of the eye requires immediate veterinary attention. It can be difficult to determine the cause, and diagnosis may involve a variety of blood tests and examinations. If untreated, anterior chamber inflammation can lead to the development of CATARACTS, iris adhesions, and GLAUCOMA.

APLASTIC ANEMIA: This condition implies ANEMIA, and also that the bone marrow does not contain the elements needed to produce red blood cells. In the cat it can be seen in conjunction with generalized bone marrow suppression of all cell lines, or it may occur with a normal bone marrow ability to produce white blood cells and platelets. It may be seen in conjunction with FeLV, but it is also seen in cats in which there is no sign of FeLV. It can be caused by certain drugs and estrogens. Therapy is supportive and symptomatic, and includes blood transfusions or only red cell transfusions and attempts to stimulate normal bone marrow function with drugs.

ARTHRITIS: Inflammation of the joints. *See* CHRONIC PROGRESSIVE POLYARTHRITIS, DEGENERATIVE ARTHRITIS, IDIOPATHIC IMMUNE-MEDIATED ARTHRITIS, and SYSTEMIC LUPUS ERYTHEMATOSUS ARTHRITIS.

ASTHMA: *See* FELINE BRONCHIAL ASTHMA.

ATAXIA: This term means lack of coordination. Sensory ataxia is the inability of the body to sense position of its limbs in space. This position sense loss is termed a *conscious proprioception deficit.* Motor ataxia is seen with lesions in the cerebellum, vestibular apparatus, or spinal cord. Ataxia is clinically manifested by a tendency to cross the limbs so that they interfere with one another, to walk on the dorsal (top) surface of the paw, to abduct the limbs (move them away from the center of the body), and/or to appear hypermetric (an overmeasurement in the gait response, observed as greater movements of the limbs than normal). *See* BALANCE DISORDERS for methods of diagnosis and treatment of vestibular and cerebellar ataxia. Intervertebral disc disease (SPINAL CORD DISEASES) is an example of spinal motor ataxia.

AURAL DISEASES AND DISORDERS: Problems with cats' ears that involve the canal and pinnae are considered dermatologic conditions. Middle and inner ear problems that affect balance are considered NEUROLOGIC DISORDERS. Because cats' ears are always carried upright and are therefore open to air circula-

Illustration 18: The cat's ear

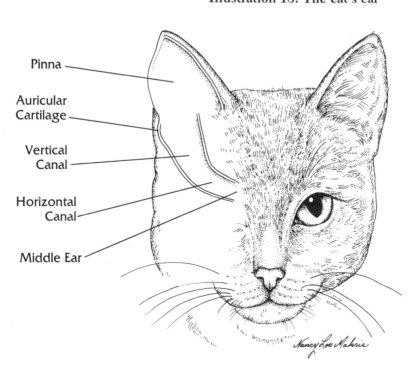

Pinna

Auricular Cartilage

Vertical Canal

Horizontal Canal

Middle Ear

tion, they are not as prone to bacterial and yeast infections as some dogs' ears are. Cats' ear canals are examined with an otoscope. The outer ear can be safely cleaned with a soft cloth or cotton swab, moistened with water or mineral oil. (*See* Illustration 18, page 179.)

PARASITIC SKIN DISEASES, EAR MITES, and other pruritic (itchy) dermatologic conditions often cause a cat's pinnae to become inflamed or abscessed due to constant scratching. *See also* FELINE SOLAR DERMATITIS, FROSTBITE, and SQUAMOUS CELL CARCINOMA.

AURAL HEMATOMA: Occasionally a cat may develop an aural hematoma (blood-filled swelling) on the pinna of an ear due to excessive scratching or irritation. Surgery to remove the clot and provide drainage is usually performed and the underlying cause corrected.

AUTOIMMUNE DISEASES: An autoimmune disease is one in which an animal's body is attacking itself in one of several ways. It may form antibodies against its own natural body components (autoimmune disease), or there may be a direct attack on the immune defense cells themselves (a classic example of this is rheumatoid arthritis, which occurs rarely in cats). The causes of autoimmune diseases are not known but are probably closely related to cancer in that there is a probable paradoxical failure of the body's immune system or a general imbalance in the immune defense system that has a basis in genetic, viral, or environmental influences, or a combination of any of these. These influences can bring about changes in the cellular components allowing the normally inhibited antibody formation to proceed at an enhanced rate and to make antibodies against its own cells—the body perceives its own cells to be foreign. Autoimmune diseases are diagnosed by the use of blood tests for specific antibodies and appropriate biopsy of affected organs. In general, autoimmune diseases are treatable and controllable but not curable. Feline autoimmune diseases include AUTOIMMUNE HEMOLYTIC ANEMIA, the PEMPHIGUS GROUP of skin disorders, rheumatoid arthritis, and SYSTEMIC LUPUS ERYTHEMATOSUS.

AUTOIMMUNE HEMOLYTIC ANEMIA: This disease, in which a cat's body destroys its own red blood cells, results in ANEMIA. It is an autoimmune phenomenon, the cause of which is unknown. It is sometimes seen in association with FELINE LEUKEMIA, but it may also develop in cats that have merely been exposed to the FELINE LEUKEMIA virus. A specialized blood test called the Coomb's test is used to diagnose autoimmune hemolytic anemia. While this test is not 100 percent accurate, a cat with a positive test result definitely has autoimmune hemolytic anemia. If a negative test result occurs, the cat may still have the disease, but other clinical signs will have to be used to support the diagnosis. As opposed to other types of anemia that progress slowly, autoimmune hemolytic anemia is of sudden onset and is characterized by listlessness, anorexia, pica (a cat with this disease may eat kitty litter), pale mucous membranes, and possibly jaundice (icterus). It is treated initially with cortisone. Blood transfusions may be necessary if a cat is not stabilized by cortisone therapy, but problems can arise because the disease may cause destruction of the transfused red blood cells. The prognosis varies: Some cats do well, others are subject to recurrent attacks, and still others do not respond well at all, especially those who are FeLV(+). Occasionally, a splenectomy is used to treat this disease.

AUTOIMMUNE SKIN DISEASES: Autoimmune diseases that affect a cat's skin include the PEMPHIGUS GROUP and SYSTEMIC LUPUS ERYTHEMATOSUS. Involvement may be widespread, involving the mucocutaneous areas (that is, mouth, anus), nail beds, and the skin. Treatment is aimed at managing the abnormal immune system.

B

BACTERIAL CYSTITIS: This bacterial infection of the urinary bladder frequently follows the FELINE UROLOGICAL SYNDROME (FUS). When bacterial cystitis occurs, it is almost always ascending from the lower urinary tract. Clinical signs include accidents in the house, straining to urinate, desire to go outdoors or to the litter tray often to urinate, and blood in the urine. The same clinical signs can occur when URO-LITHS are present. If stones have lodged in the urethra for one or two days, the symptoms may begin to include those of UREMIA. Treatment involves appropriate antibiotics as advised by the veterinarian. If treatment fails or cystitis returns, then further tests are ultimately performed. The prognosis for recovery from cystitis is good.

BACTERIAL SKIN DISEASES (PYODER-MAS): Feline bacterial skin disease (FOLLICU-LITIS or Feline Acne) is commonly seen on the chin and may be due to improper washing or, when it is the backs of kittens' necks that have become irritated, excessive licking or mouthing by the queen is the cause. Cleansing is usually both curative and preventive. Bacterial skin disease can also develop when the outer layer of the skin is broken due to a trauma, or wound, such as an animal bite or scratch that allows bacteria to enter, as in an ABSCESS or PYONYCHIA. There are several relatively rare feline bacterial skin diseases (such as actinomycosis, which affects the skin and bone, and nocardiosis, which affects the skin and lungs) that are produced by the invasion of the bacterial organism via a bite, scratch, or puncture wound. These diseases are characterized by abscesses and nodules that ulcerate and develop draining tracts usually on the limbs, ears, neck, abdomen, and tail. Treatment of these two diseases involves surgical removal and drug therapy with antibiotics. Other uncommon bacterial skin diseases can occur in cats.

BALANCE DISORDERS: The maintenance of balance and coordinated movement is mediated by a cat's central nervous system. Balance disorders are usually the result of VESTIBULAR and/or CEREBELLAR DISEASE. *Vestibular* refers to the part of the nervous system that orients most animals to their surroundings. The vestibular system maintains equilibrium by channeling information to the appropriate brain divisions, resulting in smoothly coordinated movement.

Information regarding head position is "sensed" by structures in the inner ear (vestibular system). This information is then conveyed by a nerve (vestibular/cochlear) to the brain, whereupon information regarding linear, angular, acceleratory and deacceleratory movement is relayed to other parts of the brain, resulting in balanced movement.

The coordination of movement occurs in the cerebellum. The cerebellum "smoothes out" movement. Thus, abnormalities of the cerebellum may evoke signs of lack of coordination, and disease of the vestibular system results in lack of balance.

Vestibular disease is very common. Signs include head tilts, falling, rolling, veering, stumbling, tripping, rapid eye movements, and disorientation. In addition, FACIAL PARALYSIS, uneven pupil size, unilateral head muscle atrophy, and weakness may be observed. Onset is usually sudden, and the earliest signs may be nausea and vomiting. When FACIAL PARALYSIS is present, drooling and apparent eating difficulty may also be observed. Diagnosis is by means of a neurological examination to determine where a disturbance has occurred along the complex interconnected pathway for balance or coordinated movement.

When the disturbance is outside the substance of the nervous system, it is called a *peripheral disturbance*. Peripheral disturbances most commonly seen in cats can be associated with an outer ear infection (*otitis externa*) or an inflammation of the inner or middle ear. Disturbances which are inside the substance of the nervous system (*central disturbances*) include infections, vascular insults (strokes), tumors, THIAMINE DEFICIENCY, and trauma. Treatment of a *central* process will include a complete neurological workup that may be preceded by a medicine trial. When the process is suspected to be *peripheral*, medication alone may be prescribed.

Prognosis for balance disorders varies. Most peripheral diseases improve progressively in anywhere from one to six weeks. In all neurologic diseases, *follow-up consultation with a veterinarian is extremely important. See also* ATAXIA.

BLADDER TUMORS: *See* UROGENITAL TU-MORS.

BLINDNESS: It is unusual for cats to totally lose their vision, but it can happen if there is a prolonged deficiency of taurine in a cat's diet. Such a deficiency can lead to retinal degeneration. Vision can also be lost if undiagnosed ANTERIOR CHAMBER INFLAMMATION has caused the development of CATARACTS or GLAUCOMA. Cats adjust to vision loss extremely well and often retain their ability to get around things and even jump in their own homes. In fact, cats adjust to blindness so well that it is possible for an owner not to have any idea his pet is blind unless the animal is taken into unfamiliar surroundings.

BONE TUMORS: *See* MUSCULOSKELETAL TUMORS.

BRONCHIAL DISEASE: Any cat with a persistent, chronic cough may have bronchial disease. The two major types of bronchial disease to which cats are subject are FELINE BRONCHIAL ASTHMA and FELINE BRONCHITIS. There is also a fairly rare form of *parasitic bronchial disease.* These three forms of bronchial disease can be diagnosed by means of bronchial cell samples.

BRONCHITIS: *See* FELINE BRONCHITIS.

C

CALICIVIRUS: *See* Infectious/Contagious Diseases.

CARDIAC ARRHYTHMIA: A cardiac arrhythmia is a disturbance of the heartbeat. It can occur during heart failure (due to acquired valvular disease, heart muscle disease, or congenital heart disease), or it can be the result of systemic and metabolic disease processes. Heartbeat irregularities are often detected in the course of a routine physical examination by a veterinarian, who will then usually perform an electrocardiogram (EKG). This will help evaluate the heart rhythm or help detect heart enlargement. Other tests, including a chest X ray and perhaps blood tests, will provide additional information about the cat's general health as well as better define the state of the heart. If specific diseases can be identified and treated, sometimes the arrhythmia will resolve. Some heartbeat irregularities cannot be traced to a specific causative factor. In addition, treatment may not always be necessary. It is important to maintain communication with the veterinarian so that appropriate medicines can be prescribed when indicated or changed when needed.

CARDIAC DISEASE: Once thought to be rare in cats, heart disease is now known to affect approximately 10 to 15 percent of the cat population. Although cats can be born with CONGENITAL HEART DISEASE, by far the greatest number afflicted with cardiac disease develop it after birth (ACQUIRED HEART DISEASE). Of these, heart muscle disease (CARDIOMYOPATHY) most frequently occurs. Very old cats can sometimes develop METABOLIC HEART DISEASE, which is brought about by an excess of the thyroid hormone or kidney failure.

Heart disease is often difficult for an owner to detect because cats may show no overt symptoms until the disease has progressed quite far. The first signs may be those of a generalized lethargy, depression, and loss of appetite. Because these symptoms can mimic those of numerous other diseases, it is often not until a cat develops rapid and labored breathing that heart disease is suspected.

Veterinary diagnosis of heart disease is based on a number of appropriate tests, including an electrocardiogram (EKG), chest X ray, nonselective angiogram, and sometimes an echocardiogram, an innovative form of testing that utilizes noninvasive sound waves to evaluate the heart's function and structure. All of these diagnostic tests are described in Glossary 2.

With early detection and treatment, the prognosis is good for many feline cardiac patients. In addition to treatment with appropriate medication, cats with severe heart disease should ideally be placed on low-salt diets. But because it can be very difficult for owners to get their cats to change diets, most veterinarians agree that this is not absolutely essential. Cats with heart disease should not be bred.

Left untreated, heart disease may eventually lead to CONGESTIVE HEART FAILURE. *See also* CARDIAC ARRHYTHMIA, DILATED (CONGESTIVE) CARDIOMYOPATHY, HYPERTROPHIC CARDIOMYOPATHY (HCM), RESTRICTIVE CARDIOMYOPATHY, and SEPTAL DEFECT.

CARDIOMYOPATHY: Cardiomyopathy represents the most common category of feline heart disorders. Cardiomyopathies are diseases in and of the heart muscle itself and do not primarily affect the heart valves or heart vessels. There are many forms of cardiomyopathy that range in severity and clinical manifestations.

Cardiomyopathy usually affects young to middle-aged male cats and is characterized by all the classic signs of CARDIAC DISEASE: lethargy, depression, and anorexia followed by breathing difficulty. Although a cure is not possible, early diagnosis and treatment may allow a cat to continue to lead a quality life.

Cardiomyopathies can be classified as follows:

Hypertrophic cardiomyopathy (HCM): In this situation the left ventricle becomes very thick and rigid. The heart, which has to maintain a certain degree of flexibility in order to expand (to receive blood) and contract (to eject blood), becomes too stiff to perform these functions. This can lead to pulmonary edema (fluid in the lungs) and CONGESTIVE HEART FAILURE. All breeds of cat can be affected, but there is some predilection among Persians. Early diagnosis and appropriate treatment with a diuretic (to get rid of excess lung fluid) and a medication to relax the ventricle usually allows a cat to lead a good quality life for up to two or three years.

Dilated (congestive) cardiomyopathy: When this disease occurs, all four heart chambers become very distended, flabby, and weak, and the heart's pumping action is reduced. Digitalis is given to help strengthen the pumping ability of the heart. Diuretics are added to rid the body of the excess fluid that occurs in CONGESTIVE HEART FAILURE. Only four or five years ago, the prognosis for cats with this disease was very grave. Great strides have been made in recent years, and many feline patients

with dilated (congestive) cardiomyopathy may survive happily for a period of time with medication. Early diagnosis and treatment is the key to success.

Restrictive cardiomyopathy: In this less common disease the heart muscle becomes covered with scar tissue, causing it to become stiff and unable to expand or contract adequately. Treatment must be individualized according to the extent and severity of cardiac disease. Usually, older cats are affected.

CATARACTS: Any opacification or clouding of the normally clear lens of the eye is called a cataract. Cataracts often result from debris in the anterior chamber of the eye caused by untreated inflammation. Although cataracts can be removed in cats, they usually occur in conjunction with another severe concurrent disease such as ANTERIOR CHAMBER INFLAMMATION. This concurrent disease often changes the eye so severely that cataract removal cannot improve the cat's vision.

CELLULITIS: *See* ABSCESSES.

CEREBELLAR DISEASE: *See* BALANCE DISORDERS.

CEREBELLAR HYPOPLASIA: *See* CONGENITAL NEUROLOGIC DISEASES.

CEREBRAL ISCHEMIC NECROSIS: *See* VASCULAR NEUROLOGIC DISEASES.

CERUMINOUS GLAND ADENOCARCINOMA (Ceruminous Gland Adenomas): This is a tumor that appears as large masses in the ear and ear canal, and may spread to adjacent lymph nodes. It is usually of sudden onset and is often mistaken for a severe ear infection. Surgical excision using a procedure called *ear ablation* is the therapy of choice. If a recurrence follows surgical ablation or if incomplete surgery is expected due to the size of the mass, radiation therapy is appropriate. Chemotherapy is of questionable value at the present, although some institutions are currently investigating its use in cases of ceruminous gland adenocarcinomas.

CHOLANGIOHEPATITIS: This inflammatory disease often begins in the bile ducts, gall bladder, and pancreas, and extends into the liver and liver cells themselves. The disease may progress from an acute cholangiohepatitis to chronic cholangiohepatitis and eventually to biliary cirrhosis. Very commonly, inflammation is found in the pancreas, duodenum (part of the small intestine), gall bladder, and liver at the same time. The etiology of this disease is unknown, but bacteria have been incriminated, and perpetuation of the inflammation is probably mediated by the immune system. Signs are those of classic LIVER DISEASE, including jaundice, and a diagnosis is based on laboratory tests and a liver biopsy. The prognosis depends on how far the disease has progressed when diagnosed. If cirrhosis has developed, the prognosis is very poor. As in any liver disease, there is no specific therapy. In the initial stages, intravenous fluids and antibiotics are given. In the chronic stages, corticosteroids may be added to the therapeutic regime.

CHRONIC INTERSTITIAL NEPHRITIS (CIN)—CHRONIC KIDNEY FAILURE: CIN is a condition in which chronic kidney disease has led to severely damaged kidneys, with the result that the normal nephrons are largely replaced by scar tissue. This is not a specific kidney disease but the end-stage of many different kidney diseases, including GLOMERULONEPHRITIS, HYDRONEPHROSIS, and PYELONEPHRITIS. Clinical signs are those of UREMIA, and treatment consists of supportive care.

CHRONIC PROGRESSIVE POLYARTHRITIS: This arthritic disease of cats produces multiple joint swelling and lameness. Two stages or forms of the disease are seen. The first is characterized by joint swelling with no radiographic evidence of joint erosion or destruction. The second form has severe erosion of the joint surfaces. Signs include a reluctance to walk, lameness, and swollen joints. This disease is associated with certain joint cells and the FELINE LEUKEMIA VIRUS (FeLV). The disease is currently not considered curable. It is treated supportively and with corticosteroids or other immunosuppressive drugs.

CLOUDING OF THE EYE: *See* ANTERIOR CHAMBER INFLAMMATION, CATARACTS, CORNEAL SEQUESTRUM, and GLAUCOMA.

COLITIS: Colitis is a general term meaning inflammation of the colon. Two types are commonly found in cats:
Chronic colitis: Chronic colitis is characterized by intermittent bloody, mucoid stools. It can be difficult to determine the cause of chronic colitis, and various therapies may bring only temporary relief. The cat can be treated for INTESTINAL PARASITES, dietary therapy may be used, and a number of different diagnostic tests can be performed, but the condition may return. For the most part, this is not a serious problem for a cat.
Ulcerative colitis: Ulcerative colitis can be seen, especially in Abyssinian cats, but is rare. This disease is characterized by anorexia and weight loss in addition to bloody, mucoid diarrhea. Although dietary therapy and anti-inflammatory medications are helpful in controlling the disease, it is usually chronic and requires lifelong medications.

COLOR CHANGES IN THE EYE: Blue-eyed cats such as albinos and Siamese (which are part albino) often have a reddish reflection in their eyes, causing their eyes to sometimes appear pink. This is simply a reflection from the back of the eye and is nothing to be concerned about. For other kinds of color changes see CORNEAL SEQUESTRUM and DIFFUSE IRIS MELANOMA.

COMA: *See* STATES OF CONSCIOUSNESS.

CONGENITAL HEART DISEASE: Only about 1 to 2 percent of cats with cardiac disease are born with heart defects or abnormalities. Kittens born with severely affected heart valves usually die within the first few months. Less severe congenital problems may not significantly alter a cat's natural life span. Congenital heart diseases are usually detected by a veterinarian during the kitten's first physical examination. Further tests can be performed to diagnose and evaluate the cause (see CARDIAC ARRHYTHMIA for these tests).

The one form of congenital heart disease that can be successfully treated surgically, *Patent ductus arteriosis* (PDA), is an uncommon problem.

The most common form of congenital heart disease in cats is a malformation of the atrioventricular valves. These valves normally separate the left atrium from the left ventricle and the right atrium from the right ventricle. When the valves do not meet properly due to congenital malformation, "leaky" valves result, allowing blood to flow in the wrong direction. This causes cardiac enlargement and, occasionally, CONGESTIVE HEART FAILURE.

Another form of congenital heart disease in cats is a septal defect, a hole in the septum (which divides the two sides of the heart). This hole allows the blood to flow in the wrong direction. The end result may be heart enlargement and eventually CONGESTIVE HEART FAILURE. If detected early, both of these conditions can sometimes be treated medically.

Genes for congenital heart disease can sometimes be passed along from one generation to the next, so cats with congenital heart disease should not be allowed to breed.

CONGENITAL NEUROLOGIC DISEASES:
Cats are subject to several congenital (present at birth) neurologic diseases. Among them are:

Cerebellar hypoplasia: Interuterine infection of a kitten fetus by the FELINE PANLEUKOPENIA (FPL) virus destroys the rapidly dividing cells of the external germinal layers of the cerebellum, which can result in cerebellar hypoplasia (atrophy). Affected kittens will have characteristic signs of cerebellar dysfunction including tremors and DYSMETRIA. These signs are seen as soon as a kitten starts to walk (at around four weeks of age). As the kitten grows and becomes more active, the signs become more obvious, but they are not progressive. Cats usually do not compensate for the problem, and therefore the signs will persist throughout an animal's life. Mildly affected cats may be perfectly functional as pets.

Lysosomal storage diseases: Lysosomes are cellular organelles that contain enzymes responsible for the breakdown of substances including protein, polysaccharides, and lipids. Congenital deficiencies of these enzymes can cause a buildup of these substances in the lysosomes, leading to the degeneration of cells. Affected kittens are normal until two weeks to three months of age, when tremors and DYSMETRIA develop. Neurologic dysfunction progresses to PARALYSIS, BLINDNESS, grand mal seizures (EPILEPSY), and death by one year of age in most cases. There is no treatment.

Spina bifida and associated spinal cord abnormalities: Spina bifida refers to a defective fusion of the vertebral bones so that the spinal cord is not completely encased by bone. The meninges and spinal cord may protrude. This condition is associated with a genetic defect in Manx cats, which are born without tails. Hind limb weakness and urinary incontinence are the most common neurologic signs. There is no treatment for cats affected with this abnormality.

CONGENITAL RENAL ABNORMALITIES:
In these conditions the kidneys fail to develop and mature normally, resulting in small kidneys in which normal tissue is replaced by scar tissue. There are several degrees of this failure to develop properly, including complete failure (renal aplasia) and partial failure (renal hypoplasia). The most common congenital renal abnormality in cats is hypoplasia, which usually involves only one kidney. Thus, clinical signs are often absent. Hypoplasia rarely involves both kidneys. The second most frequently occurring congenital renal abnormality in cats is polycystic renal disease. Signs include increased water intake and urine volume, and there is often a progression to depression, loss of appetite, vomiting, anemia, and other symptoms of UREMIA.

Therapy for congenital renal abnormalities is usually not needed since most cats have one normal kidney. The very rare cat with involvement of both kidneys requires treatment of uremic symptoms, general supportive care, and parenteral fluid therapy. These treatments are not curative, and most (but not all) cats with congenital renal abnormalities involving both kidneys die at an early age.

CONGENITOHEREDITARY SKIN DISORDERS: Congenital skin disorders are not common in cats, but they can occur. Two that are not confined to any particular breed of cats are *cutaneous asthenia* and *epitheliogenesis imperfecta*. There is nothing that can be done for either of these conditions.

Cutaneous asthenia, or "rubber kitten syndrome," is seen as abnormal fragility of the skin, resulting in constant lacerations and tearing from minimal trauma. It is due to a hereditary abnormality of the connective tissues of the skin.

Epitheliogenesis imperfecta is a congenital absence of the epidermis (outer layer of the skin) in various areas which may appear to be ulcerations.

Other congenital skin disorders that are hereditary in nature have no cures, and most commonly affect certain types of purebred cats are:

Alopecia universalis: This hereditary disorder affects cats selectively bred to produce the sphinx (Canadian hairless) cat. There will be little or no hair at all except for whiskers and short facial hairs, and the skin feels oily and has a rancid odor.

Hypotrichosis: Cats with this disorder are bald by six months of age and show histopathological evidence of poorly developed hair follicles. Mexican cats, Devon Rexes, and Siamese cats are subject to this disorder.

Oculocutaneous albinism ("Chediak Higashi"): Persian cats with yellow eyes and blue smoke haircoats are subject to this disorder which is characterized by a tendency to bleed spontaneously and an increased susceptibility to infection.

CONGESTIVE HEART FAILURE (CHF): This is the end result of untreated CARDIAC DISEASE (congenital, acquired valvular, cardiomyopathic, metabolic, and so forth) in which the heart is unable to satisfy the needs of the various tissues and organs because it cannot accept and/or pump an adequate supply of blood. The primary sign of congestive heart failure is severe breathing difficulty due to pulmonary edema (fluid in the lungs) or pleural effusion (fluid in the chest cavity). Occasionally, fluid can build up in the abdomen and cause abdominal swelling. CHF is a serious emergency, and a visit to the veterinarian should not be delayed. With prompt treatment the prognosis can be favorable.

CONJUNCTIVITIS: Conjunctivitis occurs when the mucous membrane next to the cornea (conjunctiva) becomes inflamed. The tissue will become very red, and there may be a lot of mucoid or purulent discharge from the eye. A cat will be uncomfortable and will often squint. Left untreated, conjunctivitis can affect the adjacent corneal tissue and, in severe cases, ulcers are formed (CORNEAL ULCERATION). Conjunctivitis is caused by a number of different infectious agents, among them calicivirus (see Infectious/Contagious Diseases), herpes virus, and mycoplasma and chlamydial organisms. It is frequently seen in very young kittens and is more apt to occur in situations where there is a lot of cat-to-cat contact, such as catteries, shelters, boarding kennels, and cat shows. Depending on the underlying cause, conjunctivitis is treated topically or with systemic antibiotics given orally. It will usually clear up with medication, but sometimes the underlying infection will remain in a cat's system, causing the conjunctivitis to recur or become chronic. Early diagnosis and treatment are beneficial.

CORNEAL SEQUESTRUM (Corneal Blackbody): A corneal sequestrum is a piece of dead corneal tissue that becomes enclosed within the live cornea. It characteristically appears as a dark brown stain on the normally clear cornea. It can be difficult to determine the cause, but any constant irritation to the cornea or lack of tears, resulting in chronic dryness of the cornea, can be factors in the formation of a sequestrum. Although sequestra interfere only slightly with vision, they can be very painful because the top layer of corneal tissue will not heal over them. They can be very difficult to heal and sometimes must be surgically removed.

CORNEAL TRAUMA: Corneal laceration, or trauma, is very common in cats. Cats that fight can sustain injuries to the surface of their eyes. Any eye injury requires immediate veterinary attention. If the wound is superficial, antibiotic treatment may allow proper healing, but many eye injuries require surgery in order to suture deep lacerations or puncture wounds. After surgery, the eye must be closely watched for infection. Without proper treatment, a cat may develop CORNEAL ULCERATION and lose an eye. With prompt veterinary attention the eye can often be saved, even when an injury is severe. *See also* the Emergencies section.

CORNEAL ULCERATION: A cat's eye can become ulcerated due to an untreated viral infection that affects the eyes or by CORNEAL TRAUMA. If the top layer of corneal cells is weakened or damaged, the eye can become infected. As bacteria grow they can enter the inner layer of the cornea and literally begin to eat it away. At the worst, more and more of the thickness of the cornea is lost, to the point that the innermost corneal layer is pushed outward by the normal pressure within the eye and appears as a small bubble on the eye's surface. This is a serious emergency that underlines the importance of having any eye injury seen by a veterinarian as soon as possible. Even the deepest ulcerations can frequently be helped with intensive medication or surgery.

CORONA VIRUSES: Corona viruses are a family of viruses classified by their appearance. They are present in all animal species in various forms (for example, they are responsible for certain kinds of respiratory problems in humans). There are several strains of corona virus in the cat, among which are FELINE INFECTIOUS PERITONITIS (FIP) virus (not highly contagious) and strains of feline enteric corona virus, which is easily spread among cats through feces. It may be asymptomatic in older kittens and adults, but causes diarrhea in young kittens (*see also* GASTROINTESTINAL DISEASES AND DISORDERS). One cat in a household may have FIP virus while others in the same house do not.

COXOFEMORAL LUXATION: Luxation, or dislocation of the coxofemoral joint (hip), is more common in cats over ten months to a year of age and is usually a result of trauma. Younger cats usually sustain a FRACTURE through the growth plate of the femur with the same type of trauma that causes dislocation in older animals. Diagnosis is based on orthopedic examination and confirmed by radiographs of the hip joint. Generally an attempt is made to correct the luxation by manipulation of the joint and limb under general anesthesia. Once the luxation is corrected, the leg is placed in a special bandage (Ehmer sling) for ten to fourteen days. Surgical correction is indicated when the luxation cannot be corrected with external manipulation, a fragment of bone is present within the hip joint, the conformation of the hip joint is poor, or ARTHRITIS was already present in the hip joint prior to injury.

CRANIAL CRUCIATE LIGAMENT RUPTURE: This uncommon orthopedic injury in the cat is usually the result of trauma. It may eventually lead to DEGENERATIVE ARTHRITIS of the stifle (knee) joint. The cranial cruciate ligament is a major ligament within the stifle joint, helping to stabilize the joint. Rupture of this ligament results in instability of the stifle joint. Injury to the cartilage within the stifle joint can occur secondarily from resultant instability. Clinical signs relate to pain in the knee joint with varying degrees of lameness. Diagnosis is based on orthopedic examination and occasionally radiographs. Treatment is generally limited to surgical stabilization of the knee joint. The prognosis depends on the age and activity level of the cat, success of the surgery, the degree of ARTHRITIS already present, and whether one or two knees are involved.

CROSSED EYES: Siamese cats are sometimes born with the hereditary abnormality of crossed eyes (esotropia). This does not seem to affect their vision much and usually is not a problem. Along with crossed eyes, many Siamese cats also have "jittery" eyes, or nystagmus, which is particularly noticeable when they are staring intently at something. Again, this does not present a problem and affects the acuity of the cat's vision only slightly.

CUTANEOUS ASTHENIA: *See* CONGENITO-HEREDITARY SKIN DISORDERS.

CYSTITIS: *See* BACTERIAL CYSTITIS.

D

DEAFNESS: Some white cats with blue eyes are born deaf. Hearing acuity can also sometimes diminish gradually as a cat ages. There is no clinical test for feline deafness, but owners may notice that an older cat is not as attentive as it formerly was or does not wake when a loud noise occurs. Cats usually compensate very well for loss of hearing by using their other senses.

DEGENERATIVE ARTHRITIS: This degeneration of cartilage in older cats is the result of the wear and tear that comes with aging. Fissures and erosions initially develop in the articular cartilage and lead to inflammation and associated joint pain. Degenerative arthritis also develops from a predisposing injury or disease such as an old traumatic injury to the joint, PATELLAR LUXATION, or a cruciate ligament tear. Clinical signs include pain with movement of the joint, lameness, mild to moderate joint swelling, stiffness, and joint crepitation (grating or crackling). Diagnosis is based on orthopedic examination and radiographs. Treatment is aimed at relieving pain with low doses of painkilling drugs. Since cats are very sensitive to these types of drugs, *only* a veterinarian should administer them. Infrequently, surgery is indicated, depending on the location of the arthritis and the number of joints involved.

DELAYED UNION AND NONUNION: Delayed union refers to a fracture that has not healed in the usual time expected for that particular type of fracture and age of the patient. Nonunion refers to a fracture in which all evidence of bone healing at the fracture site has stopped, and motion and instability are present at the fracture site.

The most common causes for delayed union and nonunion are inadequate immobilization of the fracture site for a sufficient period of time, inadequate alignment of the fracture ends, damage to the blood supply to the fracture site, and infection in the fracture site. Treatment of delayed union involves maintaining the existing fixation of the fracture site for an extended period of time until healing occurs or, if necessary, surgical intervention to stabilize and realign the fracture ends. Nonunions are treated surgically by applying rigid internal stabilization to the fracture site (that is, metal bone plates).

DEPRESSION: *See* STATES OF CONSCIOUSNESS.

DERMATOLOGIC DISEASES AND DISORDERS: Cats are subject to a number of skin diseases and disorders, and can suffer from almost all of the skin conditions that humans can, including cysts and tumors (*see* MAST CELL TUMORS, MELANOMA, SQUAMOUS CELL CARCINOMAS, for example).

Skin disorders in the cat can have many causative factors. They may develop because of bacterial, fungal, or viral invasion; they may be the result of poor nutrition or of environmental influences; or they can occur due to internal malfunctions or imbalances in a cat's own body, such as in AUTOIMMUNE SKIN DISEASES and HORMONAL SKIN DISEASES. External parasites and allergies can also cause skin problems, and they can be congenital and hereditary.

ALLERGIC SKIN DISEASES and PARASITIC SKIN DISEASES are characterized by extreme pruritus (itchiness), while many other types of skin disease are not. Skin diseases are often accompanied by alopecia (hair loss) and various kinds of sores and lesions.

Feline skin diseases are extremely difficult to diagnose because many conditions have similar clinical signs. Extensive testing, including skin scrapings, bacterial/fungal cultures, blood tests, and a complete medical workup to determine underlying factors are usually necessary. *See also* ABSCESSES, BACTERIAL SKIN DISEASES, CONGENITOHEREDITARY SKIN DISEASES, FELINE ENDOCRINE ALOPECIA, EOSINOPHILIC GRANULOMA COMPLEX, FELINE SOLAR DERMATITIS, FOLLICULITIS, FROSTBITE, FUNGAL SKIN

DISEASES, MILIARY DERMATITIS, NEURODERMATITIS, NUTRITIONAL SKIN DISEASES, PHYSIOCHEMICAL SKIN DISEASES, PYONYCHIA, STUD TAIL, and VIRUS-RELATED SKIN DISEASES.

DIABETES MELLITUS: This ENDOCRINE DISEASE results from a defect in the production or action of the hormone insulin, which is produced by the pancreas. Insulin facilitates the entry of blood glucose into tissue cells; therefore, if there is either a deficiency of insulin or a defect in insulin's actions, the glucose is unable to move into tissue cells and builds up in the bloodstream. When blood glucose levels rise to a certain point, the glucose begins to "spill" into the urine. At the same time, the body attempts to compensate for the lack of glucose-produced energy by utilizing stored fats and proteins.

In uncomplicated diabetes mellitus, cats are usually alert and may have the major symptoms of excessive hunger (polyphagia), increased thirst (POLYDIPSIA), and increased urination (POLYURIA). Although many cats with uncomplicated diabetes exhibit weight loss, others are obese and may actually gain weight. If uncomplicated diabetes mellitus is left untreated, strongly acidic ketone bodies may accumulate in the blood as a by-product of fat metabolism in the liver. The result is called ketoacidosis, which can produce extreme weakness, loss of appetite, vomiting, coma, and eventual death.

Very little is known about the causes of diabetes in cats. Feline juvenile-onset diabetes is rare. Most diabetic cats are middle to old aged, and some may have a type of diabetes similar to the mature-onset variety seen in humans. This subgroup of diabetic cats tends to be obese, nonketotic, and resistant to the glucose-lowering effects of insulin injections. Other cats may develop diabetes secondary to overproduction of cortisol or growth hormone, but these conditions appear to be rare in the cat. Administration of cortisone-like drugs or megestral acetate (Ovaban) can also induce diabetes in some cats. Overall, however, the underlying cause of the diabetes cannot be defined in the vast majority of cats.

Diabetes mellitus is diagnosed by finding elevated concentrations of glucose (with or without ketone bodies) in the blood and urine. Treatment differs according to the type of diabetes mellitus that is diagnosed but is designed to maintain ideal body weight and normal water consumption and urine output. Cats usually receive subcutaneous injections of insulin on either a once-daily or twice-daily schedule. Owners of diabetic cats must be willing and able to administer daily injections and carefully monitor their pets. The most common complication arising in insulin-treated diabetic cats is HYPOGLYCEMIA from insulin overdose.

DIARRHEA: *See* GASTROINTESTINAL DISEASES AND DISORDERS.

DIFFUSE IRIS MELANOMA: This is a slow-growing OCULAR TUMOR on the cat's iris. A cat's iris normally has a vertical slit or pupillary opening. If adhesions occur, the iris can appear to have a ragged border or can develop an abnormal position in the eye. The first signs of a diffuse iris melanoma usually do not occur until a cat is seven or eight years old. The normally golden-colored iris develops a brown coloration that gradually diffuses throughout the iris. In advanced cases there may be thickening of the iris. If left untreated, this condition can eventually lead to GLAUCOMA. In some older cats, this tumor has been known to spread to other parts of the body. The only treatment is surgical removal of the eye.

DILATED (CONGESTIVE) CARDIOMYOPATHY: *See* CARDIOMYOPATHY.

DYSMETRIA: This neurologic disorder is an inability to regulate the rate, range, and force of movement that causes the ataxic gait observed in cerebellar disease. Dysmetria usually appears as a *hypermetria,* or overmeasurement in the gait response, resulting in greater movement of the limbs than normal in all ranges of motion. This clinically resembles "goose stepping." *See also* ATAXIA and BALANCE DISORDERS.

DYSTOCIA: Difficult birth. *See* Chapter 5.

E

EAR DISEASES: *See* AURAL DISEASES AND DISORDERS.

EAR MITES *(Otodectes cyanotis):* Ear mites are very common in cats. They are very difficult to see with the naked eye but may appear as small white specks on a background of reddish-brown exudate in the ear canal opening. They cause severe itching, and the ear will often be irritated due to constant scratching. A cat with ear mites may also shake its head continually. Diagnosis is made by microscopic examination of material swabbed from the ear, which will reveal tiny white mites crawling in reddish-brown or blackish waste material. Treatment is with solutions applied in the ear two or three times a day for several weeks.

ECLAMPSIA (HYPOCALCEMIA): *See* Chapter 5.

ECTOPIC URETER: This is a birth defect in which the entrance to the ureter (which usually goes from the kidney to the bladder) is in an abnormal location, causing urine to flow into the urethra of males and females or into the vagina in the female instead of into the cat's bladder. Ectopic ureters can occur on one or both sides. Most cats affected by ectopic ureters have continuous URINARY INCONTINENCE. This condition can also be associated with HYDRONEPHROSIS and urinary tract infections. Treatment is surgical. The ureter is placed so that it enters the bladder normally, and the prognosis if fair to good in most cases.

ENDOCRINE DISEASES: Overall, endocrine disease is very rare in cats. The endocrine glands, located throughout a cat's body, are the manufacturers of hormones that, when released, travel in the bloodstream throughout the body to reach another gland or part of the body. These hormones, sometimes called the chemical messengers of the body, regulate body functions in numerous ways. Because there is a tremendous amount of interaction between hormones, it is often difficult to isolate the action of a particular hormone.

To summarize the cat's endocrine system *(see also* Table 7, opposite page):

The *thyroid gland,* adjacent to the cat's larynx (voice box), makes two main hormones, T4 and T3. The most common problem associated with the thyroid gland in cats is overproduction of the two thyroid hormones, resulting in HYPERTHYROIDISM. *(Hypothyroidism,* an underproduction of these hormones, is very rare in the cat.) HYPERTHYROIDISM is always due to a thyroid tumor, which is usually benign.

There are four *parathyroid glands* that lie in the soft tissue around the thyroid glands in a cat's neck and secrete the parathyroid hormone, important in the regulation of blood calcium. A deficiency of this hormone *(hypoparathyroidism)* causes the blood calcium to drop and results in a condition called *tetany* in which the muscles twitch and spasm in a way similar to an epileptic seizure. Although naturally occurring hypoparathyroidism is extremely rare in cats, *iatrogenic hypoparathyroidism* is relatively common after surgical removal of thyroid tumors for hyperthyroidism, since it can be difficult to identify and preserve the parathyroid glands during surgery.

Two *adrenal glands* are located at the front of each kidney. They are divided into two parts, similar to a plum or peach—the inner part corresponding to the pit and the outer to the flesh of the fruit. Each part makes different hormones. The outer part, *adrenal cortex,* manufactures cortisol/cortisone and aldosterone. The inner part, *adrenal medulla,* produces adrenaline, or epinephrine. Abnormalities or tumors of either the adrenal cortex or medulla are extremely rare in the cat.

The *pancreas* serves two distinct functions. One part of the pancreas is an endocrine gland, the other an exocrine gland that releases digestive enzymes into the small intestine to help in the absorption of food. The endocrine part of the pancreas makes many hormones, the most important of which is insulin. Not enough insulin will result in DIABETES MELLITUS. An overproduction of insulin results in signs of HYPOGLYCEMIA and can be caused by a tumor of the pancreas, but this condition is extremely uncommon in cats.

The *gonads* include the testicles in males and the ovaries in females. In the male, the testicles make testosterone, which is necessary for fertility. If there is a deficiency of testosterone, the sperm count decreases and the cat is no longer fertile. A deficiency of testosterone, produced by castration in the male, presents no clinical problems other than lack of fertility. The same holds true for female cats—a deficiency of estrogen or progesterone brought about by lack of production of the gonads or by surgical spaying simply prevents estrus, or a

TABLE 7

THE CAT'S ENDOCRINE SYSTEM

Endocrine Glands	Hormone(s)	Function
Pituitary	Adrenocorticotropic (ACTH)	Promotes growth and secretion of adrenal cortex
	Thyroid-stimulating (TSH)	Promotes growth and secretion of thyroid
	Follicle-stimulating (FSH)	Promotes growth of ovarian follicle (female) and spermatogenesis (male)
	Luteinizing (LH)	Promotes ovulation (female) and testosterone secretion (male)
	Prolactin	Promotes milk secretion from mammary glands
	Growth (GH)	Promotes growth in young cats; elevates blood glucose
Thyroid	Thyroxine (T4) Triiodothyronine (T3)	Increases metabolic rate; necessary for hair growth
Parathyroid	Parathyroid	Increases blood calcium
Adrenal cortex	Cortisol	Elevates blood sugar; increases protein and fat breakdown; necessary for stress
	Aldosterone	Controls sodium, chloride, and potassium balance
Adrenal medulla	Epinephrine (adrenaline)	Elevates blood glucose; increases blood pressure and cardiac output
Pancreas	Insulin	Promotes glucose transport from blood into cells
Gonads	Estrogens Progesterone	Necessary for fertility—females
	Testosterone	Necessary for fertility—males

heat cycle, and renders the animal sterile. Excesses of either testosterone or estrogen are very rare. In females an excess occasionally occurs due to a tumor of the ovaries.

The *pituitary gland*, located at the base of the brain, is known as the "master gland" because it controls and regulates the function of many of the other glands through the action of its six major types of hormones. Adrenocorticotrophic hormone (ACTH) is released from the pituitary and regulates the adrenal cortex which manufactures cortisol. Thyroid-stimu-

lating hormone (TSH) stimulates the thyroid gland to make T4 and T3. Growth hormone (GH) does just what it says—stimulates growth. A deficiency of this hormone in a young cat will result in dwarfism, which happens very rarely. A tumor of the GH-producing cells produces excessive circulating GH levels, resulting in a condition called acromegaly. Acromegaly, which appears to be relatively rare in cats, usually results in a type of DIABETES MELLITUS.

Other hormones secreted by the pituitary

TABLE 8

ENDOCRINE DISORDERS OF CATS

Endocrine Gland	Malfunction	Disorder(s) Caused
Pituitary	*Deficiency* of ACTH (rare in cats)	Addison's disease
	Excess of ACTH (rare in cats)	Cushing's syndrome
	Deficiency of TSH (rare in cats)	Hypothyroidism
	Deficiency of GH in young cats (rare)	Dwarfism
	Excess of GH	Acromegaly
Thyroid	*Deficiency* of T3 and T4 (very rare in cats)	Hypothyroidism
	Excess of T3 and T4	Hyperthyroidism
Parathyroid	*Deficiency* of parathyroid hormone	Hypoparathyroidism (Hypocalcemia)
	Excess of parathyroid hormone (rare in cats)	Hyperparathyroidism (Hypercalcemia)
Adrenal cortex	*Excess* of cortisol (rare in cats)	Cushing's syndrome
	Deficiency or cortisol and aldosterone (rare in cats)	Addison's disease
Adrenal medulla	*Excess* of adrenaline (very rare in cats)	Pheochromocytoma
Pancreas	*Deficiency* of insulin	Diabetes mellitus
	Excess of insulin	Hypoglycemia
Gonads	*Deficiency* of estrogen and progesterone in females; deficiency of testosterone in males	Infertility

gland are follicle-stimulating hormone (FSH) and luteinizing hormone (LH), both of which are important in stimulating ovaries and testicles. An excess or lack of these hormones is rarely found and does not appear to cause any clinical problems in the cat. The pituitary gland also secretes prolactin, which is very important in milk secretion in the lactating queen.

Basically, most overproduction of a hormone (called *hyper-*) is caused by a tumor or tumors of one of the endocrine glands. *Hypo-* describes an underproduction of a hormone and is usually of an unknown cause or idiopathic. Diagnosis of endocrine disease is made by means of a combination of clinical signs and blood tests (*see* Table 8, opposite page). *See also* DIABETES MELLITUS, HYPERTHYROIDISM and HYPOGLYCEMIA.

ENDOMETRITIS: The endometrium is the glandular, secretory portion of the uterus, and endometritis implies inflammation of the endometrium. Symptoms can be a vaginal discharge, fever, and signs similar to PYOMETRA, except that radiographically the uterus is not greatly enlarged. Treatment depends on severity and may include antibiotics and/or an ovariohysterectomy.

ENTERITIS: Inflammation of the small intestine. *See* EOSINOPHILIC ENTERITIS and PLASMACYTIC-LYMPHOCYTIC ENTERITIS.

EOSINOPHILIC ENTERITIS: This very poorly understood gastrointestinal syndrome in cats is characterized by vomiting and diarrhea which get progressively more severe, causing weight loss and anorexia. When an intestinal biopsy of a cat suffering from this disease is taken, it is found that the normal intestinal mucosa has been replaced by eosinophilis (a type of white blood cell). At this time it is not known why this occurs. Treatment with cortisone may abate the disease temporarily, but it is generally progressive and often fatal.

EOSINOPHILIC GRANULOMA COMPLEX: This is a group of related diseases that affect the skin and oral cavity of cats. The etiology of these diseases is unknown, but proposed causes include allergies, viruses, trauma, and bacteria. Attempts at identifying the underlying cause of these diseases should be made, and treatment will vary, according to the cause. Three types of lesions are recognized: the eosinophilic ulcer, eosinophilic plaque, and linear granuloma.

The eosinophilic ulcer: Lesions are well circumscribed, reddish-brown ulcers that glisten and are accompanied by alopecia (hair loss). They range from 2 × 5mm to 5 × 7mm (approximately ¼ × ½ inches to ½ × ¾ inches). There is no pain or itching associated with the lesion. Although these lesions can be located anywhere on a cat's body, the majority (80 percent) are on the upper lip and are known as "rodent ulcers." These rodent ulcers may become cancerous later in life.

The eosinophilic plaque: These are very similar to eosinophilic ulcers except that the lesions are redder and associated with intense pruritus. Most of the plaques occur on the abdomen and thighs. They may be seen in conjunction with allergies.

The linear granuloma: These are well circumscribed, raised, firm, yellowish linear lesions with hair loss, usually found on the back of the hind limbs and in the mouth. They are not painful and do not itch.

EPILEPSY (SEIZURE DISORDERS, ictus, "fit"): Seizures and seizure-like disorders are common entities in veterinary medicine. The term *seizure* refers to an involuntary paroxysmal disturbance in the normal function of the brain. Seizures may result from a variety of causes, including infections, vascular accidents (strokes), neoplasia, post-trauma, toxicity, and congenital diseases of the brain. In some instances, HYPOGLYCEMIA, LIVER DISEASE, and RENAL FAILURE may precipitate a seizure. A common seizure classification of young cats is termed *idiopathic*, since no other clinical signs are detected following a detailed neurologic evaluation.

A variety of seizure types exist. The most common is a generalized grand mal seizure which consists of an aura, prodome, ictus, post-ictus, and interictus. The aura is the time prior to the seizure during which the cat can sense its onset. Restlessness, anxiety, affectionate behavior, a "blank" expression, or other behavioral changes may be noticed by the owner. The prodome follows the aura as the cat becomes still and loses consciousness. During the ictal event, there is a sudden increase in muscle tone followed by rhythmic contractions. Stiffening and running movements of the legs, chomping, and facial twitching are often seen. Urination, defecation, hypersalivation, and eye pupil changes may also be present. This phase can last from thirty seconds to three minutes but often seems longer to an apprehensive owner! During the postictal period that follows the event, a cat may exhibit blindness, ATAXIA, confusion, depression, and fatigue, or any other kind of behavioral change. This phase can last minutes, hours, or days. It is important to note that the length of the ictus and postictus do not necessarily have a relationship to the severity of the seizure. In the interictal period that follows, the cat is normal. If there is a persistent behavioral change, gait disturbance, or visual problems, the veterinarian will be alerted to a nonidiopathic cause.

Partial or focal seizures may occur independently from or concurrently with grand mal seizures. Partial seizures are usually very short (five to fifteen seconds) but will often occur more frequently than grand mal seizures (two to twenty in an hour).

First steps in diagnosis consist of a thorough history and routine physical examination of the cat, and neurologic examination to attempt to localize and characterize the problem. The decision as to when neurodiagnostic tests should be performed varies depending on history and clinical findings.

Symptomatic therapy with anticonvulsants is frequently prescribed on a trial basis, as medications, dosages, and routes of administration are dependent on the individual cat's needs and may suddenly change. An owner must work closely with the veterinarian by observing the pet carefully and keeping a log of each seizure event. Two *emergency* situations may occur in regard to seizures: prolonged *status-epilepticus* and *sequence clustering*. See the Emergencies section for how to proceed should these events occur.

EPITHELIOGENESIS IMPERFECTA: *See* CONGENITOHEREDITARY SKIN DISORDERS.

ESOPHAGEAL DISEASE: Esophageal disease is rare in cats. Very occasionally, congenital anomalies occur, such as persistent right aortic arch. Inflammation of a cat's esophagus can result from swallowing something too large or from a reflux of stomach acid up into the esophagus, which burns it. We often see cats with esophageal irritation that is caused by too-large vitamin C tablets becoming stuck in the cat's throat and scalding it. In addition to esophageal disease, regurgitation can be caused by thoracic (chest) disease, such as LYMPHOSARCOMA in which a chest tumor becomes large enough to press on the esophagus. Primary esophageal tumors are rare in cats. Megaesophagus is also rare in cats. It is characterized by a large dilated esophagus with no motility. It is thought to be a neuromuscular disease.

F

FACIAL PARALYSIS: Diseases that interfere with the facial nerves produce a change in the cat's facial expression, such as an asymetrical drooping of the ears or lips and an inability to blink an eye on the affected side. Facial nerve paralysis can be caused by infection, trauma, and neoplasia. A middle-ear infection, the most common cause of this problem, may be accompanied by vestibular (inner ear) signs. The neuroanatomical cause of facial paralysis is ascertained by a complete neurologic examination and/or selected neurodiagnostics.

FELINE BRONCHIAL ASTHMA: This is possibly an allergic phenomenon. It occurs episodically, just as it does in humans, when the airways spasm, creating breathing difficulty. Signs of bronchial asthma are wheezing and coughing. Although the majority of cases are not emergencies and can be treated medically, an asthma attack *can* be an emergency requiring immediate veterinary attention. Diagnosis is made by means of chest X rays, blood tests, and possibly a sampling of lung cells, a procedure not done at all hospitals. Asthma can be *controlled but never cured*, as it is a state of oversensitivity of the airways.

FELINE BRONCHITIS: This infection and/or irritation of the airways causes occlusion. The result is coughing and wheezing, which can become chronic. Diagnosis is made through a sampling of secretions and possibly a chest X ray. Once the organisms causing bronchitis have been isolated, the disease can be treated with appropriate antibiotics. Cats will improve but may always have a little cough, and will be more susceptible to future bronchial infections.

FELINE ENDOCRINE ALOPECIA: *See* HORMONAL SKIN DISEASES.

FELINE ENTERIC CORONA VIRUS: *See* CORONA VIRUSES.

FELINE INFECTIOUS PERITONITIS (FIP): *See* Infectious/Contagious Diseases.

FELINE LEUKEMIA: Leukemia is an entity of malignant blood cells that is found by diagnosis in the peripheral blood and bone marrow. Although most forms of feline leukemia are caused by the FELINE LEUKEMIA VIRUS (FeLV), every cat with FeLV does *not* have feline leukemia.

There are many types of acute leukemia seen in the cat: lymphoid leukemia, nonlymphoid leukemia such as myeloid leukemia, erythroid leukemia, stem cell leukemia, and combinations called *erythremic myelosis* or *erythroleukemia*. Certain chronic forms of leukemia such as chronic lymphocytic leukemia also exist in the cat. Signs of the disease are nonspecific and include general malaise, loss of appetite and weight, and chronic diarrhea. Diagnosis is made by the use of blood tests and subsequently confirmed by bone marrow samples.

The long-term prognosis for cats with acute leukemia caused by FeLV is poor. Chemotherapy is the treatment of choice and is offered to owners who wish to pursue it, but we do not recommend it because other complications of the virus make therapy for a cat with true leukemia very difficult, requiring much supportive blood care and exorbitant expense in the face of a very poor short- and long-term prognosis. Currently, experimental and investigative therapies are being studied in the hopes of offering better treatment in the future for cats with leukemia.

FELINE LEUKEMIA VIRUS (FeLV): The feline leukemia virus was discovered in 1964 and is still under study. It can cause certain types of cancer, including FELINE LEUKEMIA and LYMPHOSARCOMA. FeLV infection does not always cause cancer in cats, but it often makes a cat more susceptible to other infectious diseases by depressing the animal's immune system and decreasing its resistance to disease-causing organisms. Cats with FeLV often have reproductive problems such as abortions, fetal reabsorptions, and the birth of weak, short-lived kittens. When apparently healthy kittens are born to a FeLV-infected queen, they may carry the FeLV infection at birth. FeLV can interfere with the body's immune system and also cause noncancerous blood and bone marrow disorders, such as ANEMIA, leukopenia (low white blood cells), and/or thrombocytopenia (low blood platelets).

The feline leukemia virus is transmitted primarily by direct, prolonged contact between infected and noninfected cats when the virus is shed in the saliva, urine, feces, and milk. Because the virus is short-lived outside a cat's body and is easily destroyed by most disinfectants, the incidence of FeLV and its related diseases is directly related to the density of the cat population and the degree of contact between cats.

This is why testing of all cats in a household is recommended and absolutely necessary if one cat in a household tests positive for FeLV, and this is why we recommend that all indoor/outdoor cats be tested periodically for the disease. If a cat is adopted into a cat-owning household, both the new and existing pets should be tested. It is also extremely important for an owner to make sure that any contemplated boarding facility have a strict FeLV testing policy. Kittens under six months of age and sick or elderly cats are more susceptible to FeLV than healthy adult animals.

Depending on these factors and on the degree of exposure, several things may happen when a noninfected cat is exposed to FeLV. It may not become infected at all or may develop an immunity to the disease. It may become infected but not ill, continuing to carry the virus. Such cats are called asymptomatic carriers. Last, a cat may become infected and develop LYMPHOSARCOMA or one of the other FeLV-related diseases after several weeks or even years.

FeLV is diagnosed by means of specific blood tests, which indicate whether or not the disease-causing agent is in a cat's bloodstream. There are two laboratory tests used to diagnose the presence of FeLV, an immunofluorescent antibody test (IFA test), or "Hardy test," and an enzyme-linked immunosorbent assay test (ELISA test), or "Kit test." These tests do not evaluate the presence of the diseases that may be caused by the FeLV virus. A positive test result indicates only that a cat is carrying the feline leukemia virus at the time that the test is performed. It does not indicate whether or not a cat has cancer, nor does it preclude the possibility that the cat may develop an immunity to the disease or develop a FeLV-related disease at some future time. If a cat is sick, other tests will be required for diagnosis of a specific disease. A negative test, on the other hand, means only that a cat has no detectable virus in its blood at the time the blood sample is taken. A cat can be in the early stages of infection, however. A negative FeLV test does not necessarily mean that a cat does not have LYMPHOSARCOMA, as between 10 and 30 percent of cats with LYMPHOSARCOMA test negative for FeLV.

We recommend that all cats who test positive for FeLV be isolated from FeLV(−) cats, that is, be kept in a separate room with separate litter pan and food and water dishes, and retested in six to twelve weeks. If the second test is positive, the cat should then have fur-

ther tests to determine what, if any, FeLV-related diseases are present. Periodic testing is recommended, even if the second test is negative.

There are several factors that owners of healthy FeLV(+) cats and their veterinarians must take into account before deciding on a course of action. If an only cat can be kept isolated from other cats, an owner may opt to keep it but must bear in mind the possibility that the pet may develop an FeLV-related disease. If there are several cats in a household, they should all be tested, and those that are FeLV(−) protected from exposure. In this circumstance, periodic testing of all of the cats is necessary in order to determine any change in their status. FeLV(+) cats should not be bred under any circumstances.

FeLV is *not* transmitted by people on clothing, hands, and so forth. Only prolonged, direct cat-to-cat contact can transmit the disease.

If a cat dies of an FeLV-related disease or if a FeLV(+) cat has lived in a household, precautions are necessary before acquiring a new cat. The entire house should be disinfected thoroughly, and at least thirty days should elapse before bringing a new cat into the household. As an added safety measure, it is a good idea to have the new cat tested for FeLV on a regular basis.

A new vaccine to protect cats against FeLV has now been developed—*see* Chapter 3 for details. *See also* FELINE LEUKEMIA, FELINE INFECTIOUS PERITONITIS, LYMPHOSARCOMA, and ONCOLOGY.

FELINE PANLEUKOPENIA: *See* Infectious/Contagious Diseases.

FELINE SOLAR DERMATITIS: This condition occurs when a white cat or one with white ears is exposed to too much sunlight for too long. A lack of protective melanin (pigment) in the skin has been proposed as a mechanism. In all-white or light-colored cats it may also affect the eyelids, nose, and lips. The skin will become red (sunburned) and eventually may ulcerate. In time it can develop into cancer—*see* SQUAMOUS CELL CARCINOMA.

FELINE UROLOGIC SYNDROME (FUS): This is the most common urinary tract problem of cats. Clinical symptoms usually include straining to urinate (STRANGURIA) and frequency of urination (POLLAKIURIA), which can progress to HEMATURIA. Cats often lick at their genital region and may urinate in odd places outside the litter pan. If obstruction of the urethra occurs, clinical symptoms include vomiting, loss of appetite, and depression. Obstruction is more common in male cats than in females. Cats of all ages can be affected, but the largest number are between one and ten years of age. All species of cats are affected.

The cause of FUS in unknown. Several factors are currently considered to be particularly important:

1) *Diet:* Dietary magnesium (a part of "ash" in the diet) has been found to induce the syndrome experimentally. The ratio of calcium to phosphorus (the other major components of "ash") is not as important but should be in the proper ratio (*see* Chapter 3). A diet containing less than 0.1 percent magnesium, 0.8 percent calcium, and 0.6 percent phosphorus (dry matter basis) is reported *not* to induce FUS. Most cat food manufacturers only report the "ash" content of their diets. Thus, the magnesium content could be too high even if the total "ash" content is low. The diets that are currently considered to be efficacious in preventing FUS and have recommended amounts of magnesium, calcium, and phosphorus are: Feline c/d (dry or wet), Feline s/d (dry or wet), Friskies Beef and Liver Buffet, and Friskies Turkey and Giblets (*see* Chapter 3). It should be emphasized that most other commercially available foods do *not* contain the amount of magnesium required to experimentally produce FUS. However, some commercial cat foods are just below these concentrations. Currently, dry cat foods other than those named above and semimoist cat foods listing more than 5 percent ash should be avoided if a cat has had FUS. This will lower the total amount of magnesium ingested each day. Canned cat foods other than those listed above should be used with caution if a cat has had FUS, since the content of magnesium may be high, even in diets listing less than 5 percent ash.

2) *Urine acidity* has been found to be important in FUS. An alkaline urine promotes the precipitation of struvite crystals in cat urine. After a cat ingests a meal, the urine becomes more alkaline, which may influence FUS. It is currently recommended that cats that have had FUS should receive urine acidifiers to prevent this postingestion alkaline urine. The two found to be efficacious are ammonium chloride powder and DL-methionine.

Other less important factors that only vaguely influence FUS negatively include obesity and inactivity for prolonged periods.

Once FUS has occurred, the veterinarian will determine whether or not obstruction has developed. If so, treatment in the hospital usually proceeds with relief of the obstruction, parenteral fluids, antibiotics, and general supportive care. If an obstruction has not occurred, treatment at home is possible and will be determined by the veterinarian. The prognosis for FUS is generally favorable.

FLEAS: *See* PARASITIC SKIN DISEASES.

FOLLICULITIS (Feline Acne): This condition is characterized by pimples or bumps on cats' chins. It may be due to improper washing or to a contact dermatitis. Proper cleansing of the skin is both preventive and curative.

FRACTURES: A fracture is a complete or incomplete break in the continuity of bone. A fracture is most commonly caused by a traumatic injury such as a fall or car accident. Infrequently, a fracture can result from a disease that causes destruction or weakening of bone, such as a bone tumor or a nutritional disease affecting the bones (*see* MUSCULOSKELETAL DISEASES and NUTRITIONAL HYPERPARATHYROIDISM). There are a number of different types of fractures:

Closed fracture: The fracture does not communicate to the outside environment. In other words, the skin is intact.

Open, or compound, fracture: The fracture site communicates to the outside environment. These fractures can be contaminated or infected, which may complicate healing.

Green-stick fracture: One side of the bone is

broken and the other is bent. This type of fracture is usually seen in young cats.

Comminuted fracture: Splintering or fragmentation of the bone is present.

Avulsion fracture: A fragment of bone that is normally at the site of insertion of a muscle or tendon is detached following an abnormal, forceful pull.

Physeal fracture: The fracture occurs through the growth plate in a young cat.

Clinical signs of a fracture may include pain or localized tenderness, local swelling, crepitus (crackling or grating) at the fracture site, inability to use a limb, and deformity of the limb. X rays are necessary to determine the type of fracture and its precise location. Treatment of a fracture should first be directed at possible injury to other parts of a cat's body, such as abdominal or chest injuries. Fracture repair is divided into conservative management, using casts or splints, and surgical repair, utilizing metal plates, pins, or wires. The location and type of fracture, degree of instability, age of the cat, and economic limitations of the owner will dictate the type of repair used. Prognosis depends on the type of fracture, associated joint injury incurred, whether the fracture is initially contaminated or infected, and whether or not the optimum means of repair was utilized based on the type of fracture and assessment of the patient. *See also* DELAYED UNION AND NONUNION. (*See* the Emergencies section for handling of a cat with a suspected fracture.)

FROSTBITE: Frostbite of the ears and other parts of the body is rare in healthy cats but may occasionally occur in outdoor cats during very cold weather. Cats' ear tips are particularly susceptible to frostbite because their hair covering is light and they are fully exposed. Toes, tail, and scrotum can also be frostbitten. Affected areas will be pale, then red and swollen, and should be bathed with warm water. Frostbitten ears will develop scaly alopecia, necrotic (dead skin) areas, and the skin may become leathery and slough off. After frostbite, there may be temporary or permanent leukotrichia (white hair), alopecia (hair loss), and scaling.

FUNGAL SKIN DISEASES (Mycoses): The most common fungal disease of cats is *superficial mycosis,* or ringworm. The fungus is contracted from the soil or other animals and is highly contagious by direct and indirect contact (for example, the hairs are infective), and the incubation period can range from four days to four weeks. Predisposing factors to infection with ringworm are immaturity, malnutrition, immunosuppression/immunodeficiency, a hot and moist climate, and poor environmental conditions.

There are no typical lesions for ringworm in cats, and the disease may manifest itself in a variety of clinical signs: hair loss, stubbled hair, abnormal redness of the skin (erythema), itching, excoriation (destruction and removal of the skin surface), raised spots on the skin, pus-filled blisters (pustules), bumps, draining tracts, dry skin, abnormal nails, and others. Diagnosis is made by ultraviolet light examination, culture, microscopic examination, and possibly biopsy. Treatment consists of oral and topical medications plus environmental cleansing. Longhaired cats may have to be shaved. Cats may carry ringworm fungus without symptoms and can therefore act as a source of infection to other pets and people.

Intermediate mycoses: There are several types of intermediate fungal infections. Sporotrichosis is an uncommon fungus skin infection caused by an organism (*Sporothrix schenckii*) found in soil, plants, water, and the gastrointestinal tract and tracheobronchial tree of rats and humans. Cats pick up this organism via wound contamination, and it is not contagious. It appears as nodules, swollen lymph nodes, draining tracts, and respiratory infection. Diagnosis is made by microscopic evaluation, culture, and occasionally by biopsy. The treatment of choice is sodium iodide.

Deep mycoses: These are primarily diseases of the respiratory tract, but they may also cause some dermatologic signs such as abscesses and fistulas (draining tracts). Diagnosis is by culture, antibody titers, and other tests. Treatment includes combined topical and chemotherapeutic techniques. Examples of deep mycoses are blastomycosis, coccidioidomycosis, cryptococcosis, and histoplasmosis.

G

GASTRITIS: This is a nonspecific term meaning inflammation of the stomach. It results from a cat ingesting something caustic or toxic. *See* GASTROINTESTINAL DISEASES AND DISORDERS.

GASTROINTESTINAL (GI) DISEASES AND DISORDERS: Gastrointestinal problems in cats are not well understood and can be difficult to diagnose. Because of the tendency of cats to compensate well for illnesses, early subtle changes are sometimes not noticed, and a veterinarian often does not see a cat until a disease has progressed quite far. In general, GI disorders in cats can have a number of different origins. In young kittens, especially, they can be caused by an infectious disease such as FELINE PANLEUKOPENIA or FELINE ENTERIC CORONA VIRUS. In cats of any age they can be due to a systemic disease such as FELINE INFECTIOUS PERITONITIS (FIP), FELINE LEUKEMIA VIRUS (FeLV)-related diseases, kidney disease, and so forth. GI symptoms also frequently develop in cats of all ages when they have swallowed a foreign object or toxic substance, or are suffering from hairballs. INTESTINAL PARASITES also usually cause gastrointestinal symptoms.

When a cat has either diarrhea or is vomiting, it is important to differentiate between an acute and a chronic condition; *and* if it is a chronic condition, it is important to determine whether or not it is accompanied by anorexia, weight loss, and lethargy. In order to aid in the diagnosis, a veterinarian will also want to know the frequency of occurrence and the type, color, and other characteristics of the vomitus or stools.

A cat with GI problems is usually given a complete examination (including a thorough under-the-tongue search—*see* acute vomiting below) and diagnostic tests such as an abdominal X ray immediately. When a cat has diarrhea or is vomiting, there are several reasons why we do not generally wait to see what will happen, as we may do with a dog. In the first place, cats are not apt to eat garbage or rotten food that would cause gastrointestinal upsets, so we must look for other sources of the problem. In addition, cats are relatively small and can become dehydrated quickly and, as we mentioned above, by the time a cat is suspected of having a problem it may have progressed quite far.

In young kittens, infectious viral diseases are the most common causes of vomiting and/or diarrhea. If these symptoms are accompanied by fever, FELINE PANLEUKOPENIA must be suspected. Milder cases of gastrointestinal upset may be due to FELINE ENTERIC CORONA VIRUS. Both of these diseases are described in the section on Infectious/Contagious Diseases. Kittens are also particularly susceptible to INTESTINAL PARASITES.

Vomiting: Vomiting in cats can be either acute or chronic.

Chronic vomiting can be due to a number of reasons. Chronic inflammatory gastric diseases can cause frequent vomiting, but they are poorly documented. One of the most common causes of chronic vomiting among cats is a tumor of the intestinal tract, especially LYMPHOSARCOMA which infiltrates into the stomach or intestine, replacing the normal intestinal cells with cancer cells.

There is a special type of chronic vomiting that occurs in older cats; they may vomit multiple times in a week, sometimes every day, yet continue to eat, do not lose weight, and generally flourish. The etiology of this type of vomiting is unknown, and in general nothing is done about it as long as the cat continues to thrive. If necessary, motility-modifying medications can be given.

Acute vomiting is most often caused by hairballs, the most common problem that all cats have regardless of haircoat length. An owner might think that a cat with hairballs has a respiratory problem because of the hacking cough, wheezing, gagging, choking, and sometimes moaning that usually precedes spitting up. Despite the violent symptoms that often accompany hairball vomiting, this is not a serious problem and can usually be controlled with lubricants (*see* the Appendix).

The other frequent cause of acute vomiting in cats is the swallowing of foreign objects, especially a long string or thread. The problem can be compounded if there is a needle on the end of the thread. One end of the string or thread usually becomes wrapped around the base of a cat's tongue, and then the free end passes down into the animal's digestive tract. The intestines and stomach will accordianate to clear out the string, causing it to act as a saw that can severely damage the cat's intestines. Cat owners should always be conscious of their pets' natural curiosity and playfulness, and keep all strings and threads out of reach. If a cat is given a toy on a string to play with, the string must always be securely tied to a solid object so that it cannot come loose and be swallowed.

Cats' innate curiosity and tendency to play with everything can cause them to swallow objects of all sorts, from pins and paper clips to twist-ties, tinsel, and small plastic bags. They may also ingest houseplant leaves, which can cause a mild stomach irritation. Some houseplants contain substances in their leaves, berries, or sap that are mildly toxic to cats. If a sufficient amount of these toxins is ingested, it can cause GASTRITIS. Owners should be aware of this, and try to train their cats not to chew houseplants (see Chapter 8) or else put the plants out of reach.

Some cats with especially huge appetites or those that have a favorite food will regularly eat their food so quickly that they immediately regurgitate it. This is not a serious problem, but an owner who becomes aware of it can help by feeding the cat more frequently with small portions of food.

Acute vomiting can also be a sign of PANCREATIC DISEASE.

Diarrhea: Diarrhea in cats is usually chronic rather than acute. It is important in the diagnosis of diarrhea to ascertain whether it is coming from the small or large intestine. If it is from the large intestine, it is characterized by an increased frequency of stools that may be full of blood and mucus and accompanied by straining. If it originates in the small intestine, there is a large volume of watery stool, but the frequency is usually not increased.

INTESTINAL PARASITES are the most common cause of diarrhea in kittens. Included among multiple other causes of chronic diarrhea in cats are a number of nonspecific inflammatory diseases of the gastrointestinal tract. As in vomiting, LYMPHOSARCOMA that has infiltrated into the intestinal tract will cause chronic diarrhea and weight loss. Chronic diarrhea is also a common symptom of HYPERTHYROIDISM in cats, especially if it is accompanied by weight loss in the face of an increased appetite. Bacterial infections such as salmonella and campylobacter can cause diarrhea, but they are rare in cats.

Little is known about the role that diet plays in diarrhea with cats, but experience has shown that sometimes in young cats it can be controlled with diet. Essentially, dietary therapy is performed on a trial-and-error basis to ascertain if there are certain ingredients or additives in some foods that might cause the problem. We also know that oversupplementation with certain minerals can create diarrhea in cats. *See also* ANAL SAC (GLAND) IMPACTION, CHOLANGIOHEPATITIS, COLITIS, EOSINOPHILIC ENTERITIS, ESOPHAGEAL DISEASE, GASTRITIS, HEPATIC LIPIDOSIS, LIVER DISEASE, PANCREATIC DISEASE, and PLASMACYTIC-LYMPHOCYTIC ENTERITIS.

GLAUCOMA: Glaucoma is a general term that refers to increased pressure within the eye. It can occur when the fluid (aqueous humor) that is constantly manufactured, circulated through the eye, and drained out fails to drain properly due to scarring, inflammation, or stoppage in the drainage area. This area, known as the iridocorneal angle, extends 360 degrees around the circumference of the eye.

In the cat, glaucoma is often secondary to ANTERIOR CHAMBER INFLAMMATION and is the result of debris clogging the iridocorneal drainage angle. If the pressure in the eye is not relieved, permanent damage is done to the optic nerve and vision can be diminished or lost completely. Signs of glaucoma are discomfort, squinting, red eyes, and dilation and clouding of the pupil. Cats often will not show their discomfort, so clouding or dilation of the pupil may be the first signs noticed by an owner. Sometimes the pressure can be reduced before damage is done to the optic nerve if treatment is started early enough. Despite prompt and intense treatment, however, many eyes with glaucoma become blind.

GLOMERULONEPHRITIS (GN): This kidney disease damages the glomerulus. The glomerulus supplies blood to the tubule that composes the rest of the nephron (*see* RENAL DISEASES AND DISORDERS for definitions of parts of the kidneys). Damage to the glomerulus ultimately leads to damage to the tubule and to the entire nephron. GN affects virtually all of the glomeruli and involves both kidneys. The cause of GN is not clear, but it is related to exposure to an antigen that is foreign to the body and that causes the body's immune system to produce an antibody. In GN, the antibody and antigen combine to form soluble complexes that circulate in the blood and damage the kidneys when they are filtered by the glomeruli. If there is an ongoing exposure to the antigen and antibody production continues, GN persists and worsens until severe kidney damage occurs. If the production of the antibodies ceases because the exposure to the antigen stops, GN can stabilize or resolve. The antigens that cause GN are rarely identified. When they are identified, they are systemic disease states such as LYMPHOSARCOMA and cannot be removed.

Clinical symptoms of GN may include fluid in the body tissues (edema) and body cavities. This is the result of glomerular damage that brings about loss of albumin (protein), which is necessary to hold fluid in the blood vascular compartment. When low-blood albumin concentration occurs, it results in loss of water from the blood to the tissues, causing edema. This is not an invariable clinical sign of GN, however. Other signs include those of UREMIA since damage occurs to the nephrons after sufficient damage of the glomeruli.

Treatment consists of diuretics, or water pills, when edema is present. Otherwise, it is aimed at supportive care, parenteral fluids, and antibiotics. Specific therapy aims at suppressing the production of antibody and/or removal of antigen(s) when possible. The prognosis is guarded.

GRANULOMAS (LICK SORES): *See* NEURODERMATITIS.

GROWTH PLATE DISORDERS: Although rare, conformational abnormalities of the limbs as a result of damage to the growth plate of immature cats (three to six-and-a-half months old) can occur due to trauma. When they do develop, they usually involve the bones of the forelimb (the radius and ulna). Damage to the growth plate of one bone results in cessation of growth of that particular bone, while the other leg bone continues to grow, resulting in limb deformities, joint damage, or a shortened limb. Surgical treatment may be required. Prognosis depends on the particular growth plate involved and the degree of deformity present at the time of diagnosis. This is an uncommon problem for cats because of their small size.

H

HAIRBALLS: *See* GASTROINTESTINAL DISEASES AND DISORDERS.

HEART DISEASE: *See* CARDIAC DISEASE.

HEART MURMUR: *See* CARDIAC ARRHYTHMIA and CONGENITAL HEART DISEASE.

HEMANGIOSARCOMA: This malignant tumor of the cells that ordinarily form blood vessels causes a proliferation of small blood vessels with no beginnings or ends and creates internal hemorrhaging and eventually a palpable mass. In cats, these tumors are most often located in the abdominal cavity and just underneath the skin (subcuticular tissue) but have also been found in the throat and nose. Surgical excision followed by biopsy is the treatment of choice, but the tumors may recur following surgery, especially if they are abdominal. The prognosis is generally poor, although it is somewhat better with the subcuticular form.

HEMATOPOIETIC TUMORS: These tumors of the blood-forming elements are the most common tumors occurring in the cat. Examples of hematopoietic tumors are FELINE LEUKEMIA and LYMPHOSARCOMA.

HEMATURIA: In this condition there is an abnormally large number of red blood cells present in the urine. Thus, the urine appears pink to dark red in color, depending on the number of red blood cells. The causes of hematuria can be BACTERIAL CYSTITIS, FELINE UROLOGIC SYNDROME (FUS), UROLITHS in the bladder and/or urethra, trauma, and the presence of tumors anywhere from the kidneys to the urethra, which are extremely rare in cats. Other clinical signs that may be present are straining to urinate (STRANGURIA), an urge to urinate often (POLLAKIURIA), and an inability to pass urine. If hematuria is suspected, the veterinarian should be consulted for tests and treatment.

HEMOPHILIA: This hereditary blood clotting disorder is due to an inherited deficiency of a needed clotting factor. It occurs rarely in cats but has been documented. The clinical signs are influenced by several factors including the severity of the deficiency and the degree of organ impairment induced by hemmorhage. There may be bleeding from the mouth, bruising, or bleeding from the gastrointestinal or urinary tract, or it may be noticed when simple surgery is performed or a small wound occurs. Specialized blood tests include factor analysis and coagulation (clotting) studies. Because this is a hereditary condition, these animals should not be used for breeding. Females usually carry the hemophiliac trait but are rarely clinically affected themselves.

HEPATIC LIPIDOSIS: The etiology of this LIVER DISEASE, which results in a fatty infiltration within the liver, is unknown. The most common sign of this disease is anorexia, which may have gone on for some time. It is not known whether or not the anorexia is caused by some other disease or by the hepatic lipidosis itself. If diagnosed early, force-feeding and general supportive care may decrease the fatty infiltration, but the disease is fatal for a large number of cats. The AMC is currently investigating causes of this serious feline disease.

HIP DYSPLASIA: Generally, hip dysplasia is not a common orthopedic disease of cats. It is a developmental disease that has several causes including genetic, environmental, and dietary factors. Several anomalies may be identified radiographically or pathologically: joint looseness (laxity), shallow joints, dislocation of the hips, erosion of the articular cartilage, remodeling of the bony surfaces of the joint, and secondary degenerative joint disease. There are some differences in the severity of clinical signs, the age of onset at which the signs appear, the rate of disease progression, and the degree of pain and associated lameness. With time, cats with hip dysplasia may develop DEGENERATIVE ARTHRITIS in their hips, which will cause pain and discomfort. Treatment is mainly symptomatic and varies with the severity of DEGENERATIVE ARTHRITIS.

HORMONAL SKIN DISEASES: Hormone-related skin diseases may occur in cats and are characterized by signs that are symmetrical on both sides of the body. They include:
Feline endocrine alopecia: This condition is characterized by bilateral, symmetrical hair loss that begins in the perineal and genital regions and then spreads. The exact cause of this condition is not known, but a sex hormone deficiency and/or imbalance is suspected by some veterinarians. Treatment consists of androgen/estrogen compounds or progesterone compounds. New information has arisen that questions the hormonal nature of this condition. Some veterinarians currently feel that it is allergic in nature rather than hormonal. *See also* ALLERGIC SKIN DISEASES.
Hypothyroidism: This is a condition that has not been documented in cats except in cases secondary to surgical excision of the thyroid gland.
Telogen effluvium: This is a condition of hair loss that may occur three to eight weeks after a stressful situation.

HORNER'S SYNDROME: This syndrome occurs when the sympathetic nervous system is disrupted along its neuroanatomical route. The classic signs of this disorder include a smaller eye pupil on the side of the involvement, protrusion of the third eyelid, a retraction of the eye globe, and a drooping of the upper eyelid. Common causes of this disorder include injury to the high thoracic spinal cord, avulsions (ripping) of the nerve plexus of the front legs, and a middle-ear inflammation. Diagnosis and treatment depend on the neuroanatomical location of the injured pathway for the sympathetic nervous system.

HYDRONEPHROSIS: This is a kidney disease resulting from obstruction to urine outflow at any level of the ureter. Potential causes include UROLITHS, tumors in and outside of the urinary tract (rare in cats), trauma with bleeding and blood clot formation in the urinary tract, and CONGENITAL RENAL ABNORMALITIES that cause obstruction in the urinary tract. Signs are often absent, but when infection is present, with or without stones, symptoms can include those of BACTERIAL CYSTITIS. Treatment aims at relieving urinary tract obstruction if possible. If one kidney is severely damaged, it can be surgically removed as long as the other kidney is normal and/or is capable of sustaining adequate renal function. The prognosis varies. It is guarded when both kidneys are involved, but when only one kidney is involved or the cause of hydronephrosis can be corrected, the prognosis is fair to good.

HYPERTHYROIDISM: This is an endocrine disorder resulting from an overproduction of the thyroid hormones T4 and T3. It commonly occurs in middle-aged to old cats and is usually caused by a nonmalignant tumor of the thyroid gland. The principal clinical signs of hyperthyroidism are weight loss, increased appetite, and hyperactivity (see Table 9, at right). Gastrointestinal upsets, malabsorption, POLYDIPSIA, POLYURIA, and cardiovascular signs are also seen frequently (see GASTROINTESTINAL DISEASES AND DISORDERS and METABOLIC HEART DISEASE).

Diagnosis is based on clinical signs and specialized blood tests. The treatment of choice for a cat with hyperthyroidism is a thyroidectomy, or surgical removal of the hyperfunctioning thyroid tissue. Although the procedure is not difficult, cats with hyperthyroidism usually suffer from systemic metabolic and cardiac imbalances, and will therefore be highly sensitive to anesthesia and potential postoperative

TABLE 9

HISTORICAL AND CLINICAL FINDINGS IN FELINE HYPERTHYROIDISM

Clinical Finding	Percentage of Cats
Weight loss	95
Polyphagia (increased appetite)	80
Hyperactivity	75
Tachycardia (rapid heart rate)	65
Polyuria/polydipsia	60
Vomiting	55
Cardiac murmur	50
Diarrhea	35
Increased fecal volume	30
Anorexia (decreased appetite)	20
Polypnea (panting)	20
Muscle tremors	15
Congestive heart failure	10
Dyspnea (difficult breathing)	10

complications. It is therefore important that particular care be taken during the entire surgical procedure. Other methods of treatment are with radioactive iodine, which destroys the hyperfunctioning thyroid tissue, or by long-term antithyroid drug therapy, which controls but does not cure the hyperthyroid state. In order to achieve a good prognosis, continued veterinary evaluation is needed.

HYPERTROPHIC CARDIOMYOPATHY (HCM): *See* CARDIOMYOPATHY.

HYPERTROPHIC PULMONARY OSTEO-ARTHROPATHY (HPOA): This is a bony disease resulting in proliferation of new bone along the shaft of the bones of the front and rear legs. Signs include lameness, reluctance to move, and swelling of the limbs. Most cats are middle-aged or older. The disease is most often associated with neoplasia (cancer) or can be due to an infection in the chest cavity. Radiographs are required to diagnose the disease. Treatment is aimed at removal of the chest disease if possible, and the prognosis depends on the type of chest disease. Since the underlying cause of HPOA is generally neoplasia, the prognosis is poor.

HYPOCALCEMIA (ECLAMPSIA): *See* Chapter 5.

HYPOGLYCEMIA (LOW BLOOD SUGAR): Hypoglycemia in cats is almost always a complication of insulin treatment for DIABETES MELLITUS. Symptoms are always neurologic because the brain requires a constant supply of blood sugar. Signs include weakness and seizures. Treatment of hypoglycemia associated with insulin overdosage includes feeding or administration of glucose-containing fluids (orally and intravenously if needed). Once the hypoglycemia is controlled, adjustments must also be made in the insulin dosage. *See also* the Emergencies section.

HYPOTRICHOSIS: *See* CONGENITOHEREDITARY SKIN DISORDERS.

I

IDIOPATHIC IMMUNE-MEDIATED ARTHRITIS: This is a very uncommon arthritis disorder caused by an immune-mediated phenomenon. Antibody complexes in the cat's circulation are either deposited or formed within the joint, causing reaction in the joint lining and fluid production. The precise cause for the immunologic basis of the disease is unknown. Signs include fever, depression, appetite loss, lameness, general limb stiffness, and swelling of the joints. Diagnosis is based on orthopedic examination, radiology, and blood tests. The disease has to be differentiated from INFECTIOUS ARTHRITIS, CHRONIC PROGRESSIVE POLYARTHRITIS, rheumatoid arthritis, and SYSTEMIC LUPUS ERYTHEMATOSUS ARTHRITIS. Treatment involves the use of steroids alone or in combination with immunosuppressive drugs.

IDIOPATHIC NEUROLOGIC DISEASES: There are several neurologic diseases of cats that are idiopathic; that is, they are of unknown cause or arise spontaneously.

Idiopathic epilepsy: Many diseases in the cat can cause seizures. Seizures of undetermined origin are called idiopathic epilepsy, and cats with idiopathic epilepsy have no other neurologic deficits. Thus the epilepsy is not associated with a potentially progressive or untreatable disease. Idiopathic epilepsy can usually be controlled with anticonvulsants. Phenobarbital is the anticonvulsant of choice for long-term seizure management in cats.

Idiopathic peripheral vestibular disease: This disease is characterized by an acute onset of vestibular signs including head tilt, nystagmus (rapid eye movement), and ATAXIA. The disease affects either the structures of the inner ear or the vestibular nerve. However, lesions have not been identified. The syndrome is occasionally associated with previous upper respiratory tract infection, but this is not a consistent finding. Clinical signs are usually reversible over a two- to three-week period. There is no treatment.

IMMUNE-MEDIATED DISEASE: An immune-mediated disease is one in which an ordinarily beneficial immune reaction against a virus or bacterium becomes harmful and causes a problem. It occurs when a foreign agent, such as a bacterium, virus, or even a drug, attaches itself to the body's cells. The antibodies that the body forms to attack the foreign agent then also attack the body's own cells, destroying them. *See* FELINE INFECTIOUS PERITONITIS (FIP).

IMMUNOLOGIC SKIN DISEASES: *See* ALLERGIC SKIN DISEASES and AUTOIMMUNE SKIN DISEASES.

INFECTIOUS ARTHRITIS: This condition results from the presence of bacteria within a joint. Bacteria may gain entrance into a joint via a penetrating injury (for example, a bite wound), bacterial septicemia in which bacteria within the bloodstream are carried into the joint, or as a complication of joint surgery. Signs include a painful joint, swelling of the joint, lameness, fever, and depression. Diagnosis is made by orthopedic examination and aspiration of joint fluid via a sterile needle, followed by microscopic examination and culture of the fluid for confirmation of the specific type of bacteria. Radiographs may demonstrate the degree of joint damage and help establish a diagnosis. Treatment with appropriate antibiotics for several weeks is necessary. Surgical therapy may be indicated to drain and flush the joint and assess the amount of damage caused by the infection. Complications of infectious arthritis include spread of the infection into adjacent bones (OSTEOMYELITIS), fusion or ankylosis of the joint, and secondary DEGENERATIVE ARTHRITIS. Prognosis is dependent on the number of joints infected, how quickly and effectively the joint infections are treated, the amount of damage to the joint caused by the infection, and the particular joint involved.

INFERTILITY: *See* Chapter 5.

INFLAMMATORY NEUROLOGIC DISEASES: Inflammatory systemic diseases often produce neurologic symptoms in cats. FELINE INFECTIOUS PERITONITIS (FIP) is a viral-induced disease. The dry form of this disease can affect a number of organs, including the liver, kidneys, eyes, and brain. Brain tissues that are most commonly affected are the meninges (membranous coverings of the brain and spinal cord) and ependyma (cellular lining of the brain ventricles). Hind-leg weakness, rapid eyeball movement, and convulsions are commonly observed neurologic signs. These signs are invariably progressive and eventually cause death or necessitate euthanasia. *See also* Infectious/Contagious Diseases.

Systemic fungal diseases: Cryptococcosis and blastomycosis are fungal diseases that may affect the central nervous system (CNS) of cats and result in neurologic dysfunction. Commonly reported neurologic signs associated with cryptococcosis include depression, circling, ATAXIA, and weakness. Although lesions of the lung are most commonly seen in cats with blastomycosis, neurologic signs such as seizures, depression, and paralysis have been reported. These conditions are often indistinguishable from each other clinically, but a diagnosis may be made by demonstrating the presence of these organisms in the CNS fluid

or from the pus of an accessible lesion. Successful treatment of cats with neurologic involvement has not been described in either disease.

Toxoplasmosis: Toxoplasmosis can cause irreversible neurologic signs such as seizures, behavior changes, and paralysis. *See* Infectious/Contagious Diseases for a complete description of this disease.

INTERVERTEBRAL DISC DISEASES: *See* SPINAL CORD DISEASE.

INTESTINAL PARASITES: Intestinal parasites are a common cause of DIARRHEA, especially in kittens. Diagnosis is usually made by a microscopic examination of a stool sample. Sometimes a blood count is also performed to help confirm diagnosis. Some cats can have perfectly normal stools while harboring parasites, so a yearly stool sample evaluation should be part of every cat's health examination. Although there are some over-the-counter deworming medications (anthelmintics) available, they are usually not very effective, and veterinary advice should be sought before attempting to deworm a cat, especially a kitten.

Roundworms (Ascarids): These are the most common feline intestinal parasites. They lodge in the small intestine and are usually not a problem for older cats, but are often present in newborn kittens who have been infected by their mothers. Although humans can get roundworms by ingesting their eggs, the worm can only complete its life cycle in the cat and will only grow into the larval stage in people.

Hookworms (Ancylostoma): Hookworms are not common in cats but can be found in very hot, humid climates. They lodge in the small intestine and can cause bloody diarrhea in severe cases. Severe ANEMIA can result.

Roundworms and hookworms are nematodes. Each has a direct life cycle in which the eggs are ingested by the cat, hatch, develop into larvae, and then into adult worms in the cat's body.

Tapeworms (Cestodes): Unlike the above parasites, tapeworms must go through an intermediate host in order for growth and larvae to develop. In the cat, the most common hosts are fleas and rodents. Flea control is therefore important if a cat has tapeworms, or the animal will reinfest itself. Tapeworms rarely cause gastrointestinal symptoms and are suspected if a cat licks its rectum excessively or scoots its rear end along the ground to get rid of the tickle caused by worm segments. This is often mistaken for ANAL SAC (GLAND) IMPACTION. These worm segments are often visible to owners as little grains or "packets" of rice around the cat's rectum. Effective medications are now available through a veterinarian to rid a cat of tapeworms.

Protozoan parasites: Coccidia and Giardia are both parasites of the small intestine that can cause watery diarrhea. Coccidia is usually a kitten parasite that can get into the kitten from the mother or from the environment. Giardia is environmental in origin and can also infest adult cats. Usually, it is endemic in wildlife around ponds or lakes, gets into the water, and is then ingested by cats who drink it. Giardia is transferable to and from humans. Coccidia is usually treated with sulfas and Giardia with metronidazole (Flagyl).

INTESTINAL TUMORS: Adenocarcinoma of the intestines is a common tumor of the feline GI tract, especially in the ileum. Surgical removal can be performed but the prognosis is guarded. *See also* MAST CELL TUMORS.

K

KIDNEY DISEASES AND DISORDERS: *See* RENAL DISEASES AND DISORDERS.

KIDNEY FAILURE: *See* RENAL FAILURE.

L

LARYNGEAL DISEASE: Severe laryngitis to the point of occlusion of the larynx can result from an upper respiratory infection. The primary signs of laryngeal disease are phonational changes and/or the complete absence of voice, which can be accompanied by gagging, choking, or wheezing sounds, noticeable on inspi-

ration of breath. Although rare, paralysis of the larynx can occur secondary to nerve damage. Laryngeal neoplasia can also cause signs similar to laryngeal paralysis. Treatment of laryngeal disease depends on the underlying cause.

LEUKEMIA: *See* FELINE LEUKEMIA and FELINE LEUKEMIA VIRUS (FeLV).

LICK SORES (GRANULOMAS): *See* NEURODERMATITIS.

LIPOMAS: These are the most common skin tumors seen in the cat. They are benign tumors of fat and can occur anywhere on the body. They are excised surgically and diagnosed by biopsy. No other treatment is usually necessary.

LIVER DISEASE: All liver diseases in cats are characterized by jaundice, or icterus, in which the white part (sclera) of the eyes and the mucous membranes appear yellow. It is also accompanied by anorexia, weight loss, lethargy, and sometimes nonspecific vomiting and diarrhea. Cats often suffer from a nonspecific toxic hepatophathy in which it is unknown whether the toxins arise from the animal's own gastrointestinal tract or from the outside environment. Regardless, the pathologic changes that take place in the liver are the same. If this type of liver disease is diagnosed early enough, possibly general supportive care may be beneficial and the liver may heal and repair itself. However, if the disease has progressed for some time or progresses rapidly, it will ultimately be fatal. As a general rule, liver disease in cats is rarely detected early enough, and the prognosis is usually guarded, regardless of the underlying disease. A definitive diagnosis is always made by means of blood tests and a liver biopsy. *See* CHOLANGIOHEPATITIS and HEPATIC LIPIDOSIS.

LOW BLOOD SUGAR: *See* HYPOGLYCEMIA.

LUNG CANCER: There are two types of lung cancer seen in cats: *primary* lung cancer, which arises in the lungs, and *secondary* lung cancer, which has metastasized from another part of the body such as the mammary glands. A diagnosis is made by X ray and specialized biopsy procedures. Coughing may be the only symptom of feline lung cancer. Surgery is the treatment of choice for primary lung cancer. Treatment for cancer that has spread from another part of the body depends on the specific diagnosis, and chemotherapy is the treatment of choice. In most cases, chemotherapy will not cure the disease but may provide prolonged good-quality life by slowing down the rate of disease progression.

LUNG DISEASE: *See* Dyspnea in the Emergencies section, PNEUMONIA, and LUNG CANCER.

LYMPHOSARCOMA (LSA): Lymphosarcoma is a malignant tumor of cells called lymphocytes that are normally found in the lymph nodes, lymphoid tissue, thymus gland, blood, and bone marrow. Most common forms affect the intestines in the abdominal cavity and the thymus gland in the chest cavity but can also involve the liver, spleen, kidneys, nervous system, eyes, nasal cavity, skin, and bladder. Lymphosarcoma is believed to be associated with the FELINE LEUKEMIA VIRUS, but *not all cats with lymphosarcoma are FeLV(+).*

Signs of lymphosarcoma vary according to the site of the disease. If it is located in the thymus, there may be difficulty breathing; if it is in the intestine or stomach, there will be gastrointestinal symptoms including vomiting, diarrhea, anorexia, weight loss, and dehydration. When the kidneys are affected, signs of RENAL FAILURE such as increased water drinking and urination and enlargement of the kidneys will occur. When the cancer is located in or behind the eyes, there will be a clouding and possible swelling of the eye, and cutaneous (on the skin) lymphosarcoma can appear to be simply an undefined skin problem.

Diagnosis is made by means of a biopsy of the affected tissue, and the treatment varies according to the location in the body. Cortisone is always used as an initial therapy, often followed by chemotherapy. Lymphosarcoma should be considered a potentially treatable disease, and the prognosis varies a great deal. If a cat that has been treated with chemother-

apy goes into remission and remains in remission for eight months (about one-quarter of all treated cats do), it will then live for several more years. In our judgment, an owner should always begin treatment and observe the response before making a decision about a cat. Although chemotherapy is presently given primarily through the larger veterinary schools and veterinary cancer specialists, many veterinarians in private practice are now giving ongoing chemotherapy treatments to cats under the supervision of cancer specialists.

LYSOSOMAL STORAGE DISEASE: *See* CONGENITAL NEUROLOGIC DISEASES.

M

MAMMARY GLAND TUMORS: Mammary gland tumors are a disease of middle-aged (nine to thirteen years of age) cats and are the third most common tumor in the cat, after HEMATOPOIETIC TUMORS and SKIN TUMORS. Eighty-five percent of feline mammary gland tumors are malignant. Researchers are just now beginning to investigate the relationship between female hormones, especially progesterone, and the subsequent development of mammary cancer. Very early spaying, before the first heat (which may occur as early as four to four-and-a-half months—*see* Chapter 5) might be preventive, but no definitive studies have been made. As it is now, mammary gland tumors may develop in cats that are spayed at five to six months of age; these tumors have rarely been reported in neutered and intact male cats. There is a genetic predisposition toward mammary gland tumors among Siamese cats, which often develop tiny, multiple tumors at seven to nine years of age that tend to recur and spread extremely rapidly, despite surgical removal. For all other cats, wide surgical excision of the tumor and biopsy is the treatment of choice, followed by chemotherapy if the cancer has spread. Once mammary tumors have developed, they most often spread to the lungs. Spaying does not appear to prevent recurrence in the cat.

Prognosis is inversely related to the size of the tumor. The smaller the tumor(s) at the time of surgical removal, the longer the survival of the cat. Thus, a cat with a tumor volume of between 1 and 8 cc (½ to 4 inches) has the best prognosis, while one with a tumor measuring 28 cc (12 to 14 inches) or more will survive only up to six months after surgery. Early diagnosis and surgical therapy is therefore very important.

Occasionally, there is mammary hyperplasia (an increase in the number of mammary gland cells) in young (six to eight months old) female cats in association with their first heat. This is not mammary gland cancer and is cured by performing an ovariohysterectomy (OHE).

A small percentage of female cats that are given Ovaban (megesterol acetate) to treat skin conditions or behavior problems may subsequently develop tumor-like nodules in their mammary glands. Removal and biopsy are indicated, although this is a benign mammary hyperplasia. Sometimes injections of synthetic progesterone are used to keep intact females from coming into heat, and there is some evidence that this drug may lead to the development of mammary cancer. Therefore, it is safer to spay a cat not intended for breeding.

MANGE, NOTOEDRIC: *See* PARASITIC SKIN DISEASES.

MAST CELL TUMORS: Mast cell tumors in cats can develop in three different parts of the body. They can appear on the skin, in the spleen, and in the small intestine.

Mast cell tumors on the skin: Feline mast cell tumors, appearing as multiple, firm, raised, light-colored skin masses, are very often found on the face and around the head. They can develop very quickly or may have been on the cat's body for some time and suddenly grew and spread. Because they are very annoying and itchy, the cat tends to scratch them, and they often ulcerate. They are diagnosed by surgical removal of one tumor, which is then examined by biopsy. The treatment of choice is cortisone given orally. Mast cell tumors are considered to be sensitive to radiation therapy, but if they are multiple and spread out on the cat's body, this is not practical. The prognosis for complete recovery is better when the tumors develop gradually.

Mast cell tumors of the spleen: Another form of mast cell tumors in the cat develops in the spleen. Signs involve chronic vomiting, and an enlarged spleen can usually be felt on palpation. Treatment involves surgical removal of the spleen, and the prognosis for recovery is fairly good.

Mast cell tumors of the small intestine: A solitary mast cell tumor can develop in the small intestine of cats. Signs mirror those of an intestinal obstruction and include vomiting, little or no appetite, and scant bowel movements. Treatment is surgical removal of the blocked area and rejoining of the normal remaining ends. After removal, a biopsy of the affected piece of intestine will reveal a mast cell tumor.

Mast cell tumors *on any part of the body* release chemical substances that cause ulcers in the duodenum, and vomiting results. Surgical removal of the affected part and antacid medications may help prolong the cat's life, but the prognosis is poor.

MASTITIS: *See* Chapter 5.

MELANOMA (MALIGNANT): A malignant melanoma is a cancerous growth of pigment-forming cells. They develop rarely in very old cats.

MENINGIOMA: *See* NEOPLASTIC NEUROLOGIC DISEASES.

METABOLIC HEART DISEASE: Metabolic heart disease can occur in cats when a tumor develops in the thyroid gland and produces abnormally high quantities of thyroid hormone that can affect the heart. Cats that develop this disease are usually older (over twelve years of age). Signs of metabolic heart disease include severe weight loss accompanied by a profound increase in appetite, increased water drinking and urination, and occasionally vomiting. Early diagnosis by means of blood tests is usually definitive. Once a diagnosis has been made, the thyroid gland tumor can be removed surgically and the disease will usually resolve. Some medical treatments have also been used successfully instead of surgery. *See also* HYPERTHYROIDISM.

METRITIS: *See* Chapter 5.

MILIARY DERMATITIS: This is a condition with multiple etiologies, including parasitism, dermatophytes (fungal), food allergies, and drug eruptions. The condition appears as small clusters of scabs on the body. Diagnosis entails identifying the cause, and treatment involves correcting the underlying cause if possible.

MUSCULOSKELETAL DISEASES AND DISORDERS: The cat's musculoskeletal system contains essentially the same parts as man's (*see* Illustration 19, below). The bones of the skeleton provide support and also serve to protect the internal organs. When bones join together to form a joint, there is a protective layer of cartilage on each bone end, or head, to prevent friction. Most of the cat's joints are hinged, except for the shoulder and hip joints which fit together like a ball and socket. Ligaments and tendons hold bones together and joints in place, and the muscles cause them to move.

Diseases and disorders can occur in any part of the cat's musculoskeletal system and have a number of different origins. Trauma, or injury, to the bones themselves may cause FRACTURES; an injury to ligaments can result in CRANIAL CRUCIATE LIGAMENT RUPTURE. Dislocation of a joint because of trauma may cause PATELLAR LUXATIONS, a dislocation of the knee cap. Disease may cause inflammation of the bones, and bacterial or fungal infection can also occur (OSTEOMYELITIS). There can also be congenital malformations of joints (HIP DYSPLASIA).

Owners should know that indiscriminate supplementation with minerals or the feeding

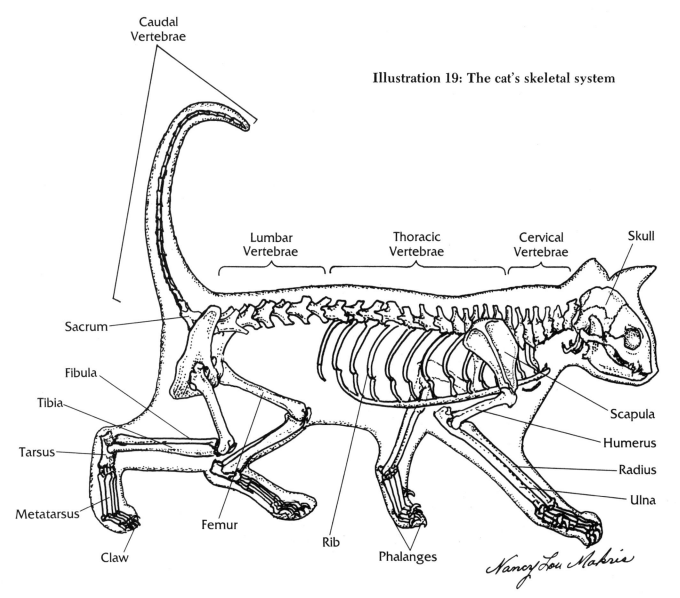

Illustration 19: The cat's skeletal system

Caudal Vertebrae

Lumbar Vertebrae

Thoracic Vertebrae

Cervical Vertebrae

Skull

Sacrum

Fibula

Tibia

Tarsus

Metatarsus

Claw

Femur

Rib

Phalanges

Scapula

Humerus

Radius

Ulna

Nancy Lou Makris

of an all-organ-meat diet may cause severe skeletal problems in young cats—*see* NUTRITIONAL HYPERPARATHYROIDISM. The wear and tear of use over the years, exacerbated by injury or disease, may lead an older cat to develop a degenerative joint disorder such as DEGENERATIVE ARTHRITIS.

Signs of musculoskeletal problems are varied but usually include one or more of the following: lameness, stiffness, swelling, joint crepitation (grating or grinding), and a reluctance to move or walk. Symptoms may be confined to one area of a cat's body, or there can be multiple involvement of many joints. Diagnosis is generally made via orthopedic examination and X rays, with other specific tests such as fluid aspiration and blood tests as required. Treatment varies widely depending on the particular disease and degree of involvement. *See also* CHRONIC PROGRESSIVE POLYARTHRITIS, COXOFEMORAL LUXATION, DELAYED UNION AND NONUNION, GROWTH PLATE DISORDERS, HYPERTROPHIC PULMONARY OSTEOARTHROPATHY (HPOA), IDIOPATHIC IMMUNE-MEDIATED ARTHRITIS, MUSCULOSKELETAL TUMORS, POLYDACTYLIA, spinal disc protrusion (in SPINAL CORD DISEASE), and SYSTEMIC LUPUS ERYTHEMATOSUS ARTHRITIS.

MUSCULOSKELETAL TUMORS: Musculoskeletal tumors in the cat can be divided into three categories: primary bone tumors, secondary bone tumors, and soft-tissue tumors that arise in the muscles or connective tissues of the body—the supporting structures of the skeleton. Signs of musculoskeletal tumors are generally quite obvious and include masses on the body, which can be large, lameness, limb or head swelling, or an inability to eat.

Primary Bone Tumors: There are three main categories of primary bone tumors that arise most commonly in the cat: osteosarcoma, chondrosarcoma, and fibrosarcoma and the related malignant fibrous histiocytoma.

Osteosarcoma occurs most often in distal limbs (those farthest from the body's center) of older cats, in the facial bones of the skull such as the maxilla (either of the two bones forming the upper jaw), the mandible (lower jawbone), or in the bony calvarium, the flat bones that make up the vault of the skull. Distal tumors in the cat are similar to those in the dog; that is, they are malignant and have a high potential for spreading to other parts of the body. Amputation of the affected limb is the best treatment, and in our experience it may allow for significant prolongation of a good-quality life. Osteosarcomas of the flat bones of the skull or of the bones of the upper and lower jaw tend to behave in a different manner. Although they can grow to a large size, they do not spread as readily, and surgical removal, if possible, is the treatment of choice. In the event that surgery is not possible, these tumors are generally slow-growing, and the prognosis in the short run may be fair, although the long-term prognosis is, of course, poor.

Chondrosarcoma is the second most common primary bone tumor seen in the cat. It arises from the cartilage of the bone and almost always develops in the bones of the distal limbs, but chondrosarcomas may also be seen in the skull or nasal bones. Again, amputation is the therapy of choice and may allow for a good-quality life for a while, although the chance of metastasis is high in this type of tumor.

Fibrosarcoma/malignant fibrous histiocytoma comprise the third most commonly occurring primary bone tumors in the cat. While the fibrosarcoma is a locally invasive tumor only, the malignant fibrous histiocytoma, which has a high metastatic potential, is a close variant, and it may be difficult for a pathologist to differentiate between the two. Amputation is the therapy of choice, followed by chemotherapy in some cases.

Secondary Bone Tumors: Secondary bone tumors are tumors that involve bone but do not arise from the bone itself. Some of the soft-tissue sarcomas, such as fibrosarcoma and malignant fibrous histiocytoma (see below), may subsequently involve and invade nearby bones. Spread of distant tumors to the bone is uncommon but not rare in the cat; and other carcinomas, such as SQUAMOUS CELL CARCINOMA, MAMMARY GLAND CANCER, and primary LUNG CANCER, may invade the bones. When possible, surgical amputation is the therapy of choice, but if the cancer is widespread, paliative therapy is all that can be done. In those institutions where radiation therapy is available, its use may give relief from pain. There is a very poor prognosis for metastatic bone cancer in the cat, however, based on the presence of an aggressive primary tumor.

Primary Soft-Tissue Tumors: Although soft tissue tumors may appear as lumps on the skin, they are actually in connective tissue beneath the skin.

Fibrosarcoma will occur in muscles and connective tissues of the trunk and thorax, and also in the soft tissue of limbs. When possible, surgical excision is the first therapy of choice, often followed by repeat surgery with or without chemotherapy or radiation following the second surgery. These tumors behave mostly as locally invasive tumors and have a low metastatic potential.

Malignant fibrous histiocytomas also occur in the soft tissue. These tumors have a higher metastatic potential than fibrosarcomas. Again, surgical excision, followed by chemotherapy, is indicated.

Angiosarcomas are tumors very similar to HE-MANGIOSARCOMAS. That is, they arise from small blood vessels in the skin and often physically resemble the other types of sarcomas. Surgical removal is the therapy of choice; however, recurrence locally is quite common, and repeat surgeries are often needed. At this time there is no efficacious chemotherapy for angiosarcomas, but research is currently in progress.

N

NASAL CANCER: Although nasal cancer is rare in the cat, it does occur. Signs include persistent sneezing with or without facial deformity. The most common nasal cancer in cats is adenocarcinoma of the nose, in which the therapy of choice is surgical removal and biopsy, followed by radiation therapy. The prognosis in these cases is poor. LYMPHOSARCOMA may also involve the nose of the cat and produce swelling. For other conditions that produce a nasal discharge and sneezing with or without facial deformity, *see* NASAL DISCHARGE below.

NASAL DISCHARGE: The primary cause of a nasal discharge in young cats is an UPPER RESPI-

RATORY INFECTION, such as rhinotracheitis or calicivirus. If the viral infection is mild, the cat usually gets better with supportive care. Occasionally, however, if the infection is severe, the internal structure of the nose can be damaged and a cat can develop *chronic rhinitis*, a chronically runny nose. This is because the internal structure of the nose has been damaged so that normal drainage cannot take place. A secondary bacterial infection may set in, and the discharge will become purulent. This condition can usually be *controlled but not cured* by the use of antibiotics. Sometimes surgical intervention becomes necessary in order to remove all of the affected portions of the nasal cavity.

In cats that do not have an upper respiratory infection, chronic nasal discharge can be caused by a fungal infection, cryptococcosis being the most common. Foreign bodies such as grass, needles, or a grub (cuterebral larvae) can become lodged in the nose, causing a nasal discharge. A nasal fracture can also create a chronic nasal discharge, as can a posttraumatic split hard palate until it heals. Abscesses of tooth roots can make a cat's nose run. In older cats that develop a bloody nasal discharge, the possibility of NASAL CANCER must also be considered. This may be accompanied by nasal deformity, depending on how far along the tumor is.

NEOPLASTIC NEUROLOGIC DISEASES: Tumors, both benign and malignant, can cause neurologic symptoms in cats.

Meningioma: This benign tumor originates from the meninges and is the most common central nervous system (CNS) tumor in cats. Meningiomas generally affect older male cats, many of which are more than ten years old. Although meningiomas are benign and often grow slowly, they cause neurologic deficits secondary to the displacement or destruction of the normal brain tissue. Neurologic signs commonly include seizures, circling, behavior changes, lethargy, collapse, BLINDNESS, ATAXIA, weakness, and intermittent nystagmus (rapid eyeball movement). If cats are not treated, there is a slow progression of neurologic dysfunction. Cats treated with steroids may re-

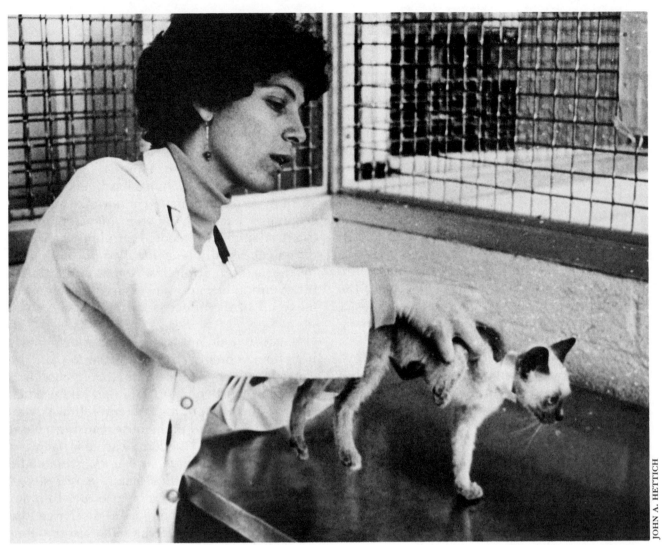

Photograph 31: Dr. Deborah Sarfaty giving a neurologic examination to a Siamese kitten

JOHN A. HETTICH

spond favorably for a temporary period of days to several weeks. Meningiomas are often visible on skull radiographs due to partial calcification of the tumor. At The AMC, a CAT scanner makes diagnosis of these tumors easier. Surgical removal is the treatment of choice. In those reported cases in which tumor resection was successful, almost all abnormal neurologic signs were restored to normal.

Lymphosarcoma: Neurologic dysfunction may also occur in cats with LYMPHOSARCOMA. Affected cats are often young and have slowly progressive neurologic dysfunction. Hind-leg paralysis is the most common neurologic sign. Many cats also have back pain. The tumor is usually outside the protective covering of the spinal cord. The onset of neurologic signs occurs when the compression interferes with the spinal cord circulation, resulting in lesions. Since the tumor is often located on one side of the spinal cord, it is common for the neurologic signs to be asymmetrical, at least at the onset of the observed disability. The weakness and ataxia are more pronounced on the side of the lesion. A myelogram is usually necessary to demonstrate the location of the tumor. It has also been found that half of the cats that have primary LYMPHOSARCOMA of the kidneys develop neurologic disease from metastasis to the brain. Corticosteroids and chemotherapeutic agents have been used to temporarily alleviate clinical signs in cats with LYMPHOSARCOMA. The effectiveness of these agents in the treatment of cats with neurologic involvement has not been established.

NEURODERMATITIS: Psychogenic (having an origin in the mind rather than the body) dermatitis and alopecia are relatively common in cats, which may obsessively lick one or more areas of their bodies, causing marked hair loss and/or skin lesions (lick sores). There is usually some historical, psychological insult such as a move, new pet or person in the household, and so forth. Treatment involves chemotherapeutic trials. Some animals recover when the insult (that is, the new animal) is removed; others require maintenance therapy.

NEUROLOGIC DISEASES AND DISORDERS: The cat's nervous system may be roughly divided into five gross structures: cerebrum, brain stem, cerebellum, spinal cord, and peripheral nerves/muscles. To understand diseases and disorders that may affect a cat's nervous system, it is necessary to define these subdivisions.

Cerebrum (cerebral cortex): This part of the brain is composed of four lobes: frontal, parietal, occipital, and temporal. Each lobe has a particular function. For example, the frontal lobes are associated with intellect, behavior, and fine motor abilities; the parietal lobes process sensory information such as pain and touch, and position sense; the temporal lobes are responsible for complex behavior and hearing; and the occipital lobes are associated with vision. The entire cerebro-cortical function is complex and integrated. Injury to the brain may cause abnormalities in one or more of these functions. Common signs include seizures, behavior change, loss of intellect, gait abnormalities, sensation difficulties, altered consciousness, and visual loss.

Brain stem: This part of the brain is also subdivided. Twelve nerves exit from the brain stem and innervate muscles of the face, mouth, and glands of the head. Within the brain stem lie a complex series of tracts that communicate information to and from the cerebrum to the nerves of the limbs and internal organs by way of the spinal cord. Dysfunction of the nerves that leave the brain stem depends on the particular nerve involved. For example, if cranial nerve two is damaged, vision is impaired; if cranial nerve seven is injured, FACIAL PARALY-SIS may ensue; if cranial nerve eight (vestibular portion) is affected, balance difficulties may occur. In short, depending on the particular function of each set of cranial (brain stem) nerves, abnormalities will be reflected by a loss of that function. Lesions of the brain stem substance create a host of abnormal signs, including head tilts, spontaneous eye movements, coma, severe gait disturbance, abnormal respiration, and abnormal heart rhythms.

Cerebellum: This part of the brain coordinates and smoothes out movement. Injury to the cerebellum may cause loss of balance or "jerky," uncoordinated body and limb function. Typically, cats will have a "drunken" gait, a high-step in the legs, a fine head tremor that may worsen when the animal is attempting to do something, and an altered stance (placement of legs far apart). Rapid eyeball movement may also be observed.

Spinal cord: The spinal cord extends from the brain stem to the outside of the skull, where it is encased by the vertebral column. The spinal cord has *ascending* (to the brain) and *descending* (from the brain) pathways. The ascending pathways convey the perception of pain and both conscious and unconscious position sense. Descending pathways include those that posture the animal against gravity and initiate movement.

Peripheral nerves: Information leaves the spinal cord by way of spinal nerves known as ventral roots (descending). Information also enters the spinal cord by spinal nerves known as dorsal roots (ascending). In this manner, the body and its limbs are constantly kept in touch with the environment. The peripheral nerves generally carry this input/output. For example, input would go to the brain and output would be received by a muscle.

Muscle/neuromuscular function: These represent the final common pathway of descending information. Different types of muscles are innervated by different parts of the nervous system. The complexity of this system is beyond the scope of this book. *See also* ATAXIA, BALANCE DISORDERS, CONGENITAL NEUROLOGIC DISEASES, DYSMETRIA, EPILEPSY, FACIAL PARALYSIS, HORNER'S SYNDROME, IDIOPATHIC NEUROLOGIC

DISEASES, INFLAMMATORY NEUROLOGIC DISEASES, NEOPLASTIC NEUROLOGIC DISEASES, NUTRITIONAL NEUROLOGIC DISEASE, PARESIS, PERIPHERAL NEUROPATHY, PLEGIA, SPINAL CORD DISEASE, STATES OF CONSCIOUSNESS, and VASCULAR NEUROLOGIC DISEASE.

NUTRITIONAL HYPERPARATHYROIDISM ("Paper-Bone Disease," Osteogenesis Imperfecta, Juvenile Osteoporosis): This disease occurs most commonly in young cats and is caused by an improper diet (an all-meat diet), resulting in loss of calcium (demineralization) from the skeletal system. Spontaneous fractures of the spine and leg bones result. Associated signs of lameness and limping are often seen. Treatment consists of a correct diet and calcium supplementation by a veterinarian. The prognosis varies and is dependent on the severity of the disease (that is, the number of fractures already sustained).

NUTRITIONAL NEUROLOGIC DISEASE: Thiamine (vitamin B_1) is thought to have a role in neuromuscular transmission and also serves as a co-enzyme for several enzymes involved in the metabolism of carbohydrates. Thiamine deficiency occurs in cats fed all-fish diets that contain thiaminase (*see* Chapter 3). Occasionally, it follows prolonged periods of anorexia. Terminally, there is irreversible damage to various parts of the brain stem. The earliest signs of the disease are ATAXIA followed by convulsions with marked head ventroflexion (head flexed toward the ground). The pupils of the eyes may be dilated and poorly responsive to light. Finally, there is semi-coma, continual crying, and opisthotonus (rigid spasms of the spine and extremities). Prompt therapy with thiamine injections in the early stages of the disease results in complete remission of signs.

NUTRITIONAL SKIN DISEASES: As discussed in Chapter 3, certain dietary deficiencies can lead to dermatologic signs in cats, in addition to other symptoms.
The B-complex vitamins:
   Biotin deficiency can lead to a thin haircoat, dry, scaly skin, and MILIARY DERMATITIS.

Insufficient riboflavin can cause alopecia, anorexia, and weight loss.

Vitamin A deficiency can result in alopecia, scaling, and a poor haircoat, as well as multiple other problems unrelated to the skin.

Vitamin E insufficiency can lead to pansteatitis (yellow-fat disease) in which excess fat underneath a cat's skin causes lumpy deposits. It is usually the result of a diet containing an excess of red tuna, cod liver oil, and so forth.

A deficiency of the essential fatty acids linoleic, linolenic, and arachidonic will eventually lead to scaly skin and hair loss.

Not enough zinc will cause a cat to develop a thin haircoat and have slow hair growth, scaly skin, and ulceration of the lips.

Dietary deficiencies in cats are easily prevented by feeding a well-balanced commercial cat food or by providing an animal source of protein and nutrients daily. *See* Chapter 3 for more about cats' nutritional requirements.

O

OCULAR TUMORS: *See* DIFFUSE IRIS MELANOMA and SQUAMOUS CELL CARCINOMA.

OCULOCUTANEOUS ALBINISM: *See* CONGENITOHEREDITARY SKIN DISORDERS.

ONCOLOGY: This is the study of tumors, both benign and malignant. The incidence of tumors in the cat is, overall, less than in the dog. However, the percentage of malignant tumors in cats is much higher—approximately 72 percent of all feline tumors are malignant, whereas only 34 percent of all dog tumors are. The difference is that the most commonly occurring tumors in the dog are skin tumors, which are usually benign, while the most commonly occurring tumors in the cat, the HEMATOPOIETIC TUMORS (LYMPHOSARCOMA and FELINE LEUKEMIA), are malignant. This does not necessarily mean that a cat with a malignant tumor is doomed, however, because once a diagnosis has been made and treatment begun, the chances are that a cat with cancer can live a relatively long, normal life with only a few minutes a week of treatment. It is important to note that, with the exception of the FELINE LEUKEMIA VIRUS (FeLV), which is contagious to other cats, feline cancer cannot be transmitted to other animals. There is no evidence to suggest that FeLV is transmittable to people.

There are two basic types of feline tumors: HEMATOPOIETIC TUMORS, which involve blood-forming elements (for example, FELINE LEUKEMIA and LYMPHOSARCOMA), and solid tumors or masses which may be external or internal and can occur anywhere on a cat's body.

There is no known single cause for cancer in any animal. There are environmental influences. For example, white-skinned cats can develop SQUAMOUS CELL CARCINOMA of the pinnae of the ear from too much of the sun's radiation. There are also familial or genetic predispositions toward cancer, as in the case of MAMMARY GLAND TUMORS in Siamese cats. Viral infections are directly responsible for other feline cancers, such as FELINE LEUKEMIA and LYMPHOSARCOMA. No research has been done as to possible dietary causes of cancer in the cat. Today, the most commonly held theory is related to the *oncogene*, which normally is dormant until some outside factor (genetic, environmental, infectious, and so forth) activates it. When the oncogene is activated, cancer can develop.

An older yet still widely held theory about cancer is that of *the failure of immuno-surveillance*. This theory holds that all living bodies have mutant, or abnormal, cells that arise either intermittently or continuously, and that a normally functioning immune system recognizes these cells as abnormal and destroys them as they are formed. Cancer would then result from one or two causes:

1) The abnormal cells escape from immuno-surveillance, as in the case of tumors that are not detected as abnormal because they are in a "sanctuary" such as the eye or the central nervous system and are therefore not exposed to the system and not recognized as abnormal until they are big enough to cause problems.

2) The immune system does recognize the abnormal cells yet fails to function properly or to mount a response of significant magnitude to destroy these abnormal cells, and allows the cancer to grow. This theory is controversial.

To unify the two theories, immune system failure could be an aftermath, rather than a causative factor, in the development of cancer. The activation of the oncogene could cause an immune system failure which would then cause cancer.

It is interesting to note that once a tumor has reached a volume of 1 cc (½ inch), the immune system is incapable of destroying it without help (for example, surgery, chemotherapy, and so forth) and, as cats age, their immune systems become less effective, which may again allow the escape of abnormal cells into the bloodstream.

HEMATOPOIETIC TUMORS (FELINE LEUKEMIA, LYMPHOSARCOMA), SKIN TUMORS, and MAMMARY GLAND TUMORS are the most commonly occurring cancers in cats. *See also* CERUMINOUS GLAND ADENOCARCINOMA, FELINE LEUKEMIA VIRUS (FeLV), HEMANGIOSARCOMA, LUNG CANCER, LIPOMAS, MAST CELL TUMORS, MELANOMA (MALIGNANT), MUSCULOSKELETAL TUMORS, NASAL CANCER, and PEMPHIGUS GROUP.

OPHTHALMIC DISEASES AND DISORDERS: Cats are fortunate in that, up to the present, they have been able to avoid many of the conformational eye problems that some breeds of dogs are prone to due to inbreeding. Exceptions are the brachycephalic, or pug-faced, cats such as Persians and Himalayans which may have eye problems associated with their eyelids rolling inwards or with excess fur irritating the cornea.

In general, cats develop eye problems as a result of infectious diseases that affect the conjunctiva causing CONJUNCTIVITIS and because of systemic diseases such as FELINE LEUKEMIA VIRUS (FeLV), FELINE INFECTIOUS PERITONITIS (FIP), and toxoplasmosis (*see* INFLAMMATORY NEUROLOGIC DISEASES), which can cause ocular inflammation (ANTERIOR CHAMBER INFLAMMATION, for example) and RETINAL DISEASES. Wounds and trauma from fighting are also frequent causes of feline eye problems (*see* CORNEAL TRAUMA).

Cats' retinas can also be permanently damaged by a deficiency of the amino acid taurine in their diet, which may result in BLINDNESS. Taurine is present in adequate amounts in almost all commercial cat foods, and this problem occurs only when a cat is fed a diet intended for dogs, a poorly balanced home-cooked diet, or a vegetarian diet. More about this in Chapter 3.

Many infectious and systemic diseases are reflected in a cat's eyes, so they are good indicators of a cat's general bodily condition (*see* Illustration 20, below). Owners should pay particular attention to any clouding, haziness, or change of color in a cat's pupil, iris, or cornea, and to any change in shape or dilation of the pupil. Redness or a discharge should always be investigated and, of course, any eye injury no matter how seemingly minor should have immediate veterinary attention. *See also*

CATARACTS, CLOUDING OF THE EYE, COLOR CHANGES IN THE EYE, CORNEAL ULCERATION, CROSSED EYES, DIFFUSE IRIS MELANOMA, GLAUCOMA, SQUAMOUS CELL CARCINOMAS, and THIRD EYELID PROLAPSE.

ORAL TUMORS: See SQUAMOUS CELL CARCINOMAS.

OSTEOMYELITIS: This infection of bone may be caused by several different types of bacteria or fungi. Introduction of the bacterial or fungal agent can be by hematogenous routes (via the bloodstream), a direct injury such as a bite or gunshot wound, or during surgical re-

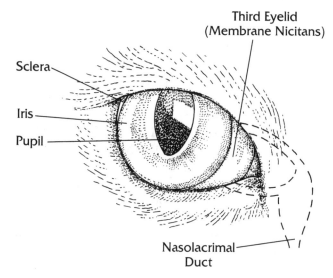

Illustration 20: The cat's outer and inner eye

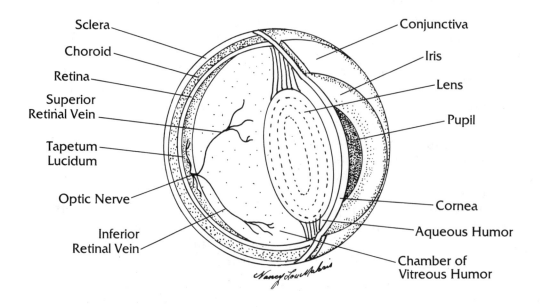

pair of a fractured bone. Diagnosis is based on history, physical examination, blood tests, and radiographs. Treatment is dependent on the acuteness or chronicity of the infection. Generally, chronic osteomyelitis cases must be treated surgically to remove dead and infected bone, promote drainage, and retrieve an accurate culture (an uncontaminated specimen) from the infected area. Appropriate antibiotics or antifungal drugs are used in most cases for osteomyelitis. The prognosis depends on the severity of the infection, chronicity, the amount of bone infected, and the type of bacteria or fungus causing the infection.

P

PANCREATIC DISEASE: Pancreatic disease is a rare and poorly documented problem in the cat's gastrointestinal tract. This is because the laboratory tests available at this time do not accurately measure pancreatic enzymes in the cat, and it is, therefore, very difficult to diagnose except by biopsy (or autopsy). In general, signs of pancreatitis in the cat are anorexia, abdominal discomfort, and acute vomiting. Pancreatic insufficiency (maldigestion), in which the digestive enzymes from the pancreas are no longer present to break down food, resulting in chronic diarrhea and an increased appetite, is rare in the cat. It can be cured by supplementation of pancreatic enzymes.

PANLEUKOPENIA: *See* Infectious/Contagious Diseases.

PAPER-BONE DISEASE: *See* NUTRITIONAL HYPERPARATHYROIDISM.

PARALYSIS: *See* PLEGIA.

PARAPARESIS: Weakness of the hind limbs. *See* PARESIS.

PARASITIC SKIN DISEASES: External parasites are a common cause of skin problems in cats. Some of these parasites are contagious to man and other animals and may also be carriers of other diseases (*see* INTESTINAL PARASITES).

JOHN A. HETTICH

Photograph 32: A severe flea infestation can cause extreme pruritis (itching).

Control is extremely important because, in most instances, these parasites do not live on cats but feed on them and live in the surrounding environment. A veterinarian is the best source of information about specific kinds of parasite-control products. Over-the-counter preparations are generally not strong enough, nor are they designed to work effectively in all geographic areas. Whatever product is used, it is extremely important that it be specifically designed for use on cats. Parasite control methods are discussed in detail in Chapter 3. *See also* EAR MITES.

Fleas: Fleas are the most common parasite found on cats. Severe infestations can cause extreme pruritus in cats of all ages, and anemia in young kittens. In addition, fleas are intermediate hosts of feline tapeworm.

Notoedric mange: This rare disease of cats resembles sarcoptic mange in dogs. It is highly contagious and is caused by tiny mites. Signs are extreme itching around the head and neck and sometimes generalized lesions. Therapy involves isolation, clipping of the hair, parasitic dips, and treatment of any secondary skin problems.

Cheyletiellosis ("walking dandruff"): This is also a type of mange, caused by mites that live on the surface of the skin and may or may not cause any signs. It may cause dandruff over the animal's back and possibly skin eruptions. It is contagious. Treatment involves isolation, topical parasiticides, and thorough cleaning of the environment, as these mites can live for up to ten days off a cat.

Demodecosis: This type of mange is extremely rare in cats and is caused by a mite that normally lives in the skin. Symptoms can involve focal or diffuse areas of hair loss and generalized scaling. It is diagnosed by skin scrapings and treated by the use of parasiticides.

Cuterebriasis: Grub or fly larvae may penetrate the skin of cats and form a cutaneous cyst. The larvae will remain in the cyst for about a month and then break out. Skin lesions appear as firm nodules that may become fluctuant and rupture, developing fistulous tracts. Treatment involves removing the inch-long larvae and treating the wound with antiseptics.

Ticks: Ticks are not found on cats as often as on dogs, but when present are usually in the thick hair and areas inaccessible to cats such as between the toes, inside the ears, and at the back of the neck. Unengorged male ticks are small and dark brown, while female ticks engorged with blood are pale gray and can swell to the size of a pea. If found, a firmly attached tick should be removed with tweezers and the small wound touched with antiseptic. If part of the tick remains in the cat, it may cause a tiny red spot that will probably clear up in a day or two.

PARESIS: This is a disturbance in the mechanism for initiating voluntary motor function; it causes weakness or paralysis, depending on the severity of the lesion. The severity increases as the location of the lesion descends in the upper motor neuron system to involve more of the pathways (*see* NEUROLOGIC DISEASES AND DISORDERS). *Paraparesis* is weakness of the hind limbs, and *tetraparesis* is weakness of all four limbs.

PATELLAR LUXATIONS: Luxation, or dislocation, of the knee cap (patella) can be congenitally or traumatically induced. The luxation is classified as either medial (displacement of the patella out of its normal femoral groove to the inner aspect of the leg) or lateral (displacement to the outer aspect of the leg). Congenital luxations can occur in certain cat breeds. Trauma-induced luxations can be either medial or lateral. Clinical signs vary according to the degree of luxation. Some cats may be in intermittent pain and occasionally limp on a rear leg, while others have a persistent severe lameness. Diagnosis is made by orthopedic examination. Treatment is determined by the severity of the luxation and the resulting lameness. Surgery is the primary means of treatment when indicated. The prognosis depends on the severity of the luxation and the particular surgical technique used.

PEMPHIGUS GROUP: This group of AUTOIMMUNE SKIN DISEASES is not common in the cat. They are manifested most often by crusting ear and eye lesions, with or without whole body skin crusting and ulcerative lesions. There may also be scaling and ulcers of the foot pads. Diagnosis is made by means of a biopsy and specialized seriologic and immunodiagnostic testing. Therapy is directed at control rather than cure. However, there are reports in veterinary medical literature of excellent responses to various kinds of therapy, ranging from immunosuppressants to cortisone and gold.

PERIPHERAL NEUROPATHY: This refers to any disorder of the lower motor neuron system that involves the spinal roots, spinal nerves, peripheral nerves, or neuromuscular junction. Diseases of the spinal roots and peripheral nerves include inflammation (polyneuritis), neoplasia (neurofibroma), trauma (root avulsion, FRACTURES), and ischemia (aortic thromboembolism). Diseases of the neuromuscular junction include myasthenia gravis and botulism. Clinical signs include PARESIS or paralysis of one or more limbs, voice change, eye blink difficulty, megaesophagus, and respiratory difficulty.

PHARYNGEAL DISEASES: Signs of pharyngeal disease in the cat are essentially those of a sore throat, including difficulty swallowing, gagging, and drooling. Sometimes cats with pharyngeal disease develop an abnormal, squeaky purr. Pharyngitis can be secondary to an upper respiratory infection or develop as a result of polyps that arise in the middle ear and grow down into the eustachian tube and extend to the back of the throat. Foreign bodies such as chicken bones and sewing needles can also cause pharyngeal problems, as can the chewing of certain kinds of houseplants with sharp, prickly leaves. Tonsillar tumors must also be suspected when abnormal pharyngeal signs are presented.

PHYSIOCHEMICAL SKIN DISEASES: Cats' skin is affected by the outside temperature and by other environmental influences. A temperature-dependent hair color change is commonly seen in Siamese cats. Cold areas induce dark hair growth while warmer areas of the body induce light hair color.

Cats are also subject to FROSTBITE when exposed to extreme cold; when continuously in the sun, light-skinned cats can develop FELINE SOLAR DERMATITIS.

Longhaired cats that develop hair mats are predisposed to a variety of bacterial skin diseases.

PLASMACYTIC-LYMPHOCYTIC ENTERITIS: This inflammatory disease mimics LYMPHOSARCOMA but is not cancerous. It is a very poorly understood disease of unknown etiology. There is no proven therapy for it. A diagnosis can only be established by an intestinal biopsy. Symptomatic therapy with antibiotics, cortisone, and dietary manipulation may help for a period of time, but the disease seems to be progressive, and eventual death can occur.

PLEGIA: Plegia is a suffix meaning paralysis. Motor plegia is the complete absence of purposeful movement. Sensory plegia is the complete absence of deep pain sensation.

PNEUMONIA: Pneumonia can be a consequence of a severe or untreated upper respiratory infection or of the inhalation or aspiration of food or medicine into the lungs, either after a cat has vomited or due to improper methods of medication. Signs of pneumonia include fever, lethargy, appetite loss, and a cough. Cats with pneumonia are treated with antibiotics on a long-term basis and frequently take a long time to improve. Severe pneumonia can be an emergency (*see* the Emergencies section).

PNEUMONITIS: *See* Infectious/Contagious Diseases.

POLLAKIURIA, or FREQUENCY OF URINATION: In this condition, a cat needs to urinate more often than normally and small amounts of urine are passed each time. It often occurs with BACTERIAL CYSTITIS, FELINE UROLOGIC SYNDROME, or when the urinary tract is obstructed.

POLYDACTYLIA: Extra, or supernumerary, toes are fairly common in cats. They have no clinical significance.

POLYDIPSIA: This is a condition in which a cat ingests more than normal amounts of water. Normal maximum daily water intake for a cat is one cup per ten pounds of body weight per day (this includes water present in the food). Polydipsia can occur with RENAL FAILURE, either acute or chronic, DIABETES MELLITUS, diabetes insipidus, and HYPERTHYROIDISM.

POLYURIA: This is a condition in which a cat's urine output is larger than normal. This almost invariably occurs with POLYDIPSIA and is a result of the same diseases.

PROTEINURIA, or ALBUMINURIA: This is the abnormal presence of albumin (albuminuria) and other abnormal proteins (proteinuria) in the urine. The condition is detected by routine urine dipsticks or by twenty-four-hour urine collections. Diseases that cause proteinuria include ACUTE RENAL FAILURE (mild proteinuria), AMYLOID GLOMERULONEPHRITIS, BACTERIAL CYSTITIS, FELINE UROLOGIC SYNDROME, and GLOMERULONEPHRITIS. Proteinuria can also occur with fever and after exercise.

Treatment consists of appropriate therapy for the causative condition or disease.

PULMONARY TUMORS: *See* LUNG CANCER.

PYELONEPHRITIS: This is an infection of the kidney(s) by bacterial organisms. One or both kidneys can become infected. Clinical signs are the same as those for BACTERIAL CYSTITIS at some time in the disease, but often there are no symptoms of note until the clinical signs of UREMIA appear, when both kidneys are in an advanced state of infection. The disease can occur with or without UROLITHS and with or without HYDRONEPHROSIS. Treatment aims at eradicating infection with appropriate antibiotics as directed by the veterinarian. If both kidneys are involved and clinical signs of UREMIA are present, then treatment includes supportive care, fluids, and appropriate antibiotics. The prognosis is variable, depending on the presence or absence of UREMIA, HYDRONEPHROSIS, UROLITHS, and so forth.

PYODERMA: *See* BACTERIAL SKIN DISEASES.

PYOMETRA: A pyometra is a collection of inflammatory material and fluid within the uterus. It is functionally considered an abscess and can only occur in unspayed females. A queen must have ovulated during her estrus period in order to develop a pyometra. The toxins from the bacteria and pus cells are what make the cat sick. Pyometras most commonly occur two to three weeks after a heat cycle. Symptoms are abdominal distention, loss of appetite, vomiting, diarrhea, depression, possible fever, and often increased thirst and urination.

Pyometras can take two forms: The cervix may remain closed and the pus accumulate within the uterus, or the cervix opens and a very purulent, occasionally bloody and sometimes malodorous discharge appears from the vagina. Diagnosis depends on history, presence of drainage through the vagina in cases of an open pyometra, and radiographic confirmation. Treatment is surgical removal of the uterus, and the prognosis is good for otherwise healthy cats. Exceptions are those cats that have suffered from toxic kidney changes due to released toxins and those cases in which the uterus has ruptured due to weakened walls or severe distention, releasing pus into the cat's abdomen. A pyometra is a surgical emergency. Other methods of treatment, not generally available, include medical therapy and drainage through the cervix.

PYONYCHIA: This is a pyogenic (pus-producing) infection of the nail bed. This disease has several distinct etiologies. It can be caused by trauma, a fungus infection, parasites, contact dermatitis, or as a complication of a declawing operation. Or it may be due to an immunologic disorder such as an autoimmune disease. It is generally not a primary disease entity but is secondary to an underlying problem. Signs are swelling, pain, redness, hair loss, exudation and crusting, split and brittle nails, and fever. Treatment consists of correcting or controlling the underlying cause.

PYOTHORAX (Septic Pleurisy): This is the accumulation of pus within the pleural space, between the lungs and the chest wall. Clinical signs are loss of appetite, fever and/or subnormal temperature, respiratory distress, pain, and obvious illness. This condition can be either chronic or acute. It can develop quickly and should be considered an emergency. It is of unknown cause but may be the result of a penetrating bite wound, a chest wound, or subsequent to PNEUMONIA. Treatment consists of in-hospital chest drains to get the pus out of the pleural cavity and lavaging (washing or flushing) with antibiotics. The prognosis is fair.

PYURIA: This is the presence of abnormally high numbers of white blood cells in the urine. It frequently occurs with HEMATURIA (which can occur without pyuria). The causes of pyuria are bacterial infections of the urinary tract. Signs of pyuria may include straining to urinate, an urge to urinate often, and an inability to pass urine. If pyuria is observed, a veterinarian should be consulted.

R

RABIES: *See* Infectious/Contagious Diseases.

RENAL DISEASES AND DISORDERS (KIDNEY DISEASES AND DISORDERS): Like humans, cats have two kidneys located in the abdomen. They act as filters for waste materials in the bloodstream, eliminating toxins from the blood. The kidneys also regulate the cat's body fluid composition and volume, and aid in the production of certain hormones which in turn regulate the production of red blood cells and assist in the formation of bones. **Parts of the kidneys:** The nephron is the functional unit of the kidney. The cat has approximately one million nephrons, each of which consists of a glomerulus that filters blood and a tubule that modifies the filtrate formed by the glomerulus. The glomerulus is a tuft of tiny blood vessels (capillaries) that filters blood to begin the production of urine. The fluid resulting from this filtration is called glomerular filtrate. The tubule is the part of the nephron that modifies the fluid that was produced by the filtration of blood. Urine is transported from the kidney to the urinary bladder via the ureters. It is then stored in the urinary bladder, which contracts to empty itself of urine when full. The urine travels through the urethra to the outside via the vagina in females and the penis in males. Male cats also have several very small prostate glands located outside the urethra and connected by tiny tubes to the urethra.

If only one kidney is damaged or rendered incompetent by virtue of disease, bacterial infection, trauma, or congenital malformation, the remaining kidney is usually able to take over and perform the necessary renal functions entirely, as long as it is healthy. However, if both kidneys become incompetent, a cat will suffer from RENAL FAILURE, and UREMIA will occur. Kidney damage can occur from birth, as in CONGENITAL RENAL ABNORMALITIES and ECTOPIC URETERS, resulting in HYDRONEPHROSIS on both sides. It can also result from a bacterial urinary tract infection such as PYELONEPHRITIS. Sometimes the kidneys can become damaged by kidney stones (UROLITHS) or RENAL TUMORS, but it is rare.

Kidney disease can be of unknown origin, such as AMYLOID GLOMERULONEPHRITIS, FELINE UROLOGIC SYNDROME (FUS) (the most common urinary tract problem of cats), and most forms of GLOMERULONEPHRITIS. Signs of kidney disease vary according to the severity of the disorder and the degree of kidney involvement. When only one kidney is affected, clinical signs may be entirely absent or extremely mild. Virtually all the signs (such as HEMATURIA, POLLAKIURIA, POLYDIPSIA, POLYURIA, PYURIA, STRANGURIA, and so forth) listed in this chapter are possible, but not necessarily all are invariably present. There are a number of tests and studies available to veterinarians in order to make a diagnosis of kidney disease (*see* Glossary 2). Treatment of kidney diseases varies widely, depending on the cause, the severity of the disease, and the amount of kidney damage already sustained by a cat. It almost always includes parenteral fluids (fluids given intravenously) and supportive care. Depending on the disease, antibiotics and diet may also be used as therapy. The prognosis for a cat with kidney disease also varies widely. *See also* BACTERIAL CYSTITIS, CHRONIC INTERSTITIAL NEPHRITIS, PROTEINURIA, RENAL SUBCAPSULAR CYSTS, and URINARY TRACT TRAUMA.

RENAL FAILURE (KIDNEY FAILURE): This is a disease state that occurs when the kidneys have been damaged. It can be abrupt (ACUTE RENAL FAILURE) or come on slowly (chronic kidney failure). In both cases, UREMIA is the end result.

RENAL SUBCAPSULAR CYSTS: Cats occasionally develop an accumulation of fluid beneath the capsule of the kidney. In most cases, the cats are older (at least ten years of age) and have chronic kidney failure. Clinical signs are those of UREMIA. In addition, one or both kidneys are enlarged without being painful. This disorder is usually treated by surgery, which aims at removing all or part of the renal capsule. The prognosis is usually good, but if advanced UREMIA is present, the prognosis may be guarded. *See also* CHRONIC INTERSTITIAL NEPHRITIS.

RENAL TUMORS (KIDNEY TUMORS): Tumors, or cancer, can arise in the kidneys themselves (primary renal tumors) or spread from other organs into the kidneys (secondary or metastatic renal tumors). Both are extremely rare in cats, with the exception of renal LYMPHOSARCOMA. Invasion of both kidneys by malignant lymphocytes is invariable when this disease occurs. More frequently, other organs besides the kidneys are involved with LYMPHOSARCOMA. Clinical signs are those of UREMIA. Symptoms of other kinds of renal tumors are frequently lacking but can include HEMATURIA and ANEMIA if the tumor bleeds excessively. Treatment is the surgical removal of the involved kidney after the diagnosis is certain, but if both kidneys are affected, as in LYMPHOSARCOMA, chemotherapy can be attempted in addition to parenteral fluid therapy and supportive care. The prognosis is always guarded.

REOVIRUS: *See* Infectious/Contagious Diseases.

REPRODUCTIVE DISORDERS: In the female cat the most efficient and safest method of preventing reproductive disorders is an early ovariohysterectomy (OHE). Uterine disorders, such as ENDOMETRITIS, PYOMETRA, and uterine tumors, as well as ovarian diseases, including tumors and abnormal hormone levels, can be totally avoided by early spaying. Ovariohysterectomy at an early age (preferably prior to the first estrus) greatly decreases the chance of a cat developing MAMMARY GLAND TUMORS, most of which are highly malignant in cats.

Male cats rarely suffer from reproductive tract disorders. Reproductive system disorders relating to breeding and birth such as infertility, mastitis, and so forth, are discussed in detail in Chapter 5.

RESPIRATORY DISEASES AND DISORDERS: The respiratory tract of a cat consists of the nose, larynx, pharynx, trachea, bronchi, and lungs. Each of these areas can become infected, diseased, or injured. Nasal disease is usually characterized by a purulent, thick NASAL DISCHARGE, while diseases of the larynx or "voice box" (LARYNGEAL DISEASE) can cause phonational changes. Problems with the back of the throat or pharynx will result in classical sore throat symptoms. In general, signs of respiratory problems consist of abnormal breathing, excessive sneezing or discharge from the nose, hoarseness, difficulty swallowing, coughing, and wheezing. A severe or untreated UPPER RESPIRATORY INFECTION is often the cause of respiratory problems. Foreign bodies can become lodged all the way down in a cat's trachea, or windpipe, and a traumatic injury, such as a bite wound or heavy blow can cause respiratory tract injury. *See also* BRONCHIAL DISEASE, FELINE BRONCHIAL ASTHMA, FELINE BRONCHITIS, LUNG DISEASE, NASAL CANCER, PHARYNGEAL DISEASES, PNEUMONIA, PULMONARY TUMORS, PYOTHORAX, and TRACHEAL DISEASE.

RESTRICTIVE CARDIOMYOPATHY: *See* CARDIOMYOPATHY.

RETINAL DISEASES: Many signs of systemic disease can be seen in the retina, which is located in the back of the eye. Cats that have severe ANEMIA, for instance, can have hemorrhages in the back of their eyes—these are usually FELINE LEUKEMIA VIRUS [FeLV(+)] cats. Also, cats with FELINE INFECTIOUS PERITONITIS (FIP) and TOXOPLASMOSIS can have changes in their retinas. These changes can lead to decreased vision or even loss of vision. The amino acid taurine is also extremely important in maintaining proper retinal health. Without a daily dietary source of this amino acid that cats cannot manufacture in their own bodies, the retina will degenerate, causing eventual BLINDNESS (*see* Chapter 3 for more about this). Retinal diseases in the cat are not visible to the naked eye and can only be detected by means of a thorough ophthalmic examination.

RHINOTRACHEITIS: *See* Infectious/Contagious Diseases.

RINGWORM: *See* FUNGAL SKIN DISEASES.

RODENT ULCER: *See* EOSINOPHILIC GRANULOMA COMPLEX.

S

SEIZURE DISORDERS: *See* EPILEPSY.

SEMI-COMA: *See* STATES OF CONSCIOUSNESS.

SEPTAL DEFECT: *See* CONGENITAL HEART DISEASE.

SKIN TUMORS: *See* LIPOMAS, MAST CELL TUMORS, MELANOMAS (MALIGNANT), and SQUAMOUS CELL CARCINOMAS.

SLIPPED SPINAL DISCS: *See* SPINAL CORD DISEASE.

SPINA BIFIDA: *See* CONGENITAL NEUROLOGIC DISEASES.

SPINAL CORD DISEASE: Intervertebral disc protrusion/extrusion may occur in cats, commonly older animals. The onset of neurologic signs is usually acute. A majority of intervertebral disc protrusions occur in the lower back. The signs of extruded disc material include crouching in the rear legs, mild to severe hind limb weakness and ATAXIA, back pain, urinary and fecal incontinence, and paralysis of the tail. In general, the more function that is lost in the limbs, the more severe the spinal cord compression due to a "slipped disc." Proprioception is lost first, followed by mild to moderate to severe motor dysfunction and sensory loss. Complete loss of proprioception, motor function, and sensation in the limbs suggests near complete or complete loss of normal spinal cord functions. The prognosis is poor in these instances. Many gradations exist. A veterinarian or veterinary neurologist should be consulted prior to making any medical or surgical decision about treating a cat with this disorder.

SPLENIC TUMORS: *See* MAST CELL TUMORS.

SQUAMOUS CELL CARCINOMAS: There are three distinct types of squamous cell carcinomas (cancers) seen in cats. In order of frequency, they occur on the skin, the mouth, and the conjunctiva of the eye.

Squamous cell carcinomas of the skin: Squamous cell carcinomas of white pigmented skin can be caused by excessive exposure to sunlight. Cats with any white areas, especially the ears, who live in very sunny climates such as Florida, the Caribbean, southern California, and so forth, and are exposed over a period of years to the strongest rays of the sun (between 10 A.M. and 2 P.M.) can develop chronic dermatitis that will eventually become cancerous. The condition can be diagnosed by means of a biopsy. Protection from the sun's rays can be preventive. Treatment consists of radiation therapy and/or amputation of the affected area (usually the ear tip).

Squamous cell carcinomas of the mouth: This type of carcinoma is becoming more common. It begins with an invisible tumor inside the mouth—on the gum, under the tongue, and so forth—that grows extremely rapidly (within a period of only three or four months) until it becomes so large that it interferes with a cat's ability to eat or even close its mouth. These cancers usually cannot be successfully removed surgically because of their size. They are said to be sensitive to radiation therapy, but in our experience radiation therapy has provided no relief, nor has chemotherapy. Therefore, we have to state that there is no known effective treatment for this type of carcinoma.

Squamous cell carcinoma of the conjunctiva: Squamous cell carcinoma does occur in the conjunctiva of the eye, although infrequently. The only effective therapy is enucleation (complete removal) of the eye and its contents.

STATES OF CONSCIOUSNESS: The ascending reticular activation system (ARAS) functions to "arouse" the cerebral cortex and awaken the brain to consciousness. Disturbances of consciousness can result from lesions in the ARAS. Depression occurs when a cat responds slowly or inappropriately to verbal stimuli. Stupor or semi-coma implies that a cat is unresponsive except to vigorous and repeated stimuli that may necessarily be painful. Coma means complete unresponsiveness to repeated noxious stimulation.

STRANGURIA: This is the symptom of straining to urinate. It can occur with a bacterial urinary tract infection and with FELINE UROLOGIC SYNDROME, with or without blockage of the urethra. Stranguria is usually accompanied by an increased frequency of urination (POLLAKIURIA) and HEMATURIA. A veterinarian should be consulted if symptoms are observed.

STUD TAIL: This skin disease is most commonly seen in sexually active tomcats. The supracaudal gland is a modified sebaceous (oil) gland located on top of the tail where it meets the body. Hyperactivity of the gland occurs when a male becomes sexually aroused and a waxy accumulation causes hair loss. There is no pain or itching. Castration is not usually effective, and treatment involves cleansing the area and/or oral medication.

STUPOR: *See* STATES OF CONSCIOUSNESS.

SYSTEMIC LUPUS ERYTHEMATOSUS: This disease is rare in cats, and as far as we now know, there is no age, breed, or sex predilection for it in cats. The most common signs of lupus in the cat are skin lesions, persistent skin infection, fever, enlarged peripheral lymph nodes, ANEMIA, oral ulcers, and GLOMER-ULONEPHRITIS. Lupus is diagnosed by means of special immunologic tests for the presence of specific antibodies, an antinuclear antibody test, and also through biopsy of affected organs (usually the skin in cats). While it is not considered curable, it is treatable. We use immunosuppressive therapy with corticosteroids and possibly other drugs if the disease is aggressive and active, along with supportive care. When the disease is more benign and not causing potential life-threatening illness, we may recommend less intensive drug therapy.

SYSTEMIC LUPUS ERYTHEMATOSUS ARTHRITIS: This rare arthritis often involves multiple joints and is one of several conditions associated with SYSTEMIC LUPUS ERYTHEMATO-SUS. The disease is very infrequently found in the cat. Diagnosis is based on orthopedic examination, blood tests, radiographs, and microscopic examination of aspirated joint fluid.

Treatment with immunosuppressive drugs such as corticosteroids is required. With proper drug therapy, the disease can usually be controlled.

T

TETRAPARESIS: Weakness in all four limbs. *See* PARESIS.

THIAMINE DEFICIENCY: *See* NUTRITIONAL NEUROLOGIC DISEASE.

THIRD EYELID PROLAPSE: Like many other animals except humans, cats have a third eyelid, or nictating membrane, which is situated below the eye on the nasal side. This membrane serves as a protective mechanism. When a cat senses danger to the eye, it can pull the eyeball back into its orbit (something that humans cannot do), and the third eyelid then comes across and covers it as an added protection. Under most circumstances, this membrane is kept in its normal position beneath and adjacent to the eye by fine, delicate nerves. Problems can develop if these tiny nerves become inflamed or traumatized, allowing the third eyelid to cover one or both eyes. The cause of this phenomenon is unknown, but the result can be very upsetting to a cat owner who sees only a pinkish membrane covering his pet's eye and may think that the eye is gone or badly injured. Although a prolapsed third eyelid can occur because of an injury and should always receive veterinarian attention, if there is no detectable underlying cause, it will usually repair itself in a month or two.

TOXOPLASMOSIS: *See* INFLAMMATORY NEU-ROLOGIC DISEASES and Infectious/Contagious Diseases.

TRACHEAL DISEASE: In general, signs of tracheal disease in the cat are a chronic cough and perhaps severe breathing difficulty. Although it is rare, cats can suffer from a collapsed trachea. This is a structural defect in which the tracheal tube sags inward, rather than staying open to permit passage of air. Foreign bodies, such as a small bone, stick, or straw, can become lodged in a cat's trachea and must be removed surgically or with long forceps. There are also parasitic diseases of a cat's trachea that can usually be treated medically.

TUMORS, EYE: *See* DIFFUSE IRIS MELANOMA and SQUAMOUS CELL CARCINOMA.

TUMORS, URINARY TRACT: *See* RENAL TUMORS and UROGENITAL TUMORS.

U

ULCERS: *See* MAST CELL TUMORS.

UPPER RESPIRATORY INFECTIONS (URI): *See* Infectious/Contagious Diseases.

UREMIA: This is a constellation of abnormalities in body fluid composition and volume caused by both acute and chronic RENAL FAILURE. Typical signs of uremia include increased water intake (POLYDIPSIA), increased urine volume (POLYURIA), lack of appetite, VOMITING, DEPRESSION, lethargy, and ANEMIA. These symptoms will vary in severity depending on the degree of kidney damage.

URINARY INCONTINENCE: Urinary incontinence is the loss of urine in any unaccustomed or undesirable area. Most urinary incontinence is involuntary and can be due to a number of very different causes, including a congenital defect such as an ECTOPIC URETER, a neurologic disorder, or a spinal disease. It is rarely the result of the loss of sex-steroid hormones after an ovariohysterectomy or castration operation in cats. Sometimes urinary incontinence is not of physical origin but is the result of a behavior problem (submissive or excitement urination, or sexual marking—*see* Chapter 8). It can be very difficult to ascertain the cause in many instances of urinary incontinence. If the cause is determined to be physical, treatment will depend on the specific condition and may include drugs to control the abnormality.

URINARY TRACT TRAUMA: Urinary tract trauma can occur as the result of a number of accidents, including being hit by an automobile or bicycle, or a fall from a height. A sign of a problem after a known accident can be blood in the urine (HEMATURIA). If blood clots have formed in the urinary tract, obstruction is possible, causing straining to urinate (STRANGURIA) or inability to urinate. Sometimes the bladder can be ruptured and urine may accumulate in the abdominal cavity. Ultimately, signs of UREMIA will appear if the obstruction involves the urethra or both kidneys or if the bladder has ruptured. Treatment aims at supportive care, parenteral fluids, antibiotics, and removal of any obstruction. Brisk hemorrhage must be controlled by surgery.

URINARY TRACT STONES: *See* UROLITHS.

UROGENITAL TUMORS: The most common identified urogenital tumor in cats is cancer of the bladder, which is quite rare. The most common symptom is unrelenting cystitis and/or HEMATURIA, which is not responsive to appropriate medical therapy. Dye studies of the urinary tract and bladder should be performed, followed by surgical exploration and biopsy to confirm the disease.

Other primary tumors of the urogenital system can involve the kidneys and the vulva/vagina. These are extremely rare.

UROLITHS (URINARY TRACT STONES): Feline uroliths occur most commonly in the bladder but can be in any part of the urinary tract. They can be in the urethra after they pass from the bladder or be located in both places. Uroliths are rarely present in one or both kidneys. There are several types of stones in cats. The most common type of urolith (stone) is struvite (more than 70 percent), with fewer reports of ammonium urate, uric acid, calcium phosphate, and calcium oxalate stones. The cause of uroliths is unknown, but urinary tract infections, impedance of urine outflow, and diet are all known influences. Clinical signs of uroliths may include HEMATURIA, PYURIA, obstruction of the urethra, straining to urinate (STRANGURIA), increased frequency of urination

(POLLAKIURIA), and ultimately UREMIA if the obstruction is complete.

Treatment aims at increasing urine volume via increased water intake and controlling bacterial infection *if* it is present. Dietary management and urine acidification also form an important part of the treatment. Dietary management to dissolve struvite stones can be attempted along with efforts to control infection, but dietary management for other than struvite stones has not been proven to be efficacious. The vast majority of uroliths in cats are struvite. Thus, a trial of dietary dissolution seems justified if the urolith does not cause urethral obstruction. Simultaneously, the urine should be acidified, which promotes urolith dissolution. If bacterial infection is present, antibiotics should also be used. Uroliths that do not dissolve in thirty days should be removed by surgery. Thereafter, prevention of uroliths can be attempted with dietary manipulations, ongoing use of acidifiers, and control of infection. See FELINE UROLOGIC SYNDROME (FUS) for details of these preventive measures.

UTERINE INFECTIONS: *See* ENDOMETRITIS, METRITIS, and PYOMETRA.

UTERINE PROLAPSE: *See* Chapter 5.

V

VASCULAR NEUROLOGIC DISEASE: Cerebral ischemic necrosis is a neurologic disease caused by vascular compromise in the brain. Cats are acutely affected with neurologic dysfunction that often affects one side of the cerebral cortex more than the other (lateralization). Clinical signs include DEPRESSION, aggression, ATAXIA, circling, BLINDNESS, jerky movements of the face or limbs, and weakness. Although weakness and visual deficits may always persist, a cat often adapts to these deficits and appears normal within days or weeks. The disease is nonprogressive. The brain lesion is most profound in the area supplied by a major vessel called the middle cerebral artery. The cause of the vascular compromise is unknown. The prognosis for life in these cats is usually good, but residual signs such as seizures and aggressive behavior may affect the animal's compatibility as a pet.

VESTIBULAR AND/OR CEREBELLAR DISEASE: *See* BALANCE DISORDERS.

VIRUS-RELATED SKIN DISEASES: Systemic viral diseases can often cause skin disorders. FELV has been known to cause a number of skin diseases such as chronic, recurrent pyodermas (abscesses), eosinophilic ulcers, itching, lymphoid hyperplasia (large lymph nodes), and skin cancers. Feline herpes causes an ulcerative stomatitis (oral lesions) and dermatitis, while cats with CALICIVIRUS may develop swollen feet with erosion of the foot pads and interdigital webs, and mouth ulcers. Treatment of the underlying viral cause is necessary to clear up these skin disorders.

VOMITING: *See* GASTROINTESTINAL DISEASES AND DISORDERS.

W

WARFARIN POISONING: Cats can accidentally ingest rat poison when they catch and eat a mouse or rat. Warfarin and similar chemicals found in rat poison can cause serious bleeding problems in cats. The poison interferes with vitamin K and the production of several blood clotting factors. Clinical signs may be varied and include ANEMIA, pale mucous membranes, nosebleeds, difficulty breathing, gastrointestinal or urinary bleeding, and bruising. In most cases, the problem can be controlled with vitamin K injections, blood transfusions, and prevention of further exposure to the poison. *See also* the Emergencies section.

About The
Animal Medical Center

The Animal Medical Center is known worldwide for its pioneering approach to pet care and veterinary medicine. *Town and Country* magazine recently called it the world's best hospital, animal or human. It is the hospital where New Yorkers from all walks of life take their sick or injured pets. Even at midnight there are likely to be pet owners bringing everything from dogs and cats to birds, reptiles, and other exotic animals to The AMC for treatment.

It had its beginning in 1910 as a clinic for treating the pets and work animals of the poor living on New York's Lower East Side. Founded by the New York Women's League for Animals under the leadership of Ellin Prince Speyer, the clinic treated six thousand animals in its first year. In 1914, with the help of a donation from James Speyer, the Ellin Prince Speyer Hospital for Animals was founded at 350 Lafayette Street. In 1955, the Speyer Hospital received a large grant from the estate of Alfred H. Caspary to build the Institute of Veterinary Research adjacent to the hospital. Several years later, with the help of another grant from the Caspary estate, the Speyer Hospital and the Institute of Veterinary Research were combined in a new building at 510 East 62nd Street in the Rockefeller University/New York Hospital/Cornell Medical Center area, enabling the facility to be in close proximity to the other medical institutions with which it works closely.

High-Quality Services
for Sick Animals

In its charter, The AMC was dedicated "to establish high-quality medical, surgical, laboratory, and nursing services for sick animals." This aim has been well met. Over seventy veterinarians with specialties in a wide spectrum of fields, assisted by a devoted staff of trained paramedical personnel, treat more than sixty thousand animal patients a year. Support systems such as a pharmacy, medical library, and computer system for the storage of clinical data help to make the Center's operations run smoothly.

227

The Center never closes. It is open twenty-four hours a day, 365 days a year, and provides the only full-service veterinary emergency operation in the New York metropolitan area during the hours of 5 P.M. to 8 A.M. Nearly fifteen thousand emergency cases are handled by The AMC annually.

New avenues of care for pets are constantly being explored and implemented. In the past year, The AMC has established an innovative Oral Medicine and Surgery Service in which a team made up of a dentist and a veterinary surgeon apply dental techniques to animals that previously were used only in human dentistry. An Exotic Animal Clinic recently opened at The AMC, under the direction of Dr. Kathleen Quesenberry (one of our contributors). Already a wide variety of pets, from iguanas to pythons, rare birds, and ferrets, has been treated.

To Improve the Quality of Care Through Study

The AMC's unique location in the midst of a densely populated pet-owning area and its consequent large caseload make it possible for The AMC to carry out all research into new methods of diagnosis and treatment by observing and treating naturally occurring disease and performing clinical and comparative studies. The AMC does not support any research programs in which diseases are artificially induced. Currently, AMC research programs include investigations into improved methods of treatment of cancer and of cardiac, ophthalmologic, and kidney disease.

The Donaldson-Atwood Cancer Clinic, for example, works closely with the Memorial Sloan-Kettering Cancer Center in developing innovative therapies for treating cancer in pets and is actively engaged in studying the comparative aspects of oncologic therapy that may eventually help in the treatment of human cancer patients. Four thousand cases are diagnosed and treated annually in the Clinic.

In keeping with its commitment to employ the best diagnostic methods available in veterinary medicine, The AMC now houses the only CAT (computerized tomography) scanner available for animals on the eastern seaboard and has recently purchased one of the few echocardiographs available for veterinarians in the Northeast.

AMC staff members regularly receive grants to enable them to further their research into particular areas of veterinary medicine, and many are the recipients of awards recognizing their work.

Postgraduate Teaching

The third aim set down in The AMC's charter is "to develop postgraduate teaching facilities for veterinarians." Each year between twenty and twenty-five veterinarians, graduates of veterinary medical colleges in the United States and abroad, join The AMC as interns to further their training. Competition is stiff to be accepted for the Center's postgraduate training, and the number of applicants is many times greater each year than the number of positions to be filled. Following a year of rigorous training, these interns may continue their work at The AMC as medical or surgical residents. After residency, some veterinarians join the staff of The AMC, while others go on to private practice or return to veterinary medical colleges to teach. Many AMC graduates are internationally known for their work.

In addition, The AMC runs a continuing education program for its staff veterinarians and area practitioners. Lectures and workshops covering a wide range of veterinary specialties are covered. Other educational programs for veterinarians and veterinary medical college students are also offered, often in cooperation with organizations such as the American Animal Hospital Association and the American Veterinary Medical Association.

One Step Further

In addition to providing the best possible medical care for pets and furthering the development of even better animal medical care through research and the training of veterinarians, The AMC goes one step further: It also ministers to pet owners and other animal lovers.

Since 1982, The AMC has had a full-time clinical social worker on the staff. Susan Phillips Cohen is the Director of Counseling and the chairperson of The AMC Institute for the Human/Companion Animal Bond. She works with pet owners to help them understand and cope with their grief and bewilderment at a pet's death or sudden illness, and to aid them in making difficult decisions about hospitalization, surgery, and euthanasia. She also runs workshops and self-help groups for bereaved pet owners. In 1983, two social work interns expanded the Center's Human/Companion Animal Bond program personnel. In addition, The AMC's Pet Outreach Program, in which volunteers bring cats and dogs to visit the residents of nursing homes, mental institutions, senior citizen centers, and hospices, has met with tremendous success.

Another unique AMC program, The Animal Behavior Therapy Clinic (ABTC), was established in 1978. Under the directorship of Dr. Peter L. Borchelt, The ABTC is dedicated to the diagnosis and treatment of behavior problems in pet animals. Seminars and courses for pet owners on various aspects of pet behavior are also given on a regular basis.

The AMC is always striving to find ways to make pet ownership more viable for people. Some recently innovated programs illustrate this. The AMC's Surviving Pet Maintenance and Placement Program is designed to take the worry out of what will happen to a pet if an owner is no longer able to care for it. Designed specifically to meet the needs of older pet owners, the program assures that a pet will be well cared for for the rest of its normal life should its owner become ill or die. Another program, Accessible Care for Animals (ACA), is aimed at improving veterinary services for people with disabilities. The AMC has also recently installed TTY (teletypewriter) equipment so that hearing-impaired or deaf pet owners can call the Center. There are also three veterinarians on staff who are fluent in American Sign Language.

The Human Element

None of these impressive facts and programs would combine to work as well as they do to fulfill The AMC's primary aim to provide high-quality care for sick animals if it weren't for the people involved.

In more than two years of visiting The AMC at all hours of the day and evening to interview veterinarians and collect material for this book and its companion volume, *The Complete Book of Dog Health*, I saw The AMC staff at work. I saw a lot of pats, kind words, and TLC for the animals. I saw a veterinarian carrying one of her patients around in her arms because she thought it was in need of some extra affection. Doctors often interrupted interviews to answer pages, attend to patients, and reassure anxious owners. The dedication, enthusiasm, energy, concern, and responsibility of all the people who staff The AMC, coupled with their professional ability, is what makes The Animal Medical Center a very special place.

Fall 1985   Elizabeth Randolph

APPENDIX

Medications

DAVID P. AUCOIN, DVM

Throughout this book, references are made to various medications or drugs that veterinarians may prescribe either to treat disease, to relieve pain or discomfort, or to sedate/tranquilize cats so that they can be treated or operated on. These medications or drugs may be used by a veterinarian during the course of treatment or may be sent home with an owner to give the cat as directed. There are detailed instructions on how to give various forms of medicine to a cat in Chapter 13.

Cats and Medication

It is important for a conscientious cat owner to realize that just because a cat is sick it does not necessarily mean that it requires drugs in order to get better. Cat owners should be aware that veterinarians are apt to give fewer medications to cats than they do to dogs. There are three basic reasons for this.

1) In general, cats are difficult to medicate, especially at home. The struggle and ensuing stress involved in medicating a cat at home often offsets any good effects that the medication might have. Thus, a doctor will often medicate a cat in the office when necessary, rather than ask that medication be given at home.

2) Cats are overtly sensitive to many medications, especially those that require metabolism in order to work. They are usually slow metabolizers of drugs; therefore, it is impossible to predict how long a drug that requires a cat to metabolize it into a harmless product before it can be eliminated from the body will continue to have an effect on the cat.

3) Cats have remarkable healing powers. They tend to get better with rest and loving care and often require nothing additional.

It is especially valuable if owners can obtain the *generic name* of any medication used in treating a cat, whether in the doctor's office or at home. There are several reasons why it is important to know exactly what kind of medicine (rather than a brand name) an animal has been given: if another doctor is seen in the future, if treatment with a particular medication is successful, and if there is an idiosyncratic reaction (individual hypersensitivity) to a specific drug, which is not uncommon in cats. Because there are often many different brands of a given drug, a brand name alone may be extremely difficult to identify. This information should be obtained if a cat is treated in an emergency clinic by a doctor other than its regular veterinarian so that the cat's own doctor will know what has been given. Having said that, it is interesting to note that some drugs, such as Valium, are usually referred to by their brand names, not by their generic names.

Common sense should always prevail when it comes to medicating a cat. If an owner has given a cat medication before and had difficulty either with the form of the medicine (for example, pills or capsules) or with a particular type (for example, anti-

231

biotic or tranquilizer), the doctor should be told. The medicine can often be given in a different form or dosage. Unfortunately, however, many frequently used medications have an alcohol base (elixirs) when they are in liquid form, and cats often cannot tolerate the taste of alcohol and refuse the medication. If an animal seems to be having a bad reaction to a medicine, an owner should not be afraid to stop giving it until the doctor can be consulted. *No medication is so important that an animal will suffer irreparable harm if a dose or two is missed.* This does not mean, however, that the medicine should be stopped entirely for two weeks or until the next doctor appointment comes around. The veterinarian should also be consulted if a medication is not having the desired effect. Under no circumstances should an owner take it upon himself to increase the dosage of any medicine. In every instance the veterinarian should be consulted as soon as possible if difficulties arise.

Over-the-Counter Products and Drugs

Because of cats' sensitivity to certain medications, *no drug should ever be given to a cat without a veterinarian's advice.*

Products that contain acetaminophen or phenacatin (which is metabolized into acetaminophen), such as Tylenol analgesic and other aspirin substitutes, and many cold remedies *are toxic in any amount for cats.* Fifty percent of all ten-pound cats would die within forty-eight hours from one single dose of Tylenol; double strength would kill all of them within two days. At last count, there were almost three hundred different over-the-counter remedies containing either acetaminophen or phenacatin on the market, many of which are not clearly labeled as to ingredients. That's why we repeat again: NEVER GIVE A CAT ANY OVER-THE-COUNTER MEDICATION WITHOUT FIRST CONSULTING A VETERINARIAN.

Aspirin: Although there are safe doses of aspirin for cats, it should never be given to a cat except as directed by a veterinarian.

Flea-control preparations: Cat owners should be aware that kittens are especially sensitive to many over-the-counter flea-control preparations. It is best to obtain any such products from a veterinarian, or check with the doctor before using any commercial product. Always use a product labeled specifically for cats.

Kaopectate: For simple diarrhea not accompanied by vomiting or other signs of illness (see "Gastrointestinal Diseases and Disorders" in the Encyclopedia), 1 cc (about 16 drops) of Kaopectate diarrhea remedy every four hours is usually effective for cats. As we discussed in Chapter 13, a syringe is the easiest and most accurate way to give a cat liquid medication.

Hydrogen peroxide: Giving a cat enough hydrogen peroxide to make it throw up is a relatively harmless way to induce vomiting *if a cat is known to have eaten something noncorrosive, such as human medications, antifreeze, or rat poison.* Vomiting should *never* be induced if a cat is known or suspected to have eaten anything corrosive, such as gasoline or oil products (the distinctive smell will usually indicate this) or anything with a lye base, such as drain cleaner. More about poisons in the Emergencies section. An overdose of hydrogen peroxide will not do any permanent damage to a cat but will simply make the animal very sick to its stomach.

Tranquilizers and Anesthetics

The methods of giving general anesthetics, preoperative testing, and postoperative care, are all discussed in detail in Chapter 4. Owners should realize, however, that even if only local anesthetics are to be used for a simple procedure (which is very rare), cats almost always need to be tranquilized in order to be worked on. A cat will probably be given a combination of one or more sedatives/tranquilizers, which will be metabolized according to the animal's own system, the amount of sedative given, and so forth. Here at The AMC (and at most veterinary hospitals) cats are routinely kept in the hospital until they have completely regained consciousness after anesthetic. In some situations (an emergency clinic, for example) a cat may be released to its owner while still not entirely out of the anesthetic/tranquilizer. In these cases the cat may be very dopey and may thrash around and vocalize while coming out of the anesthetic. These are perfectly normal reactions. As we mentioned above, an owner should find out the name of the tranquilizer given in case of a bad reaction and for the information of the regular doctor.

Medications Used in Veterinary Medicine

It is also important for cat owners to realize that almost all the drugs used in feline veterinary medicine have an equivalent in human medications and are probably available in human pharmacies. The only difference is in a particular species' reaction to and metabolization of a specific medication, and in FDA approval of the drug for a given species of animal. Thus, there is no great mystery surrounding veterinary medications, and they can usually be found listed in any standard reference pertaining to human medicines. The following list consists of some medications commonly used in feline veterinary medicine and the side effects that may occur when these medicines are used. This may help cat owners to know what to expect and ask intelligent questions of their veterinarians.

Some Medications Often Used for Cats, by Type: Their Generic Names, with Simplified Pronunciations, Most Common Trade Names, and Side Effects.

NOTE: DOSAGES ARE PURPOSELY OMITTED, AS THEY VARY DEPENDING ON USE.

In general, unless instructed otherwise by a veterinarian, all medications should be given with food. A common side effect of almost all medication in cats is gastrointestinal upset, including appetite loss, diarrhea, and vomiting. Cats often salivate excessively when given any medication, spitting foam all over. This is not a toxic reaction but is merely due to the bad taste of the medicine. It will usually let up with continued use of the medicine. Some medications also cause dopiness or hyperactivity. If any of these side effects is excessive or a cat is exhibiting symptoms that it didn't prior to being medicated, owners should stop the medication and check with the veterinarian. Barring this, all medications should be continued up to the full amount prescribed, even after the cat seems better.

ALLERGY MEDICATIONS:
Side effects: Increased water consumption, urination, appetite.
Contraindications: Excessive amounts of any of the above.
Metrevet (mét ra vet)
Temeril-P (tém er ill)

ANTIBIOTICS—used to kill bacteria:
Side effects: Loose stool/diarrhea and/or vomiting. Excessive salivation: foaming.
Contraindications: Excessive dose or inappropriate duration of any/all of the above.
Amoxicillin (a mox i síll in)

Ampicillin (am pi síll in). Trade names: Omnipen, Princillin
Cephadroxil (sef a dróx ill). Trade name: Cef-a-tabs
Cephalexin (sef a léx in). Trade name: Keflex
Cephalothin (sef á loe thin). Trade name: Keflin
Chloramphenicol (clor ám fen i col)
Erythromycin (er ith roe mýe sin)
Gentamicin (jen ta mýe sin)
Lincomycin (lin koe mýe sin)
Metronidazole (me troe ní da sole). Also used for worming. Trade name: Flagyl
Neomycin (nee oh mýe sin). Trade name: Biosol
Penicillin G (pen i síll in)
Sulfadiazine/trimethoprim (sol fa dýe a zeen/trye méth oh prim) Also used as a urinary anti-infective. Trade names: D. Trim, Tribrissin
Sulfadimethoxine (sul fa dye meth óx een). Trade name: Bactrovet
Sulfisoxazole (sul fi sóx a zole). Trade name: Gantrasin
Tetracycline (tet ra sýe kleen). Trade name: Panmycin
Ticarcillan (tye kar síll in)

ANTICONSTIPATION MEDICATIONS:
Side effects/contraindications: Diarrhea.
Bisacodyl (bis a kóe dill). Trade name: Dulcolax
Cephulac (céf u lak). Trade names: Lactulose
Laxatone or Petromalt
Psyllium (síl e um). Trade names: Metamucil, Siblin

ANTICONVULSANT MEDICATIONS:
Side effects: Increased water consumption, urination, and appetite. Cat will be very sedated for one to two weeks, after which sedation will wear off.
Contraindications: Inform veterinarian if cat is *not* initially sedated.
Phenobarbital (fee noe bár bi tal). Also used as a tranquilizer.

ANTIDIARRHEA MEDICATIONS:
Side effects/contraindications: Constipation.
CMP (Corrective Mixture of Paregoric)
Neopectolin®: contains neomycin and pectolin

ANTIFUNGAL MEDICATIONS:
Side effects/contraindications: Vomiting/diarrhea.
Griseofulvin (gri see oh fúl vin). Trade name: Fulvicin

ANTI-INFLAMMATORY MEDICATIONS:
Side effects: Gastrointestinal upsets.
Aspirin. Use only buffered aspirin; for example, Bufferin or Ascriptin.
Steroids. *See* separate listing.

ANTIMITE MEDICATIONS:
No major side effects.
Amitraz (a mi tráz). Trade name: Mitaban
Cerumite (sir yóu mite)

BRONCHODILATORS—used for breathing difficulty, coughs, asthma:
Side effects/contraindications: Gastrointestinal upset. Can cause cats to become "hyper"—tense, excitable, hopped-up.
Theophylline (thee óff i lin)
Aminophylline (am in óff i lin)—metabolized into theophylline.
Oxtriphylline (ox trýe fi lin). Same drug as theophylline.

HEART DISEASE MEDICATIONS, including DIURETICS:
Note: Dosage will vary as disease progresses.
Side effects: These are all very potent drugs and may cause severe side effects. If owners see any of these side effects, they should never give more medication and should always stop and consult with the veterinarian. Side effects can include anorexia, vomiting, diarrhea, lethargy, and weakness due to lowered blood pressure. When diuretics are given, owners should expect increased water intake/urination

Captopril (káp toe prill). Trade name: Capoten
Digoxin (di jóx in). Trade names: Cardoxin, Lanoxin
Hydralazine (hye drál a zeen). Trade name: Apresoline
Propranolol (proe prán oh lole). Trade name: Inderal
   DIURETIC:
Furosemide (fur óh se mide). Trade name: Lasix

HORMONES—used to treat endocrine system imbalance disorders:
Side effects: Few reported side effects.
Levothyroxine (lee voe thye róx een)—replacement therapy for hypothyroidism
Oxytocin (ox i tóe sin)—used for queening/milk production problems. Trade name: Pitocin
Stanozolol (stan óh zoe lole). Trade name: Winstrol
Testosterone (tess tóss ter own)

SHAMPOO:
Benzoyl Peroxide (bén zoe ill). Trade name: Oxydex

STEROIDS—used as anti-inflammatory agents:
Side effects: Increased water consumption, urination, food consumption.
Contraindications: Severity of any of the above.
Dexamethasone (dex a méth a sone). Trade name: Azium
Hydrocortisone (hye droe kór ti sone). Trade name: Topiderm
Prednisone (préd ni sone). Trade name: Meticorten
Triamcinalone (trye am sín oh lone). Trade name: Vetalog

TRANQUILIZERS (sedatives, anti-anxiety medications):
Side effects: As a group, there is a great deal of variation from cat to cat on how long these medications last. Owners must determine their own cat's tolerance and tell the veterinarian. If a cat is sedated for more than eight to ten hours, it is too much; but if a cat is given a lot of medication and is still lively, the medicine needs to be changed or its dosage altered. Most tranquilizers are short-acting, with a two- to four-hour effect.
Acepromazine (a se próe ma zeen)
Diazepam (dye áz e pam). Trade name: Valium
Ketamine. Trade name: Vetalar
Phenobarbital

ULCER/ANTIVOMITING MEDICATIONS:

*Note: Often due to hairballs; therefore, Laxatone®
and Petromalt®, also used for constipation, are
often used.*
Side effects/contraindications: Excessive vomiting.
Cimetidine (sye mét i deen). Trade name: Tagamet
Prochlorperazine (proe klor pér a zeen). Trade
name: Compazine

URINARY ACIDIFIERS/ANTI-INFECTIVES:

Side effects/contraindications: Vomiting, anorexia.
Aluminum Chloride ⎱ Combined trade name:
Methionine   ⎰   Uroeze
Sulfadiazine/trimethoprim (*see also* Antibiotics)

WORMING AGENTS:

Side effects: These agents are no longer purgative
but very parasite-specific and should cause no side
effects. Possible side effects are vomiting/diarrhea.
Dichlorvos (dye klór voss). Trade name: Task
Mebendazole (me bén da zole). Trade name:
Telmintic
Metronidazole (*see also* Antibiotics)
Piperazine (pí per a zeen)
Praziquantel (pray zi kwón tel). Trade name:
Droncit
Pyrantal Paomate (pi rán tel páy o mate). Trade
name: Nemex
Thenium Closylate (thén ee um klóe si late). Trade
name: Canopar

Some Terms Commonly Used in Veterinary Medicine

Abdominal: Pertaining to the "belly" cavity containing the stomach, intestines, liver, kidneys, urinary bladder, uterus, and so forth.

Abscess: A collection of pus anywhere in the body, usually surrounded by inflamed, damaged tissue.

Acquired disease/disorder: A condition that develops after birth, as opposed to one that is present at birth (congenital).

Acute: Of sudden or rapid onset, as opposed to chronic.

Adreno-: Pertaining to the adrenal gland.

Alopecia: Hair loss.

Analgesia: Loss of sensation of pain.

Anasarca: Fluid in limbs or under the skin.

Antibody: A protein the body will manufacture in response to a disease organism or to a vaccine. It helps to fight off the disease in the future. *See also* Antigen.

Antigen: A substance that the body recognizes as "foreign," such as a bacterium or virus, against which it produces an antibody.

Arthro-: Pertaining to joints.

Atopy: An allergic reaction to inhaled allergens which usually appears as a skin problem.

Aural: Pertaining to the ear.

Autoimmune disease: A disease in which the body destroys its own tissues.

Benign: A tumor or growth that is not cancerous or malignant.

Brachycephalic breeds: Breeds of cats with short noses and pushed-in faces (for example, Persians).

Carcinoma: A cancer that arises in the epithelium, the tissue that lines the skin and internal organs of the body.

Cardio-: Pertaining to the heart.

Cardiology: The study of the diseases, functions, and structures of the heart.

Castration: Neutering of a male cat by surgical removal of the testicles.

Chronic: A condition that continues or recurs and often lasts a long time, as opposed to one that is acute.

Clinical signs: Overt symptoms or signs visible to the naked eye.

Coagulation: Clotting, as blood.

Congenital: A condition or disease present at birth that may surface later in life. Not necessarily hereditary.

Cyst: An abnormal sac filled with liquid.

Dermatology: The study of diseases of the skin and their diagnosis and treatment.

Edema: Abnormal collection of fluid in tissue spaces (*see* Anasarca).

Effusion: Abnormal fluid buildup in a body cavity.

Encephalo-: Pertaining to the brain.

Endocrinology: The study of the endocrine glands and the hormones they secrete.

Entero-: Pertaining to the intestines.

Estrous cycle: The regularly occurring heat cycle of a female cat.

Estrus: The actual heat period.

Etiology: The cause(s) of a particular disease.

Fibroma: A nonmalignant tumor of connective tissue.

Gastro-: Pertaining to the stomach.

Gastroenterology: The study of diseases of the stomach, intestines, liver, and pancreas.

Hematoma: A blood-filled swelling; blood clot outside the blood vessels.

Hepato-: Pertaining to the liver.

Hereditary: A disease or condition present at birth that can be traced back to ancestors or parents. It can surface later in life.

Homeostasis: Physiological equilibrium.

Hydration: Balance of water in the body.

Hyper-: An overproduction, as in hyperthyroidism.

Hyperplasia: Enlargement.

Hypo-: A deficiency or underproduction, as in hypothyroidism.

Hypoxia: A deficiency of oxygen in the tissues.

Idiopathic: Of unknown cause.

Incubation period: The time between infection and the onset of disease symptoms.

-itis: Inflammation of, as in pancreatitis.

Kcal (kilocalories): One thousand calories or one Calorie (C).

Malignancy/malignant: Descriptive term(s) used to describe a cancer that can spread (metastasize) to other parts of the body.

Metastasize: Spread to other parts of the body, as in cancer.

Metastatic cancer: Cancer that has spread from one location to another part of the body.

Metr-: Pertaining to the uterus.

Mycosis: A disease caused by a fungus.

Myo-: Pertaining to the muscles.

Neonatals: Newborns.

Neoplasia: Abnormal cell growth; tumor or cancer.

Nephro-: Pertaining to the kidneys.

Nephrology: Study of disorders of the kidneys.

Neuro-: Pertaining to the nervous system.

Neurology: The study of diseases, functions, and structures of the nervous system.

-ology: A term meaning "the study of".

Oncology: The study of tumors.

-opathy: Disease or dysfunction of.

Ophthalmo-: Pertaining to the eye.

Ophthalmology: The study of diseases, functions, and structures of the eye.

Orthopedics: The study of bones and joints.

-osis: A diseased condition, as in hydronephrosis.

Otic: Relating to the ear.

Oto-: Pertaining to the ear.

Ovariohysterectomy (OHE, "spay"): The neutering of a female cat by surgical removal of the ovaries and uterus.

Pancreat-: Pertaining to the pancreas.

Perianal: Beside or around the anus.

Perineum: Region between the anus and the urethral opening.

Pneumo-: Pertaining to the lungs.

Primary cancer: Cancer arising in the area of the body in which it is found.

Pruritus: Itching.

Pulmono-: Pertaining to the lungs.

Pyo-: Pus in, as in pyometra.

Queen: Female cat that gives birth to kittens.

Renal: Relating to the kidneys.

Sarcoma: Malignant tumor of the cells that make up the body tissues.

Thoracic: Pertaining to the chest cavity that contains the heart, lungs, and major blood vessels.

Toxic: Poisonous.

Trauma: A sudden physical injury or wound; a shock.

Uremia: Buildup of poisons in the bloodstream due to kidney failure.

GLOSSARY 2

Some Tests/Procedures/ Equipment Often Used in Diagnosing/Treating Feline Diseases/Disorders

Acupuncture: A traditional Chinese healing system in which symptoms are relieved by the use of thin metal needles inserted at specific points.

Angiogram: A process in which dye is injected into a vein and then an X ray is taken in order to see the blood vessels.

Aspiration: The process of removing fluid or other matter from any part of the body using a fine sterile needle and syringe.

Barium series: GI diagnostic tests for which a cat must usually fast for twenty-four hours and is then given a white chalk-like liquid orally (barium), and X rays are taken of the GI tract. The white barium will highlight abnormalities or stoppages in the GI tract.

Biochemical profile (SMA-20): A series of blood tests evaluating the function of internal organs such as the liver and kidneys.

Biopsy: Examination by a pathologist of a piece of tissue that has been surgically removed to confirm a diagnosis of a condition or disease process. This is not confined to the diagnosis of a malignant cancer.

Blood tests: A diagnostic tool in a number of feline illnesses. A small amount of blood is removed and tested for various components, for example, CBC (complete blood count); platelet count; RBC (red blood cell count); WBC (white blood cell count); biochemical profile; and so forth.

Blood transfusion: The placement of whole blood or plasma directly into a cat's vein via a catheter.

Bone marrow aspiration: The removal of a small amount of bone marrow for evaluation under a microscope (*see* Aspiration).

Bronchoscopy: The process of examining the trachea and bronchi and/or removing tissue or foreign bodies using a special instrument (bronchoscope).

BUN (blood urea nitrogen): A blood test of kidney function. The normal in the cat is 10 to 20 mg. percent.

Casts (urinary): The element in the urine that is created when proteinaceous material in the urine is compressed in the nephrons (*see* "Renal Diseases and Disorders" in the Encyclopedia) to form a "cast" of the tubule that it forms in. A few granular casts in the urine are normal.

Catheter: A flexible tube used to remove or insert fluids.

Catheterization: The process wherein a urinary catheter is passed up the urethra to enter the bladder. Catheterization is done with sterile equipment. It is sometimes needed to relieve obstructions of the urethra. It may also be done to obtain a urine sample for diagnosis or to monitor urine output.

CBC (complete blood count): Blood test to inspect white and red blood cells and their status.

Chemotherapy: The treatment of disease with chemicals given orally or by injection.

Coagulation studies: Studies of the clotting ability of the blood.

Coomb's test: A specialized blood test used to diagnose autoimmune hemolytic anemia.

Creatinine: A blood test of kidney function in the cat. Normal is less than 1.0 mg percent.

Culture: Process by which specimens collected from a patient and incubated in a laboratory medium are examined for bacterial or fungal growth.

Cystocentesis: A procedure wherein a urine sample is obtained by aspiration of urine directly out of the bladder (*see* Aspiration).

Cystogram: An X-ray study that directly evaluates the size and contour of the urinary bladder. Air is injected by a urinary catheter into the urinary bladder, then a small amount of contrast material (opaque to X rays). The study is usually performed under sedation.

Cytology: The study of the function and structure of cells by microscopic examination, as in vaginal cytology.

Dietary therapy: Control of diet/food intake as a tool for treating various diseases.

Diuretics: Medications/drugs that increase the output/volume of urine.

Dye studies: The injection of a dye into a part of the body prior to taking X rays in order to highlight abnormalities and so forth.

Echocardiogram: A test using ultrasound (sound waves), which are noninvasive and reflect back from the heart and are transcribed by special recording paper. This test enables a veterinarian to see both the inside and outside of the heart and determine its function and structure without surgery.

Electroencephalogram (EEG): Brain function evaluation using an electroencephalograph, which records the electrical activity occurring in the brain.

Electrocardiogram (EKG): Heart function evaluation using an electrocardiograph, an instrument that records the electric currents traversing the heart.

Endoscopy: Visualization of the GI tract by use of a special instrument (endoscope).

Enzyme-Linked Immunosorbent Assay (ELISA test, "kit test"): A laboratory method used to diagnose the presence of FeLV.

Exclusion diagnosis: The process of making a diagnosis by ruling out everything else that could cause the problem.

Immunofluorescent Antibody Test (IFA test, "Hardy test"): A laboratory method used to diagnose the presence of FeLV.

IM: Intramuscular, as an injection.

Intravenous fluids: Fluids given via a catheter directly into a cat's vein.

Intravenous Pyelogram (IVP): An X-ray study to evaluate the size, contour, and function of the kidneys and ureters. The urinary bladder is also evaluated by this study.

IV: Intravenous, as an intravenous injection.

Lavaging: Washing or flushing with repeated injections of water or water mixed with medications.

Myelogram: A dye study of the spinal cord.

Otoscope: An instrument used to examine a cat's ears.

Palpation: Examination of the body with the hands and fingers.

Parenteral fluids: Fluids not given orally; given either subcutaneously (SQ) or intravenously (IV).

PO: By mouth (*per os*).

Radiation therapy: Treatment using X rays.

Radical surgery: Surgery aimed at removing all traces of a disease or growth.

Radiograph: X ray.

Skin scrapings: The removal of thin layers of skin for microscopic study.

SMA-20: Biochemical profile.

Speculum: An instrument used to hold open a body cavity for examination, such as the vagina, nostril, etc.

Spinal tap: The removal of fluid from around the spinal cord by aspiration.

Stool sample: The collection of feces for microscopic examination in order to identify intestinal parasites.

Subcutaneous (SQ): Beneath the skin, such as injected fluids or medications.

Tracheoscopy: An examination/visualization of the trachea using a tracheoscope.

Urethrogram: An X-ray study that directly evaluates the size and contour of the urethra. The bladder is filled with sterile fluids, and a contrast is injected into the urethra through a catheter placed in the very end of the urethra to outline the urethra. The study is usually done under sedation.

Urinalysis: A test of kidney function that examines the urine chemicals, concentration of solutes, cellular elements, and formed elements (casts).

Vaginal swab/culture: A collection of matter from the vagina on a swab for microscopic examination and/or culture.

X-ray examination: Examination of skeleton/internal organs by the use of radiographs/negative prints that reveal abnormalities inside the body.

Bibliography

Introduction

Books:

CAT CATALOG, Judy Fireman, editor; New York: Workman Publishing Co., 1976.

THE DELL ENCYCLOPEDIA OF CATS, Barbara Shook Hazen. New York: Dell Publishing Co., 1974.

SIMON AND SCHUSTER'S GUIDE TO CATS, Gino Pugnetti; Mordecai Siegal, U.S. ed. New York: Simon & Schuster, 1983.

A STANDARD GUIDE TO CAT BREEDS, Richard H. Gebhardt, consultant editor, Grace Pond and Dr. Ivor Raleigh, editors. New York: McGraw-Hill Book Co., 1979.

Cat Registries:

American Cat Association (ACA), 10065 Foothill Blvd., Lake View Terrace, CA 91342. Susie Page, Sec.

American Cat Fanciers' Association (ACFA), Box 203, Point Lookout, MO 65726. Ed Rugenstein, Sec. *(Second largest)*

Canadian Cat Association, 14 Nelson St. W., Ste. 5, Brampton, Ont., Canada L6X 1B7. Susan Plante, Registrar.

Cat Fanciers' Association Inc. (CFA), 1309 Allaire Ave., Ocean, NJ 07712. Thomas H. Dent, Executive Manager. *(Largest)*

Cat Fanciers' Federation, 9509 Montgomery Rd., Cincinnati, OH 45242. Barbara Haley, Recorder.

Crown Cat Fanciers' Federation, Box 783, Gibbons, Alberta, Canada T0A 1N0. Elaine Wiley, Secretary.

The International Cat Association, P.O. Box 2988, Harlingen, TX 78551. Georgia Morgan, President.

United Cat Federation, 6621 Thornwood St., San Diego, CA 92111. David Young, Sec.

National Breed Clubs:

Abyssinian Cat Club of America, 2304 Meridan St., Falls Church, VA 22046. Ruth Bauer, Sec./Treas.

Abyssinian Midwest Breeders, P.O. Box 1253, Oak Brook, IL 60521. Sue McDonald, President.

Amerikat Society (American Shorthair Breed Club), 804 Gannon Ave., Madison, WI 53714. Tom Herbst, Sec./Treas.

Atlantic Himalayan Club, Inc., 16 Cortland St., Roseland, NJ 07068. Connie Schweinberg, Membership Chairman.

Balinese Breeders and Fans of America, 685 Nicolson Ave., Santa Clara, CA 95051. Leslie Lamb, Membership Chairman.

The Cornish Rex Society, 720 Fisherville Rd., Fisherville, KY 40023. Carol Barbee, President.

Devon Rex Breed Club, 211 Sunset #4, West Linn, OR 97068. Karen King, Sec.

Devons West Breeders Assoc., 4126 107th Pl., NE, Kirkland, WA 98033

International Ragdoll Cat Association Inc., 156 Iowa, Riverside, CA 92507. Ann Baker, Owner.

Japanese Bobtail Breeders Society, 4406 Alta Vista, Dallas, TX 75229. Debra Fredrickson, President.

Korat Cat Fanciers Association, 400 N. Sunset Blvd., Gulf Breeze, FL 32561. Rosemary Voelker, Secretary.

Les Amis des Cartreux, 5195 Winters Chapel Rd., Doraville, GA 30360. Andrea Hawkins, Sec./Treas.

Long Island Ocelot Club, P.O. Box 66040, Portland, OR 97266.

Maine Coon Breeders and Fanciers Association, P.O. Box 791, Pacific Grove, CA 93950. Suzanne Servies, Corr. Sec.

National Siamese Cat Club Inc., 525 E. 89th St., New York, NY 10128. Stephanie Karageorge, Sec./Treas.

Ocicats International, 2008 Midwood Pl., Charlotte, NC 28205. Bill McKee, Sec.

The Persian Quarterly, 4401 Zephyr St., Wheat Ridge, CO 80033–3299.

The Ragdoll Lovers Cat Club, 5510 Ptolemy Way, Mira Loma, CA 91752. Georgann Chambers, Corr. Sec.

Siamese Cat Society of America, Inc., 2588–C South Vaughn Way, Aurora, CO 80014. Sam Scheer, Sec.

Silver and Golden Persian Fanciers, 1133 W. Berkeley, Springfield, MO 65807. Nancy L. Wallis, Secretary/Editor.

Singapura Fanciers' Society, 82 W. Catalina Dr., Oakview, CA 93022. Hal Meadow, Sec.

Snowshoe Cat Fanciers of America, 720 Jefferson Ave., Defiance, OH 43512. Jim Hoffman, President.

Snowshoes International, 720 Jefferson Ave., Defiance, OH 43512.

Somali Cat Club of America Inc., 10 Western Blvd., Gillette, NJ 07933. Mrs. Evelyn Mague, President.

Turkish Angora Club of the Future, 34 Warren Rd., Ashland, MA 01721. Patricia Joyce, Sec./Treas.

United British Shorthair Breeders, P.O. Box 22707, Tucson, AZ 85734. Nora Wilson, Sec.

National Referral Services:

American Breeders Association and Referral Service, 33222 N. Fairfield Rd., Round Lake, IL 60073.

CHAPTER 3: KEEPING YOUR CAT HEALTHY

Books About Natural Foods/Cooking for a Cat:

DOG AND CAT GOOD FOOD BOOK, Terri McGinnis, DVM. San Francisco: Taylor & Ng, 1977.

DR. PITCAIRN'S COMPLETE GUIDE TO NATURAL HEALTH FOR DOGS AND CATS, Richard C. Pitcairn, DVM, Ph.D., and Susan Hubble Pitcairn. Emmaus, PA: Rodale Press, 1982.

KEEPING YOUR PET HEALTHY THE NATURAL WAY, Pat Lazarus. Indianapolis/New York: Bobbs-Merrill Company, 1983.

THE HEALTHY CAT AND DOG COOK BOOK, Joan Harper. Chicago: Soodik Printing Company, 1975.

Natural Pet Food Manufacturers:

"Cornucopia"
Veterinary Nutritional Associates, Ltd.
229 Wall Street
Huntington, NY 11743

The Iams Company
Box 855
Lewisburg, OH 45338

Foods of Nature Pet Food
Jones Manufacturing Co.
P.O. Box 1515
Covina, CA 91722

CHAPTER 8: FELINE BEHAVIOR

Doctoral-level Animal Behaviorists and Veterinarians with Animal Behavior Training
Who Specialize in Pet Behavior Problems (listed by state):

CALIFORNIA
Ian Dunbar, Ph.D.
Animal Behavior Clinic
San Francisco SPCA
2500 16th Street
San Francisco, CA 94103

Benjamin C. Hart, DVM, Ph.D.
Lynette A. Hart, Ph.D.
Behavioral Service
Veterinary Medical Teaching Hospital
University of California—Davis
Davis, CA 95616

Richard H. Polsky, Ph.D.
Animal Behavior Counseling Service
11251 Greenlawn Avenue
Culver City, CA 90230

COLORADO
Stephen W. Horn, Ph.D.
Consultants in Animal Behavior
55 Hoyt Street
Lakewood, CO 80226

Jack C. Hunsberger, Ph.D.
Animal Behavior Consultants
5034 S. Youngfield Ct.
Morrison, CO 80465

Philip N. Lehner, Ph.D.
Suzanne Arguello, MS
Animal Behavior Associates, Inc.
P.O. Box 8473
Fort Collins, CO 80525

FLORIDA
Walter F. Burghardt, Jr., DVM, Ph.D.
Behavior Clinic for Animals
447 South Federal Highway
Deerfield Beach, FL 33441

GEORGIA
Sharon Crowell-Davis, DVM, Ph.D.
Teaching Hospital
College of Veterinary Medicine
University of Georgia
Athens, GA 30602

John C. Wright, Ph.D.
P.O. Box 180 MU
Macon, GA 31207

INDIANA
Eric Klinghammer, Ph.D.
Animal Behavior Advisory Service
Battle Ground, IN 47920

MARYLAND
Ginger Hamilton, Ph.D.
Consultants in Animal Psychology
1508 Vivian Court
Silver Springs, MD 20902

MICHIGAN
Eli Barlia, Ph.D.
Hunters Creek Animal Behavior Clinic
P.O. Box 10
Metamora, MI 48455

NEW YORK
Peter L. Borchelt, Ph.D.
Animal Behavior Clinic
The Animal Medical Center
510 East 62nd Street
New York, NY 10021
        and
Animal Behavior Consultants, Inc.
108–25 63rd Road
Forest Hills, NY 11375

Kathryn A. Houpt, VMD, Ph.D.
Animal Behavior Clinic
New York State College of Veterinary Medicine
Cornell University
Ithaca, NY 14853

NORTH CAROLINA
Margaret Sery Young, Ph.D.
Donna S. Brown, Ph.D.
School of Veterinary Medicine
North Carolina State University
Raleigh, NC 27606

OHIO
Robert M. Andrysco, Ph.D.
P.O. Box 12410
Columbus, OH 43212

David Hothersall, Ph.D.
David Tuber, Ph.D.
Animal Behavior Associates
1853 H. Kenny Road
Columbus, OH 43220

PENNSYLVANIA
Victoria L. Voith, DVM, Ph.D.
Animal Behavior Clinic
School of Veterinary Medicine
University of Pennsylvania
Philadelphia, PA 19104

CHAPTER 9: CATS AS COMPANIONS

Traveling with a Cat:

Pet Express, members Independent Pet and Transportation Assoc. (IPATA)
    Pet relocation experts. Pamphlets on shipping a cat by air domestic/international. Shipping service, flight reservations, boarding, and so forth.
    Write to: Pet Express, P.O. Box 40160, San Francisco, CA 94140.

The ASPCA Animalport
    24-hour service, 365 days a year. In-transit services. Shipping, pickups, boarding, transfers, veterinary service.
    Air Cargo Center, Building 189, Kennedy International Airport, Jamaica, NY 11430. (718) 656-6042.

"Touring With Towser"
    A guide of 2,000 independent hotels and motels, and 4,000 chain locations that will accept pets. Addresses and telephone numbers included.
    Send $1.25 to: Gaines TWT, P.O. Box 8172, Kankakee, IL 60902.

"Traveling with Your Pet"
    Travel tips and regulations for 177 nations/dependencies and the U.S., plus special tips on containers, and so forth.
    Send $4.00 to: ASPCA Education Dept., 441 East 92nd St., New York, NY 10028.

CHAPTER 10: WHEN A CAT DIES

Books Specifically About Death of a Pet:

A SNOWFLAKE IN MY HAND, Samantha Mooney. New York: Delacorte Press/Eleanor Friede, 1983. A sensitive and touching book about living with cats who have cancer. For teenagers and adults.

CHARLOTTE'S WEB, E. B. White. New York: Harper & Row, 1952. A charming book about a friendship which transcends death. For adults and children.

PET LOSS, Herbert A. Nieburg and Arlene Fischer. New York: Harper & Row, 1982. A guide for adults and older children on how to deal with the loss of a pet.

General Books on Death:

These books have proved helpful to many pet owners even though not specifically about the death of a cat.

EXPLAINING DEATH TO CHILDREN, Earl Grollman. Boston: Beacon Press, 1967. The advice of specialists from many fields.

ON DEATH AND DYING, Elisabeth Kübler-Ross. New York: Macmillan Publishing Co., 1969.

THE TENTH GOOD THING ABOUT BARNEY, Judith Viorst. New York: Atheneum, 1971. How to say goodbye to a departed cat. Simple enough for young children but effective for anyone.

HOW TO SURVIVE THE LOSS OF A LOVE, Melba Colgrove, Harold Bloomfield, Peter McWilliams. New York: Bantam Books, 1977.

THE BEREAVED PARENT, Harriet Sarnoff Schiff. New York: Penguin Books, 1978.

WHEN BAD THINGS HAPPEN TO GOOD PEOPLE, Harold S. Kushner. New York: Schocken Books, 1981.

CHAPTER 11: EXOTIC CATS

Sources of Commercial Diets for Exotic Felines:

NOTE: These products differ somewhat in protein, fat, and mineral content.

Spectrum Frozen Feline Diets
Animal Spectrum Inc.
5801 Locust Street
Lincoln, NE 68516
800-228-4005

Nebraska Brand Feline Food
Central Nebraska Packing Company
P.O. Box 550
North Platte, NE 69101
Order through: Animal Spectrum Inc.,
800-228-4005

Zu/Preem Feline Canned Diet
Zu/Preem
Hill's Pet Products Inc.
P.O. Box 148
Topeka, KS 66601
Order through: Animal Spectrum Inc.,
800-228-4005

Reliable Protein Products and Feline-Fare (RPP)
1736 East 23rd Street
Los Angeles, CA 90058
213-748-1153

Index